Gendering Criminology

GENDERING CRIMINOLOGY

Crime and Justice Today

Shelly Clevenger and Jordana N. Navarro

UNIVERSITY OF CALIFORNIA PRESS

University of California Press
Oakland, California

Names: Clevenger, Shelly, author. | Navarro, Jordana N., author.
Title: Gendering criminology : crime and justice today / Shelly
    Clevenger and Jordana N. Navarro.
Description: Oakland, California : University of California Press,
    [2021] | Includes bibliographical references and index.
Identifiers: LCCN 2020055785 (print) | LCCN 2020055786 (ebook) |
    ISBN 9780520298286 (paperback) | ISBN 9780520970472 (epub)
Subjects: LCSH: Crime—Sex differences. | Sex discrimination in
    criminal justice administration. | Sexual minorities—Crimes
    against.
Classification: LCC HV6158 .C54 2021 (print) | LCC HV6158 (ebook) |
    DDC 364.081—dc23
LC record available at https://lccn.loc.gov/2020055785
LC ebook record available at https://lccn.loc.gov/2020055786

Manufactured in the United States of America

30 29 28 27 26 25 24 23 22 21
10 9 8 7 6 5 4 3 2 1

This book has been a labor of love for all those who have ever felt treated differently based on who they are or whom they love. I dedicate this book to all warriors for equality and to my daughter, Iris, whom I hope will grow up to smash the patriarchy in her own way. RESIST. PERSIST. CHANGE THE CULTURE.
Shelly Clevenger

This book is dedicated to all individuals battling various forms of systemic oppression every day—especially the Black community and LGBTQIA+ people—who continue to see their humanity challenged and disregarded by a system that should protect them and their loved ones. This book is also dedicated to my husband, Jaret, and sons, Colton and Jackson, as well as the many wonderful friends in my life who supported these efforts through the ongoing pandemic: Bex, Bree, Eisely, Kevin, James, Joan, and Sarah. I hope this text inspires others to see how social constructs shape our everyday world and how they harm people simply for being who they are. To that end: RESIST. PERSIST.
CHANGE THE CULTURE!
Jordana Navarro

Contents

Contents

Preface

New Language for a New Way of Thinking

The goal of this book to help the reader understand the impact of gender, gender identity, sexual orientation, and race on crime and victimization. We employ an intersectional approach, meaning that we want the reader to consider all the aspects of who a person is and how that can impact their life. We feel that at this current time this is more important than ever. We want to shed light on the fact that there is bias and hatred based on the identity of a person, and it is important to understand how identity affects a person's experiences. We focus this book on gender and gender identity, but we also talk about other factors that can influence a person's life experiences.

In this book, we want to be inclusive of all people and sensitive to all populations. You will see some terms being used that may be unfamiliar or different than you would normally see. The reason is that we want all people to feel included and seen as well as to humanize people who often are not given that respect by society or the system. First, we use the term **criminal-legal system** and not "criminal justice system." This is to convey our belief that the current system does not deliver justice for many of the people that take part in it. They may be individuals against whom an offense was committed and/or individuals who are arrested, tried, and convicted. We feel there is a problem with the system and that it needs to be changed. Until the system can deliver justice to all people, we will refer to it as the criminal-legal system. This term conveys that it is a system operating under the law to criminalize people, but it is not a system of justice.

Second, we use the term **system-involved person** or **individual** instead of "offender" or "person who committed a crime" or some variation thereof. We also use the term **incarcerated individual** or **person** instead of "inmate." The reason for these changes is that there is often a stigma attached to the term *offender*, and even after a person serves their time, that stigma exists. We believe in restorative justice and that for most people who are involved in the system, there is hope for redemption. However, readers will notice the use of the term *offender* in some places when the theorists we are quoting use that term.

We also have altered language in this text in relation to the terms *victim* and *survivor*. Readers will notice terms such as "person against whom an offense was committed" or "person who experienced [a crime]." This is our way to acknowledge that a person has been victimized, without using a value-laden term such as *victim*. This language is a response to the fact that many individuals who have been victimized do not like or prefer the term victim, or do not describe themselves as victims. Many individuals prefer the term *survivor*, as it emphasizes that they survived what happened to them. That term is often viewed as more empowering for individuals than victim is. However, as the criminal-legal system and federal government use the term "victim" in their official proceedings and reports, we decided to use the above language as a compromise to acknowledge both survivors and the language used by the system. We fully support individuals who have been victimized and how they choose to refer to their experiences and themselves.

We use the acronym **LGBTQIA+**, which stands for "lesbian, gay, bisexual, transgender, queer/questioning, intersex, asexual" as well as those who do not identify with the previous terms or who are gender fluid. We cover these terms in chapter 1 of this text. We use this acronym to let our readers know that we want all people to feel included and acknowledge all.

We believe that language has power, and although this may seem like a small change, choice of language is one way that we can work to change the culture and help people who feel disenfranchised or left out to know that they are seen. We want our readers to think not only about their own identities, as well as those of others, and how identity can affect lived experiences, but also how they can work to make changes for the better within their own lives and communities.

The Story of Gender

Definitions, Origins, and Current Issues

LEARNING OBJECTIVES
▶ Understand terms related to gender, sexual orientation, and identity.
▶ Explain how gender, sexual orientation, and identity shape perceptions of the self and others.
▶ Apply chapter content to contemporary issues related to gender and sexual orientation.

This chapter will cover terms pertaining to gender and identity. These topics lay a foundational framework for the rest of this book. Understanding what each term means as well as its context is important for connecting the relationship between gender identity and crime and victimization. Throughout this chapter and the book, we use the term **LGBTQIA+** in order to include all people. LGBTQIA+ stands for "lesbian, gay, bisexual, transgender, queer or questioning, intersex, asexual," and the + represents anyone who does not identify as any of those, such as people who identify as gender fluid or pansexual (which will be discussed later in the chapter) (GLAAD, 2021). However, this is not a definitive list. The acronym is always evolving and changing as people and society evolve and change. As of the writing of this book, this is the abbreviation that we felt was most inclusive. This chapter will acquaint you with the meaning behind these different terms as well as introduce you to the current issues facing the LGBTQIA+ communities in terms of crime and victimization.

UNDERSTANDING GENDER

Although the terms *gender* and *sex* are sometimes used interchangeably, they are not equivalent. **Gender** is a

MEDIA BYTE 1.1   Gender Reveal Parties

Search for at least five news stories related to gender reveal parties. Attempt to find news stories from a wide array of outlets and vantage points that discuss gender reveal parties in terms of broader trends related to gender identity. If you have questions about sources, please contact your instructor.

After reading the stories, answer the following questions on the impact of this new trend on individuals and their gender identities.

1. Explain whether you believe gender reveal parties contribute to gender stereotypes and the foundation for your belief.
2. Explain whether you believe these parties should be "sex reveal parties" and the foundation for your belief.
3. Discuss methods other than colors that expectant parents could use to reveal the biological sex of their unborn child.
4. Explain whether these parties are exclusionary and the foundation for your belief.

human-created construct or idea, whereas the term *sex* is grounded in the biological differences between females and males. Unlike the term *sex*, gender and what constitutes "masculine" and "feminine" are culturally specific. In other words, societies differ in terms of the behaviors and roles they assign to each gender and whether they recognize genders outside of the binary. The process of socializing an individual toward these behaviors and roles begins before a child is even born, even though parents cannot know their child's gender until that individual is born and able to express it. For example, in the United States, specific colors are associated with gender. This association is currently strongly seen in children's clothing (pastel shades like pink for girls, stark primary shades like blue for boys) and toys (the overabundance of dolls for girls, "action figures" for boys).

The continued confusion between biological sex and gender is most clearly seen in the recent trend of "gender reveal" parties hosted by expectant parents. In these parties, expectant parents reveal the (assumed) gender of their unborn baby with the corresponding gendered colors (see Media Byte 1.1). However, illustrating that gender is *culturally* specific as well as *time* specific, color associations were the reverse in the pre–World War II era. In this period in the United States, blue was associated with femininity and girls, while pink was associated with masculinity and boys. This association began to shift during the baby boom generation (Maglaty, 2011). The fact that biological sex and gender are conflated from birth, despite their difference, reinforces the fact that gender is a sociocultural concept.

In recent years, conceptualizations of gender have begun to shift within the United States. More specifically, a sizable percentage of the population no longer views gender as just femininity or masculinity standards—instead, this concept is becoming more fluid. It includes individuals who express themselves in diverse ways. Yet, despite this shift, most people in the United States continue to perceive gender as aligning with the categories of sex (female and male). As a result, it is not surprising that dominant systems within society (like the criminal-legal system) are still structured according to that prevailing mindset. Because gender shapes an individual's experiences even before birth, this book will provide a "gendered lens" to criminology. In this chapter, we present an overview and exploration of gender, gender identity, sexual orientation, and overall identity to illustrate how these essential concepts shape an individual's life experiences, including involvement in the criminal-legal system. Our use of *criminal-legal system* instead of *criminal justice system* emphasizes that the workings of this system do not always lead to "justice"—particularly for marginalized populations.

As mentioned, one of the methods to reinforce gender at a broad sociocultural level is through styles of dress. For example, it was not long ago when women were required to wear skirts in workplaces or barred from many kinds of employment altogether. These themes and trends stem from conceptualizations of what it means to be "feminine" and "masculine" within contemporary Western culture. To frame and understand these patterns, seminal work in gender studies introduced two key terms that named these trends: *emphasized femininity* (or ideal forms of "womanhood"), which is associated with attractiveness, chastity, nurturance, and passivity, and *hegemonic masculinity*, which is associated with attractiveness, independence, sexual prowess, and strength. For example, men are expected to dress in a masculine way, which typically means wearing pants and shirts, or a suit and tie for business and formal occasions, without many embellishments (Crane, 2001). It is not gender congruent, or aligning with dominant conceptions of Western masculinity, for men to wear lace, ruffles, or a skirt as everyday dress. However, again, because gender is culturally specific, the kilt is a traditional style of dress among men in Scotland, with significant historical and cultural meaning.

Like men, women are expected to dress in gender-congruent ways, which in Western culture means skirts or feminine styles of pants and shirts. In contrast to men, women do not typically wear ties. In addition to avoiding "masculine dress," women also must style themselves so that they always remain within societal bounds of "decency" in their appearance (Crane, 2001). For example, the United States Congress continues to maintain rules forbidding women to bare their shoulders within the congressional chamber (Zillman, 2017). Gender permeates every aspect of our life, even in the language we use (e.g., *he, she, they*), which has implications for how we perceive ourselves, how others see us, and the experiences and opportunities that arise from those interactions.

An example of gender influencing life experiences is evidenced by the work of Schilt (2006). This research revealed that transgender men (individuals assigned female at birth but who identify, live, and work as males) benefitted professionally from their change in gender. They were treated better overall at work and made more money than women. Participants in the study also noted significant differences in how their coworkers and bosses treated them. More specifically, coworkers and bosses listened to the participants immediately when expressing an idea and opinion, and the participants were not questioned when they made a comment or suggestion. Participants also reported that they felt more respected and valued at work. They reported having instant credibility just by being in the room, in contrast to what they previously experienced when working as women.

In addition to gender, ethnicity, race, and residency status play overlapping roles in shaping life experiences. For instance, a participant in Schilt's (2006) study, who identified as a Black man, reported that he was viewed as intimidating and frightening to people. Thus, he had to navigate social life as a Black man in the United States, where implicit and overt biases can lead individuals to act scared or wary of others different from themselves. Although others' implicit and overt biases also impact Black women, the participant reported that he had not had to deal with them as much before starting to live as a man. This finding underscores the complex and overlapping stratification system within the United States. The participants in Schilt's study gained social privilege associated with their gender, but these benefits were not universal across demographic backgrounds. "Performing gender" is a careful balance that includes many factors for individuals every day.

Gender also affects the risk of becoming a justice-involved individual. More specifically, Western culture socializes boys with more freedom, and deviant behavior, including crime, is more tolerated for boys than for girls (Hagan, 1989; Hagan, Gillis, and Simpson, 1985, 1991). Given that deviancy perpetrated by boys is more tolerated, there are more opportunities for offending and victimization. Not surprisingly, research continues to show that adolescent boys commit a sizable portion of "street crime" and many cybercrimes like hacking (Adam, 2005).

Societal gender constructs also shape the rearing of young girls. For instance, in patriarchal households, fathers (or male guardians) may emphasize controlling the movements of young girls (by establishing curfews, for instance). This parenting style often includes implicit or overt deference to the father as "the head of the household," which may not be as pronounced for male children. In other words, there are two types of rules in many Western households corresponding to dominant gender ideals: one for boys and one for girls. Because of differences in oversight and societal conceptions rationalizing boys' deviance as "boys being boys," it is not surprising that young men are at heightened risk to engage in or experience crime.

The previous paragraphs provide a "thousand-foot view" of how gender, as a broad construct, shapes social life. However, there are several other constructs related to gender identity that are important for readers to know. In the following sections, we will review these terms so to show how differences in identity can shape our experiences.

DEFINING THE WORDS THAT EXPRESS OURSELVES TO OTHERS

As discussed, many use the terms *gender* and *sex* interchangeably, and it is commonly believed that the sex assigned at birth determines one's gender. However, sex assigned at birth, gender, and who we love can all be different. What is often called **gender identity** is an individual's own psychological experience of gender. This is the gender we consider ourselves to be as a person. Individuals whose gender identity aligns with their sex assigned at birth (female/feminine, male/masculine) are referred to as gender normative, or **cisgender**. When gender identify and assigned sex differ, different terminology is used to respect the individuality of the person. For example, an individual who chooses to not to conform to gender constructs is described as **gender nonconforming.** In the following pages, we will review the various terms individuals use to describe themselves to establish the foundation for how these words inform their self-perceptions, how others view them, and the life experiences we all encounter. But first, we will review three broad terms (gender binary, gender expression, sexual orientation) that shape those subsequent conversations.

Gender Binary

The term **gender binary** refers to the perception that gender comprises only two categories: feminine or masculine. In a gender-binary system, an individual selects one of the two genders and adheres to the norms of that gender. Most societies around the world have been historically gender binary, and this remains the norm today as gender-binary thinking still permeates through laws, opinions, and beliefs across the globe. For example, many nation-states structure their criminal-legal systems and the associated incarceration facilities according to the gender-binary system, which assigns individuals a gender based on the sex assigned at birth (male or female). Basing incarceration housing decisions on sex assigned at birth is problematic for individuals who do not identify with they were assigned at birth or with the gender-binary system in general (see chapter 5 for a complete discussion).

The reliance on using sex assigned at birth to structure expected behaviors and life experiences has led to societal conversations about how this negatively impacts LGBTQIA+ individuals. A recent example is the discussions in the

---

MEDIA BYTE 1.2   **Bathroom Protections for Transgender Students**

Read the "Dear Colleague" letter here: https://www2.ed.gov/about/offices/list/ocr/letters/colleague-201605-title-ix-transgender.pdf. After reading the letter, please read at least five news articles related to the repeal of these protections from a range of reputable news outlets. If you have any trouble finding sources or the letter itself, contact your instructor. After reading this information, reflect on and explain your thoughts about the following questions:

1. Do you think the repeal of these protections will affect transgender students?
2. Place yourself in the shoes of a transgender student. How do you think you would feel seeing these protections repealed by government officials?

United States vis-à-vis public bathrooms. These conversations center around whether people can use the bathroom that corresponds with their *gender* rather than the sex assigned at birth. For example, should an individual who identifies as a man be allowed to use a men's bathroom even if the sex assigned at birth was female? To be more inclusive, some businesses and institutions have established "gender-neutral" bathrooms. (See Media Byte 1.2.)

While national dialogue continues to focus on increasing inclusivity in living spaces, large systems based on antiquated classification, like the criminal-legal system, are not easy to change. During the legal process, system-involved individuals have no say in their incarceration facility. This can be problematic because correctional facilities, detention centers, and some psychiatric treatment centers often separate their service populations into sex-assigned-at-birth categories. Therefore, regardless of a person's gender, whatever sex-assigned-at-birth category is listed on their birth certificate or driver's license is where that individual goes upon arrival at the facility. (See Active Learning Assignment 1.1 and Case Study 1.1.) Aside from the harm caused by *misgendering* individuals for significant periods, research shows that individuals in LGBTQIA+ communities are often poorly treated by other incarcerated individuals and staff as well as being at additional risk for assault (both physical and sexual) and suicide (Amnesty International, 2019).

Up to this point, we have focused discussion on individuals whose gender aligns (from a societal standpoint) or differs from their sex assigned at birth. However, **non-binary** individuals, or gender non-binary individuals, identify outside of both genders. The idea of being non-binary is not new, as there have been individuals who identified as non-binary throughout history (Mogul, Ritchie, and Whitlock, 2011). However, due to social stigma and pressure to adhere to a binary system, individuals may not feel comfortable or safe openly

---

ACTIVE LEARNING ASSIGNMENT 1.1

Medical Forms and Inclusivity

Planned Parenthood provides several resources on their website to help transgender people access care and learn about health services offered (https://www.plannedparenthood.org/learn/gender-identity/transgender). However, questions remain as to whether there should be other categories on medical paperwork aside from sex assigned at birth, such as gender identity, to be more inclusive and precise in responding to patients' needs. After exploring the information, reflect on the following questions and be prepared to discuss them in class:

1. Do you believe medical forms should include other methods of identification aside from sex assigned at birth? Why or why not?
2. Imagine that you are checking into a medical facility, and the form you receive does not provide options for you to accurately describe how you see yourself. How would this make you feel?
3. How might such medical forms be detrimental for individuals who are incarcerated?

CASE STUDY 1.1

Medical Care and Treatment in a Gender Binary World

Gender identification can limit navigation in various social spheres. One is medical care and benefits. For example, individuals who identify as male but were assigned the sex of female at birth (and retained female genitalia or reproductive organs) are sometimes not screened for breast or cervical cancer, while individuals who identify as women but were assigned the sex of male at birth may be invited to have breast and cervical cancer screenings (Sanchez and Adams, 2018). This kind of oversight, which stems from binary gender identification, can be potentially deadly to these individuals.

The differential treatment stems from the classification system that is reflected in the paperwork for accessing NHS resources. Medical forms with categories only for the sex assigned at birth or categories that confuse gender with the sex assigned at birth can negatively affect the treatment transgender people receive—as well as people who identify outside the realm of female and male entirely. Students are encouraged to think about these situations as they read the following discussion prompts:

1. How might such gender-binary paperwork affect you if you were a transgender individual?
2. What is your opinion of this NHS initiative?

---

expressing themselves. In addition to non-binary and gender non-binary individuals, other individuals may use any of the following terms to self-identify outside of the typical two-group classification system: *genderqueer, gender bender, bi-gender, beyond gender, pan-gender, agender,* or *polygender* (GLAAD, 2021).

Gender Expression

Gender expression is how one shows the world their gender. An individual may express their gender through their clothing, hairstyle, way of speaking, and mannerisms. However, the terms *gender expression* and *gender identity* are not interchangeable. It would be inappropriate to draw assumptions about the latter based on the former, given that the only way to know an individual's gender identity is from the person directly. Avoiding assumptions is especially important because we often make assumptions based on our vantage point and privilege, which may not apply to the other person. For example, we might assume that a person assigned male at birth, who dresses in women's clothing, who wears makeup and a wig, identifies as a woman. However, that individual may work as a drag queen and performer; thus, their *expression* is part of their occupation—not how they identify themselves. In another example, a woman with short hair and styled in masculine clothing, who works in a male-dominated field such as construction, may incorrectly be assumed to self-identify as a man based on her outward appearance. However, that person may simply enjoy that manner of dress or that profession but does self-identify as a woman. (See Active Learning Assignment 1.2.)

In addition to clothing, different communication styles are related to gender. For example, perceptions of masculinity are associated with dominating conversations and group interactions as well as interrupting people when they are talking. In contrast, communication styles that appear more submissive, empathetic, and caring are often associated with femininity (Robinson and Smith-Lovin, 2001). However, despite these broad patterns, many factors shape how individuals see themselves. Indeed, different communication styles may be related to culture or personal style or be situation-specific—as well as to gender. For instance, a woman may act in a traditionally masculine way at work because she believes it is required for advancement or most appropriate for the particular job. However, outside that environment or with a different audience (such as friends and family), that same individual may use a different communication style, one that does not equate to how that person identifies as an individual. In other words, while behavior can give us an indication of someone's

---

ACTIVE LEARNING ASSIGNMENT 1.2

Drawing Gender

Draw a line down the center of a blank piece of paper. Then draw a picture of what you think of when you hear the term *masculine* on one side of the line, and *feminine* on the other side. Present your work to the class or a peer. Explain your images and why you associate them with femininity and masculinity.

gender identity, it is inappropriate to assume gender identity based solely on appearance and behavior.

Sexual Orientation

Like sex assigned at birth and gender identity, sexual orientation is not synonymous with gender. An individual's **sexual orientation** refers to their self-perception of their sexual attraction to others, which has no bearing on their gender. Sexual orientation can also change throughout a person's lifetime. Moreover, a person may be sexually attracted to members of the same sex but not identify as gay or lesbian or even act upon those feelings. Young people, in particular, may have a sexual attraction to the same sex but choose to pursue sexual relations with the opposite sex to avoid homophobia in their community or family. Yet, as these young people grow up, they may feel more comfortable and safer engaging in sexual relations with individuals of the same sex.

Sexual orientation is an individual's attraction to another person, which can stem from various (overlapping) connections: emotional, physical, sexual, and spiritual. This attraction exists apart from someone's gender or gender expression. Considering the various points of attraction, some prefer the term *affectional* or *affection orientation* because it provides a holistic picture of one's desire of others. Updated terminology is relevant because, just as in the case of sex assigned at birth, sexual orientation has historically been viewed as a binary choice (opposite sex versus same sex). Yet, individuals' attractions vary outside of those fixed choices. For example, *bisexual* people are attracted to individuals of both the opposite and the same sex. On the other hand, *asexual* people do not experience sexual attraction to individuals of any gender. In contrast, *pansexual* people are attracted to any gender identity and sexual orientation; they are also referred to as *polysexual*, *omnisexual*, or *ambisexual*. In summary, gender and sexual orientation are fluid and not easily captured through a rigid binary system of classification (GLAAD, 2021). Yet, the fixed binary system structures many life experiences.

Transgender

Transgender is a term used to describe individuals who have a gender identity that is different from their sex assigned at birth. The term *transgender* can mean different things to different individuals. A transgender person may choose to alter their body hormonally or surgically to reflect their gender identity. However, identifying as a transgender individual does not necessitate permanently changing one's body; many transgender people live their lives as their chosen gender without any permanent alterations.

As society has progressed in its overall thinking, the meaning of *transgender* has changed. For instance, in the past, some definitions of *transgender* included any individual who behaved in a way counter to (or had characteristics that were not of) their sex assigned at birth (Norton and Herek, 2013). The problem with these definitions is that they could include individuals who did not self-identify as transgender. Another practice that has (rightly) faded from the everyday discourse is using the term *transsexual* as an equivalent to *transgender*. This term, like the word *homosexual*, is now considered offensive because the medical community used it to diagnose individuals, via the Diagnostic and Statistical Manual (DSM), with "disorders" like gender identity disorder (later called gender dysphoria). As discussed throughout this chapter and this book, the methods societies use to classify and structure individuals (by gender, race, or other characteristic), which impact individual life experiences, are social constructs. Thus, this historical process was, and remains, hugely offensive, because it assumed that these "divergent" methods of identification were the result of mental disorders that required treatment, rather than reflecting the rigid and incorrect binary gender system. Transgender individuals do not need to be diagnosed or treated for disorders. (See Case Study 1.2.)

Cisgender

The term *cisgender* was created in the 1990s as a contrast to the term *transgender*. **Cisgender** refers to individuals whose gender identity aligns with the sex assigned to them at birth. For example, an individual who was assigned the sex of female at birth and is living as and identifies as a woman would be considered a cis woman. *Cis-* is Latin for "on this side of," whereas *trans-* means "on the other side of." Although it was created a few decades ago, the use of *cisgender* has increased within academia and national conversations about gender inclusivity. Aside from being used to self-identify as female/woman or male/man, the word also makes it possible to acknowledge the significant privileges and rights that cisgender individuals experience compared with LGBTQIA+ people (Serrano, 2016).

A significant goal of this book is to underscore how gender structures life experiences. Related to that overall goal are discussions of privilege differences (invisible "propellers" or "barriers") that people encounter in their everyday lives. Put another way, privilege is an unfair advantages or unearned opportunities that some people acquire based solely on membership in a particular group. In terms of gender identity, cisgender people have cisgender privilege in that they never have difficulty accessing their bathrooms of choice or navigating within spheres designed around the binary sex classification system (e.g., women's or men's clubs). In addition, they are not signaled out to speak for an entire community and are not asked intrusive questions about their identity. Moreover, a cisgender person typically does not have to worry about relationship rejection or physical attack because they are living their life in a way that

Caitlyn Jenner

Caitlyn Jenner, who was previously known as Bruce Jenner, was famous before coming out to the world as a transgender woman in 2015. Jenner was a gold medalist and set a world decathlon record at the 1976 Summer Olympics. Jenner was a public figure for decades after winning the gold medal. She had several endorsement deals, such as being a spokesperson for Wheaties, as well as various speaking engagements. She also worked in the television and movie industry. However, she is most recently famous from starring in the popular reality show *Keeping Up with the Kardashians.* Jenner's (then) marriage with Kris Jenner was a constant feature of that show. During a substantial portion of the show, until April 2015, Jenner was living as a man.

In 2015, it was revealed that Jenner was living as a woman, and her name was Caitlyn. One of Jenner's first public appearances post-announcement was on Diane Sawyer's *20/20*, where they discussed the transition from a man to becoming a woman. Jenner explained what the process was like for her family. Her candid discussion about living as a transgender woman was featured and recognized in a variety of outlets. For example, she appeared on the cover of *Vanity Fair.* At the 2015 ESPY Awards, she received the Arthur Ashe Award for Courage, which is awarded to people who transcend sports. Past recipients include Muhammed Ali and Nelson Mandela. In her acceptance speech, Caitlyn talked about raising awareness for rights and issues specific to transgender people. This call was further emphasized in Jenner's television series, *I Am Cait,* which documented her new life.

While many have heralded Caitlyn Jenner's efforts to call attention to issues specific to the transgender community, such as greater public consciousness, the praise has not been universal. Some point out that Caitlyn Jenner's experiences as a white transgender woman of significant wealth and social capital are much different from those of transgender people encountering various barriers related to overlapping systems of oppression (e.g., ableism, racism) or financial insecurity. These barriers limit the ability of many transgender people to live their lives in alignment with their gender identities. While Caitlyn was able to obtain hormones and afford surgery easily, many others are not due to limited access or financial resources.

Please search for (and watch) the full *20/20* interview with Diane Sawyer and Caitlyn Jenner. If you are unable to locate the video, please speak with your instructor. After watching the video, please reflect on the following questions and be prepared to discuss the following questions in class:

1. Do you believe that Caitlyn coming out as a transgender woman helped the transgender community receive more acceptance? Why or why not?
2. Do you think that Caitlyn's race, power, and privilege affected the experience she had in her transformation? Please explain.
3. How do you think that this experience would be different for a transgender woman of color who was not a celebrity?
4. What is your reaction to hearing Caitlyn's story?

does not conform to their sex assigned at birth. For individuals who are not cisgender, the latter is a palpable reality.

In addition, a cisgender individual can usually obtain employment, housing, government assistance or benefits, and medical care without fear of how their gender expression or identity will influence those decision outcomes. Even something as simple as obtaining a driver's license or work identification card is free of hidden barriers for cisgender people. In contrast, transgender and gender non-binary individuals face challenges if they want such documents to reflect their true identities. In high-stress settings, like a hospital or law enforcement agency, cisgender individuals do not have to worry about how they are classified. Yet, for other populations, misgendering has real consequences like undue stress, anxiety, and fear.

Compounding this problem, it is often a complicated process to get these documents changed to reflect different ways of identifying. Depending upon the agency, state, or nation, an individual may have to show proof that a particular surgery was performed or provide a doctor's letter indicating that a change is warranted. Some states, nations, and agencies may not allow a change at all regardless of surgery status, while others permit changes without documentation. Further complicating this process is that these entities vary on what documents can be changed. Thus, an individual's driver's license may differ from their birth certificate. To outsiders, the challenges associated with this may not seem obvious, but differing information across key identifying documents can pose severe problems with securing employment and loans. For example, an individual's birth certificate and driver's license are both used to verify the right to work within the United States. Thus, these variations present cumbersome difficulties that cisgender individuals do not face because of cisgender privilege.

Aside from the fear of being denied benefits, employment, job offers, and promotions because of discrepancies relating to gender identity on official documents, individuals who do not identify as cisgender can experience challenges with more common events like getting through airport security or interacting with law enforcement. Cisgender persons do not face these challenges as they can quickly identify themselves without fear of being accused of lying or falsifying documents or being denied needed assistance as a result of differing gender identity across official documentation (Spade, 2011).

When considering cisgender privilege, it is also important to note that other classification categories, such as ableism, classism, racism, and residency status, work hand in hand to alter life experiences. People's background and current status can confer different levels of privilege within society, which can also relate to financial resources. For example, requiring a doctor's letter or surgery to change official documentation inherently constrains individuals with limited access to doctors or limited financial means to pursue operations. These requirements are more easily met by those of higher social capital and the corresponding financial means.

The challenges experienced by gender-nonconforming people have a ricocheting effect on their lives. For example, they may experience difficulty in securing employment with health benefits, which subsequently limits their ability to obtain documentation and surgery that is sometimes necessary to have their identification materials accurately reflect who they are. Aside from difficulties obtaining gender reassignment surgery, individuals pursuing this surgery may have to undergo counseling and take hormones, which are additional costs that cisgender people do not experience. A lack of healthcare coverage means that many individuals are not able to take these steps. For instance, research shows that 91 percent of transgender or non-binary individuals reported wanting counseling, hormones, and/or puberty blockers. However, only 65 percent said they received these treatments (James et al., 2016). Likewise, in studies evaluating transgender men's and women's access to surgery, rates ranged from 8 percent to 25 percent for chest surgery (both men and women) and from 4 percent to 13 percent for genital surgery. Participants noted that the main obstacles were access to doctors and clinics and the ability to pay for these items (Kailas et al., 2017; Sineath et al., 2016).

Because many transgender individuals are not able to financially access these treatments and procedures to facilitate their transition, some turn to illegal markets for hormones and surgeries. Accessing illegal markets is dangerous as formal regulation agencies do not oversee them, and patients may be assisted by unqualified doctors, which in turn can lead to severe sickness or even death. As elsewhere, individuals battling multiple systems of oppression (including classism and racism) are the most vulnerable (Amnesty International, 2019).

The disproportionate use and impact of illegal markets on individuals who are of people of color or financially insecure align with broader research on white privilege. Akin to cisgender privilege, white privilege is the free benefits white individuals receive just for being white. White privilege and cisgender privilege intersect to structure life experiences. Therefore, cisgender white people are more advantaged than cisgender people of color. This prevailing pattern is grounded in ample research across various topics within criminology and criminal justice. For example, research has found that a white person is less likely than a person of color to be stopped by police, to experience police brutality, and to be killed by police (Stinson, 2020; Wertz et al., 2020). White individuals are also less likely to grow up in socially disorganized neighborhoods and to be blocked from employment or housing as a result of systemic inequality (Peterson and Krivo, 2010). Likewise, cisgender individuals are less likely than individuals who are not cisgender to face arrest, harassment, and physical violence by law enforcement officials (Mallory,

ACTIVE LEARNING ASSIGNMENT 1.3

Identifying Cisgender Privilege

Please read "White Privilege: Unpacking the Invisible Knapsack" by Peggy McIntosh (1988) either at https://nationalseedproject.org/about-us/white-privilege or from your institution's library or your instructor. After reading this article, think of all the ways that an individual identifying as cisgender experiences privilege, and create a list reflecting these thoughts. Share your list with a partner or the class.

MEDIA BYTE 1.3   Cisgender Privilege

Please read at least five news articles from reputable sources about cisgender privilege. After reading those articles, answer the following questions and be prepared to share them with the class. If you have any questions about appropriate sources, please ask your instructor.

1. What is your opinion of cisgender privilege? In other words, do you believe it exists and that it creates an environment of different life experiences?
2. Do you personally identify with any forms of cisgender privilege? Please explain.
3. Do you believe that cisgender individuals are aware of their privilege? Please explain.

Hasenbush, and Sears, 2015). (See Active Learning Assignment 1.3 and Media Byte 1.3.)

Intersex

The term **intersex** refers to individuals born with reproductive anatomy that is not "typical or standard," in medical professionals' opinions, for males and females. *Intersex* was initially a medical term, but many within this community have embraced this term to describe themselves. For example, a person may be intersex who (outwardly) appears female but (internally) has male reproductive anatomy or vice versa. Individuals would also be considered intersex by medical professionals if they have the following: an abnormally small penis, unusually large clitoris, lack of vaginal opening, or divided scrotum that resembles a labium. *Intersex* also applies to individuals who have sex chromosomes that are not exclusively male (XY) or female (XX) (that is, XXY). Finally, medical professionals might consider individuals to be intersex if they

---

ACTIVE LEARNING ASSIGNMENT 1.4

United Nations Intersex Awareness Campaign

The United Nations Intersex Awareness campaign is designed to educate the world about the realities of intersex individuals, as well as dispel the myths and misconceptions that surround this term. Review the United Nations Intersex Awareness campaign website (https://www.unfe.org/intersex-awareness/). If the website is not active, please contact your instructor for another site. After exploring the site, answer the following questions:

1. What is your opinion about this campaign?
2. Imagine you are the parent of an intersex child. Would the "Advice for Parents" section be helpful? In your explanation, please identify any areas for improvement.
3. Imagine you are the leader of a nation. Would the "Advice for Governments" section be helpful? In your explanation, please identify any areas for improvement.
4. Examine the "Intersex Voices" section of the website. Explain whether and how it changed your perceptions of intersex individuals.

---

have over- or underproduction of sex-related hormones or an inability to respond to sex-related hormones altogether (American Psychological Association, 2006; Intersex Society of North America, 2008).

According to the United Nations (UN, 2017), 1.7 percent of the population is born intersex. While some individuals know they are intersex, others may not. The latter individuals may live their entire lives unaware of being intersex, if there are no visible physical differences from others or if their guardians did not inform them (Intersex Society of North America, 2008). A controversial issue that also arises with guardians is that they, in consultation with medical professionals, may authorize surgical procedures on their intersex children when they are young so that they conform to standards of "male" or "female." While some surgeries may be medically necessary to avoid potentially life-threatening or painful physical conditions, controversy emerges if surgery is not grounded in medical necessity but based on a desire to make the child "fit in." Such a decision is especially problematic as numerous, excruciating surgeries may be required and can result in serious long-term consequences for the child, such as infertility, chronic pain, a decrease or loss in sexual sensation, incontinence, mental anguish, and suffering (UN Free and Equal, 2017; see Active Learning Assignment 1.4). As awareness of the intersex population increases, many parents are electing not to pursue surgery for their children and deciding to raise them as gender-neutral or letting the children decide their own identity and whether they want any surgical changes to their body. (See Media Byte 1.4.)

```
MEDIA BYTE 1.4       Perspectives from Intersex Individuals
```

Please watch the YouTube video "Growing Up Intersex" (https://youtu.be/
I9a1rXOpluc). If this video is no longer available, contact your instructor for a
comparable video. After watching the video, answer the following questions and
be prepared to share your thoughts with the class:

1. What most surprised you about the stories you heard? Please explain.
2. What is your reaction to the experiences these intersex individuals had?
   Please explain.

Why Representation Matters

After discussing key concepts in understanding gender and sex assigned at
birth, we now shift the discussion to how misunderstandings about these
terms negatively impact the lives of those in LGBTQIA+ communities and why
representation matters in all spheres of interaction. The first critical consideration is how to account for and study this area of individuals' lives ethically.
Currently, many studies (and government and social service agencies) use self-
report methods that prompt individuals to identify their gender from a prese-
lected list. However, if that list is not exhaustive, an individual may not "fit" any
of its categories. The lack of fit is particularly problematic for essential forms of
identification (such as a driver's license). For example, Department of Motor
Vehicles forms list "male" or "female," which excludes and marginalizes intersex individuals (and does not acknowledge the range of ways individuals identify in terms of gender). A related ethical concern is that individuals may be
driven to select categories based on social desirability pressures and to avoid
judgment or intrusive questioning from outsiders about what gender they identify with. In both cases, the affected individuals face barriers that cisgender
individuals typically do not face (hence cisgender privilege) and may feel
excluded or marginalized as a result. Problems with gender categories also
occur when individuals access law enforcement following a crime or in the
placement of justice-involved individuals. (See Case Study 1.3.)

CURRENT ISSUES IN GENDER AND CRIME

Privilege comes in many forms. We have discussed privilege associated with
gender, which will be a dominant theme of this book, as well as privilege associated with race. However, disabled people also suffer from unique challenges
associated with the social construct of "disability" that can magnify other
forms of stratification. Likewise, the language surrounding immigration and

Selecting Gender on Facebook

As greater public awareness and understanding have increased about issues related to gender and sex assigned at birth, companies have followed suit and tried to be more inclusive of how people self-identify. For example, Facebook now has fifty-six different options for users to self-identify their gender (see table CS 1.3 for list). This Facebook tool easily allows individuals to identify their gender with just a click of a box. While it is a seemingly small step, the goal is to send a message of inclusivity and support to individuals within LGBTQIA+ communities.

Table CS 1.3   Facebook Gender Selections

Agender	Gender Questioning	Trans Person*
Androgyne	Gender Variant	Trans Woman
Bigender	Genderqueer	Trans Woman*
Cis	Intersex	Trans*
Cis Female	Male to Female	Trans* Female
Cis Male	MTF	Transfeminine
Cis Man	Neither	Transgender
Cis Woman	Neutrois	Transgender Female
Cisgender	Non-binary	Transgender Male
Cisgender Female	Other	Transgender Man
Cisgender Male	Pangender	Transgender Person
Cisgender Man	Trans	Transgender Woman
Cisgender Woman	Trans Female	Transsexual
Female to Female	Trans Male	Transsexual Female
Female to Male	Trans Man	Transsexual Man
FTM	Trans Man*	Transsexual Person
Gender Fluid	Trans Masculine	Two-Spirit
Gender nonconforming	Trans Person	Woman

Users interested in these categories must edit their "Contact and Basic Information" and select Custom from the menu for Gender (see figure CS 1.3). After choosing Custom, the list of options will appear. If the desired option is not present, Facebook allows users to suggest another. In addition to identifying gender, Facebook users can also designate a pronoun preference.

Case Study 1.3 *continued*

Figure CS 1.3. Facebook's gender menu.

· Gender identities in the list with various meanings have an asterisk beside them—for example, "trans*." The use of the asterisk is very deliberate as it conveys a different sense than just the word *trans* or *transgender*, which refers to only trans men and trans women. *Trans** refers to multiple groups and aims to be more inclusive. Thus, users may select trans* to identify themselves and to convey membership in a community with many other individuals beyond that specific designation.

After reviewing the Facebook list, please answer the following questions and be prepared to share with the class:

1. What are your thoughts about Facebook's categories in terms of being inclusive?
2. Do you think Facebook's list is exhaustive? Why or why not?
3. Why is it important to be inclusive on widely used social media platforms?

residency status also carries privilege, which can intensify differential treatment in everyday interactions. Given the role of these overlapping systems in shaping daily interactions, we now shift the conversation to examining how these social constructs and statuses shape individual experiences in the criminal-legal system: first, in terms of immigration and residency; then, in terms of justice-involved LGBTQIA+ youth.

Overlapping Stratification Systems: Gender and Residency Status

One of the most controversial issues within the past decade has been immigration. While this topic superficially appears gender-neutral, research indicates that women are treated differently than men in terms of immigration, residency status, and obtaining citizenship. For example, Salcido and Menjivar

---

ACTIVE LEARNING ASSIGNMENT 1.5

Applying for US Citizenship

Check out the webpage "10 Steps to Naturalization" at https://www.uscis .gov/citizenship/learn-about-citizenship/10-steps-to-naturalization. Click on "Step 3. Prepare your Form N-400, Application for Naturalization." Read through the application at https://www.uscis.gov/n-400. Then answer the following questions:

1. What is your initial reaction to the application?
2. In examining the questions, do you believe the process is gendered? Why or why not?
3. Do you think that most immigrants can complete this application? Why or why not?
4. Do you think that most immigrants will be successful in gaining citizenship if they complete this form? Why or why not?
5. Do you think the application and citizenship process influences whether people decide to live in the country without proper documentation?

(2012) found that immigrant women were treated differently compared to immigrant men. Moreover, research shows that LGBTQIA+ people are more likely to suffer disparaging treatment compared to cisgender people. The number of individuals affected is significant: an estimated twenty million women and girls in the United States are immigrants (American Immigration Council, 2019).

One reason for the disparate treatment is that the US Citizenship and Immigration Services agency is not set up to acknowledge and assist women becoming citizens. Women who immigrate are often considered "dependents" of men, as men are thought of as the head of the household (American Immigration Council, 2019). Thus, even though many immigrant women are the ones financially supporting their families, they encounter a disadvantage based purely on their gender. On the other hand, men face an advantage based solely on their gender. (See Active Learning Assignment 1.5.)

This incorrect assumption about dependency is present throughout the immigration system and leads to different experiences for women going through the naturalization and citizenship process. For instance, women applying for visas are often forced to rely on men as the designated primary visa holders. This constraint remains true even if the woman is applying for an employment visa in a high-demand field that pays very well (Salcido and Menjivar, 2012). The primary method through which immigrant women can obtain legal status in the United States is having a man petition for them in a family-based immigration application and process (American Immigration Council, 2019).

MEDIA BYTE 1.5   Criminalizing Asylum-Seeking Women

Read at least three news articles from reputable outlets about the ankle monitor-ing of asylees. If you have difficulty finding sources, please contact your instruc-tor. After reading the materials, answer the following questions, explaining your beliefs. Be prepared to share your answers with the class.

1. Do you think that asylees should be electronically monitored?
2. Do you think the differential treatment to women asylees is warranted?
3. Do you think women fleeing violence should be treated differently from other populations seeking entry?

Women asylum seekers often encounter unique barriers that stem from their gender. For example, women who harbored guerillas often faced more difficulty establishing residency than men who were *part of* and *served* in gue-rilla armies. These women are punished despite research that shows many of them harbored guerillas after being threatened with rape or physical violence if they did not comply (American Immigration Council, 2019). Relatedly, asylum claims from women fleeing domestic abuse need to provide proof that they lived with the individual who abused them. This proof can be in the form of bills, a deed, or statements, which assumes that the woman had access to finances or that the documentation could be acquired before fleeing. Even if the woman can provide the documentation, however, it does not guarantee her asylum will be granted. For example, in some cases where threats were aimed at a woman's husband, he would be granted asylum but not she (Salcido and Menjivar, 2012). As with many decisions related to justice involvement, a single one can have a ricocheting impact. In this case, if a woman is unsuccessful at establishing lawful residency, she is exposed to possible apprehension, arrest, incarceration, and deportation (see Media Byte 1.5).

System-Involved LGBTQIA+ Youth

In examining issues in gender and identity studies, it is essential to acknowl-edge that there is a crisis for many LGBTQIA+ youth within various spheres of social life: the criminal-legal system, the educational system, the medical sys-tem, and occupational pursuits. LGBTQIA+ youth confront differential treat-ment based on their identity, which can manifest as the denial of opportunities and services or direct forms of ostracization like bullying. Indeed, one in five LGBTQIA+ youth report experiencing bullying, and over half report physical harassment or abuse in school that stems from prejudices tied to their gender or sexual identity (Human Rights Campaign, 2013). To compound these nega-tive experiences, LGBTQIA+ youth of color who are bullied in school often have to interact with the criminal-legal system if they have defended themselves or others during traumatic experiences. These LGBTQIA+ children face the added consequence of possible referral to the criminal-legal system, with lifelong consequences, for arguably preexisting systemic failures.

The **school-to-prison pipeline** is the channeling of youth from school to the criminal-legal system (juvenile or adult). The pipeline begins with disciplinary problems in school, which leads to law enforcement referrals. Or it can begin through suspension and expulsion, which puts youth on the streets and thereby increases their chances of interaction with the criminal-legal system. Students are often funneled into the pipeline for offenses that occur on school property or at school events. These events can range in severity but tend to fall into one of five categories: affray (fighting in a public area and/or disturbing the peace), communicating threats, disrespect or insubordination, disruptive behavior/disorderly conduct, and petty larceny (Fabelo et al., 2011). Depending on the school's policies, committing one of these offenses could lead to disciplinary action that would change the course of the child's life.

Zero-tolerance policies are in effect within 94 percent of US public schools (Skiba et al., 2011). These policies mandate severe responses—usually expulsion and referral to law enforcement—if students engage in or become involved in certain offenses. Other severe consequences include suspension or some other punishment as designated by the school. Schools employ zero-tolerance policies for different offenses, not always just unprovoked violence. For example, some policies can be applied to youth who were defending themselves. While zero-tolerance policies are designed to deter violence, there is a dearth of empirical evidence pointing to their effectiveness (González, 2012). Moreover, as previously noted, these policies further harm youth who already experience barriers to securing equitable treatment within educational institutions. Considering the disparaging treatment often experienced by marginalized youth, it should not be surprising that research has found that these policies have resulted in a disproportionate number of suspensions and expulsions for children of color. Research shows youth of color are disciplined differently in schools than are their white peers (Bell and Puckett, 2020). Black boys are often wrongly assumed to be older than they are, believed to be guilty of engaging in deviance, and encounter more incidents of police violence than white boys do. This discriminatory treatment also extends to Black girls: research has found that Black girls are viewed as needing less protection, support, and comfort than white girls (Epstein, Blake, and Gonzalez, 2017). This differential treatment is suspected to stem from societal perceptions that Black girls are "tougher" and in less need of these responses. For children of color who identify as part of the LGBTQIA+ communities, these overlapping systems of oppression (heterosexism, racism, and so on) can be severely detrimental to their educational experience—especially if they experience unfair treatment in school and run afoul of zero-tolerance policies (Human Rights Campaign, 2013).

Another issue related to the school-to-prison pipeline is the number of LGBTQIA+ children who end up in the foster care system. Children are given up to the system for a multitude of reasons or can become system-involved if they are already intertwined with the juvenile-legal system. Since the criminal-legal system is not responsive to backgrounds of involved individuals, juveniles who identify as part of LBGTQIA+ communities may experience additional trauma. This trauma may stem from experiencing harassment or rejection based on their sexual orientation, gender identity, or gender expression, which in turn may lead to more exclusion, isolation, depression, and anxiety than cisgender youth experience. The point is that LGBTQIA+ youth, as well as youth of color, are likely to find themselves in systems that are not equipped to address the systemic inequalities they confront in the course of daily life.

In terms of system involvement via foster care, research has shown that LGBTQIA+ youth are more likely to experience harmful and damaging interactions with those working in the child welfare profession than cisgender and heterosexual youth are. LGBTQIA+ youth were twice as likely to report poor treatment within the foster care system as other groups. Moreover, LGBTIA+ youth were twice as likely to be placed in group homes and three times more likely to be hospitalized because of emotional trauma than heterosexual and cisgender youth were (Wilson et al., 2014).

Aside from the initial adverse treatment within the foster care system, LGBTQIA+ children are also more than twice as likely as heterosexual or cisgender children to be moved from their first caregiver or foster family—often due to the family's request (Berg, Mimiaga, and Safren, 2008; Dettlaff et al., 2018). Foster parents may not understand or want to understand the issues of LGBTQIA+ youth. The same can be said about individuals working in the child welfare field whose job it is to assist families with these transitionary periods. In other words, the negative experiences LGBTQIA+ youth report experiencing from child welfare workers can stem from those individuals' personal biases, lack of education in relevant topics, or overall incompetency in addressing issues specific to LGBTQIA+ youth. Unfortunately, LGBTQIA+ children suffer from these deficits, which are outside their control, experiencing emotional and physical consequences associated with rejection, loneliness, and depression (Ragg, Patrick, and Ziefert, 2006). (See Active Learning Assignment 1.6.)

Research shows that involvement in the child welfare system is also linked to sex trafficking and commercial sex, with high rates for LGBTQIA+ youth of color. A report issued by the US Department of Health and Human Services Administration (2013) revealed that between 50 percent and 90 percent of those who experienced sex trafficking had been involved in child welfare services. This relationship likely stems from the impermanence of housing and the traumatic background experienced by many LGBTQIA+ youth "aging out" of child welfare services. Youth without stable homes and who are grappling with the residual impacts of trauma are likely to be targeted by traffickers. As

---

ACTIVE LEARNING ASSIGNMENT 1.6

Explore a Guide for Foster Parents

To assist foster parents with understanding the needs of LGBTQIA+ youth, organizations and agencies have prepared guides like the following: https://www.childwelfare.gov/pubPDFs/LGBTQyouth.pdf. If this guide is not available, please ask your instructor for an alternative.

   After reading the guide, please answer the following questions and be prepared to share your answers with the class:

1. What misconceptions about LGBTQIA+ youth are covered in this guide? Please provide examples.
2. What are the risks to LGBTQIA+ youth as a result of being rejected by their family?
3. In what ways can a foster parent create a welcoming home for LGBTQIA+ youth?
4. How can you support LGBTQIA+ youth in your community?
5. If a foster parent follows the tips and suggestions listed, do you think that could prevent a child from running away or being recruited by traffickers? Why or why not?

---

mentioned, LGBTQIA+ youth are especially likely to have unstable housing and a history of trauma. Consequently, these youth are vulnerable to traffickers who promise to meet their basic needs. Once that relationship is established, however, these traffickers often use coercive tactics (like physical and psychological abuse) to retain control for exploitation purposes (Polaris Project, 2019).

MOVING TOWARD QUEER CRIMINOLOGY

The information presented in this chapter has shown that there are many individuals within society with specific needs and issues related to their gender or overall identity. It is vital for the criminal-legal system, academics, and society to acknowledge that this is a salient need and to act to assist people within the LGBTQIA+ communities. Within the past decade, there has been a movement within academia to be more inclusive regarding those within the LGBTQIA+ communities, which led to the creation of queer criminology. **Queer criminology** is a subfield of criminology in which scholars address topics of importance to LGBTQIA+ people. A goal of queer criminology is to support LGBTQIA+-identifying researchers and activists who will ultimately be able to change the systemic forms of oppression discussed throughout this chapter and book. In other words, queer criminology is dedicated to political and systematic change within society and the criminal-legal system so that LGBTQIA+ individuals do not experience injustices across various spheres of social life (Ball, 2016a; Buist and Lenning, 2016).

Although this subfield endeavors to include all people within multiple groups, some have contested the use of the term *queer*. However, the word *queer* is often used to refer to any difference or challenge to heteronormativity, gender, and/or sexuality norms and binaries (Jagose, 1996; Sullivan, 2003). Moreover, the term *queer* has also been historically connected to politics and activism. Thus, its use in the queer criminology movement is activist-oriented and is meant to include all who have been left out or marginalized.

The use of *queer* has a secondary purpose: it reclaims once-derogatory language that was meant to isolate LGBTQIA+ individuals. Initially, *queer* was a term that was used to insult or harm someone, but it was reclaimed in the 1980s and 1990s by the individuals that word sought to disparage. Those individuals took the term *queer* as part of a movement to push for equality across various spheres of social life, and the meaning attached to the term has since shifted to positive. However, critics of these early queer movements cite various inequalities in that time: the exclusion of people of color, the exclusion of transgender individuals, and the promotion of issues based on privilege (Jagose, 1996; Sullivan, 2003). Regardless of these disagreements, the queer criminology field continues to advocate for inclusivity and raise awareness of the unique barriers faced by LGBTQIA+ people.

As previously mentioned, LGBTQIA+ individuals are at risk for violence based on homophobia and transphobia, which they are unlikely to find assistance for or compassion about in the criminal-legal system (see chapter 8). Instead, many individuals within LGBTQIA+ communities face persecution, arrest, harassment, and victimization at the hands of the criminal-legal system (Buist and Lenning, 2016; Mogul, Ritchie, and Whitlock, 2011). Unfortunately, the criminology field has not been a forceful ally in addressing these systemic issues; instead, the field often actively worked to perpetuate myths and stereotypes regarding LGBTQIA+ people through research, findings, and categorizations that classified same-sex relations as "deviant" and/or as part of a "disorder." Perhaps most disturbingly, some work was used in the criminalization of acts, thus making individuals who committed them "criminals" and subject to punishments and incarceration (see chapter 5). Unfortunately, despite advances in thinking, criminologists have not worked to replace these harmful and destructive labels but instead have remained silent on issues related to sexuality and gender identity (Woods, 2014).

As research has advanced, new issues related to LGBTQIA+ individuals underscore the vital role of queer criminology in shaping discourse about equality and inclusivity. New lines of research include anti-gay violence and entrapment by law enforcement, criminalization of consensual same-sex activities, and police raids on establishments where gay, lesbian, and transgender individuals congregate (Buist and Lenning, 2016; Mogul, Ritchie, and Whitlock, 2011; Moore, 2001). To bring attention to these and other issues of LGBTQIA+ experiences, criminologists, researchers, and students within the field need to actively seek to include LGBTQIA+ individuals in their research, teaching, and activism. If more data is collected about individuals within LGBTQIA+ communities, it could be used to influence policy and assist agencies that work with system-involved individuals, as well as to help practitioners who work with individuals from LGBTQIA+ populations.

Queer criminology and other fields of study that raise the voices of those who have been silenced in mainstream criminology and society are necessary as they allow for different perspectives and experiences to be heard and considered (Ball, 2016b; Belknap, 2015; Buist and Lenning, 2016). Many of the scholars and researchers who have embraced queer criminology and its associated activism are graduate students and early career academics without tenure. This provides much hope for the future as new scholars embrace new areas of study. However, it also provides an obstacle to the growth of this emerging area as young scholars in the field of criminological research and teaching may face resistance from scholarly organizations, universities, academic departments, colleagues, and students in the courses that are being taught. There may be anti-LGBTQIA+ sentiment within these groups, and scholars may face pressures to conform. Individuals wanting to do this research and teach this material may be guided down a path that would be considered "safer" or more traditional to obtain tenure and academic recognition and to be taken more seriously as a teacher-scholar (Ball, 2016b; Belknap, 2015; Buist and Lenning, 2016; Dalton, 2016). (See Active Learning Assignment 1.7.)

The suggestion often made to graduate students and junior scholars not to devote much research energy or teaching within the area of queer criminology is likely the result of sparse representation or positive depictions of LGBTQIA+

ACTIVE LEARNING ASSIGNMENT 1.7

Queer Criminology

Please listen to the following program, "Queer Criminology," which includes stories that illustrate the need for this approach: https://youtu.be/oZOiFE2Ec7w. If this program is not available, please contact your instructor for an alternative. After listening to the program, answer the following questions and be prepared to share your answers with the class:

1. What are your thoughts on the emerging area of queer criminology?
2. Do the stories that are shared show a need for queer criminology? Why or why not?
3. Please provide some examples from this program about how individuals within LGBTQIA+ communities are treated differently.
4. Why do you think people within LGBTQIA+ communities are treated differently in the criminal-legal system?
5. What positive effects on system-involved people are likely if queer criminology becomes more mainstream? Please explain.

individuals within the criminology field. Moreover, queer criminology, as discussed, did not emerge as an academic pursuit in the same way as more traditional areas like policing. Thus, to change its reputation long-term, Belknap (2015) suggests that queer criminology follow the path of Black criminologists. They have been strategic in the publications and representations of their work, as well as in taking leadership positions within higher education and professional organizations. Finally, Black criminologists have done considerable work pursuing grant funding to improve the criminal-legal system as change agents (Gabbidon, Taylor Greene, and Wilder, 2004). This has allowed Black scholars to have a voice within the discipline in a way that they did not before. While arguably, there is still room for improvement, their path can serve as a model for other marginalized groups that are advocating for change.

SUMMARY

This chapter has explained and discussed the differences in terms relating to gender, gender identity, sexual orientation, and overall identity. While many view gender in binary terms, there are other ways to view and express gender, as presented in this chapter. While gender has been one of the most identifiable characteristics, the way that someone expresses themselves, how they act, or their profession does not necessarily reflect their gender identity. There are many variations and nuances when it comes to understanding gender. It is also essential to understand the connection of gender and perceived gender identity to the treatment that one experiences in society. Cisgender individuals experience life much differently than transgender or gender non-binary individuals.

Two of the current issues relating to gender are immigration and LGBTQIA+ youth in the system. Research has shown that immigration status has a very gendered nature, affecting how one receives residency status or asylum, with men often coming out ahead. Likewise, LGBTQIA+ youth in the criminal-legal and foster care systems often have a very different experience than heterosexual and/or cisgender youth. In school, LGBTQIA+ youth are often teased and harassed and may face dire consequences for retaliation through zero-tolerance policies that contribute to the school-to-prison pipeline. Also, LGBTQIA+ youth are often mistreated and have differential experiences in the foster care system. They experience unstable housing as they move from home to home, usually at the request of the foster parent. Among child welfare workers and foster parents there can be a lack of understanding of what LGBTQIA+ youth need and want, which makes these youth particularly vulnerable to recruitment by sex traffickers.

Overall, this chapter has provided an overview of different identities and ways that people see themselves. Despite advances in thinking, however, there is still differential treatment of individuals based on their gender, sexual orientation, and identity, which means that there is still work to be done. The emerging area of queer criminology seeks to bring more attention to the issues of LGBTQIA+ individuals within the criminal-legal system. However, there are often challenges for those who want to research and teach in this area as more traditional and mainstream areas of criminology are favored. Yet, through the persistence of scholars researching and teaching in this area, there will be more information published and disseminated to students, which will continue to bring many of the topics discussed in this text into greater focus.

The Why and How

2

Theories of Gender, Crime, and Victimization

KEY TERMS
- ► biosocial theory
- ► criminology
- ► deterrence theory
- ► feminist pathways theory
- ► labeling theory
- ► life course and development perspective
- ► rational choice theory
- ► routine activities theory
- ► self-control theory
- ► social control theory
- ► social learning theory
- ► strain theory
- ► victimology

LEARNING OBJECTIVES
- ► Understand the premise and key components of various criminological perspectives.
- ► Explain how gender and gender norms and roles work in conjunction with various criminological perspectives to explain crime.
- ► Apply chapter content to contemporary issues related to gender and crime.

The question of why individuals engage in crime has intrigued academics and practitioners from across disciplines since the late 1800s. It was during this period when the discipline was formally named **criminology,** which is the scientific study of crime. As criminology grew throughout the years, the lens of interest widened to understanding victimization (that is, **victimology**) before, during, and after criminal events (Mendelsohn, 1976). To better understand both perpetration and victimization, criminologists have proposed many theories that have both withstood the test of time and proved to be adaptable to new arenas of criminal activity (such as the internet).

In this chapter, we review often-cited criminological theories, but through a gendered lens. In other words, we explain the basic premise of each perspective but also discuss the applicability of each framework across genders (that is, cisgender and non-cisgender). In some these instances, the authors express their viewpoints on the subject because there is a shortage of research across perspectives, particularly concerning the non-cisgender community.

BIOSOCIAL THEORY

Perhaps the earliest, and most controversial, explanation of the genesis of crime originated from scholars who focused on understanding whether specific biological markers were indicative of criminality—then referred to as biological criminology (e.g., Lombroso, 1911). However, this early work quickly lost favor within the academy as rational choice perspectives grew in popularity. Moreover, given the potential dangers associated with this line of research being misrepresented and misused, social scientists quickly abandoned its pursuit (Wright and Cullen, 2012). Despite its rise and fall, this framework has been revitalized by scholars who investigate the role of biology and the environment (i.e., **biosocial theory**) in the manifestation of criminal behavior (Biosocial Criminology Association, https://www.biosocialcrim.org/). Contemporary work has focused on prenatal and perinatal risk factors and engagement in delinquency (Barnes and TenEyck, 2017) and using the biosocial perspective to identify why response to programming aimed at reducing deviance varies across youth (Vaske, 2017). This theory can also be used to frame support for forced sterilization or promotion of soft sterilization (such as IUDs [intrauterine devices]) for system-involved women, poor women, or women deemed not fit to reproduce.

While this theoretical field is growing, there remain serious ethical concerns about whether subgroups can be inadvertently harmed through this line of research; for example, poor women of color are most often harmed by forced sterilization programs (see Case Study 2.1).

DETERRENCE THEORY

Deterrence theory, or what many colloquially refer to as the "backbone" of the criminal-legal system, purports that criminal behavior can be "deterred" by ensuring that engagement in such activities is not perceived to be in one's best interest. Put another way, deterrence theorists argue that humans are oriented toward behavior that is both desirable and unlikely to cause painful individual consequences. Thus, to prevent the onset of crime, the criminal-legal system needs to be designed such that the potential effects of criminal activity offset any motivations toward deviant behaviors. To create this imbalance, deterrence theory emphasizes that punishment must be swift, certain, and severe (Loughran, Paternoster, and Weiss, 2016; Pratt et al., 2017).

While deterrence theory gained widespread support in early criminology, subsequent empirical research has mostly produced mixed or weak support for the merits of the perspective. Of the components that have been evaluated, scholars have paid particular attention to the "certainty" component. In a review of this research, Loughran and colleagues (2016) concluded that the

---

CASE STUDY 2.1

Sterilization of the Poor and Black in North Carolina

Sterilization programs targeted at specific groups of people are an opportunity to apply biosocial theory to the social world. Between 1929 and 1974, North Carolina sterilized an estimated 7,600 people through the state-sponsored eugenics board. This process was not unique to North Carolina; thirty states had similar laws and boards that were staffed by respected doctors, lawyers, and social workers. The push for sterilization was grounded in assorted reasons that denied these individuals their agency and humanity, such as they were criminal, lazy, promiscuous, and financially insecure. Therefore, to avoid future generations with such traits, sterilization was "necessary." Historical records show that these sterilization programs operated for significant periods of time and

targeted marginalized members of society, specifically the Black community (Price and Darity, 2010). The women typically did not consent: these procedures occurred during other medical procedures like childbirth. For example, a fourteen-year-old Black girl gave birth to a child who was the result of rape, and she was sterilized against her will after giving birth. She did not find out until years later when she was married and was trying to start a family with her husband (Fowler, 2020). In 2010, the North Carolina Justice for Sterilization Victims Foundation was created. In 2013, the state awarded the 177 remaining living people who had been sterilized $10 million in damages.

1. What is your opinion of eugenics boards?
2. Do you think that the biosocial reasoning is strong enough justification to sterilize someone? Please explain.

---

evidence supporting the inverse relationship between the certainty of punishment and engagement in criminal activities was weak. Likewise, although some attention has been paid to the severity of punishment, findings have been inconsistent. In one noteworthy example utilizing college students, Pogarsky (2002) found that the severity of punishment was a significant factor in the investigation of considering criminal engagement. In contrast to certainty and severity of punishment, however, celerity, or swiftness, has rarely been considered, given methodological challenges experienced by researchers.

Deterrence theorists would likely assert that this framework is particularly robust because it addresses criminal activity before onset as well as acts to mitigate later offending. In terms of the former, individuals who refrain from engaging in deviance in recognition of the swift, certain, and severe response by the criminal-legal system are said to have experienced primary deterrence (Loughran, Paternoster, and Weiss, 2016). For example, a driver is running late for work and contemplates running a red light. As the driver approaches the intersection, he notices a law enforcement officer sitting at the intersection and does not continue with the idea. In this example, the driver specifically stopped before committing an offense when he realized he would experience swift, certain, and severe punishment by the criminal-legal system.

Components	Primary Deterrence	Secondary Deterrence
Swiftness of Punishment	The individual does not engage in the offense, because the action is not in their best interest in the reflection of swift, certain, and severe punishment.	A system-involved individual does not engage in the offense because the action is not in their best interest in the reflection of swift, certain, and severe punishment.
Certainty of Punishment		
Severity of Punishment		

Figure 2.1. Deterrence theory. Figure created by authors.

The tenets of deterrence theory also apply to system-involved individuals who refrain from engaging in subsequent deviance (that is, secondary deterrence). For example, a community-monitored individual (via check-ins with parole or probation officers, required counseling sessions, and ankle monitoring) who committed a sexual offense is contemplating engaging in a contact offense (a physical or sexual offense against a person) at a local school. As the individual thinks through this course of action, he realizes that his monitor is certain to go off as he approaches the school, which would result in a swift, certain, and severe response by law enforcement. Because he fears violating the terms of his release, the individual does not engage in the contact offense.

Despite the substantial footprint of deterrence theory in criminal-legal policy, the effectiveness of the perspective in framing engagement in and deterring crime has not been strongly supported in the literature. While this lack of support may be related to the elusive "tipping point," or the point at which the certainty of punishment is perceived and internalized among the wider population (Loughran, Paternoster, and Weiss, 2016), it could also be that the origination of crime goes beyond the potential consequences of such actions. For example, individual decisions on what steps are in one's best interest, in the reflection of possible outcomes, may have a nexus with gender.

Although deterrence theory is an essential theoretical perspective in terms of shaping the criminal-legal system, it has rarely been evaluated through a gendered lens (Smith and Paternoster, 1987). Many of the studies that focus on the applicability of deterrence theory across genders, although noteworthy, are dated (pre-2000s) (e.g., Finley and Grasmick, 1985). In contrast, other studies include gender as merely a control variable. Aside from these exceptions, typically only traditional binary categories have been used in studies. In other words, to the best of our knowledge, investigation on the applicability of deterrence theory beyond the conventional binary categories of "men" and "women" is absent from the literature.

In one early investigation assessing the role of gender within a deterrence theory context, scholars evaluated whether girls and boys responded differently to police interaction. Its findings suggested that contact with law enforcement acted as a potential deterrent for girls' delinquency. However, this effect was not present for boys. Ultimately, the scholars noted this behavior was likely reflective of a difference in risk aversion between girls (more risk aversive) and boys (less risk aversive). The authors concluded that deterrence theory provided a more meaningful framing of offending by girls than by boys (Keane, Gillis, and Hagan, 1989).

While the study by Keane and colleagues indicated deterrence theory may vary across genders, this overall finding was not supported in similar research. For example, an earlier study by Smith and Paternoster (1987) asserted that deterrence theory, among other theoretical frameworks, was as applicable in framing offending by women as offending by men. Consequently, these researchers stated that the call for theoretical perspectives specific to women's offending was ill-advised and unwarranted.

Fast-forwarding to the present day, an abundance of scholarly attention has called into question whether deterrence theory presents a holistic picture of the origins of crime. For example, in one thorough synthesis of the literature, scholars found that the critical components of deterrence theory were only weakly related to crime. Moreover, when other essential theoretical concepts were assessed, beyond those specified in deterrence theory, the impact of certainty, celerity, and severity on crime essentially became moot. While scholars do not advocate for the dismissal of deterrence theory, current thinking supports integrating this perspective with other frameworks (Pratt et al., 2017). We agree with this call, particularly given the conflicting findings regarding the critical components of deterrence theory across genders, including the complete absence of investigation beyond conventional binary categories.

CONFLICT AND CRITICAL THEORIES

The 1950s brought theories that incorporated conflict into the earlier criminological perspectives. For example, Thorsten Sellin's (1938) theory of culture conflict posited that there is a conflict between different cultural groups and subcultures. For example, this can occur when immigrants come into a country because there is pressure to assimilate from the broader culture, but individual desires to maintain customs and traditions are also important. Within this theory, cultural differences are used as a justification for the crimes committed as having been legal or acceptable in the previous culture but not in the new culture. For example, the physical punishment or abuse of women is tolerated or legal in certain countries but not in the United States. This creates a culture conflict as the individual who broke the law may not see their actions as wrong based upon their upbringing and life in the former country. (See Case Study 2.2.)

Honor Killings

Honor violence occurs against women by men who are related to them to reclaim family "honor" that they believe the women have tarnished. In certain cultures, a woman can dishonor her family by being too promiscuous, being too American (if an immigrant), having premarital sex (even if raped), dressing inappropriately, or not obeying. Male relatives will physically abuse or kill the woman to bring honor back to the family name. This practice is rooted in cultures that believe that women are objects, belongings, and the property of men. The United Nations (2010) estimates that five thousand women and girls are murdered each year in honor killings. However, people murdered in honor killings can also be individuals who identify as LGBTQIA+, who would dishonor the family with their sexual identity or sexual orientation.

Please reflect on the information about honor killings and answer the following questions. Be prepared to share your answers with the class.

1. Do you think that an immigrant committing an honor killing or honor violence should be punished? Why or why not?
2. Would your answer be different for a person who had immigrated to a place where honor violence is legal or not enforced? Please explain.

George Vold, often considered the founder of conflict or critical theory, wrote about the issues that occur between groups in 1958. This theory, which ultimately stems from the works of Karl Marx, views conflict as a natural component of society's social process involving a struggle to maintain or gain power. In other words, different groups in a society are bound to have conflicting interests and clashing politics. For a society to effectively use the conflict and flourish, there needs to be a compromise between groups. The focus of this theory is on crime that results from conflicting group interests, including things such as ethnic clashes, political protests, and labor disputes. While this theory did not initially focus on gender, it is applicable today to the power struggle that is often seen between men and women. More specifically, given that men control and dominate most aspects of society in terms of social capital and power (that is, patriarchy), marginalized groups such as LGBTQIA+ people and women may be at odds with them. These groups are trying to make changes through social movements, politics, and activism to reduce the amount of power that men wield when making decisions that impact others.

The 1960s brought about a substantial change in criminological theory, as there were three significant events related to social change: the Vietnam War, the growth of a counterculture, and the rising political protests aimed at eliminating discrimination and racism. The Vietnam War affected American society by creating legitimate doubts about the motives and credibility of those in power. The development of a counterculture that centered on the middle and lower classes in terms of its refusal to abide by the "established standards" of activism also contributed to the advancement of criminological theory. The resulting social conflict was placed at the forefront of emerging perspectives during this time, especially after people began to see that a viable approach to fighting for equality was through civil disobedience, which often meant breaking the law. While these movements were not focused on gender, they paved the way for the feminist movement soon to come.

Related to social power, Austin Turk (1969) believed that the problem of explaining crime was in how criminality was defined. Like his predecessors, he found that society is characterized by conflict arising between different groups trying to establish control over one another. However, he emphasized that when defining "criminality," the critical interaction occurs between those who enforce the law and those who violate the law. In the process of conceptualizing crime, various social factors such as cultural and social norms (that is, widely held unwritten rules of behavior) and the criminalization process also influence what is considered legal or illegal. Turk believed that the assignment of the label *criminal* to an individual had less to do with their actual behavior and more to do with their relationship to authority. In terms of gender, women were less likely to be criminalized in the 1960s and 1970s; instead, they were institutionalized. If a woman engaged in a crime or acted out of character, she was thought of as "mentally ill" or "sick" and in need of treatment.

Richard Quinney's (1970) theory of social reality was also a product of the 1960s. He believed that everyone experienced a different reality. In other words, our reality stems from our socioeconomic status, race, gender, and so on. For example, financially insecure people encounter a different reality than those of higher socioeconomic means. Likewise, cisgender people experience a different reality than LGBTQIA+ individuals. Quinney's perspective can be true of various social stratification categories as people were treated differently in the 1960s relative to now.

In 1971, William Chambliss and Robert Seidman developed a conflict theory about the legal system. Within this perspective, the complexity of society and the idea that several groups are always in conflict with one another are essential components of this framework. The premise of the perspective is that the ruling class uses the law as a proxy for coercively controlling others, which is about money and power. In essence, those with wealth and power have their norms or values reflected in society, ensuring that their interests are served. Chambliss and Seidman believed that the relationship between those in power and the use of the law as a tool affected numerous institutions, including law enforcement and legislatures. This can be seen in the structure and nature of laws that are passed. From a gendered and race perspective, those with the most social capital are white cisgender men, and thus they can influence the passage of laws that support that point of privilege. In recent years, however, the makeup of power is shifting. (See Media Byte 2.1.)

MEDIA BYTE 2.1   More Women of Color Elected to Congress

Please read the following article about the growing numbers of women of color elected to Congress: https://www.washingtonpost.com/nation/2019/01/04 /women-color-congress-are-challenging-perceptions-political-leadership/? noredirect=on. If this article is no longer available, please ask your instructor for a similar one. After reading the article, please answer the following questions:

1. Do you believe that increasing the diversity and inclusivity of Congress will change the power structure within society? If so, please explain. If not, please explain.
2. Do you think that increasing the diversity and inclusivity within Congress will change crime control policies? Please explain.
3. How does this shift in Congress compare to conflict and critical theory? Please explain.

As conflict and critical theories have evolved, individuals have continued to apply them to examine differences in power. One such method is reviewing the treatment of individuals by the criminal-legal system to see how those in power and those without power are treated. Critical criminologists have also applied these theories to understanding the wealth differential within society and the crimes of the powerful. More specifically, some critical criminologists are interested in how those in power engage in crimes but seem to avoid severe (if any) punishment for their actions. Likewise, in terms of gender dynamics, some critical criminologists study the power differentials in sex trafficking and rape. Broadly, contemporary critical criminology theorists are interested in understanding the detrimental treatment of those without power.

Cultural Criminology

Cultural criminology is a product of the critical criminology movement, as it is focused on examining culture and society, and how culture and society impact the understanding and views of crime. Ferrell and Sanders (1995) are credited with founding cultural criminology. The basic underlying assumption of this theoretical perspective is that "crimes" are constructed out of symbolic inter-actions among groups and people. Given that crimes are socially constructed, there are continuing variations in their meaning and perceptions that shape interpretations. In other words, cultural criminologists view the conception and definition of crime as complex.

From a cultural criminology perspective, the meaning of crime, criminality, and crime control are shaped by everyday influences like the media. Ferrell and

Sanders (1995) posited three requirements for cultural criminology. First, researchers need to understand the critical role of media in shaping the crime and justice beliefs of the people in a particular society. Second, scholars need to focus on studying and evaluating the legal and moral authorities that dictate what is acceptable in the media. Third, researchers should be aware that crime cannot be understood without examining the powers that shape policy and the meaning of crime itself. Put another way: one cannot investigate media content without taking into consideration the individuals charged with creating and disbursing that media to society. Given the nature of this theory, traditional models of study, such as survey research, are likely dated. Instead, ethnographies are better suited to capture system-involved individuals' perceptions, their subcultural interpretations of life, and the emotions involved in crime (such as surprise or ambiguity). In examining how things are portrayed, the goal is to understand why society may view gender, race, and sexuality in ways that harm individuals at the micro level.

Convict Criminology

Convict criminology emerged in the 1990s from five interrelated movements: theoretical developments in criminology, writings in victimology and constitutive criminology, the failure of the system-involved individuals' rights movement, the authenticity of insider perspectives, and the growing importance of ethnography (Richards and Ross, 2001). The basic tenet of convict criminology is that system-involved individuals should be recognized in the criminal-legal process, whether it be via working within education, policy-making, or research fields. This tenet is grounded in the belief that system-involved individuals are stripped of their humanity in the criminal-legal process through the language used and their treatment before and after involvement. Thus, as people first and foremost, they have critical insights to share, given their lived experience of being incarcerated and interacting with the criminal-legal system. Moreover, they are uniquely positioned to provide input on ways to better the system that others not directly involved cannot. In the same manner that former law enforcement officers, lawyers, and corrections officers who have earned doctoral degrees are celebrated, those who have been incarcerated and paid their debt to society also bring unique perspectives to academia as well as the criminal-legal system overall, which should be celebrated as well.

Interest in convict criminology has significantly expanded since 2011. It has become a formal division in the American Society of Criminology, and it has become a more standard subject within criminology. Although journals and research books do not necessarily include this perspective as a theoretical paradigm, it is relevant and related to critical and conflict theories. For example, research on system-involved individuals has highlighted the potential problems these returning citizens have in the hiring process. In one study, Ross and colleagues (2011) found that system-involved individuals interviewing for faculty positions reported that their experiences were positive but included some tension.

Additionally, departments seeking to hire individuals with personal expertise in convict criminology struggled with securing funding from donors, grants, and the state (Ross et al., 2011). Individuals with PhDs who were formerly incarcerated may also face barriers to research, such as obtaining funding or access to correctional facilities. Despite these obstacles, however, system-involved individuals are exceptionally suited to building rapport with individuals who are incarcerated or returning to society after state control. With the growth in convict criminology, there are many areas ripe for investigation, especially in the areas of gender and sexual identity. For instance, one area deals with studying responsive programming that meets the diverse needs of individuals who are incarcerated or under other methods of state control and accounts for their identities and life histories, and how this programming can in turn reduce recidivism as well as improve policies and education.

FEMINIST THEORIES

For much of early criminology, scholars focused on understanding crime perpetrated by men (Miller and Mullins, 2017; Smith and Paternoster, 1987). If women were included in studies, they were often used as comparisons or were kept at the periphery. This pervasive pattern led to the now-famous statement by Chesney-Lind (1986) that the approach of early criminological research was "add women and stir." However, as large-scale social events occurred, such as the women's liberation movement, interest in understanding factors that contributed to offending by and victimization of women grew (Sharp, 2009). This increased interest eventually led to the founding of the criminology subdiscipline referred to as feminist criminology, where "theories of gender are as much a starting point . . . as are theories of crime" (Miller and Mullins, 2017, 217).

There are several branches of feminist thought, which all consider how various systems of oppression (e.g., ableism, racism, sexism) intersect to affect the lives of women every day. These branches include liberal, Marxist, socialist, radical, and postmodern feminisms. Although each branch slightly differs in its approach, feminist criminologists assert that given the way that gender shapes and underscores the entirety of individuals' lives, it is a necessity to view criminal activity also through a gendered lens. Moreover, it is important to consider not only gender but also how other facets of one's self-identity (e.g., disability, ethnicity, sexual orientation) intersect with gender to affect life choices and decisions (Belknap, 2016).

Aside from calling attention to the role of gender in the structuring of social life, feminist criminologists remain influential voices in addressing bias reproduced through academia. This bias is especially apparent in early criminological research that relied on long-held stereotypes about femininity (e.g., irrationality, passivity) to explain offending by women. To address the challenges in explaining offending by and victimization of women and to overcome reliance on these assumptions, feminist criminologists advocate for nuanced perspectives rather than broad theories that purport to explain crime across many different contexts (Miller and Mullins, 2017). One such view, and perhaps one of the most significant contributions of feminist criminology, is feminist pathways theory.

Feminist pathways theory was a groundbreaking contribution to the broader criminology discipline because it specifically focuses on the unique macro- and micro-level factors that affect offending by and victimization of women. Like the life course development perspective discussed later in this chapter, feminist pathways theory asserts that early adverse life events can have lasting and profound effects on women and girls. In other words, early trauma, such as abuse, or interaction with the criminal-legal system, such as truancy, can set young women down a path toward later offending and/or victimization (Pasko and Chesney-Lind, 2016; Simpson, Yahner, and Dugan, 2008). This has led some to refer to the connections between offending and victimization as "blurred boundaries" in which victimization can propel women and girls toward offending, and offending can propel women and girls toward experiencing victimization (Miller and Mullins, 2017).

As interest in understanding women's routes to criminality grew, specific pathways were identified. Indeed, in Daly's pivotal 1994 publication, which described the review of forty felony cases involving women who broke the law, five distinct pathways to criminal engagement were identified: (1) "street women" are women who have been addicted to drugs and involved in street-level crime (such as petty theft, sex work); (2) "harmed and harming women" are women from dysfunctional childhood homes in which there was abuse and whose trauma manifests through their delinquency in later adolescence; (3) "drug-connected women" are women who have participated in the illegal drug market—whether as consumers or sellers, or both; (4) "battered women" are women who have violently offended within the context of an abusive relationship; and (5) "other women" are women who have offended out of a desire to obtain resources associated with a mainstream lifestyle and who do not align with any of the other groups (cited in Simpson, Yahner, and Dugan, 2008; cited in Wattanaporn and Holtfreter, 2014).

Although feminist pathways theory is in its infancy, compared to other long-standing frameworks, scholars have found that the approach is particularly useful in understanding women's criminality and victimization. For example, in a study investigating Daly's (1994) pathways, Simpson and colleagues (2008) interviewed 351 women who were incarcerated about their personal histories. After data collection, the scholars found that their results closely mirrored the pathway categories established by Daly. Given these findings, the scholars concluded that feminist pathways theory, although not widely utilized yet, is highly applicable in the understanding of women's criminality and victimization and the "blurred boundary" between the two.

In addition, feminist criminologists have also focused on investigating gendered social patterns in women's lives that affect engagement in crime. This work is readily seen in the utilization of opportunity theory, which considers situational characteristics that impact the likelihood of a criminal event. For example, again in recognition of the overlap between system-involved individuals and those who have crimes committed against them, think of a woman who is abused by her partner and who has limited social support and resources (situational characteristics) to extricate herself from the violence. Seeing no other recourse to stopping the violence, the woman kills her partner (the offense). In this example, there is a direct link between the victimization and the attack as well as critical situational characteristics that explain further why the homicide happened. Moreover, again, this coincides with the "battered women" pathway established by Daly (1994) and is supported in contemporary research (Simpson, Yahner, and Dugan, 2008; Wattanaporn and Holtfreter, 2014). (See Media Byte 2.2.)

Not only is feminist pathways theory providing insight into women's criminality and victimization, but the pathways perspective is also being applied to explain offending and victimization among LGBTQIA+ youth (Palmer and Greytak, 2017). As discussed by Buist and Lenning (2016), just as gender influences the pathways women encounter throughout their lives, so too do gender identity and sexual orientation shape the paths of LGBTQIA+ individuals. For example,

---

MEDIA BYTE 2.2   **Applying Feminist Pathways to Understanding Crime**

Please read the following article about homeless runaway girls' entrance into prostitution: https://www.nytimes.com/2013/09/16/nyregion/stubborn-cycle-of-runaways-becoming-prostitutes.html. If the article is not available, please contact your instructor for an alternate reading. After reading the article, answer the following questions:

1. Does feminist pathways theory apply to this crime? Please discuss how it does or does not apply.
2. What do you think can be done to prevent young girls from entering into crime as a result of running away?
3. Why do you think girls are disproportionately targeted? Please explain.

LGBTQIA+ youth may be forced to leave their homes or become targets at school for bullying. As discovered through studies on feminist pathways, these experiences can be especially traumatic and set these individuals "on a path" toward offending or experiencing victimization. In one informative study illustrating that point, data from more than eight thousand LGBTQIA+ youth were collected, and the results indicated that LGBTQIA+ adolescents who were victimized experienced more negative school consequences (detention, suspension, expulsion) than cisgender adolescents. Moreover, the findings indicated that LGBTQIA+ youth who were victimized encountered more formal entities of social control (e.g., law enforcement) than cisgender adolescents did (Palmer and Greytak, 2017).

LABELING THEORY

Unlike many other criminological theories in the 1960s, **labeling theory** framed criminal engagement as stemming from interactions and meaning-making in society—heavily drawing from the sociological framework of symbolic interaction. In other words, individuals' conceptions and responses to crime and criminals are the results of a more extensive process of social interactions (Bernburg, 2009; Triplett and Upton, 2016). More precisely, these theorists argue that negative labels assigned to individuals sanctioned by others, typically formal entities of social control, can have lasting consequences in terms of self-perception and pro-social opportunities. Essentially, whereas deterrence theorists argue that sanctioned individuals will avoid subsequent engagement in crime given the potential repercussions presented to them (secondary deterrence), labeling theorists assert it is precisely the "labeling" of individuals as criminals and deviants that causes subsequent criminal behavior. Although this perspective was promising and provided an interesting counter to the tenets of deterrence theory, it quickly lost support within academia because of what critics argued were its vagueness and untestable concepts—leading to its demise in the 1980s (Bernburg, 2009; Paternoster and Iovanni, 1989; Triplett and Upton, 2016). However, the perspective has recently been resurrected by scholars (Lopes et al., 2012).

To describe the labeling process, theorists focus on two types of deviance: primary deviance and secondary deviance. The concept of primary deviance is typically associated with minor forms of antisocial behavior that do not have lasting impacts on the offending individual. For example, an individual, Adam, uses an illicit substance on occasion, but no one in his social network is aware of the behavior. He does not suffer any significant consequences because of the usage, and there is no change to his self-perception. Many prominent labeling theorists do not focus on primary deviance, in contrast to secondary deviance, because it is theorized that most individuals engage in some form of deviance during their lives (Bernburg, 2009; Lopes et al., 2012). (See Media Byte 2.3.)

MEDIA BYTE 2.3   **We Are All Criminals**

Write down a list of characteristics you associate with the terms *criminal* or *felon*. After completing your list, visit www.weareallcriminals.org and read the confessions of individuals who committed crimes but were never caught. After reading the confessions, compare your list of characteristics to the people profiled on the site.

Do your conceptions of *criminal* and *felon* align with real-life cases? If so, explain areas of overlap. If not, discuss the differences between your notions and real-life accounts of undetected criminality.

Secondary deviance is typically associated with antisocial behaviors that are alleged to stem from reactions to being labeled (Triplett and Upton, 2016). For example, one day Adam's coworker notices an illicit substance sitting in plain sight in his workbag. After the coworker notifies management, law enforcement arrives and places Adam under arrest. Adam is convicted of possession of cocaine and is fired from his workplace. Due to the stigma associated with being a "drug user" and a "felon," Adam has difficulty securing another job after resolving his case with the criminal-legal system. Moreover, Adam's family members and friends treat him differently—some even going as far as to avoid interacting with him. Consequently, Adam spends more time with friends who are using illicit substances. Then, he starts to identify with the labels many associate with him. Several months later, Adam starts using cocaine again.

According to the tenets of labeling theory, Adam's subsequent drug use stemmed from the significant consequences he experienced as a result of being labeled. After his conviction, the labels assigned to Adam (drug user, felon) carried a significant social stigma, which influenced and shaped the resulting interactions he had with others. The consequences of these labels were so dramatic that Adam could not secure employment, and his social network marginalized him. These experiences indicate that the labels likely became Adam's master status. In other words, individuals' perceptions of Adam (and perhaps Adam's self-perception) were associated with the labels of "drug user" and "felon" and any other characteristic was minimized. From a labeling theory perspective, the experiences related to these labels inevitably led to Adam feeling excluded. Given his exclusion from conventional society, it is not surprising, from a labeling theory perspective, that Adam's participation in deviant groups and behavior increased (e.g., secondary deviance) (Bernburg, 2009). (See Active Learning Assignment 2.1.)

An examination of the literature finds very little research investigating the applicability of labeling theory through a gendered lens. While there is some

ACTIVE LEARNING ASSIGNMENT 2.1

Thinking about Labels and Gender

In a small group of two or three students, construct a list of negative labels assigned to individuals of various genders. After creating this list, determine the negative consequences that can result from each label—both from a personal and professional standpoint. After completing the list, discuss whether there are any patterns in labels across genders. Provide at least two to three ideas of how society can combat consequences associated with negative labeling.

crucial research addressing gender within a labeling theory context, these studies are typically dated (likely because of the rise and fall of the perspective) or consider gender only as a control variable (Bernburg, Krohn, and Rivera, 2006). Nevertheless, early studies underscore the importance of using labeling theory within a gendered context.

In one noteworthy study investigating labeling theory through a gendered lens, scholars assessed whether parental appraisals and youth self-appraisals affected delinquency of boys and girls. Using data from the National Youth Survey, Bartusch and Matsueda (1996) found that while the tenets of labeling theory functioned similarly for boys and girls in terms of negative parental appraisals affecting youths' self-appraisals and delinquency, there were notable variations as well. Specifically, they found that the impact of negative appraisals by parents and self on girls was not as consequential as on boys. On the other hand, if parents were alerted to prior delinquency by youth, these previous transgressions were less likely to result in negative appraisals of boys than of girls. In explaining these differences, and particularly the gender-gap in criminal engagement, Bartusch and Matsueda (1996) suggested that assessments by parents and self of youth as "deviants" may discourage boys and girls from behaving in gender incongruent ways. In other words, girls may feel pressured to rid themselves of negative appraisals that challenge societal conceptions of femininity; however, negative appraisals might motivate boys toward delinquency, given societal notions of masculinity.

In contrast to many other criminological frameworks of the time, labeling theorists also applied this perspective to the LGBTQIA+ community (Woods, 2014). Indeed, one of the most influential labeling theorists of the time, Howard Becker, specifically referred to one's attraction to others of the same sex assigned at birth as a deviant label in his text *Outsiders* (1963). He discussed the impact of that label on LGBTQIA+ individuals and how the resulting social stigma shaped their life choices. While this early research had noble intentions, thoughtful scholars have raised concerns about the potential harm that can result from associating criminal engagement or victimization with one's identity or sexual orientation. Indeed, as discussed by Woods (2014), there needs to be more "queering" of criminological theory. Still, scholars must remain vigilant in that work to ensure that communities are not marginalized or further stigmatized in the process.

Life Course and Development Theories

During the 1980s, scholars sought innovative ways to understand the origins of crime beyond the dominating sociological framework (McGee and Farrington, 2016). Out of this interest emerged the **life course and development perspective,** which asserted that the onset of criminal behavior was best understood through examining the whole of someone's life rather than focusing on periods of interest, such as adolescence (Elder, Johnson, and Crosnoe, 2003). In other words, unlike perspectives that focused on time-stable traits (such as low self-control), life course and development theory, much like labeling theory, viewed criminal engagement as arising from a process. Given this viewpoint, the perspective is particularly suited to data derived from longitudinal research rather than cross-sectional studies that capture social patterns at one point in time. In reviewing this perspective, there is no one set theory that all scholars refer to, but rather a constellation of frameworks that mostly view crime over the life course through the same lens: the social pathways individuals are on are complex and dynamic, and life experiences can alter these trajectories in favorable or unfavorable ways at any time. Thus, life course and development perspectives can provide insight not only into the onset of crime, but also into persistence in and desistance from crime (McGee and Farrington, 2016).

While various perspectives fall under the broad theoretical category of life course and development, they all mainly focus on the following aspects of social life: social pathways, transitions, and trajectories. Accordingly, all individuals are on social pathways moving toward desired goals and objectives—their overall trajectory. As we move, significant life events (transitions) can alter our trajectory such that it becomes necessary to reorient ourselves on a new pathway (Elder, Johnson, and Crosnoe, 2003). (See Active Learning Assignment 2.2.) For example, Patterson, DeBaryshe, and Ramsey (1990) theorized that the onset of crime was the result of dysfunction within the home (weak parenting), which then led to negative experiences in school (academic and social failure), which in turn "set someone on a path" toward delinquency.

In her seminal study, Moffitt (1993) investigated whether pathways could be established for juveniles who were system-involved to identify the factors that led to their onset, persistence in, and desistance from crime. Through this work, she identified two different pathways with different etiologies to crime over the life course: (1) "life-course-persistent offenders" and (2) "adolescence-limited offenders." Juveniles aligning with the first category were typically born with deficits in neuropsychological functioning that manifested through abnormalities in cognitive abilities, behavioral development, and

ACTIVE LEARNING ASSIGNMENT 2.2

Imagining Transitions and Trajectories

Reflect on your life up to this point and all the significant events that have occurred (only the ones you feel comfortable disclosing). Identify the events that you consider transitions and explain how they altered the trajectory of your life. Then, think about what future events you anticipate experiencing that might lead to future transitions and changes in trajectory. Display these thoughts in whatever format you like: bullet points, a comic book about you, a PowerPoint/Prezi presentation, a timeline, or some other format.

After completing this display, discuss whether life course and development theory is a viable approach to framing why individuals abstain from or engage in crime. Be sure to justify your answer completely.

temperament. According to Moffitt, these problems were then typically worsened by home environments in which parents were ill equipped to care for their children. The cumulative result of these life experiences contributed to a general antisocial disposition among these juveniles, which then led to their criminal engagement at an early age that persisted through early adulthood before generally declining.

In contrast, the onset of crime by juveniles aligning with the adolescence-limited pathway ultimately stemmed from a gap between biological and social maturity. Given that gap, these juveniles followed the social behavior and cues of more deviant peers (mimicry) whom they perceived as socially successful. This fundamental difference in the etiology of criminal engagement (general antisocial disposition versus immaturity/modeling behavior) explains why youth aligning with the adolescence-limited pathway had a later onset and desisted sooner from crime than life-course-persistent youth.

There is limited research assessing life course and development perspectives across genders. Moreover, the literature is silent on the applicability of this approach outside conventional binary gender categories, which is surprising given the vastly different experiences of cisgender youth and LGBTQIA+ youth. Nonetheless, the research that has investigated this perspective across genders is noteworthy. One example is Moffitt and Caspi's (2001) investigation of the two pathways identified by Moffitt among boys and girls. Before beginning their investigation, they noted a dearth of research addressing the applicability of life-course taxonomies across genders. After conducting their study, which found striking similarities in alignment with each pathway among boys and girls, they dismissed the need for a gender-specific theory. For example, regardless of gender, youth with deficiencies in neuropsychological functioning and inadequate home environments are aligned with the "life-course-persistent offender" pathway. Moreover, regardless of gender, immature youth from conventional backgrounds who modeled the behavior of deviant peers aligned with the "adolescent-limited offender" pathway. To underscore their point that life course and development perspectives are applicable across genders, they cited research that produced similar results: that boys and girls aligned to similar trajectories regarding the onset, persistence, and desistance of crime (e.g., Fergusson, Horwood, and Nagin, 2000).

Rational Choice Theory

Although the basis of **rational choice theory** dates back to the founding of criminology itself, the theoretical framework encapsulating those early ideas about criminality did not originate until the 1980s (Akers, 1990; Cornish and Clarke, 1986). The theorists credited with proposing the framework, Cornish and Clarke, argued that crime ultimately originates from calculated decisions that individuals make as they navigate their everyday world. (See Active Learning Assignment 2.3.) Interestingly, the conception of rationality, although a hallmark of the perspective, became the focus of critics who alleged that certain crimes and outcomes were inherently irrational (such as crimes of passion, and sexual violence rooted in power and control). Responding to these criticisms, Cornish and Clarke (1986, x) cautioned against using conceptions of rationality heavily grounded in economics and asserted that the rationality demonstrated by individuals engaging in crime was on a much lower level, as in the following examples: "(1) offenders who take account of only few benefits and risks at a time, (2) those who give only limited time and effort to a decision, especially when under the influence of drugs, alcohol or strong emotions, (3) those unduly influenced by the rewards of crime, not its potential costs, (4) those who might consider only the chances of being apprehended not the punishments that await them, and (5) those who react almost instantly to an insult or challenge."

ACTIVE LEARNING ASSIGNMENT 2.3

Applying Rational Choice to You

Create a list of all your assignments due in the next month in chronological order. Then, create a list of all your obligations over the next month in chronological order. Finally, create a third list of all your professional/work obligations in the next month in chronological order. After creating your three lists, create a master list that organizes all your obligations from most important to least important, giving reasons for the differences in importance. As you create your master list, document your reasons for each decision.

After you are finished, write a summary of the process you went through to rank your activities for the next month.

As previously discussed, there is a symbiotic relationship between rational choice theory and deterrence theory. From a rational choice perspective, crime stems from perceived opportunities and decisions about those perceptions every day, which vary by offense type and situational characteristics. To combat this social problem, then, the perceived consequences of crime must be so high that it is considered an irrational course of conduct regardless of situational characteristics—that is, deterrence theory. Thus, the rational choice perspective is unique from other frameworks reviewed in this chapter because its goal is to explain *crime* and not the individual engaging in the crime (Akers, 1990). Moreover, given this focus, Cornish and Clarke assert that the perspective was never intended to be a grand theoretical explanation, but rather a perspective to aid in crafting policy designed to deter crime. Yet some have countered that the tenets of rational choice theory align very well with critical concepts represented in other frameworks like social learning theory (which is discussed later in this chapter) (Akers, 1990).

Unlike other theoretical perspectives, there has been some exploration into applying rational choice theory across genders, albeit only within the binary context. For example, in one study, university students were asked whether they would engage in a crime under certain conditions such as chance of arrest and cost-benefit considerations (Tibbetts and Herz, 1996). Ultimately, the scholars found that motivations toward criminal behavior differed between men and women significantly. More specifically, while there was notable overlap in the factors that motivated both genders to shoplift (such as low self-control, prior offending, and perceived pleasure), the magnitude of the effect of low self-control and resulting pleasure was significantly higher for women than for men. Similarly, while there was overlap in the factors that motivated both genders toward drunk driving (such as prior offending and perceived pleasure), the two groups also differed in that moral belief acted as a significant deterrent among women but not men.

Routine Activities Theory

The **routine activities theory** falls within the rational choice framework described above but differentiates itself by identifying specific situational characteristics related to the genesis of crime (Cohen and Felson, 1979). This perspective, which is also focused on explaining *crime* rather than the person who commits crime or the person against whom the crime was committed per se, frames these incidents as resulting from a convergence of three factors: (1) a person with the potential to engage in a crime, (2) a suitable target, and (3) the absence of a capable guardian.

The framework arose during a time when the economic climate in the United States was improving, and yet crime remained problematic (the 1960s–1970s). Ultimately, Cohen and Felson (1979) found that individu-

---

ACTIVE LEARNING ASSIGNMENT 2.4

Applying Routine Activities Theory to the Everyday World

Over the weekend, go to a heavily congested area (e.g., mall, movie theater). While you are there, take notice of behavior that may increase someone's vulnerability to crime (e.g., listening to music, not paying attention to the surroundings, talking on the phone). Also, take notice of valuables left out in the open or blatantly displayed to others. Finally, pay attention to any forms of guardianship around—whether it be official guardians (e.g., attendants) or informal guardians (e.g., witnesses).

   After spending some time at the location, write up your observations in terms of the three components of routine activities theory: (1) the proximity to individuals that might offend at the site, (2) suitable targets at the location and what made them vulnerable to crime, and (3) capable guardians in the area and what made them capable. When doing your observation and write-up, consider the ways that gender and race may influence routine activities.

---

als' everyday routines (patterns in coming and going, place of work, socialization) mattered for understanding both personal and property crime. (See Active Learning Assignment 2.4.) Since its conception, the routine activities theory has been used to provide insight into various offense types—both from a perpetration and a victimization perspective. Moreover, it is one of the few views that has been applied to investigate cybercrime. To explain the perspective more fully, each component of the framework warrants a brief discussion.

   This theory and rational choice theory intersect in that both assume individuals who break the law engage in conscious decisions every day about whether to participate in crimes (Cohen and Felson, 1979; Cornish and Clarke, 1986). While the individual considering the offense is the focus within the rational choice framework, the individual is rarely studied within routine activities theory (Mustaine and Tewksbury, 2009). Instead, routine activities theorists typically focus on the other two elements of the perspective: target suitability and lack of guardianship. In terms of target suitability, theorists investigate the characteristics of individuals or places that increase their vulnerability to experiencing crime. Therefore, how this component is conceptualized will vary across studies and offense types. Unlike target suitability, however, there is an ongoing debate surrounding the idea of guardianship and what constitutes its presence.

   As interest in routine activities theory has grown, disagreement has surfaced about whether the conception of "guardianship" has drifted away from its original meaning (Hollis, Felson, and Welsh, 2013). According to Felson (2006, 80), guardianship refers to someone who "keeps an eye on the potential *target* of crime." In other words, guardianship is not met by increasing the difficulty of accessing the target (by target hardening, for example), but rather is apparent when the person who would commit the crime is deterred from carrying out the crime as a result of its presence. While the ongoing debate surrounding this concept is outside the scope of this chapter, from a routine activities perspective, the role of guardianship is vital for addressing the genesis of crime.

To illustrate the applicability of this perspective, particularly within the virtual environment, we offer the example of a recent study that we conducted. As mentioned, scholars have identified several factors that make individuals as well as property vulnerable to people breaking the law across various offense types and domains (offline and online). We conducted a study on cyberbullying within social networking sites as framed by routine activities theory (Navarro et al., 2017). Findings from this study showed that not only was the use of social networking sites problematic on its own, as it increased one's vulnerability to experiencing cyberbullying, but that specific behavior within these sites was especially risky. These findings were amplified by the discovery that there was no capable guardianship within these platforms to deter people from harming others.

Although routine activities theory has not been widely evaluated across genders, the importance of gender in understanding the origin of crime from this perspective cannot be understated. Indeed, as noted by scholars within the field, not only is gender a significant factor in assessing target suitability across many offense types, but routine activities are inherently associated with one's background as well (Popp and Peguero, 2011).

In one innovative study, gender and risk of experiencing violence at school were investigated within a routine activities theory context (Popp and Peguero, 2011). The scholars found that gender was a consistent risk factor for experiencing victimization. Moreover, the routines associated with student life affected victimization risk differently for boys and girls. More specifically, higher victimization risk among boys was associated with participation in clubs, but for girls, higher victimization risk was associated with the involvement in intramural sports.

In their explanation of these findings, the scholars theorized that participation in extracurricular activities, which is typically favored by girls, may place them in vulnerable positions for targeting by people engaging in crime. In discussing these findings, the scholars called for more attention to the role of gender, aside from its function as a control variable, in studies framed with routine activities theory. Moreover, when gender is considered, going beyond conventional binary categories is essential. Indeed, innovative research indicates that considering gender identity and sexual orientation, which also inherently affect routine activities, is also necessary for assessing vulnerability to people engaging in an offense (Costello, 2018).

Self-Control Theory

Self-control theory, or what has come to be referred to as the general theory of crime, falls within the control theory family of understanding criminal behavior. It is like other theoretical perspectives discussed in this chapter in that the focus of understanding the origins of crime is centered on the individual breaking the law. Moreover, akin to other views (such as life course and development), deviant dispositions that act as motivations toward crime are thought to stem from problems in childhood. Finally, this perspective, like deterrence theory, is based on the notion that humans are inherently pleasure-seeking beings who must be confronted with controls to counteract those inclinations. However, unlike other perspectives, self-control theory is one of the few frameworks that purports to be a viable explanation of the origins of crime regardless of culture or subgroup. Indeed, not only has self-control been applied across various settings, but it, along with routine activities theory, is also applicable to cybercrime (Gottfredson and Hirschi, 1990).

Unlike rational choice theory and routine activities theory, which are grounded in the rational thinking of people who break the law, Gottfredson and Hirschi (1990) assert that the genesis of crime stems from a lack of self-control that arises from ineffective parental management during childhood. Put another way, children who grow up in homes in which there are few consequences for poor decision making are more inclined to become adults who cannot resist the immediate gratification crime provides. According to these theorists, the inability to control oneself is only one facet of understanding crime; the other crucial piece is opportunity. For example, while an individual with low self-control may drink excessively, the chance to engage in drunk driving is inherently absent as long as access to a vehicle is missing.

Although some critics say that self-control theory is tautological—that it is circular or self-explanatory logic—proponents of this perspective argue that it has broad applicability across various settings. Moreover, Gottfredson and Hirschi (1990) assert that having low self-control does not predispose someone toward criminal activity; the other essential factor in the equation is an opportunity. While this issue remains a challenge for scholars, Akers (1991) has suggested it can be overcome by investigating independent indicators of low self-control (such as excessive drinking, excessive smoking, volatility) such that the issue of tautology becomes moot.

It has been asserted that self-control theory explains criminal activity across various cultures and groups, so some scholars have evaluated that claim by assessing the perspective across genders. In perhaps one of the earliest attempts to evaluate the applicability of low self-control across genders, Burton and colleagues (1998) found that the premise of the framework was indeed applicable to crime perpetrated by men and women but in slightly different ways. For instance, while low self-control and opportunity mattered for criminal engagement among women, opportunity was not a significant factor for men. The importance of these factors remained even when rival theoretical concepts were considered. This finding is supported by earlier research that found that, while women were generally more risk-averse than men, those with low self-control were still more prone to engage in criminal activity such as driving under the influence (Keane, Maxim, and Teevan, 1993). In a review of the research, Gottfredson (2017) noted that research has mostly found that low self-control is applicable across different cultures, groups (based on criminal history, gender, race/ethnicity, etc.), and offense types.

SOCIAL CONTROL THEORY

Control theories are based on the premise that humans are inherently pleasure-seeking individuals who, if left to their own devices, are likely to engage in crime—mainly when the risks of pain to their person are low. Thus, **social control theory** emphasizes the importance of effective and strong socialization toward conventional attitudes and beliefs, as these can have lasting effects on one's life and, conversely, the absence of these checks can have devastating consequences. Thus, unlike virtually every other theory within criminology, social control theory frames both why individuals do engage in crime as well as why they do *not* (Gottfredson, 2017).

According to Gottfredson (2017), social control theory has dominated criminological thought for decades. Indeed, most strongly associated with the work of Hirschi (2004), social control theory broadens the ideas of self-control theory and postulates that individuals are "restrained" from engaging in deviance as a result of the following factors: (1) attachment to significant others, (2) commitment to conventional goals, (3) involvement in conventional activities, and (4) beliefs. Put succinctly, individuals refrain from engaging in crime because they have too much to lose in terms of their connections to and opportunities in the broader society. And, to reverse that logic, individuals with weak bonds to society or who are immersed within a deviant lifestyle have virtually nothing to lose. Each component specified by Hirschi warrants further discussion.

The attachment to and influence of significant others in the trajectory of one's life are recognized across many theoretical perspectives within criminology (such as labeling theory, life course and development theory, self-control theory, social learning theory). Indeed, closely associating with deviant peers and the resulting effects of those interactions were the foundation of Sutherland, Cressey, and Luckenbill's (1995) differential association theory, which is discussed later in the chapter. Therefore, it should not be surprising that it is a principal component of social control theory.

Within social control theory, attachment to significant others, while including friends, more directly refers to the principal roles guardians and parents play in rearing children toward leading pro-social lives, which also connects this perspective to the ideas presented through the self-control framework (Gottfredson, 2017). Indeed, from this perspective, parents are critical to modeling pro-social behavior and enforcing sanctions to instill self-control in their children. Parents are also vital in helping their children form secure and valued attachments to institutions that function as social control (such as belief in the morals on which the legal system rests, belief in law enforcement) and socialization agents (such as schools).

The next component, commitment to conventional goals, concerns the pro-social objectives one envisions for their life (Gottfredson, 2017). For many people, these goals consist of acquiring a strong education and becoming professionally successful. These goals may also include having a healthy and stable marriage, which may or may not include children. Ultimately, these goals restrain engagement in criminal activity, because perpetrating a crime impedes or even prevents accomplishing some or all of these objectives. For example, Mary plans to pursue a law degree after college. She dreams of becoming a federal prosecutor like her father and then starting a family when she is ready. Although she struggles financially for years, she never considers engaging in anything nefarious because the consequences of such action would destroy her life goals.

The third component is involvement in conventional activities and is closely related to the above component. This "bond" refers to one's connection to society through pro-social activities such as community activities, extracurricular activities, and workplace activities (Gottfredson, 2017). For example, Mary is a valued member of the debate team at her institution. She is also the president of the pre-law society on campus. If she were to engage in a crime, she would likely be blocked from participating in these activities.

The fourth component refers to one's general belief in the righteousness associated with obeying the law (Gottfredson, 2017). Put another way, individuals who believe that crime is simply wrong and that a stable society entails everyone following the rules are unlikely to engage in criminal activity. For example, Mary avoids engaging in crime because she ultimately believes that crime is wrong—it does not align with how she was raised, she would lose everything she has worked for, and she believes in the law.

Social control theory, as in the case of self-control theory, has been widely tested across various cultures and groups. Overall, studies show the applicability of both perspectives within multiple contexts, to the extent that they are both referred to as general theories of crime. Although both approaches operate similarly for men and women, studies have found that there is some variation of the magnitude of the effect. For example, in one study assessing the tenets of social control theory across system-involved men and women, scholars found parental attachment and involvement in everyday activities was not as consequential for men as it was for women (Alarid, Burton, and Cullen, 2000).

Although social control theory remains a dominant perspective in criminology and has undergone substantial testing by scholars within the field, its applicability to individuals identifying outside of the gender binary and as noncisgender remains unaddressed. One notable exception is Sarah Strauss's (2007) doctoral dissertation, which examines the relationship between same-sex desire, suicide, and school climate within a social control theory context.

SOCIAL LEARNING THEORY

Social learning theory, which is similar to control theories, frames criminal behavior as ultimately stemming from a failure in pro-social socialization. This failure leads individuals down a path where crime is learned through the following process: interactions with significant deviant others (component 1: differential association), where crime is accepted and normalized (component 2: definitions), which is then punished or reinforced (component 3: differential reinforcement), and which is ultimately repeated by the observer (component 4: imitation) (Akers and Jennings, 2016). Given the importance of this perspective in criminology, each component will be discussed further.

Differential association, or the power of others' influence on our behaviors, is a salient concept in criminology. Within the context of social learning theory, but also like control theories, differential association refers to significant individuals in one's life who act as socialization agents and steer one towards or away from crime. Today, the concept of differential association has widened to include "virtual" associations as well. Thus, if one associates with others who instill and support pro-social behavior, engagement in deviance is less likely (Akers and Jennings, 2016).

The first component of social learning theory heavily influences the second: definitions. Indeed, it should be readily apparent that the strong influence of significant others in the socialization process also dramatically affects the attitudes and beliefs one holds. According to social learning theorists, one's feelings regarding deviance—and whether it is acceptable or not—are an essential indicator of whether problematic behavior is likely to manifest. As hypothesized by Akers and Jennings (2016), individuals are expected to engage in crime when they hold strong beliefs towards deviance and weak beliefs toward conformity.

The third component of social learning theory is taken from the work of prominent behavioral psychologists, such as B. F. Skinner (1953), who investigated the role of operant conditioning processes like punishment and reinforcement in the overall learning process. Put another way, this component, differential reinforcement, refers to the effect that punishment (positive or negative) and/or reinforcement (positive or negative) has on individual behavior (Akers and Jennings, 2016). In terms of punishment, positive actions include any *un*desirable consequence of criminal engagement (such as incarceration) that deters subsequent actions; in contrast, negative punishment includes anything desirable that is removed from an individual who broke the law (such as loss of network)—again, to deter subsequent actions. In terms of reinforcement, positive actions include any desirable consequence for the individual that results from breaking the law (such as money, respect, status); in contrast, negative reinforcement comprises anything *un*desirable that is removed because of the individual's criminal behavior (such as a rival gang's withdrawing from home turf). From a social learning theory perspective, individuals are more likely to engage in deviant behavior when reinforcements outweigh punishments.

The final component of social learning theory, imitation, is the repetition of behavior by observers of what they have learned. According to social learning theorists, imitation is likely to occur when the balance toward deviance outweighs the presented costs (Akers and Jennings, 2016). For example, imagine a child who observes domestic abuse perpetrated by their father against their mother throughout childhood. Because of this, the child grows up within a network of other children who have favorable beliefs (impacting definitions) toward the perpetration of domestic abuse (differential association). After a brief incarceration for perpetrating domestic abuse (negative punishment = removal of personal freedom; positive punishment = incarceration), all charges are dropped (negative reinforcement). Given the few consequences experienced by the individual who abused their partner, it is likely that the abuse will continue (imitation).

Given the emphasis on socialization within social learning theory, which inherently accounts for the differences in socialization between boys and girls, this framework is purported to be a viable approach to understanding the gender gap in crime as well as crime across various contexts (Higgins, 2006). As such, social learning theory has undergone a significant amount of empirical inquiry throughout the years, which mostly demonstrates its applicability across multiple settings. However, like other perspectives, while the general theory functions similarly regarding men and women, there are slight differences worth noting. For example, in one study assessing dating violence within a social learning theory context, some key components were more important for men than for women and vice-versa (Tontodonato and Crew, 1992). Specifically, there was a significant correlation across genders between relationship violence and knowledge of violence in other relationships as well as substance use. However, among men only, the use of violence was also significantly correlated with parental domestic abuse and approval of intimate partner abuse. In contrast, among women only, while parental domestic abuse did not achieve statistical significance, there was a significant correlation between the use of violence and experiencing child abuse.

It is important to note that these findings were closely mirrored at the multivariate analysis stage of the study. For example, among men, approval of abuse significantly increased the likelihood of perpetrating dating violence. In terms of women, knowledge of others' utilization of dating violence retained its importance and increased one's probability of perpetration; however, while experiencing child abuse nearly reached statistical significance, it ultimately failed to cross the threshold. Overall, individuals who used drugs frequently were most likely to perpetrate dating violence in both models. Again, these results support the framing of social learning theory, but they also highlight slight gender variations as well.

Although Akers's (2016) social learning theory has yet to move outside the gender binary, there is good reason to expect that the framework would be applicable. In a review of the literature, studies utilizing the psychology-based social learning theory found that the internalization of beliefs and norms through socialization did indeed have an impact on subsequent behavior. For example, a study synthesizing research on substance abuse among LGB individuals specifically found that differences in socialization within that subculture might have contributed to different substance-use patterns in comparison to cisgender individuals (Green and Feinstein, 2012). Unfortunately, there is a shortage of research that examines whether criminology's social learning theory can aid, in a similar vein, the framing of criminal perpetration or victimization within LGBTQIA+ communities.

STRAIN THEORY

Initially proposed by Robert K. Merton (1938), a structural-functionalist, classic **strain theory** argues that crime stems from individuals' reactions to the immense pressure to achieve cultural goals despite varying means of ability. In other words, from a classic strain perspective, individuals (regardless of culture) generally identify similar overarching life goals, one of which is economic success (Agnew, 2016). However, as is well known, depending on one's socioeconomic status, the *ability* to achieve economic success significantly varies (e.g., access to quality education, employment, social capital). From a classic strain theory perspective, individuals who are blocked by limited resources from achieving their goals are likely to experience strain (through negative feelings such as anger) and may react to that strain by engaging in crime; these are called *innovators* (Merton, 1938). At the other end of the spectrum are *conformers,* or those with access to the means to achieve cultural goals.

While some individuals conform or innovate, Merton also noted other reactions to strain. For example, individuals who aspired to cultural goals but accepted that the means to achieve those goals were inaccessible to them might *ritualize.* In other words, they might accept what was possible to achieve given their circumstances. Other individuals could reject both the cultural goals and means by living on the outskirts of society, which Merton referred to as *retreatism*. Finally, individuals could *rebel* and work to replace both the goals and means. Although strain theory has since broadened, Merton's original theory primarily related to financial resources and relative deprivation; therefore, it was particularly useful in explaining crime in areas struggling with various social problems related to resources.

In the 1990s, Robert Agnew (1992) broadened and expanded strain theory to provide a more holistic understanding of the origin of crime. In what is referred to as general strain theory, Agnew identified three sources of strain aside from one's economic position: (1) failure to achieve positive stimuli, (2) loss of positive stimuli, and (3) the presence of negative stimuli. Moreover, he noted that strains could be objective (generally shared reactions across a population) or subjective (varying responses across the population) with the latter typically resulting in problematic feelings. Following the work of Merton, Agnew (2016) hypothesized that individuals experiencing strain from one of these sources could react by engaging in crime. However, like Merton, he believed the relationship was not causal. In other words, crime was only one path individuals could take, and not the *only* reaction.

Before discussing the applicability of strain theory across genders, it is crucial to briefly illustrate Agnew's sources with the following example. Imagine a couple that is divorcing because of infidelity by both parties. The husband is distraught by the wife's actions, and he becomes violently abusive during their last weeks together. As he is hitting her one night, he shouts, "If I can't have you, no one will." She manages to escape to her new partner's house and does not see her ex-husband for several weeks. After several weeks, her ex-husband shows up at her new partner's home and kills everyone inside. Then he kills himself before the police can arrive. In this example, all three sources of strain are present: the husband's anger associated with the failure to achieve a happy marriage (failure to achieve positive stimuli), the husband's anger related to the departure of his wife, whom he still loved (loss of positive stimuli), and the husband's anger toward his wife's new partner, whom he hated (presence of negative stimuli).

Several years after Agnew introduced general strain theory, Broidy and Agnew (1997) explored the utility of the perspective across genders. They concluded that the gender gap might reflect the different types of strains experienced by men and women and their reactions to those negative feelings. For example, given the types of strain experienced by women and their typical reactions, it was unlikely that they would engage in violent crime. Instead, women's problematic reactions to strain typically manifested within the family or were self-directed in the form of self-harm.

Broidy and Agnew provide several reasons why general strain theory is highly applicable in framing crime perpetrated by women. First, in terms of failure to achieve positive stimuli, they note studies that show that women typically want close interpersonal relationships and are also increasingly concerned about financial security. However, given well-known cultural and structural barriers, the scholars note that these goals are difficult for women to achieve—especially compared to men. As a result, women may innovate and engage in financially motivated crime to resolve the strain. Second, in terms of loss of positive stimuli, the scholars note that women tend to place a high value on their social involvement with others, such that constraints on their behaviors or movements can cause significant strain. Finally, the presence of negative stimuli is readily seen in the fact that a majority of family violence and sexual violence cases involve women. Thus, the scholars note that while general strain theory is applicable across genders, there are important contextual differences between men and women in the types of strain experienced and the reactions to those strains.

General strain theory has been shown to be applicable not only within the gender binary but outside it as well. For example, in a study investigating the relationship between strain and suicidality between LGBQ and heterosexual youth, Button (2015) found that the presence of negative stimuli (that is, victimization) increased the risk of suicide for both groups. These results mirror a similar study by Button and Worthen (2014) in which victimized youth (that is, those experiencing strain) were at greater risk of experiencing various challenges in academic, personal, and other life domains. Again, while general strain theory is widely applicable across various groups, these studies demonstrate slight variations worth noting as well.

SUMMARY

From the start of civilization, humans have engaged in horrific crimes against each other. While many of these crimes may appear senseless, theoretical perspectives in criminology provide critical insight into the genesis of crime. Yet even decades after the founding of criminology, the debate regarding whether long-standing theories are applicable across genders continues. Indeed, even in theoretical perspectives purported to be gender neutral, key factors do slightly vary across men and women. Perhaps what is even more critical to resolve, however, is the near absence of research into whether traditional criminological perspectives are applicable outside of conventional binary categories. Although this book will not solve these gaps, we will endeavor to explore criminology from multiple gender vantage points.

"Manly" Crimes

The Relationship between Masculinity and Criminality

KEY TERMS

- ▶ aggrieved entitlement
- ▶ defense
- ▶ cyberabuse
- ▶ excuse
- ▶ family annihilation
- ▶ first-degree murder
- ▶ hate homicide
- ▶ hegemonic masculinity
- ▶ involuntary manslaughter
- ▶ intimate partner abuse
- ▶ mass murder
- ▶ second-degree murder
- ▶ toxic masculinity
- ▶ voluntary manslaughter

LEARNING OBJECTIVES

- ▶ Understand hegemonic masculinity, toxic masculinity, and how these terms frame criminal engagement by men.
- ▶ Explain how gender concepts related to men's criminal engagement work in conjunction with major criminological perspectives to frame crime.
- ▶ Apply chapter content to contemporary issues related to masculinity and crime.

On April 20, 1999, the students at Columbine High School were in the middle of a normal day. However, that typical day ended at 11:19 a.m. when two teenagers slaughtered thirteen individuals and injured twenty-four others before killing themselves. Since that time, many school shootings have occurred in the United States, and many individuals who have engaged in mass murder have referred to the massacre at Columbine High School as their inspiration (Thomas, Levine, Cloherty, and Date, 2014).

Although the Columbine High School shooting was not the first school shooting, it was significantly different from earlier ones. The earlier attacks typically occurred in urban schools and did not have the indiscriminate violence seen recently (Rocque, 2012). Additionally, since the Columbine High School shooting, there has been a definite pattern of deeply internalized anger and rage that is intertwined with masculinity among individuals who engage in this offense. Given that this pattern has existed throughout the years since Columbine, it is safe to say that society can no longer ignore the connection between crime, particularly violent crime, and masculinity (Kimmel, 2017). This chapter presents an in-depth exploration of the relationship between crime and masculinity to address a long-standing question within the criminology: what drives men to engage in crime?

GENDERING CRIMINOLOGY: HEGEMONIC MASCULINITY AND CRIME AS GENDERED PERFORMANCE

Criminological scholars have long called attention to the gender gap within crime, or the overrepresentation of men among those engaging in criminal activity (Lauritsen, Heimer, and Lynch, 2009). According to the Federal Bureau of Investigation's Uniform Crime Report (2015), men represented 73 percent of all arrestees in 2015. This FBI statistic has remained consistent through time, ranging from 73 to 79 percent between 1995 and 2014. Scholars from across the theoretical landscape have offered perspectives as to why men are overrepresented among criminals. For example, theorists hailing from biosocial criminology have pointed to biological differences between men and women, such as testosterone (Beaver, Barnes, and Boutwell, 2015). Feminist criminologists have noted that restrictions placed upon women before the feminist movement had hindered women's participation in crime (Adler, 1975). Other theorists have argued that men's overrepresentation among individuals engaging in criminal activity is a function of adhering to ideal gender characteristics (Messerschmidt, 1997).

To begin to understand the relationship between gender and crime, one must start with the pivotal work of Raewyn Connell (1987) and the concept of hegemonic masculinity. Connell and Messerschmidt (2005) describe **hegemonic masculinity** as "the pattern of practice (i.e., things done . . .) that allowed men's dominance over women to continue" (832). In other words, hegemonic masculinity is the societal conception of ideal characteristics associated with masculinity, which in turn drives individual behaviors as men strive to achieve those ideals. Within Western culture, hegemonic masculinity is typically associated with aggressiveness, heterosexuality, sexual prowess, and strength, both emotional and physical. Since hegemonic masculinity is the ideal way to "do gender," or to "do masculinity," all other expressions of gender, like femininity, are inherently subordinated to it (Connell, 1987). For example, in doing masculinity, or behaving in a masculine manner, a person would act stoically, emotionally strong, and stable.

Connell's work on hegemonic masculinity is still immensely important for understanding the role of gender in social interactions, and it led to scholars applying the concept to criminality. One important example is Messerschmidt's (1997) text *Crime as Structured Action: Gender, Race, Class, and Crime in the Making*. In that text, he proposes that individuals strategically engage in crime to assert their masculinity when there are few other resources available to them, such as financial capital or social capital. From his

---

ACTIVE LEARNING ASSIGNMENT 3.1

Thinking about Masculinity

In a small group, write down some characteristics associated with masculinity. Then discuss your lists in the group and create a group list of agreed-upon features. After the instructor collects these lists and displays them, the class should reflect on the role of gender socialization in guiding behavior. Be sure to consider the positive and negative consequences of adhering (or not) to the various characteristics.

---

perspective, crime is a type of symbolic capital, or resource, that men use if confronted with a threat that challenges their masculinity.

To illustrate how hegemonic masculinity affects criminal engagement, imagine a young man, Joe, is spending time with a woman, Alice, at a local bar. After several minutes, another man, Steve, approaches Alice and starts questioning her as to why she is with "loser" Joe. Instantly angry, Joe stands up, but Steve shoves him back down, which is yet another direct challenge to his masculinity (that is, strength). At this point, the entire bar is watching the conflict unfold and has watched Steve challenge Joe. In this situation, Joe is likely to engage in crime (such as assaulting Steve) as a response to the public challenge to his masculinity and the lack of other practical options to disengage from the argument. (See Active Learning Assignment 3.1.)

In addition to the relationship between hegemonic masculinity and criminality, scholars have also focused on how extreme adherence to masculine societal ideals, referred to as **toxic masculinity**, affects criminal engagement (Haider, 2016). While hegemonic masculinity is associated with aggressiveness, toxic masculinity is associated with a tendency toward violence (Kupers, 2005). While hegemonic masculinity is associated with sexual prowess, toxic masculinity is associated with an entitlement to sexual intimacy regardless of consent (Connell, 1987). Finally, while hegemonic masculinity is associated with subordination of other gender expressions, toxic masculinity is associated with the outright dominance of others through such things as homophobic attitudes and misogynistic beliefs. Thus, while adherence to hegemonic masculine ideals is damaging in that it contributes to systemic oppression, adherence to toxic masculine ideals is even more destructive in that it fuels hate and violence. One only needs to browse anti-feminist areas of cyberspace to see that the adherence to toxic masculine ideals is a reality for many men, particularly incels, or involuntary celibates (Ging, 2017).

The internet has produced many benefits for society, such as the ability for like-minded individuals to gather and share ideas online despite geographical distance. Regrettably, this benefit has also allowed deviant individuals to congregate online and share antisocial viewpoints under the cloak of anonymity.

CASE STUDY 3.1

Elliot Rodger, Incel

On May 23, 2014, in Santa Barbara, California, Elliot Rodger murdered six individuals and injured fourteen others in the act of retribution for years of sexual and social rejection. Before committing his mass murder, Rodger uploaded a YouTube video detailing his grievances against his intended targets. Although Rodger discusses his anger toward men in the video, he spews considerable hatred toward women who rejected him for "alpha males." After the crime, an image of Elliot Rodger depicted as a saint began circulating in online discussion boards frequented by incels.

In this case study, students should watch the following video of Rodger and answer the noted questions.
https://www.nytimes.com/video/us/100000002900707/youtube-video-retribution.html.

1. Describe how Elliot Rodger conceptualized masculinity. In other words, what did he seem to believe was important to him as a man?
2. Apply the discussion of toxic masculinity to statements made by Elliot Rodger. How do his comments underscore this extreme form of hegemonic masculinity?

Some of these individuals include those referred to as incels. A cursory review of discussion boards within the toxic landscape reveals a consistent theme: women are inferior to men and exist for sexual pleasure. Some incels even go as far as to encourage rape (Ging, 2017). Considering these views, it is not difficult to see the relationship between toxic masculinity and criminality, particularly after studying the case of Elliot Rodger (see Case Study 3.1).

Although not all crime stems from adherence to toxic masculinity, scholars argue that these antisocial gender ideals set up the framework for the manifestation of violence among men who feel emasculated. Kimmel (2017) refers to this as **aggrieved entitlement**, which he describes an individual's anger stemming from the belief that someone of inferior status wrongly received something that was due to them instead. For example, Elliot Rodger showed aggrieved entitlement through his discussion of women giving themselves to "obnoxious" other men (that is, of inferior status) and how this was an injustice to him. While aggrieved entitlement does not equate to criminality, it is a strong undercurrent in gendered expressions of violence like mass shooting].

Various gender concepts are essential for understanding what propels men to engage in criminal activity. By considering the role of gender in the perpetration of crime, one can also begin to understand the persistence of the gender gap. However, it is essential to reiterate that gender is an important undercurrent of social behavior and not a replacement for the criminological perspectives discussed in chapter 2. In other words, scholars can consider the role of gender in conjunction with various criminological theories.

Table 3.1 Emphasizing Gender Constructs in Criminological Theories

Theory	Connection to masculinity
Labeling	A young man engages in primary deviance to assert his masculinity (**HM**) to his peer group. Once caught and labeled, he keeps offending (secondary deviance) because he associates only with hypermasculine criminals who view crime as inherent to masculinity (**TM**). He also continues to engage in crime to avoid his own victimization (from others who would perceive him as "weak").
Life course development	A man experiences a disruption that has profound implications for how he views his masculinity: he discovers his wife is leaving him for another woman (**HM**). He shows up at his wife's place of employment and kills several people—including his wife and her lover. Before he kills his wife, however, he makes a point to tell her that if he cannot have her, he will make sure that no one will (**AE**). While serving time (change in trajectory), he continues to act out violently towards others, particularly effeminate men (**TM**).
Rational choice	A woman receives a promotion at work that a man feels entitled too (**AE**). He decides to throw a celebration for her, where he places drugs in her cocktail. After she manages to get home, he breaks into her residence and repeatedly violates her while she is unconscious—all while telling her that she deserves it (**TM**). Several days later, he posts explicit content of the encounter online under anonymous names, which go viral. The woman quits and moves to escape the constant harassment.
Routine activities	A man (potential system-involved person) takes a love interest out on a romantic date where he lavishes her with expensive food. After the date is over, he walks her to the door and asks to come inside "for a nightcap." She refuses his offer, but he insists and pushes his way inside while yelling that she owes him, given the date (**AE, TM**). Once inside, he rapes her because he knows she lives alone (suitable target, lack of guardianship). As he is leaving, he tells her not to bother with the police because he will claim it was consensual.
Self-control	A group of boys repeatedly taunts a classmate by calling him derogatory names (**HM**). The parents of the boys engaging in the abuse and taunting dismiss these events by saying that "boys will be boys" and do not step in even as the attacks escalate (ineffective parental guardianship; opportunity). At one point, the boy's peers sexually assault him in the restroom while screaming homophobic slurs (**TM**). The young boy commits suicide.
Social control	A boy grows up in a socially disorganized neighborhood with various social problems. Within the home, most of his family members have cycled in and out of prison (attachment to significant others). As such, they believe that power and respect are associated with violence (**TM**). Moreover, men are the protectors and providers of their families (**HM**). The boy works within the illegal drug market and sets his sights on being a significant distributor in the future (lack of commitment to conventional goals). To work towards this goal, he stops attending school and is on the streets a lot (lack of involvement in conventional activities). At a few points, his violence escalates into murdering his competitors, whom he believes are encroaching on "his" turf (**AE**). From his perspective, the "normal rules" of society are not applicable in his world (beliefs).
Social learning	A young boy grows up in an extremely abusive household. Throughout his childhood, he watches his father abuse his mother in many ways. Moreover, he associates with other children who are also from abusive homes (differential association). As such, the boy internalizes beliefs that women are inferior to men, and violence is sometimes necessary to keep control of one's house (**TM**) (definitions). Then, one day, his father murders his mother as she tries to escape with another man. During his trial, the boy's father claimed it was his right to kill his wife because she "belonged to him" (**AE**). He ends up pleading to manslaughter for a reduced sentence. In terms of the boy, throughout his relationships, he is abusive and receives very few consequences (differential reinforcement; imitation).
Strain	A soon-to-be indicted professional executive is distraught (negative emotion) about his potential prison sentence (presentation of negative stimuli) for money laundering, which will remove him from his family for decades (loss of positive stimuli). He believes strongly that the man handles protecting and supporting his family (**HM**). Also, from his perspective, he only engaged in the crimes to balance out advantages wrongfully given to others (**AE**). Because he cannot fathom his family going through life without him, he murders his wife and children before committing suicide (reaction to strain).

SOURCES: Connell, 1987; Kupers, 2005.

NOTE: Abbreviations for gender constructs: **AE** = aggrieved entitlement (Kimmel, 2017); **HM** = hegemonic masculinity; **TM** = toxic masculinity

To explore the relationship between masculinity and the origins of crime, the remaining pages of this chapter will present overviews of relevant research across various offense types: nonviolent, violent, and cyber. Additionally, because the performance of gender varies in social environments, the last section includes research on masculinity and crime within prisons. The aim of this chapter is not to dismiss other theoretical explanations of crime but to recognize how gender is a powerful undercurrent in individual decisions throughout life.

MASCULINITY AND NONVIOLENT CRIMES

Although the performance of masculinity is evident in the perpetration of violent crimes, as a man forcefully asserts dominance, a relationship between gender and engaging in nonviolent crimes exists as well. Nonviolent crimes include a wide swath of illegal activity; the following subsections note the more widely reported crimes. Unfortunately, many of these topics are still sparsely researched in terms of gender and perpetration. However, several notable studies have produced exciting results.

Arson

The FBI (2017e) classifies arson as a property crime given that the term means the intentional destruction of property through fire; however, this offense can quickly escalate to involve severe violent crime like homicide. According to the FBI's uniform crime reporting (UCR) expanded tables, more than thirty-six thousand arson offenses occurred during 2015. These offenses produced an average of $14,182 in damage for that year (FBI, 2015). While these figures refer to all arson offenses broadly, states typically include multiple charging options based on case severity. For example, in South Carolina's 2017 legal code, arson charges differ based on injury and the property targeted (S.C. Code Ann. § 16–11–110). In South Carolina, arson in the first degree is possible when death or serious bodily injury occurs. In contrast, second-degree and third-degree arson are based on the type of property targeted in the offense, in which an injury must not have occurred. Individuals who engage in arson at locations that affect foreign or interstate commerce are criminally liable at the federal level as well (18 U.S.C. § 844).

A review of the FBI's crime data (2019b) show that most individuals arrested for arson were 18 years old or older (5,105) compared to minors (1,264). Additionally, 71 percent of individuals arrested were white and 78 percent were men. Moreover, ten-year arrest trends indicate that men remain overrepresented among arrestees (FBI,2019b) given they represented 49 percent of the population in 2010 and 2019 (US Census Bureau, 2019). While whites are slightly underrepresented in arrests relative to their population in 2019 (76.3%

of the US population), readers should remain cautious about drawing too many inferences from these statistics, given the known disparities in policing and sentencing across demographic categories, but especially ethnicity/race, that are discussed throughout this text. Aside from these demographics, evidence shows that people who engage in arson may suffer from psychological issues that propel their actions, such as personality disorders, psychotic disorders (such as schizophrenia), or very rarely, sexual interest in fire setting, known as pyromania (Dalhuisen, Koenraadt, and Liem, 2015; Labree et al., 2010; Lindberg et al., 2005). Scholars have also noted a relationship between excessive alcohol use and arson (Burton, McNiel, and Binder, 2012). However, not all individuals engaging in arson have a mental illness or substance abuse. Scholars have found that some individuals engaging in arson perpetrate their offenses for economic reasons, to avoid the detection of other crimes, to enact revenge, or for an organization or a mission (such as organized crime, terrorist organizations) (Labree et al., 2010; May, 2014).

Given the differing motivations of individuals engaging in arson, scholars have focused on whether there are different subtypes, such as nonpsychotic and psychotic. In one notable study, evidence showed several differences between the two (Dalhuisen, Koenraadt, and Liem, 2015). More specifically, findings showed that typical nonpsychotic individuals engaging in arson were employees, in a relationship, and younger than their psychotic counterparts. Moreover, nonpsychotic individuals engaging in arson and psychotic individuals engaging in arson differed in their childhood histories. For example, psychotic individuals engaging in arson were more likely to have had contact with inpatient mental health services than nonpsychotic individuals engaging in arson were. On the other hand, nonpsychotic individuals engaging in arson were more likely to have grown up in an abusive home than psychotic individuals engaging in arson were.

Much of the research on arson focuses on men, which makes intuitive sense as they are overrepresented in this category of crime. Unfortunately, the influence of gender in the perpetration of arson is still understudied with one crucial exception. In that noteworthy exception, Roe-Sepowitz and Hickle (2011) compared men and women who engaged in arson, which resulted in several interesting findings. They found that men who participated in arson were more likely to be gang members, have histories of delinquency, and have a mental illness diagnosis than women who engaged in arson. In contrast, women who engaged in arson were more likely to be chronically tardy/truant, maltreated, and runaways than men who engaged in arson. While these findings do not specifically analyze the role of hegemonic masculinity per se, there is reason to believe in the viability of that line of research.

Reiterating the work of Messerschmidt (1997), men with access to few resources may strategically engage in crime to "do masculinity." However, to successfully perform masculinity, this process often necessitates observers or a group (such as a gang), who confers status upon the individual. Thus, for gang-affiliated individuals engaging in arson, it is possible that their crimes are about "performing masculinity" in front of peers (Creighton and Oliffe, 2010). While this hypothetical is unexplored, there are indications in earlier work that gender does seem to matter for the behaviors of individuals engaging in arson.

Burglary

The act of entering a structure unlawfully, regardless of force, to engage in illegal activity is burglary (FBI, 2017e). Individuals may burgle to commit theft or another crime such as assault or sexual violence. As with arson, states typically have multiple charging options based on offense severity. For example, in Florida's 2017 legal code, charges of burglary vary based on the presence of others in the structure, on whether the individual perpetrating the act gets or has a dangerous instrument, and on whether injuries occur during the offense (FL Stat § 810.02). For instance, a charge of burglary in the first degree is possible for an individual who burglarizes an occupied home while carrying a firearm whether or not injury results. As with arson, this offense is chargeable at the federal level in cases where foreign or interstate materials are present at the burgled location (18 U.S.C. § 103).

A review of FBI UCR data shows that burglary makes up a substantial percentage of property crimes from 2000 to 2019; however, the total number of offenses have decreased in recent years: 2000, slightly more than 2 million; 2010, about 2.2 million; 2019 about 1.1 million. Data also show that most burglaries occur at residences and particularly during the daytime. In terms of background characteristics, most people arrested for burglary in 2019 were adults (105,738) (FBI, 2019b). A review of the ethnicity and race of those arrested shows that about 68 percent of people arrested were white. As in the case of arson, about 80 percent of the people arrested in 2019 for burglary were men (FBI 2019b).

Much of the research on burglary has highlighted the role of rationality in perpetration. In other words, evidence shows that people who burglarize are motivated to commit crime, to use a routine activities theory term, and rationally choose high-value targets with the least risk of possible detection. Individuals who burgled consider a range of factors in this calculation, such as indications of wealth publicly visible (such as cars, home improvements) and whether there are quick escape routes to avoid detection (such as fences, proximity to side streets) (Kopp, 2014). Some of this calculation occurs during an individual's regular job for cable or construction companies (Mullins and Wright, 2003). Although sexually motivated individuals who burgle tend to be impulsive, evidence suggests some of these individuals also plan their offenses (for example, by watching the target ahead of the crime) (Schlesinger and Revitch, 1999).

There is a shortage of research on the role of masculinity in the perpetration of burglary within criminology; Mullins and Wright (2003) argue that this area of research is ripe for investigation. They note that the study of this topic is overdue because gender is a recognized influence on engagement in street crimes like burglary. Their findings support this claim, given the notable gender differences in the behaviors of men and women who burgled in terms of onset and desistance. Although the scholars do not specifically refer to hegemonic masculinity, their findings show that men who burgled engaged in offenses to secure financial resources that enabled their autonomy. Moreover, in their reporting of what would lead them to stop burglarizing, men noted several statements that directly align with hegemonic masculine ideals: employment with great financial and personal autonomy, established formal relationship, and fatherhood. Thus, even though discussion about hegemonic masculinity is absent per se, evidence derived from this study shows a connection between gender and burglary.

Drug Offenses

Individuals who consume, produce, or distribute illegal substances expose themselves to criminal liability at the federal and state levels. At the national level, individuals risk violating the United States Controlled Substances Act (US Code §§ 21–13). At the state level, charges and the associated punishments vary depending on offense characteristics. For example, in Tennessee's 2017 legal code, offenses and penalties vary depending on the type of substance at issue, with Schedule I drugs carrying the most severe sanctions (TN Code § 39–17–417).

The FBI's (2016b) National Incident-Based Reporting System (NIBRS) data show that drug offenses make up most of the reported crimes against society. For instance, in 2016, there were over 700,000 reported drug and narcotic offenses, representing 87 percent of all crimes classified as "crimes against society" (the others in this category include animal cruelty, gambling, pornography/obscenity, prostitution, and weapons law violations). NIBRS data also show that most individuals arrested for drugs/narcotics were adults (920,650), while arrests of juveniles totaled to 79,673. In terms of race, 73 percent of arrestees were white, 25 percent were not white, and a small percentage were of an unknown race (3%). Finally, drug and narcotics arrests included more men than women (72% vs. 27%).

Unlike other areas of nonviolent crime, scholars have explored the relationship between gender and drug use. In one noteworthy study, scholars found that using marijuana aligned with hegemonic masculine ideals (Haines et al., 2009). More specifically, men reported engaging in marijuana use because it aligned with masculinity and promoted bonding. Some also believed that using marijuana mitigated group conflicts. Finally, while men considered marijuana use among men as acceptable, this belief did not always transfer to women. In other words, some men viewed marijuana use among women as deviant and incongruent to femininity.

Later research reached similar conclusions on the role of gender in delinquency and substance use. Within that study (Sanders, 2011), findings showed that men engaged in substance use because it aligned with masculinity, and it asserted autonomy to authoritative sources. Individuals using substances also reported engaging in delinquency, although it is not clear which behavior came first, and that interaction increased with hypermasculine men. Since hypermasculinity aligns with antisocial behavior, it is not surprising that the increased interaction had lasting adverse effects on respondents' trajectories. Although there is a lack of information on this topic, these studies show that gender does influence substance use.

Fraud

Fraud is a vast category of nonviolent crime that includes bank fraud, credit card fraud, fraud against the government, insurance fraud, mail/wire fraud, securities fraud, tax fraud, and welfare fraud. Individuals engaging in fraud potentially expose themselves to criminal liability at both federal and state levels, with a range of sanctions depending on the offense.

According to FBI NIBRS (2019b) data, there were 475,040 fraud offenses reported in 2019. Given the nature of the crime, it is not surprising that most individuals perpetrating fraud were adults (200,202) rather than juveniles (8,862). Moreover, an examination of these individuals' backgrounds shows that about 43 percent were white, and most were men (62%; among reports where sex assigned at birth was known). While the connection between fraud, a white-collar crime, and masculinity may not be readily apparent, this area of criminal activity has a connection to underlying gender ideals.

As discussed in the opening of this chapter, hegemonic masculinity is typically associated with aggressiveness, heterosexuality, sexual prowess, and strength (Connell, 1987). Society dictates that men should be pillars of not only physical but emotional strength. Moreover, masculinity is associated with autonomy and self-sufficiency. For men with families, they are the providers and protectors, particularly concerning financial well-being. For men without families, they need to show autonomy and self-sufficiency to others to assert masculinity—particularly as they look for partners. Considering these sociocultural pressures, engaging in white-collar crimes like fraud is an extreme (albeit illegal) way of adhering to gender ideals. Indeed, research on men who engaged in white-collar crime has found that most rationalized their offenses by noting community and family obligations (Klenowski, Copes, and Mullins, 2011).

Theft

An individual who deprives another of their property engages in theft (FBI, 2017e). Theft is a broad category that includes offenses such as cargo theft, motor vehicle theft, and simple theft (larceny). As in all other crimes, theft charges vary based on incident characteristics. For example, in Alabama's 2017 legal code, the entirety of chapter 8 outlines theft offenses. These crimes include theft of fuel, shopping carts, and traffic signs. Moreover, some legal codes outline theft of property (lost or not), theft of trademarks, and theft of services (AL Code § 13A-8). In short, the criminal sanctions associated with theft are diverse and rely on a holistic understanding of the exact incident that took place.

According to the FBI's 2019 UCR data, there were more than 4 million thefts in 2019 in the United States (2019b). Additionally, there were 612,187motor vehicle thefts. In terms of situational characteristics, most cases of larceny-theft involved taking items from motor vehicles (about 1.1 million) or shoplifting (904,975). Most larceny offenses resulted in a loss of over $200 (1,956,531).

Adults made up most of those arrested for larceny (479,255) and motor vehicle theft (40,335) in contrast to minors (55,581 and 7,974, respectively) in 2019 (FBI). About 77 percent of individuals arrested for motor vehicle theft were men, but there was a fair split in arrests for larceny between men (57.4%) and women (42.6%). Finally, most individuals in both crimes were white (66.3% for larceny; 67.6% for motor vehicle theft).

Considering that larceny and motor vehicle theft are both street-level crimes connected to the display and pursuit of wealth, it is not surprising that scholars have found a relationship between these offenses and hegemonic masculinity. For example, in one noteworthy study on the gendered nature of motor vehicle theft, many individuals who engaged in this offense reported growing up in families where members were involved in crime (O'Connor and Kelly, 2006). Given their environment, engaging in crime was an acceptable avenue to get tangible indicators of success like cars. Cars are attractive targets because they provide autonomy, another ideal associated with dominant gender norms, and are inherently associated with masculinity (think of "hot rods," "muscle cars"). Finally, taunting police and showing off stolen vehicles to others is a method to earn status as well as engage in bonding, but these "public performances" were not acceptable for women participating in this offense. Scholars have documented similar gendered patterns among individuals who engage in larceny.

In a study focused on street theft, evidence showed a strong gender undercurrent to decisions about perpetration (Copes and Hochstetler, 2003). Men engaged in theft to secure resources to support a lifestyle of autonomy and self-sufficiency. Additionally, adherence to several hegemonic masculine ideals was particularly powerful among individuals breaking the law in this regard: a desire for autonomy, the pressure to support others, and rejection of authority. The influence of gender was also present in the discussion of perpetrating theft within social groups. Within these groups, resisting engagement in theft or deviance in general often resulted in emasculation by others. In other words,

Table 3.2   The Connections between Hegemonic Masculinity and Nonviolent Crime

Crime	Definition	Connection to masculinity
Arson	Any willful or malicious burning or attempt to burn, with or without intent to defraud, a dwelling house, a public building, motor vehicle or aircraft, personal property of another, etc.	Studies have found that men who engage in arson are more delinquent and more likely to be gang members than women who engage in arson (Roe-Sepowitz and Hickle, 2011). Therefore, men may engage in their offenses to gain status and respect and perform masculinity within their hypermasculine peer groups.
Burglary	The unlawful entry of a structure to commit a felony or theft; . . . the use of force to gain entry need not have occurred.	Evidence shows that men who burglarize are motivated to secure financial wealth to ensure their autonomy and give resources to their dependent others. Thus, they burgle to fulfill their self-perceived duties as men (Mullins and Wright, 2003).
Drug offenses	The violation of laws prohibiting the production, distribution, and/or use of certain controlled substances and the equipment or devices used in their preparation and/or use.	Findings show that drug use is more socially acceptable among men than women (Haines et al., 2009; Sanders, 2011). Moreover, using substances contributes to bonding among men and mitigates conflict. Finally, drug use may lead to delinquency and association with hypermasculine men, which further reinforces the gendered usage of substances.
Fraud	A deliberate scheme to obtain financial or similar gain by using false statements, misrepresentations, concealment of vital information, or deceptive conduct.	Research shows that men engage in fraud as an illegal way to adhere to masculine gender ideals—namely, to provide for others (Klenowski, Copes, and Mullins, 2011).
Larceny / theft	The unlawful taking, carrying, leading, or riding away of property from the possession or constructive possession of another.	Research shows that street theft among men is aimed to generate respect among peers and secure financial resources to enable an autonomous lifestyle (Copes and Hochstetler, 2003). Because masculinity and "control over one's destiny" are valued, conventional paths to get financial resources are rejected.

SOURCE: Crime definitions cited verbatim from the FBI Uniform Crime Reporting Program, 2010, https://ucr.fbi.gov/crime-in-the.u.s/2010/crime-in-the-u.s.-2010/offense-definitions.

men who engaged in street theft acknowledged the expectation that they must confront risks associated with these offenses with bravery to support themselves and others.

MASCULINITY AND VIOLENT CRIMES

Adherence to toxic masculine ideals sets the stage for the manifestation of violence, particularly when underscored with aggrieved entitlement (Kimmel, 2017). Although violent outbursts disconnected from gender do occur, disregarding gender as part of the equation is shortsighted. Considering that many of these outbursts target those perceived to be inferior to the hegemonic men (such as women and LGBTQIA+ individuals), we discuss offenses perpetrated by men targeted at those groups. For discussion of crimes perpetrated by women, readers should refer to chapter 4. For discussion of the victimization of men, readers should refer to chapter 7.

Homicide

Before discussing the connection between gender and homicide, an explanation of criminal homicide charges, types, and prevalence rates is necessary. In terms of charges, there are two broad categories of homicide: murder (which includes first degree and second degree) and manslaughter (which includes voluntary and involuntary) (Fox, Levin, and Quinet, 2018). **First-degree murder** is the intentional killing of another with malice and premeditation. For example, a husband discovers his wife is cheating on him with another man and plots to kill them both. To avoid detection, the husband disables the brakes on the family car, and that results in a fatal car accident that kills his wife and her lover. In this case, the husband's actions included malice and premeditation. A first-degree murder charge is also possible in cases where the homicide is exceptionally cruel and heinous (such as sexually sadistic homicide) or where it occurred during a dangerous felony (such as an armed robbery that goes awry, known as "felony-murder rule").

Malicious but unplanned homicides, which are not especially heinous or the result of engaging in a dangerous felony, are **second-degree murders**. For example, a husband murders his wife after learning she intended to leave him. The husband did not plan to kill his wife, yet he displayed malice in his actions. First-degree murder and second-degree are distinguished by the presence of premeditation, however slight. In other words, if an individual plans for one minute, it is premeditation, just as if they had planned for months.

Charges of manslaughter also vary on culpability. **Voluntary manslaughter** is chargeable when a homicide results from an extremely emotional event like an intense argument. However, unlike murder, this intense interaction mitigates an individual's criminal culpability. For example, two brothers get into an emotional argument that escalates into a physical fight. During the altercation, a severe injury occurs, and one of the brothers dies.

In contrast to other forms of homicide, **involuntary manslaughter** occurs when there is a gross disregard for the safety of others either through an overt act or an omission. For example, a father sees his child suffer a severe burn after touching a hot stove but does not pursue medical treatment out of fear of authorities. During the next few days, the child develops an infection that leads to sepsis and death. Because the father did not act and grossly neglected his duties as a parent, involuntary manslaughter is a proper charge, but others are also possible.

Deciding what charges are applicable and provable based on the evidence is the role of prosecutors. Most homicide cases, as in criminal cases in general, never reach trial due to plea bargaining, where the defense and prosecution negotiate mutually agreeable terms that typically include reduced charges or sentences (Fox, Levin, and Quinet, 2018). If cases do continue to trial, juries often can consider lesser included offenses in addition to the most severe charge. For example, a jury hearing a first-degree murder case may also have the choice to convict the individual of second-degree murder or voluntary manslaughter. Each state varies in its rules about considering lesser included offenses at trials. Many factors affect homicide case outcomes.

Individuals charged with criminal homicide may also influence case outcomes by how they respond to the accusations. For example, individuals may respond to homicide charges by acknowledging responsibility while asserting a justification for their actions (that is, a **defense**, such as self-defense of oneself or self-defense of others; Fox, Levin, and Quinet, 2018). Individuals may also respond to homicide charges by asserting an **excuse**, which means they are not responsible for their actions because something mitigated their guilt (for example, they were under duress or they were suffering a psychotic break). Overall, state laws outline the process for administering justice, which includes everything from classifying offenses to the rules of criminal proceedings. For example, in addition to first-degree murder and second-degree murder, Tennessee's 2018 legal code also includes reckless homicide and vehicular homicide as potential charges (39 TN § 13–2, 2018).

Homicide tends to instantly capture societal attention despite its being less common than other violent crimes. According to the FBI's Crime in the United States Preliminary Report (2017c), there were 6,591 homicide arrests (for murder and nonnegligent manslaughter) in the first six months of 2017, but over 400,000 violent crime arrests. A review of previous years shows a similar trend, with homicide arrests making up a small percentage of violent crime arrests. For example, according to 2016 data, there were 16,459 homicide arrests but over 1.2 million violent crime arrests (FBI, 2016a). Likewise, according to 2015 data, there were 15,181 homicide arrests but over 1.1 million violent crime arrests (FBI, 2015). Another consistent pattern in these data is the overrepresentation of men among arrested individuals (figure 3.1).

In most homicide cases, individuals engaging in this offense target adults (4,694), but a small number target juveniles (460) (FBI, 2016b). Unsurprisingly, individuals who perpetrate homicide are typically also adults (4,632) and rarely juveniles (365). Most individuals that perpetrated and were victimized in homicides were men (4,598 and 3,904, respectively). However, women who were victimized outnumber men who were victimized across most types of crimes against persons except for homicide: assault, human trafficking, kidnapping/abduction, sex offenses, and non-forcible sex offenses.

There are several types of homicide where the connection to masculinity is particularly profound: family annihilations, hate homicides, school shootings, and workplace shootings. Many of these homicides typically manifest as non-random **mass murders** where an individual kills at least four loved ones at a

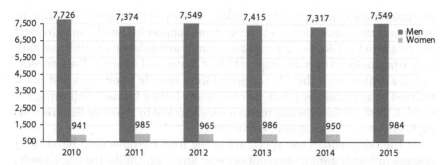

Figure 3.1. Arrests for homicide, including nonnegligent manslaughter, from 2010 to 2015, by gender. Source: Federal Bureau of Investigation, 2010–2015, *Crime in the United States,* https://ucr.fbi.gov/crime-in-the-u.s.

specific location within a short amount of time (Fox, Levin, and Quinet, 2018). Individuals who engage in these offenses usually target people out of an intense sense of aggrieved entitlement (Kimmel, 2017), which often connects back to hegemonic masculine ideals.

Family Annihilations

According to FBI NIBRS data, about 15 percent of homicide offenses involved family members in 2016 (FBI, 2016b). Homicide scholars focused on **family annihilations,** or the murder of a partner and at least one child, have found several prominent patterns throughout the years (Websdale, 2010). One consistent pattern is that fathers are overrepresented among individuals perpetrating family annihilations. In terms of individuals who are targeted, women are overrepresented among those killed by their partner; this is referred to as femicide. Other examinations of the prevalence of these mass murders show more than ten incidents occur annually (Fridel, 2017; Liem et al., 2013). Moreover, further inspection of these cases shows patterns in the lives of individuals who perpetrate these crimes, which have a connection to masculinity.

To develop an understanding of what motivates individuals to murder family members, influential scholars like Neil Websdale have created notable profiles. In Websdale's (2010) critical work on family annihilations, *Familicidal Hearts: The Emotional Styles of 211 Killers,* he names two main categories to classify individuals who engage in these offenses: civil reputable hearts and livid coercive hearts. He also created one category for those not aligned with either group (intermediate hearts).

A civil reputable (CR) heart, according to Websdale, engages in family annihilation to prevent his loved ones from experiencing grief and pain. In a family annihilation perpetrated by a CR, there is likely a forthcoming traumatic event known to the CR that would shatter the family, such as his upcoming arrest or insurmountable financial debt. Because the duty of the father, according to hegemonic masculine ideals, is to protect and support his family, an individual aligning with the CR category engages in family annihilation to fulfill that duty by sparing his loved ones an imagined life of shame and struggle. Thus, an individual aligning with the CR category forces suicide upon his loved ones, referred to as suicide by proxy, before usually killing himself. Following the murder, third parties typically report feeling shocked by the event because usually there were no prior episodes of violence.

At the other end of the spectrum is the livid coercive (LC) heart, who engages in family annihilation out of anger and rage. Unlike the CR, an individual aligning with the LC category usually engages in family annihilation as a reaction to a divorce or separation. This type of family annihilation is typically not shocking to outsiders as usually there have been prior episodes of violence within the house. The behavior of the LC, including the final expression of violence, stems from a firm adherence to hegemonic masculine ideals that underscore men's dominance within and outside the home. The LC simply cannot fathom a life without his family, because they are his and his alone. Thus, the LC murders his family out of a sense of aggrieved entitlement and rage. Sometimes the LC will murder shared children in front of their mother to inflict cruel punishment on her, referred to as a murder by proxy, before killing her. Like the CR, an LC typically commits suicide.

Hate Homicides

Individuals who perpetrate homicides based on legally recognized biases toward others engage in **hate homicides** (Fox, Levin, and Quinet, 2018). Individuals who perpetrate hate homicide expose themselves to federal and state sanctions that recognize various categories of protection. For example, at the national level, the Matthew Shepard and James Byrd, Jr., Hate Crimes Prevention Act of 2009 punishes crimes motivated by bias toward a person's color, disability, gender (including gender identity), national origin, race, religion, or sexual orientation (US Code § 18–249, 2017). Certain state legal statutes recognize other protection categories as well. For instance, according to Maryland's 2017 legal code, individuals who harass the homeless simply because they are homeless are chargeable under the state's hate crime statute (MD Crim Law Code § 10–304, 2017).

Unfortunately, the prevalence of hate homicides is extremely difficult to figure out due to various methodological challenges (Fox, Levin, and Quinet, 2018). First, finding motivations in extreme violence is not always possible—particularly in cases where the individual perpetrating the offense has committed suicide. Secondly, the reporting of hate crimes to federal authorities is still voluntary. Finally, these offenses are underreported by individuals who are victimized out of fear of authorities (if the people who experienced the violence is undocumented, for example) or retaliation (if the person who engaged in the offense is a neighbor, for example). Therefore, official statistics about the scope of the problem give an incomplete picture at best.

Aside from these challenges, statistics show that hate crimes are not rare events. FBI statistics show more than 5,800 hate crimes occurred in 2015, which involved 7,173 people who were victimized (FBI, 2015). Eighteen of these incidents resulted in the murder or non-negligent manslaughter of another. However, to underscore the difficulty with figuring out the full scope of the problem, evidence from the National Crime Victimization Survey (NCVS) shows more than 200,000 victimizations occurred in 2015 (Masucci and Langton, 2017). In fact, data indicate more than 200,000 victimizations consistently occurred annually between 2004 and 2015.

As in family annihilations, scholars have developed a typology to frame why individuals engage in hate crimes such hate homicide. Research has found four types of hate crimes: thrill-seeking hate crimes, defensive hate crimes, retaliatory hate crimes, and mission-oriented hate crimes (Fox, Levin, and Quinet, 2018). In each of these types, a strong connection to gender is present, and individuals use violence to show dominance over others viewed as inferior. Defensive and retaliatory hate crimes relate to aggrieved entitlement, while thrill-seeking hate crimes are just to perform toxic masculinity.

In thrill-seeking hate crimes, an individual is motivated by feelings of excitement as well as the desire to exert power over others. To connect this type of hate activity to hegemonic masculinity, and specifically toxic masculinity, individuals engage in thrill-seeking hate crimes to show dominance over another perceived to be inferior. Moreover, the sometimes brutal nature and group involvement typical of these incidents ensure there is an observation of the "performance."

In a defensive hate crime, violence stems from a desire to defend oneself or one's property from perceived encroachment or a slight by others. For example, the individuals who brutally murdered Matthew Shepard did not want him present within the community and abhorred LGBTQIA+ people. Therefore, they reacted with violence to the threat that they perceived from Shepard's mere presence within their community.

Unlike the previous two types, a retaliatory hate crime often results in an escalation of violence. In this type of hate crime, an individual has typically experienced an adverse event that motivates them to seek revenge. The target for the attack could be the original system-involved person or an individual connected to them. For example, imagine a young Latino man robs another young man. In the following weeks, the robbed individual intentionally assaults young Latino men who cross his path. To connect this to toxic masculinity: the robbery emasculated the individual who was victimized, and his later violence is a response to those negative feelings.

Finally, mission-oriented hate crimes are rare but are the most likely hate crime to involve homicide. In these cases, individuals engage in violence

ACTIVE LEARNING ASSIGNMENT 3.2

Mapping Hate

Explore the Southern Poverty Law Center's Hate Map at https://www.splcenter.org/hate-map. After exploring the map, select one state and report on three groups in it. Name the type of bias motivating each group and note any information showing a strong adherence to toxic masculinity.

because it is part of a broader mission. For example, groups such as the Aryan Nation that are based on beliefs of superiority and engage in hate crimes based on their hatred of others align with this classification. To connect this type of hate crime with gender, these groups often include hypermasculine men who believe that they are superior to various other "inferior" groups. These groups also typically reject mainstream society and support violence to affirm masculinity and superiority over others. (See Active Learning Assignment 3.2.)

School Shootings

Unfortunately, schools have increasingly become environments where aggrieved individuals express anger and rage against others (Kimmel, 2017). However, due to variations in the collecting and reporting of information, the reported prevalence of violence within schools varies widely (Fox, Levin, and Quinet, 2018). One of the primary sources of information about crime in schools is an annual joint report released by the Bureau of Justice Statistics and the National Center for Education Statistics. It reported forty-two violent deaths from July 2016 to June 2017 (Wang et al., 2020). However, this figure includes twenty-eight homicides, thirteen suicides, and one death resulting from legal intervention. Moreover, not only are incidents on school grounds counted but also events that take place at school activities or during the travel to and from activities and school.

Mass shootings, although devastating and horrific, are relatively rare events. For example, one database tracking incidents from 1982 to 2019 shows seventeen mass shootings at schools (Follman, Aronsen, and Pan, 2019). The Gun Violence Archive shows a total of forty-four mass shootings involving the homicide of four or more people in any location between 2016 and 2020. This number increases to seventy-two if one considers the mass shootings involving the homicides of three or more people (Gun Violence Archive, 2020).

Despite the apparent similarities in college and K–12 school shootings, scholars have found several notable differences between individuals engaging in each type. In terms of individuals engaging in K–12 school shootings, typical incidents usually involve boys and firearms (Fox, Levin, and Quinet, 2018;

Kimmel, 2017). Frequently in these cases, individuals perpetrating school shootings are responding to feeling marginalized in society. In typical college shootings, an older man is the perpetrator (Fox, Levin, and Quinet, 2018). Given the life period of these events (19–24 years old), the emergence of severe mental illness is a potential contributing factor. In the typical case, the individual is older, sometimes a graduate student, and has experienced an adverse event like failing out of an advanced degree program. It is vital to reiterate, though, that mental illness is not a *causal* factor in perpetrating extreme violence; in fact, individuals struggling with a mental illness are at increased risk of victimization rather than perpetration (Fox, Levin, and Quinet, 2018).

Regardless of setting (college or K–12), gender is a strong undercurrent in both types of school shootings. To underscore that point, in a mass shooting database maintained by Follman, Aronsen, and Pan (2019), *all* of the school shootings noted were perpetrated by men. In K–12 school shootings, scholars have found that the individuals who engage in these shootings are incapable of reconciling feelings of entitlement with their environment (Fox, Levin, and Quinet, 2018; Kimmel, 2017). These youth typically feel entitled to certain status and treatment by others and experience intense feelings of rage when their reality does not align with that expectation. Moreover, their reality may encompass bullying by others that is emasculating and further contributes to feelings of anger and rage. These feelings then manifest in the ultimate expression of dominance and power, a school shooting, that, not surprisingly, often includes the use of a weapon that expresses dominance and power.

Many individuals who perpetrate college shootings display aggrieved entitlement (Fox, Levin, and Quinet, 2018; Kimmel, 2017). This aggrieved entitlement could stem from feelings of being "wrongly" denied specific "owed" experiences, which are "given" to inferior others. For example, in the case of Elliot Rodger (Case Study 3.1), he felt entitled to the sexual intimacy that other college men were experiencing. He could not reconcile why women did not pursue him as they pursued other "obnoxious" men. For Rodger, experiencing constant rejection was emasculating, and he responded by exerting his dominance through extreme violence.

Workplace Shootings

Following family annihilations, workplace shootings are the next most frequent displays of extreme violence (Fox, Levin, and Quinet, 2018). According to the Bureau of Justice Statistics' NCVS data, about 572,000 work-related violent incidents occurred in 2009 (Harrell, 2011). In terms of mass murder, available databases show thirty-eight workplace mass shootings have occurred from 1982 to 2019 (Follman, Aronsen, and Pan, 2019). In nearly all of these cases, individuals perpetrating these events were men (about 98%) and were eighteen years old or older (95%).

Table 3.3   The Connections between Masculinity and Homicide

Crime	Description and key concepts	Connection to masculinity
Family annihilation	Usually, the homicide of a partner and one or more children; can also be defined broadly as the murder of multiple family members. Types include civil reputable, intermediate, and livid coercive.	Individuals engaging in family annihilation experience an adverse event that is destructive to their self-perceptions of masculinity. For the civil reputable, there is coming devastation or shame upon the family, and the homicide is an effort to fulfill the role of "provider" and/or "protector." For the livid coercive, the family is dissolving, and the homicide is a manifestation of anger over abandonment.
Hate homicide	A homicide motivated by an individual's bias against the targeted person. Types include thrill-seeking, defensive, retaliatory, and mission-oriented.	Individuals engaging in this offense view others as inferior, particularly gay men, and engage in homicide to "perform masculinity" to others. Recognized motivations of hate homicide are a need to feel powerful over others, to defend oneself against a perceived slight, to obtain revenge, or to fulfill a broader mission.
School shooting	A homicide at school, a school event, or while traveling to or from school or a school event. There are subtle differences between K–12 school shooters and college shooters.	Emasculated and marginalized men and boys experience intense feelings of aggrieved entitlement, and a school shooting is the manifestation of rage resulting from those feelings.
Workplace shooting	Specific coworkers may be targeted for revenge and/or murder, or the goal may be to punish the business or corporation (murder by proxy).	Individuals who engage in workplace shootings have experienced an adverse event, such as denial of a promotion or loss of a job, that caused feelings of aggrieved entitlement and intense anger. Because of those feelings, the individual takes revenge on those whom he believes have wronged him.

SOURCES: Fox, Levin, and Quinet, 2018; Kimmel, 2017; Messerschmidt, 1997; Websdale, 2010.

As in the prior types, there is a strong connection to aggrieved entitlement and masculinity in workplace shootings. In typical cases, individuals perpetrating a workplace shooting have experienced adverse events that have had devastating repercussions for how they view themselves (Fox, Levin, and Quinet, 2018; Kimmel, 2017). For example, an "owed" job may have been lost to an "inferior" other. Or an "owed" promotion did not materialize for the individual but did for an "inferior" other. For men whom society socially constructs as providers, these adverse events within the workplace can be extremely emasculating because they restrict their ability to gain autonomy and to support others. As mentioned, coupled with feelings of emasculation, these individuals also experience intense feelings of entitlement to certain things in life (such as the American dream) over less-deserving others (such as foreign-born workers). Thus, workplace shootings are the ultimate manifestation of anger and rage resulting from feelings of emasculation and entitlement. The targets are usually the source of anger and rage. However, individuals engaging in workplace shootings may also murder others as a method to inflict added punishment on the business or corporation (that is, murder by proxy) (Fox, Levin, and Quinet, 2018).

Intimate Partner Abuse

Intimate partner abuse (IPA) is a global social problem crossing all demographics. Although there is no universal definition of the problem, IPA refers to a spectrum of abusive behavior in which one exerts coercive control and power over another (see figure 3.2). Since the 1970s, research into IPA has grown exponentially. This growth is due to the greater recognition of the prevalence of the problem. For instance, recent FBI (2016b) NIBRS data shows that a substantial percentage of crimes against persons (about 26%) occurred within the family. Specifically, about 26 percent of assaults, 15 percent of homicides, 4 percent of human trafficking cases, 22 percent of abductions and kidnappings, and 24–27 percent of sex offenses involved familial ties. Statistics derived from other national studies underscore the scope of the problem.

In the most recent iteration of the Centers for Disease Control and Prevention's National Intimate Partner and Sexual Violence Survey (Smith et al., 2018), findings showed that IPA is a reality for many individuals, particularly women. Specifically, more than a third of women reported surviving abuse that included a wide gamut of types: psychological abuse (36.4%), physical abuse (30.6%), sexual abuse (18.3%), and stalking (10.4%).

Data from the earlier NISVS collections shows that no category of women is immune from experiencing IPA. In terms of ethnicity and race, about 38 percent of white women reported victimization within their lifetimes, whereas the percentages were considerably larger for some of the other ethnic/racial groups included in the study: 56.6 percent of women who identified as multiracial, 47.5 percent of American Indian or Alaska Native women, 45.1 percent of Black women, 34.4 percent of Hispanic women, and 18.3 percent of Asian or Pacific Islander women (Smith et al., 2017). In many of these cases, particularly sexual abuse and stalking offenses, men are the perpetrators. Considering these findings and the notorious underreporting of domestic abuse, it is essential for scholars to continue investigating this social problem. One line of research is the connection between gender and IPA.

To begin to understand the connection between gender and IPA, one must first understand the progress scholars have made in showing the distinct types of relationship abuse. One of the most enduring debates within the IPA field centers on whether offenses are gendered expressions of violence or gender-neutral. This debate arose out of conflicting results from extensive national surveys that showed gender symmetry in IPA perpetration in contrast to the man-to-woman perpetration pattern seen in small-scale investigations at shelters. (For an example of man-to-woman IPA, see Active Learning Assignment

---

ACTIVE LEARNING ASSIGNMENT 3.3

Intimate Partner Abuse and Music

Find a music video that displays intimate partner abuse perpetrated by a man toward a woman. Closely watch the content and name any features associated with gender roles like femininity, hegemonic masculinity, or toxic masculinity. After dissecting the video, write a brief report that answers the following questions:

1. Describe the characteristics projected by the men in the video, including the man who perpetrates the intimate partner abuse, and explain how these align or not with hegemonic and/or toxic masculinity.

2. Describe the characteristics projected by the women in the video, including the woman who experiences the intimate partner abuse, and explain how these align or not with societal conceptions of femininity.

3. Discuss how this music video challenges and/or reinforces dominant conceptions of gender and gender relations.

3.3.) To resolve this conflict, scholars suggested that both findings were legitimate and simply the result of different research methodologies (extensive national surveys versus surveys at shelters).

To address this debate, Michael P. Johnson (1995) created a typology to classify relationship violence that would account for these different findings. His typology consisted of four categories of relationship violence. The first type, common couple violence (CCV), is a relationship marked by violence of various levels of severity. In this type of relationship, men and women engage in violence equally but do not abuse each other to exert control. CCV, unlike the other types named by Johnson, is the type of relationship abuse that is often uncovered through large-scale national surveys.

Intimate partner terrorism (IPT) is at the opposite end of the spectrum. In this type of abuse, Johnson notes that men are significantly more likely to perpetrate violence toward women. Unlike CCV, individuals within an IPT relationship use violence, which can be very severe, to control and dominate their partner. More specifically, individuals use violence to compel a level of compliance that they feel entitled too (typically as men). Thus, unlike CCV, IPT is a profoundly gendered expression of abuse. Considering the gendered nature and severity associated with IPT, it makes intuitive sense why scholars were uncovering different patterns of perpetration and victimization at shelter surveys.

The next two types both relate to IPT but in separate ways. The third type of relationship abuse that Johnson found is mutually violent control (MVC). MVC is like IPT in that it refers to a relationship in which two "intimate partner terrorists" are trying to control each other through violence; however, this is rare. Finally, Johnson noted that violent resistance (VR) is a type of relationship abuse that often appears in self-defense. In other words, although there is violence within the context of a relationship, it materializes out of the desire to defend oneself from the abusive partner. This type of violence, unfortunately, often occurs in cases where women kill their partners to prevent future abuse.

As Johnson's typology shows, certain forms of IPA have a strong connection to gender and particularly masculinity. IPA research has supported this connection. For example, scholars have found that a firm adherence to traditional gender norms increases the likelihood of abuse (Herrero et al., 2017). Moreover, individuals who abuse their partners have distorted feelings about the acceptability and appropriateness of their violence (Garcia et al., 2017). Put another way, these individuals are more likely to believe that violence is acceptable. Finally, and unsurprisingly, individuals holding sexist beliefs are more likely to accept relationship abuse (Herrero, Rodríguez, and Torres, 2016).

Scholars' findings that a firm adherence to traditional gender norms increases the odds of IPA align with broader studies on masculinity. As we have seen, these studies found that hegemonic masculinity corresponds with ideals like aggressiveness and autonomy (Connell, 1987), with toxic masculinity taking these characteristics to extremes (Kupers, 2005). Therefore, women who are assertive or desire to be autonomous via employment present challenges to men who closely adhere to hegemonic masculine ideals. For hypermasculine men endorsing violence to assert masculinity, domestic abuse is likely when they are confronted with few other resources. Similarly, hegemonic masculine men may engage in sexual violence in situations where another challenges their masculinity and there are few other resources available to them (Messerschmidt, 1997).

Sexual Violence

Sexual violence, like IPA, includes many disturbing behaviors (see table 3.4). Also, as in IPA, research shows underreporting is a serious inhibitor to understanding the full scope of sexual violence within society. For example, according to FBI NIBRS data (2016b), there were about 89,000 sex offenses reported in 2016. Of these offenses, about 60,000 involved adult perpetrators, and slightly more than 18,000 involved juvenile perpetrators. Whites made up about 65 percent of all reported individuals perpetrating a sexual offense. Unsurprisingly, more of these individuals were men (77,832) than women (5,096). In contrast to official reports to law enforcement, NISVS 2015 estimations show that 3.9 million men and 5.6 million women had experienced sexual violence within the previous year (Smith et al., 2018). For most individuals who were victimized, these traumatic experiences occurred before twenty-five years of age (FBI, 2016b). As previously mentioned, a majority of the individuals perpetrating a sexually violent offense were men regardless of their target's gender.

Scholars have spent considerable time exploring the connection between gender and sexual violence. While some, such as biosocial criminologists,

Table 3.4   Types of Sexual Violence

Nonconsensual distribution of pornography	The sharing of explicit content in a public forum without the depicted individual's consent.
Sexual assault	The forcing of an individual into a wide range of behavior such as nonconsensual penetration and touching.
Sexual coercion	The forcing of an individual into sexual activity through promises of rewards (e.g., money) or threats of punishment (e.g., demotion).
Sexual extortion	The forcing of an individual into sexual activity by blackmailing.
Rape	The forcing of an individual to penetrate or be penetrated though anal, oral, or vaginal intercourse.

SOURCE: Fisher, Cullen, and Turner, 1999.

suggest that the perpetration of sexual violence stems from men's innate biological drives to reproduce, others argue that this offense is simply about dominance and entitlement. Typologies set up to frame sexual violence support the latter view because explicit expressions of dominance and entitlement are visible in each category: for instance, power rapists and anger rapists (Groth, Burgess, and Holmstrom, 1977). Within these two categories are the following subtypes, which all have connections to gender dynamics: power-reassurance rapists, power-assertive rapists, anger-retaliatory rapists, and anger-excitation rapists.

Individuals aligning with the first type, power-reassurance rapists, engage in sexual violence to perform masculinity to address their feelings of inadequacy. In these offenses, the individual engaging in the offense has watched their target for a considerable amount of time and planned the attack carefully. This individual is among the least likely to physically harm their target because he imagines the offense is akin to a consensual act. In other words, these cases may involve individuals forcing their target to act as if they are consenting to their rape. These responses then affirm that individual's self-perception of their masculinity: that even an initially nonconsenting woman cannot resist their advances. As disturbing as this belief is, it aligns with broader toxic masculine ideals (such as sexual prowess) and beliefs that women are objects of sexual pleasure for men.

Individuals aligning with the second type, power-assertive rapists, engage in sexual violence to perform masculinity due to feelings of emasculation. However, unlike power-reassurance rapists, these individuals perform masculinity through violence by degrading the people they victimize. Put another way, the targets of these offenses are likely to be harmed because violence is a means of dominating someone viewed as inferior and as a sexual object. The individual who perpetrates this offense does not care about their target or injuries to their target; what matters is exerting power and control over another. Again, these underlying motivations align well with broader conceptions of hegemonic masculinity and toxic masculinity: the idea that "real men" are dominant and that other inferior groups exist (or even want) to conform to their wishes.

Individuals aligning with the third type, anger-retaliatory rapists, engage in sexual violence as an act of retaliation or revenge. In these offenses, something has happened that has enraged these individuals, and their responses center on targeting another for punishment. The method used by individuals engaging in this offense to "punish" is sexual violence. These offenses typically appear as blitz attacks, where the incident occurs very quickly and violently. Harm to the individual targeted is likely to occur. In considering the nature of this offense (whose purpose is retaliation and revenge), there is a visible connection to previously discussed gender concepts like aggrieved entitlement. As in prior types, this offense applies to both women and LGBTQIA+ people. For example, an individual aligning with anger-retaliatory rape may target a random individual who appears connected with the source of their rage (such as women or LGBTQIA+ people) to enact revenge for some adverse life event that has occurred.

Individuals aligning with the last type, anger-excitation rapists, engage in sexual violence because they are excited by inflicting pain on others. Typically, these individuals have abnormal and deviant sexual interests, referred to as paraphilias, that influence their modus operandi. Despite this condition, however, these individuals are typically careful in how they carry out their crimes. They are likely to use deception to lure people in or target individuals in precise locations to minimize detection. During the actual event, these individuals may force their target to recite certain statements while they torture them for sexual excitement. The event itself may last a brief period but more often occurs over extended periods (hours or days). Given the planning, it is unlikely that there will be much evidence left after the offense. Considering the brutality and torture of anger-excitation rapes, the individuals targeted are unlikely to survive. Thus, there is a significant crossover between anger-excitation rapists and sexually motivated serial killers (also known as "lust killers") because both types are sexually motivated and unlikely to stop unless caught (Fox, Levin, and Quinet, 2018). Although the underlying connection to hegemonic masculinity is not as evident in this type, it would be a mistake to conclude that gender is not relevant.

Indeed, even for individuals driven by paraphilias, there is still a powerful desire to exert power and control over others in their crimes that relate to hegemonic masculine ideals. For example, consider the case of John Wayne Gacy, otherwise known as the Killer Clown, who had experienced considerable childhood trauma at his father's hands. In adulthood, Gacy became a prolific lust

Table 3.5   The Connections between Masculinity and Sexual Violence

Rapist type	Motivation	Connection to masculinity
Power-reassurance	An individual engaging in power-reassurance rape victimizes others to affirm his own masculinity because he feels marginalized and socially isolated. In these cases, harm is unlikely to occur because the individual wants to believe the act is consensual.	An individual breaks into a woman's house while she is sleeping. He wakes her up and forces her to engage in role-playing, in which he needs her to act as if they are secret lovers. During the event, he needs her to say things that affirm his masculinity. After the act is completed, he continues to act as if it was consensual and then leaves.
Power-assertive	An individual engaging in power-assertive rape victimizes others to affirm his own masculinity because he feels emasculated and/or believes that sexual intimacy is an entitlement. In these cases, harm is likely to occur because the individual wants to take possession of the individual's 's body through sexual violence.	An individual takes a woman out on a date. After the date, the pair grabs some drinks at a local bar. At one point, the individual follows the date into the bathroom and tries to start sexual intimacy. The date refuses the individual, and this enrages him. He grabs her, slams her against the wall, and rapes her despite her protests.
Anger-retaliatory	An individual engaging in anger-retaliatory rape victimizes others out of anger and revenge. In these cases, the individuals being victimized may be the actual objects of anger or may represent the objects of anger (e.g., a random member of a specific group). The presence of aggrieved entitlement is strong in these occurrences: the sexual violence is punishment for slighting the individual engaging in the offense. Considering the strong undercurrent of anger, harm is likely.	A woman fires a man from his place of employment. He blames his employer for all his troubles and becomes increasingly enraged. Over the next several weeks, the fired employee sexually victimizes several women in random blitz attacks. During the attacks, he repeatedly yells at the women that it is "their fault" as beats and sexually violates them to the point of near-death.
Anger-excitation	An individual engaging in anger-excitation rape victimizes others through sexually violent torture as the ultimate expression of control and dominance. In these cases, the motivation to control and dominate another may stem from childhood trauma that the individual has carried into adulthood. There is a significant crossover between these individuals and serial killers, meaning that death to the person being victimized is extremely likely.	An individual methodically watches a local jogging path for several weeks and takes note of the women who are frequent visitors. After several weeks, he jogs along the path himself and pretends to pass out as his target approaches. As his target bends down to help him, he jumps up to knock her unconscious and drag her away before anyone notices. Over the next several hours, the individual sexually tortures the woman and repeatedly makes her beg for her life. He kills her after 36 hours of brutal and sadistic treatment.

SOURCE: Groth, Burgess, and Holmstrom, 1977.

killer who targeted young men for his sadistic torture sessions (Fox, Levin, and Quinet, 2018). In reflecting on his crimes, one can easily see that while Gacy had paraphilic disorders (such as sadism), his deep-seated need for power and control over others also motivated him. This need for power and control stemmed from Gacy's childhood, in which his father's abuse repeatedly emasculated him. Thus, dominating others through sexual torture was a method by which Gacy felt masculine and powerful in adulthood.

MASCULINITY AND CYBERCRIME

Given the developing nature of research on cybercrime, particularly in comparison to opportunities for research on "offline" crime, there is not much information on the connection between gender and these offenses. However, given the likelihood that individuals engaging in various offline crimes have simply moved to or supplemented with online activities, there is reason to believe existing gendered patterns of behavior hold in cyberspace as well as physical space. Thus, while there has been no exploration into the connection between hegemonic masculinity and hacking per se (to the best of our knowledge), there is reason to believe a link exists given the gendered nature of theft (a similar behavior). The following table presents potential connections between hegemonic masculine ideals and various cybercrimes by associating these behaviors with their closest offline comparable offense. To illustrate the strong likelihood of a tie, the rest of this chapter will explore the connection between hegemonic masculinity and cyberabuse between partners, because (as table 3.6 illustrates) relationship violence can be a motivating factor across all forms of online crime.

Cyberabuse is a broad term encompassing two closely related offense types: cyber dating abuse (cyberDA) and cyber intimate partner abuse (cyberIPA). While both these terms describe the same broad behavior, abuse of a partner, scholars typically use cyberIPA to refer to formal adult relationships. In contrast, cyberDA is typically used to refer to informal relationships more prevalent among youth and young adults (Navarro and Clevenger, 2021). Regardless of type, research findings underscore the role of gender norms in the perpetration of cyberabuse, as in offline abuse.

As discussed in the IPA section, this offense is associated with adherence to traditional gender norms. Put another way, individuals who abuse others are likely to firmly adhere to hegemonic masculine ideals that associate men as being the head of the household, the provider, and the protector of the family (Connell, 1987; Herrero et al., 2017). To these individuals, the role of women is to care for and support men while nurturing children. Women who do not conform to those expectations or who directly challenge the roles of men may experience abuse as an attempt by hegemonic men to force compliance. This violence may be isolated offline; however, given how technology permeates every aspect of social life, abuse is increasingly moving online.

Early research on the prevalence of this problem shows that many people experience offline and online abuse in various forms (Belknap, Chu, and DePrince, 2012). For example, research has found that men who abuse their partners block their access to technology or have used technology to threaten them. Studies have also found that these individuals exploit benign forms of technology for harmful purposes (Woodlock, 2017). For example, individuals who engage in abuse use email platforms, social media, and text messaging.

Table 3.6 Suggested Relationships between Masculinity and Cybercrimes, Based on Closest Offline Comparable Offense

Crime	General definition	Connection to masculinity
Cyberabuse	The use of technology by one partner to exert coercive control over another; includes a spectrum of behavior	Hegemonic masculine men control and monitor partners' movements via technology because they feel that doing so aligns with their role; they believe they are entitled to the information. This behavior may also occur if the relationship is threatened, and the individual perpetrating the abuse perceives the potential loss of control.
Cyberfraud	The use of technology to deceive another to gain something that one is otherwise not entitled to	Hegemonic masculine men may engage in cyber (financial) fraud, cyber identity theft, or similar online offenses to conform to traditional gender ideals by achieving status and wealth. Hegemonic masculine men may also engage in cyberfraud to punish a romantic partner for challenging their authority or role within an (abusive) relationship. An example of the latter is masquerading online as the targeted individual, a type of cyber identity theft, to destroy relationships.
Cyber-harassment	The intentional use of technology to harm or threaten another; may occur once or multiple times	Hegemonic masculine men may engage in cyberharassment to supplement offline abuse or as a response to a sense of aggrieved entitlement. In the former situation, the cyberharassment often takes multiple forms. It is intended to create omnipresence in targeted individuals' lives, such that these individuals act per expectations or are in a near-constant state of fear. In the latter case, hegemonic masculine men may engage in cyberharassment if they feel a sense of aggrieved entitlement stemming from the wrongful denial of something of value (e.g., money, sexual relations) by another who they believe should enthusiastically acquiesce.
Cyber-intrusion	The use of technology to gain unauthorized access to something online, such as a social media site	Hegemonic masculine men may engage in cyberintrusion, such as hacking, to gain respect and status among peers. As noted in the literature on burglary and theft, hegemonic masculinity is associated with confronting risks with bravery and skill. Men are respected by others and seen as "real men" when they upheld these ideals. Likewise, a form of social status currency among individuals who hack is the degree to which they compromise exceedingly difficult targets successfully. Cyberintrusion, as in other forms of cybercrime, may also be connected to gender through cyberabuse. In other words, a hegemonic masculine man may engage in cyberintrusion to control and watch his partner.
Cybersexual abuse	The use of technology to photograph/record explicit content without consent, to distribute explicit content without consent, or to incite sexual abuse	Hegemonic masculine men may engage in cybersexual abuse as part of a broader pattern of coercive control over another or as a reaction to a sense of aggrieved entitlement. In the former case, men may photograph/record sexual intimacy to show their friends as proof of their masculinity, or men adhering to toxic masculine ideals may photograph/record sexual content to ensure the targeted person's compliance in the relationship. In the latter case, given that toxic masculinity is strongly associated with sex and violence, men firmly adhering to these ideals may incite others to perpetrate sexual violence against an individual whom they perceive to have wronged them. For example, an aggrieved man posts under his supervisor's name (a woman) that she wants to engage in a rape fantasy with a stranger. After collecting responses, he sends these individuals her address.

| Cybertheft | The use of technology to get something illegally, such as through digital piracy or unauthorized access to a site | As in the case of cyberintrusion, cybertheft can be motivated by a desire to obtain respect and status among other individuals engaging in this crime or by a desire to exert control over another. The former case closely aligns with earlier discussion on individuals who hack, as well as individuals who pirate, who gain status by displaying bravery, knowledge, and skill in conducting their offenses. These characteristics are associated with "real men" and not "script kiddies," who need aid in conducting their crimes. Cybertheft may also be motivated by a sense of aggrieved entitlement in which a technology-savvy individual steals something of value from another whom he perceives to have wronged him. |

SOURCES: Connell, 1987; Kimmel, 2017; Messerschmidt, 1997.

Individuals who abuse their partners also use sophisticated forms of technology, like GPS monitoring, to create a threatening omnipresence in their lives. Aside from these forms of cyberabuse, the individuals have also used technology to conduct financial cybercrimes (such as account establishment and account takeovers) and sexually violent cybercrimes (Clevenger and Navarro, 2019; Woodlock, 2017). Alarmingly, similar methods of victimization have been found by cyberDA studies involving youth (Draucker and Martsolf, 2010). The varied nature of cyberDA and cyberIPA is one of the reasons why it is exceedingly difficult to determine the actual scope of the problem.

Unfortunately, given the breadth of behavior that is possible within the spectrum of cyberabuse, it is difficult to assess how prevalent these offenses are online. However, cyberstalking research has shed some light on cyberIPA. In terms of stalking prevalence by partners across the lifespan, national studies have found that about 10 percent of women reported victimization while about 2 percent of men noted experiencing this offense (Smith et al., 2018). Although there is debate about whether the internet has spawned a new type of stalking behavior, one that is unknown to the target, research continues to show that many individuals who stalk are intimate partners (Catalano, 2012). Likewise, cyberDA research shows alarming victimization percentages, with several studies returning a range of 12 percent to upwards of 50 percent of respondents noting problematic experiences (Stonard et al., 2014). Because these experiences typically occurred within the broader context of partner abuse, the connection to gender that was outlined in the IPA section applies. Specifically, hegemonic masculine men and, even more so, men adhering to toxic masculinity, use cyberspace to further their abuse.

Research applying Johnson's (1995) typology of abuse to relationship dynamics in cyberspace further underscores the connection between gender and cyberDA and cyberIPA. In that study, respondents noted various cyberabuse incidents not grounded in gender, which most closely aligned with Johnson's common couple violence category (Melander, 2010). In these cases, the experiences were minor disputes without any firm grounding in a desire to control. On the other hand, respondents also noted several cyberabuse incidents involving various degrees of severity that mirrored intimate partner terrorism. Aside from capturing these two types, findings showed that technology-enabled mutually violent control exists in cyberspace. Finally, results also showed a type of violent resistance in cyberspace where individuals use technology to challenge the person asserting control over them and end toxic relationships.

Considering the strong connection between gender and many of the offline crimes noted in this chapter, it makes intuitive sense that a link between gender and various cybercrimes exists. Exploration of the connection between gender and cyberabuse underscores this likelihood. However, there is a shortage of information on the role of gender, specifically hegemonic masculinity, and perpetrating cybercrime. Although men are overrepresented among individuals violating the law in many of these offense types (such as cyberabuse, cyberfraud, cyberintrusion, and cybertheft), more information is needed on exactly what is *motivating* their actions. While we present several hypothetical connections based on the closet comparable offline crimes, this line of research is ripe for investigation.

SUMMARY

Throughout this chapter, we presented information showing that a firm adherence to hegemonic masculine ideals, and more so toxic masculine ideals, is a pronounced undercurrent to perpetrating offline and online crimes. Moreover, aggrieved entitlement, which itself relates to broader gender norms, also influences the likelihood of criminal engagement. These general points align with the notion that crime is a gendered performance, especially among those with few other resources to assert themselves. Therefore, to understand the origins of these "manly" crimes, criminologists need to examine the role of gender and socially constructed gender ideals.

"Ladies Only"

An Examination of Women and Crime

KEY TERMS

- ▶ acutely psychotic filicide
- ▶ altruistic filicide
- ▶ drug mule
- ▶ embezzlement
- ▶ fatal maltreatment filicide
- ▶ infanticide
- ▶ john school
- ▶ jumped in
- ▶ larceny-theft
- ▶ liberation hypothesis
- ▶ maternal filicide
- ▶ migrant worker
- ▶ multiple marginalities
- ▶ Munchausen syndrome by proxy
- ▶ neonaticide
- ▶ paternal filicide
- ▶ pink-collar jobs
- ▶ prostitution
- ▶ spouse revenge filicide
- ▶ status offenses
- ▶ suicide-filicide
- ▶ trafficked
- ▶ trained in
- ▶ unwanted child filicide

LEARNING OBJECTIVES

- ▶ Understand gender concepts related to criminal engagement by women.
- ▶ Explain how gender concepts related to women's criminal engagement work in conjunction with major criminological perspectives to frame crime.
- ▶ Apply chapter content to contemporary issues related to females and crime.

In this chapter, we discuss issues pertaining to system-involved women. However, a majority of the research on this topic reflects the experiences of cisgender women. While attention on intersectionality is increasing, there is substantial work left to do. Thus, readers should bear in mind that the experiences of transgender women, as well as women with multiple important intersecting identities (such as Black transgender women), are much less represented in the research that is noted throughout this chapter and book.

To begin our discussion on women's involvement in criminal activity, it is essential to consider how the focus on this topic started. Historically, statistics show that women are less involved in crime than men are. Moreover, women are more likely to be arrested for petty offenses: misdemeanors and lesser felonies. As in other areas of social life, gender does not exist in a vacuum; class and race can also impact the arrests of women. Financially insecure or marginalized women have always been the most likely to be arrested and punished in court. Overall, women who engaged in gender-incongruent behavior—behavior not "becoming" of a woman or not aligning with the dominant gender norms presented in chapter 3—were also more likely to be punished for those crimes. For example, in adultery laws of earlier generations, women were more likely to be charged and penalized than men. Men were often not charged or punished severely. If they were charged, they did not suffer the same consequences as women did. Men and women also differ in their motivations for criminal engagement. Because women are more likely to suffer periods of financial insecurity and are at higher risk of homelessness than are men, they have historically been driven to crime to support themselves and their families. For instance, many women who were imprisoned in the 1700s and 1800s were incarcerated due to begging, prostitution, or theft.

In examining the role of system-involved women, a pattern emerges across time. Unlike system-involved men, women tend to be arrested for petty or property offenses where there is potential economic gain. A critical concept that frames this pattern is **multiple marginalities.** The term describes the intersection of class, gender, and race that pushes women to the fringes of society where there is limited opportunity for economic success (Vigil, 2002). Indeed, the lack of opportunity at the fringes of society coupled with the pressure to financially support themselves and their families leads women to commit crime. Girls as well as adult women have specific pressures and needs that can place them on a pathway toward crime. More specifically, girls may experience abuse and neglect, which might cause them to run away from their homes. Behavior such as truancy and running away, in turn, exposes girls to potential intervention by the criminal-legal system, where they are more often adjudicated for those acts than are boys.

Whereas the previous chapter investigated the role of masculinity and crime, this chapter will focus on the role of gender in contributing to women's engagement in crime. We will discuss system-involved girls and specific crimes in which women represent a significant (if not the largest) share of individuals who violate the law (such as being drug mules, embezzlement, larceny-theft, and sex work). Although men comprise most perpetrators of murder, we revisit homicide in this chapter in terms of the subtypes in which a more significant percentage of women are represented: filicide, infanticide, and neonaticide.

GIRLS AND CRIME

The prevalence of arrests involving girls decreased by 53 percent between 2006 and 2015, as did the number of delinquency cases involving status cases for girls (OJJDP, 2019). According to the Office of Juvenile Justice and Delinquency Prevention (OJJDP), which examined information from three national data collections from law enforcement, there were an estimated 921,600 arrests of individuals under the age of eighteen in 2015. Of those arrests, girls accounted for 269,900 of incidents, which amounts to less than one-third overall. However, that overall finding varies based on specific offense statistics. For example, girls were arrested in 40 percent of juvenile larceny-theft cases, 40 percent of cases involving liquor law violations, 7 percent of juvenile simple assault cases, and 35 percent of disorderly conduct cases. In terms of violent crime, girls were also arrested in 6 percent of juvenile murder cases and 11 percent of robbery arrests. In terms of crimes against society, as referred to by the FBI, more girls than boys were arrested for sex work and related offenses (76%) (Ehrmann, Hyland and Puzzanchera, 2019).

A closer examination of **status offenses**, which are noncriminal incidents if committed by an adult but are punishable if committed by a juvenile (e.g., alcohol use, running away, truancy, ungovernability, violating curfew), the report reveals that girls comprised 55 percent of cases (OJJDP, 2019). Girls' engagement in status offenses likely relates to issues within the home that they are more like to encounter than boys. For example, girls are more likely to be sexually abused, the abuse is likely to start at a young age, and the abuse is likely to last a significant period (Flowers, 2001). Considering that girls are more likely to be sexually abused by a family member, often one with whom they reside (RAINN, 2021b), their running away or truancy may be a form of escape. Girls who are abused carry significant trauma as a result of the abuse, which may influence their involvement in status offenses. In addition to running away from home or violating curfews to escape the abuse, girls may begin to use substances to self-medicate. Finally, girls' so-called ungovernability may be related to abuse or their general home life, as this can manifest from anger connected to trauma.

Historically, research on girls as juvenile justice system–involved individuals has compared them to boys (Hoyt and Scherer, 1998). Within this research, scholars have examined connections between crimes committed by girls and academic achievement, education, hopelessness, and low self-esteem, as well as the connection between system-involved girls and histories of trauma and substance abuse (Cauffman et al., 2007; Kakar, 2005). This research has shown that various other factors contribute to girls committing crime, such as early involvement in crime, parent criminality, and parental transitions (Leve and Chamberlain, 2007), and unwanted pregnancies. Finally, mental health may also be a factor for system-involved girls (Dixon, Howie, and Starling, 2004). After presenting a broad overview, we will now examine the connection between gender and criminal engagement among girls and women within specific crimes and settings.

Girls and Gangs

In the 1990s, laypersons began to recognize the role of girls in gangs. A cover story in *Newsweek* about girls' involvement in gangs prompted conversation in broadcast media programs like the *Oprah Winfrey Show, Geraldo,* and *Larry King Live.* However, to holistically understand girls' involvement in gangs and growing presence within crime overall, it is essential to discuss the seminal work of Freda Adler's (1975) *Sisters in Crime* and the **liberation hypothesis.** According to Adler's hypothesis, greater access and involvement of women in various spheres of social life would lead to young women assuming new roles and leaving their historically assumed roles. Some of these new roles likely would include deviance and crime. In Miller's (1975) investigation of this topic during the 1970s, results showed that girls' involvement in gangs was nationwide, but was often only nominal and comprised a smaller percentage of overall gang membership relative to boys.

The involvement of girls in gangs has continued over time, with research uncovering different percentages of membership. While Miller found that, nationally, girls made up less than 10 percent of all gang members, Moore (1991), who examined girls' involvement in gangs across barrios in Los Angeles, estimated that one-third of all youth involved in gangs were young women. Curry, Ball, and Fox (1994) found that girls comprise about 3.6 percent of gang members, whereas Howell (2007) and Howell and Griffiths (2018) estimate that young women make up less than 10 percent of the overall gang population. In general, girls' involvement in gangs tends to coincide with living in larger cities (Howell and Griffiths, 2018).

Research has shown that crimes committed by girls in gangs are often less severe than crimes by boys in gangs. However, girls do commit violent offenses as well as experience violence stemming from their involvement in gangs. For instance, research shows that girl gang members engage in more crime than girls and boys not involved in gangs, which underscores that gangs themselves are criminogenic and violent (Miller and Decker, 2001). Compared to boy gang members, though, girl gang members are often less violent, as they may not participate in physical fighting or violent offenses as often or in the same manner as their male counterparts. However, fighting can be a way to achieve status for girls as well as boys in gangs, and, once that status is achieved, the gang member often fights less. Girls may fight once or twice to establish themselves but then refrain from regularly engaging in fights or violent behavior. Violence in various forms is also often part of the initiation into gangs. Girls can be jumped in by being beaten by the other gang members, or they can be trained in, which means having sex with several gang members. However, those who are trained in are often not viewed as equal to those that are jumped in (Portillos and Zatz, 1995). Gang members may also perceive or refer to these girls as "slutty" despite the purpose of being trained in was to show allegiance to the group.

Girls' motivations for joining a gang often align with broader motivations for criminal engagement by women: to secure monetary resources. In other words, girl gang members are often living in poverty-stricken neighborhoods without many legitimate opportunities for conventional personal and professional success, and thus they seek out existing illegitimate means like gangs (Campbell, 1990; Joe and Chesney-Lind, 1995; Miller, 2001). Aside from providing financial security, gangs can be a source of comfort and serve as a surrogate family for girls who desire feelings of belonging and community that are absent at home. Not only may these feelings be absent at home, but girl gang members often have a history of physical and sexual abuse—sometimes from their home lives. Thus, gang membership can be an escape from an unwanted home environment as well as provide an opportunity for girls to show that they can defend themselves from their abusers (Joe and Chesney-Lind, 1995).

WOMEN AND CRIME

According to the FBI's *Crime in the United States* report for 2015, 2,238,335 women were arrested in that calendar year, which amounted to 26.9 percent of all arrests. An examination of the percentage for women in each specific crime (table 4.1) shows that they were less likely than men to be arrested for all crimes except embezzlement. Even with embezzlement, however, arrest percentages for men and women are very close (50.2% for women, 49.8% for men). The percentage of women arrested for embezzlement is interesting as this has been traditionally thought of as a white-collar crime and dominated by men. Yet, the percentages of men and women embezzlers have been close during the past decade. Additionally, although men still represent most arrests for larceny-theft (56.8%), women are not far behind (43.2%).

While statistics show that men still outpace women in arrests, there has been an increase in the number of women who are incarcerated. Indeed, women comprise more of the prison population than ever before in history.

Table 4.1 Crime in the United States, 2015

Offense	Total arrested	Men arrested	Women arrested	% men	% women
Number of arrests	8,305,919	6,067,584	2,238,335	73.1	26.9
Murder / non-negligent manslaughter	8,533	7,549	514	88.5	11.5
Rape	17,504	16,990	514	97.1	2.9
Robbery	73,230	62,721	10,509	85.6	14.4
Aggravated assault	288,815	221,993	66,822	76.9	23.1
Burglary	166,609	135,064	31,545	81.1	18.9
Larceny-theft	900,077	511,557	388,520	56.8	43.2
Motor vehicle theft	59,831	47,169	12,662	78.8	21.2
Arson	6,802	5,460	1,342	80.3	19.7
Violent crime	388,082	309,253	78,829	79.7	20.3
Property crime	1,133,319	699,250	434,069	61.7	38.3
Other assaults	831,684	598,00	233,684	71.9	28.1
Forgery and counterfeiting	42,681	27,596	15,085	64.7	35.3
Fraud	102,339	62,721	39,618	61.3	38.7
Embezzlement	12,247	6,093	6,154	49.8	50.2
Stolen property	68,341	53,621	14,720	78.5	21.5
Vandalism	147,191	115,695	31,496	78.6	21.4
Weapons: carrying, possessing, etc.	111,316	101,366	9,950	91.1	8.9
Prostitution and commercializing vice	31,534	11,355	20,179	36.0	64.0
Sex offenses (except rape and prostitution)	39,393	36,361	3,032	92.3	7.7
Drug abuse violations	1,144,021	886,022	257,999	77.4	22.6
Gambling	3,607	2,883	724	79.9	20.1
Offenses against family and children	72,418	51,598	20,820	71.3	28.7
Driving under the influence	833,833	625927	207,906	75.1	24.9
Liquor laws	204,665	145,238	59,427	71.0	29.0
Drunkenness	314,856	253,565	61,291	80.5	19.5
Disorderly conduct	298,253	214,118	84,135	71.8	28.3
Vagrancy	19,414	15,080	4,334	77.7	22.3
All other offenses (except traffic)	2,471,772	1,826,711	645,061	73.9	26.1
Suspicion	1,045	802	243	76.7	23.3
Curfew and loitering law violations	33,908	24,329	9,579	71.8	28.2

SOURCE: FBI, 2015, *Crime in the United States: 2015*, https://ucr.fbi.gov/crime-in-the-u.s/2015/crime-in-the-u.s.-2015.

ACTIVE LEARNING ASSIGNMENT 4.1

Women Arrestees: Is It What You Expected?

Please examine table 4.1, "Crime in the United States, 2015." Then answer the following questions on your own, in a small group, or in the class as a whole:

1. Are the statistics on crimes committed by women what you expected? Why or why not?
2. Which crime or crimes did you think would have higher or lower numbers? Please explain your answer.
3. Why do you think that women have lower arrests in almost every crime? Please explain.

When examining the differences between 1980 and 2014, the total number of women incarcerated in the United States has risen by 700 percent (FBI, 2015). In 1980, 26,378 women were incarcerated. In 2014, the number increased to 215,332. Women's involvement within the criminal-legal system has also increased. For instance, the total of women under all types of supervision by the criminal-legal system—jail (109,100), prison (106,232), probation (966,029), and parole (102,825)—is 1.2 million (Sentencing Project, 2020).

Several factors have likely led to the increase in the number of women within the criminal-legal system. These include harsh sentences required by drug laws, issues in reentry that specifically affect women (such as the fact that many women incarcerated are mothers), and extensive alteration of law enforcement efforts that may now include focusing on women. Unfortunately, this increase in supervision has affected the most vulnerable women in society because those who are incarcerated tend to be women of color and to have insecure financial backgrounds, as well as histories of abuse or trauma. For example, Black women are incarcerated at two times the rate of white women, and Hispanic women 1.2 times the rate of white women (Sentencing Project, 2020).

Women and Nonviolent Crime

Larceny-Theft: The Gendered Nature of Shoplifting

The statistics released by the FBI in *Crime in the United States* (2015) reveal that men still commit more **larceny-theft** (56.8%) than women, but women are not far behind (43.2%). Larceny-theft, according to the FBI Uniform Crime Report (2017e), is "the unlawful taking, carrying, leading, or riding away of property from the possession or constructive possession of another." Men and women shoplift at about equal rates, and there is no typical profile. Research indicates that individuals aged 35–54 or who are financially insecure are more likely to shoplift than those in other age brackets and those in middle or upper socioeconomic classes (Dabney, Hollinger, and Dugan, 2004). This does not mean individuals from across the socioeconomic spectrum do not shoplift. Research by Blanco and colleagues (2008) indicates that people from all economic groups shoplift. Moreover, individuals who shoplift are most likely to be white (78%). The behaviors of individuals who shoplift are also sometimes contrary to popular media depictions. For instance, individuals who shoplift may also buy items on the same trip, indicating their actions may not be deliberate.

Although FBI (2015) statistics indicate that men shoplift at a slightly higher rate than women, shoplifting is often thought of as stereotypically women's offense. That belief can be traced back to the gendered notions of responsibilities within society. In general, shopping is believed to be a woman's task as it aligns broadly with the idea that overseeing a home is a woman's responsibility or "women's work." Moreover, shopping is something that would fall into the "second shift," the term Arlie Hochschild (1989) uses to refer to "family and house" work that a woman does after her paying job has ended for the day.

Given that women are expected to go shopping and procure the necessary items for their family and household, this responsibility may influence engagement in crime. In other words, financially insecure women and girls, who may not have access to, or are too fearful to commit other more daring or violent crimes, might be more comfortable with the ritual of shopping and the environment of retail establishments. Although there is an argument that the emancipation of women has freed them from household responsibilities, research continues to show that women do most of the household purchasing (e.g., 94% of home items, 51% of electronics; Silverstein and Sayer, 2009). As a result, shoplifting is often within the comfort zone of many girls and women.

In terms of *what* they steal, girls and women often steal things that they want or believe that they need but may not be able to afford (clothes, cosmetics, jewelry). They are also influenced by advertising campaigns explicitly aimed at them and may spend time in stores with such items, which thereby increases their desire for those commodities (Campbell, 1981). Seeing all these things that they want and feel they should have may lead to stealing them. Women and men often steal the way they shop. Women often enjoy browsing around the store when doing their shopping. When shoplifting, women often browse before stealing and may steal multiple items in different departments while shopping. When men shop, they often go straight for the items they need and get out of the store quickly. The same can be seen in their shoplifting behaviors: they take the items they want and get out (Campbell, 1981). (See Case Study 4.1.)

Researchers have identified some underlying causes of shoplifting among women. Women may shoplift as a result of personal issues, mental

---

CASE STUDY 4.1

Winona Ryder and Shoplifting

In December 2001, Winona Ryder was arrested for shoplifting over $5,560 worth of merchandise in Saks Fifth Avenue in Beverly Hills, California. She was caught on tape stashing a cashmere Marc Jacobs sweater, hair accessories, and several pairs of socks into shopping and garment bags. Security officers detained her until police arrived. At her trial in 2002, she was found guilty of felony grand theft and felony vandalism but not guilty of commercial burglary. Security staff testified that after Ryder was apprehended, she said she was preparing for a movie role. Prosecutors revealed that she had narcotics in her possession at the time of arrest, but her physicians had prescribed them all. During the trial, it was revealed that Ryder was suspected of shoplifting previously at other stores, but

no additional charges were ever filed against her.

She was sentenced to three years of supervised probation and received 480 hours of community service, which she completed at the City of Hope. Ryder also paid more than $10,000 in fines and restitution. In 2004, the judge reduced the charges to misdemeanors and put her on unsupervised probation through December 2005 because of good behavior.

After reading about this case and doing additional research if you wish, please answer the following questions:

1. What is your opinion on this case?
2. Do you think that Ryder shoplifted as a result of drug use? Why or why not?
3. Do you think that Ryder's sentence stemmed from her celebrity status? Why or why not?

MEDIA BYTE 4.1   **Winona Ryder Fifteen Years Later**

Watch this brief interview with Ryder as she talks about her shoplifting: https://youtu.be/U_sqNg-wuSm4. After watching the clip, please answer the following questions:

1. Discuss why you think Ryder committed theft.
2. Do you think that she is sorry for what she did? Why or why not?
3. Do you think that when people watch Ryder on the screen that they consider her a criminal or think about this incident of shoplifting? Why or why not?
4. How would the different feminist criminological schools of thought explain her crime?

---

health issues, eating disorders and/or substance abuse issues (Lamontagne et al., 2000). Put another way, women who shoplift may be reacting to these issues or trying to cope with their stress. Likewise, adolescent girls may shoplift as a result of peer pressure, the thrill associated with stealing, or financial insecurity (Lo, 1994: Kelley, Kennedy, and Homant, 2003). (See Media Byte 4.1.)

Drug Trafficking

When examining drug offenses or viewing drugs use and offending as depicted in media, men and women are typically thought of and depicted in positions of stark power differences. Men are often seen as the brains and the power within the operation, while women are the body, in supportive roles that are without power (Fleetwood, 2015). This duality is evidenced in drug trafficking, where women often serve as **drug mules,** or drug couriers or carriers, transporting drugs for someone else either domestically or internationally. Women use a variety of strategies as drug mules. They can put the drugs in objects when traveling, such as containers or diapers, or hide them inside the seams of luggage. They also may put the drugs on or inside their bodies: strapping the drugs to themselves, swallowing the drugs in capsules or bags, or inserting the drugs anally or vaginally. When a drug mule is apprehended, it most often as a result of authorities discovering the hidden drugs (Caulkins, Burnett, and Leslie, 2009; Green, Mills, and Reed, 1994; Harper, Harper, and Stockdale, 2000).

Women who work as drug mules or couriers are often portrayed in the media as being weak and unexperienced in the drug trade, which men in power are happy to exploit (Anderson, 2005; Maher, 1997). They may also be portrayed as addicted to drugs or at the mercy of pimps and dealers (Anderson, 2005; Maher, 1997) because they need protection (Seddon, 2008; Schemenauer, 2012). In terms of research on this topic, many studies focus on women even though the majority (about 70%) of drug mules are men (Fleetwood, 2010), and FBI (2015) arrest statistics indicate that 77 percent of those arrested for drug abuse violations are men (see table 4.1). Yet, despite those statistics, research focuses on women, and the perception of drug mules always being women continues. This continuing practice may also stem from the publicity tied to cases involving women as drug mules in contrast to men who are dealers or pimps.

Women work as drug mules for a variety of reasons. The lack of legitimate opportunities for economic success and achievement among women may lead them to work as drug mules. Put another way, women may view working as a drug mule as a way to get out poverty, escape abuse, improve their lives, and provide financial stability for themselves and their families. Although the practice carries significant risk, working as a drug mule provides women with an opportunity to earn large amounts of cash quickly in contrast to earning an income through conventional routes (Adler, 1993; Davies, 2003; Fleetwood; 2010; Olmo, 1990). The fast and practical nature of earning money quickly through this route is, thus, attractive to financially insecure women (Campbell, 2005). Through this work, women can provide a future for themselves and their families. Moreover, as women work and earn more money, they can advance to higher levels of socioeconomic status and capital (Campbell, 2008).

Past traumatic experiences, like abuse and victimization, can set women on a pathway to becoming a drug mule either as an adult or a child (Geiger, 2006;

McCartan and Gunnison, 2010). For example, Fleetwood (2010) found that women often became initially involved in trafficking and working as drug mules after suffering a victimization experience: they were pressured, tricked, or threatened by their intimate partners or family. In addition, women who serve as drug mules are frequently victimized by their drug-dealing partners even if they had not been victimized previously (Huling, 1995; Huling, 1996). It is argued that the victimization stems from the partners perceiving the women serving as mules as cheap, expendable, and easy prey.

Although poverty, abuse, and victimization are recognized reasons why women agree to carry drugs, these are often not taken into account as "mitigating circumstances" during their involvement in the criminal-legal system— reasons that could function to reduce their charges or sentence. The war on drugs and the mandatory minimums that resulted from it have resulted in harsh punishments for women (Bush-Baskette, 2004). While drug offenses and imprisonment are often thought to have hit men the hardest, women have also suffered worldwide because of the global initiative to fight drug trafficking.

The United Nations Office on Drugs and Crime (UNODC) has stated that drug trafficking is a worldwide issue and one that has affected women. UNODC's *World Drug Report* (2015b) indicates that arrests of women involved in drug trafficking have increased in India, China, Zambia, and Nigeria since 2010. Europe and Central Asia have also seen increases in imprisonment for drug charges (Iakobishvili, 2012), as has Latin America (Giacomello, 2013). (See Media Byte 4.2.) While individuals arrested for drug trafficking in the United States are typically incarcerated, other countries have implemented significantly more extreme punishments. For example, in China, Indonesia, Iran, Kuwait, Saudi Arabia, Sri Lanka, Vietnam, Singapore, and Malaysia, an individual arrested for carrying drugs can be put to death. In some countries (such as Iran, Malaysia, and Singapore), the *only* penalty for trafficking drugs is death (Pinto, 2015). In other words, women caught transporting drugs in these countries can be put to death.

MEDIA BYTE 4.2   **Drug Mule Smuggles Drugs in Breast Implants**

Authorities at a German airport stopped a Colombian woman who was in pain from recent breast implants and found that they contained smuggled cocaine: http://www.businessinsider.com/r-germany-catches-woman-smuggling-cocaine-in-breast-implants-2016–3. After you read the article, answer the following questions:

1. What is your reaction to this case?
2. Do you think that there will be more women smuggling drugs in this fashion? Please explain.

Embezzlement

Embezzlement is the taking of property (usually money) that belongs to another person or business by a person who is in a position of trust. The individual who embezzles is typically an employee, agent, or someone who works for that organization in some capacity. Embezzlement can be committed in a variety of ways, but it often involves the theft of money. For example, people who embezzle can use a company credit card for their personal use or transfer money from business accounts into their personal account. They can create and submit phony invoices for reimbursement, write out a check to themselves, or inflate their actual wages so that they make more money (Simmons-Brown, 2015).

As seen in table 4.1, the FBI's *Crime in the United States* data, more women than men were arrested for embezzlement in 2015. Moreover, FBI data from 2005 show that women represented 50 percent of arrests for embezzlement then. Since 1964, arrests of women for embezzlement have been on the rise (Simon and Anh-Redding, 2005). This increase, scholars argue, is due to the increase in the number of women within the workplace, which creates more opportunities for them to commit embezzlement. Additionally, as women obtain more upper-level managerial and administrative jobs (white-collar employment), other pathways of criminal engagement, like fraud and forgery, arise (Dodge, 2009). The increased number of women entering the workforce, rather than staying home as mothers and housekeepers, led some early scholars to suspect their participation in crime would increase (Adler, 1975).

While those scholars argued that women's increased representation in crime stems from more significant involvement in the workforce and social life outside the home, others have countered this notion. These scholars argue that the women engaging in these crimes occupy low to mid-level positions in traditionally **pink-collar jobs**, or jobs that are "reserved for women," because the amounts that are taken are not especially large (Daly, 1989; Holtfreter, 2005). For example, research on this topic has found that many of the women who embezzled had pink-collar jobs such as bank tellers or store clerks and stole small sums (averaging $1,000–$2,500; Daly, 1989). This view of women's involvement in embezzlement also considers that women are more likely to be "stuck" in lower-level, lower-paying jobs without equal opportunities for advancement relative to men. Thus, the inertia women encounter in advancement may factor into their decisions to embezzle, as they may face financial or emotional strain, or both.

Women who embezzle not only often steal smaller amounts, but do so over a long time, which lessens the risk of detection. The loss is usually noticed only after large sums of money are missing or unaccounted for in records. It can also be difficult for auditors or company accountants to determine precisely who took the money or where it went. Individuals who embezzle may alter the documents and not leave a paper trail. They may also not take vacation time because they are worried that someone would discover what they are doing (Dodge, 2009).

Interestingly, although technology has provided multiple benefits to society, the increased use of computers in businesses and organizations has aggravated this problem. Computers and technology can be used to facilitate or commit embezzlement, which some have argued has led to an increase in embezzlement (Rosoff, Pontell, and Tillman, 2007). However, even without a computer, there are at least two hundred ways to commit embezzlement (Sifakis, 2001). These multiple pathways speak to the rationality behind this crime and the notion that potential perpetrators (to use a routine activities theory term) will figure out how to embezzle money—often in effortless ways.

As previously mentioned, women's motivation to embezzle often differs from that of men. For women, their engagement in crime is often altruistic as they want to help their family or friends, or overcome financial insecurity themselves (Daly, 1989; Forsyth and Marckese, 1995). Women who embezzle often rationalize their actions because the money benefitted their children or family members. These women also perceive embezzling as a viable way to pay for essential items that correspond to their roles as mother, daughter, girlfriend, and wife. Women who embezzle may have a "Joan of Arc" sense of self. In other words, they will do whatever is necessary, even "burn at the stake," or in this case, face imprisonment, to provide for their loved ones. From their perspective, they are making the ultimate sacrifice—putting themselves in danger—to provide for their children and loved ones by not only purchasing everyday supplies but also paying for education and medical necessities (Zeitz, 1981).

The motivations of women who embezzle stand in contrast to the typical drive of men who embezzle. Men who embezzle are often motivated by a need to safeguard their reputation, social position, and status. Thus, like women who embezzle, men's engagement in this crime stems from dominant gender norms, but men's are associated with masculinity (such as autonomy and independence; Connell, 1987). Whereas women who embezzle are often stealing funds to care for and protect loved ones, men who embezzle are often stealing to cover debts or pay for a lavish lifestyle (Zeitz, 1981). Women's involvement in embezzlement can be viewed within the dominant gender ideal that women should care for others before themselves—even to their detriment.

To reiterate, the objective of criminology is to understand the social causes and reactions to crime as well as the people involved. In pursuing that objective, social scientists seek to establish broad patterns through various forms of research, both quantitative and qualitative. However, individuals can deviate from what is "typical." (See Case Study 4.2 and Media Byte 4.3.) Considering that, it is not surprising that some studies find that women engage in embezzlement for reasons that are not altruistic: greed for material possessions, to afford things they desire, or to fuel addictions (Dodge, 2009). Research also

CASE STUDY 4.2

Rita Crundwell, Municipal Embezzler

Rita Crundwell was arrested on April 17, 2012, for embezzling $53.7 million across two decades. In 2013, at the age of sixty, she pled guilty to fraud and was sentenced to nineteen years and seven months in prison, making this the biggest municipal fraud case in United States history. She was only five months short of receiving the absolute maximum penalty under the law. Crundwell was the former city comptroller for Dixon, Illinois, the childhood home of President Ronald Reagan.

The fraud began in 1990, although authorities suggest it may have started in 1988. Crundwell was very good at hiding her tracks, so the exact start date is not known. She used the money to finance her quarter-horse breeding business and lavish lifestyle, which does not align with gender norms previously discussed. Crundwell initially started working for the city as a high school student and eventually became the comptroller, a position that she occupied for almost thirty years. She had only a high school education and had planned to attend college. However, when the city's first comptroller, Darlene Herzog, encouraged her to stay and said she would mentor her, Crundwell stayed on to learn the ropes. Because the comptroller was appointed rather than elected, she was able to keep her job for many years due to the outward perception that she was good at her job and an excellent fit for the city.

Many have wondered how she was able to steal so much for so long without anyone noticing. The reason can be attributed to Dixon's unusual style of government. The power of governing is split among five people, which includes the mayor and four part-time commissioners. The pay for these positions is small ($9,600 for the mayor

and $2,700 for the commissioners), which means that they have full-time jobs and are rarely at the city courthouse. Most of the individuals in these positions are everyday citizens and not necessarily familiar with governmental workings and procedures. By the late 1980s, as comptroller, Crundwell was controlling all the city's money. She wrote the checks, deposited money, requested reimbursements, and paid the bills. If a project needed funding, that company or individual appealed to Crundwell. She had a lot of power, autonomy, and discretion: she completely controlled the finances of Dixon. This, coupled with the lack of oversight in government, allowed her to steal money for decades without anyone noticing.

Finally, a coworker noticed a discrepancy in bank activity while filling in for Crundwell. Swanson saw that tens of millions of dollars were being taken from Dixon's operating budget and placed into an account that was registered to Crundwell. By the time she was caught, the city was borrowing money to pay day-to-day operating expenses because she was stealing so much. Swanson took the evidence to the mayor, who eventually contacted the authorities, and Crundwell was arrested.

Crundwell's property was seized, which included four hundred prize-winning horses, frozen horse semen (a valuable commodity for breeding), her ranch and home, a luxury motor home, horse trailers, vehicles, jewelry, and designer clothes and purses, as well as a vacation home in Florida. The money from the sale of those items went back to the city, totaling close to $11 million. Crundwell's federal prison wages are being garnished as well: she pays Dixon $65 a month in restitution.

MEDIA BYTE 4.3   *All the Queen's Horses:* Documentary
about Rita Crundwell

Watch the trailer for the documentary about the Rita Crundwell case at https://
www.allthequeenshorsesfilm.com/trailer. Then answer the following questions:

1. Did this documentary raise awareness about embezzlement? Why or why not?
2. Will viewing this trailer and/or the documentary influence the way that people think about the gender of individuals who engage in embezzlement? Please explain.
3. Do you think that individuals who view this trailer and/or the documentary will think about Crundwell's gender when watching it or will they just see an individual who violated the law? Please explain.
4. Will people be likely to villainize her for her crime because she is a woman. Justify your response.

MEDIA BYTE 4.4   Women Who Embezzle

Read the following articles that detail two stories of women who embezzled and answer the questions below. If these articles are no longer available, please contact your instructor.

Jessica Mixon:

https://www.theledger.com/article/LK/20070209/News/608091237/LL

Cynthia Mills:

http://pittsburgh.cbslocal.com/2017/09/28/cynthia-mills-sentencing/

1. Based on what you have read, what were the motives for these two women? How were their motives similar and different? Please explain.
2. Do you find anything shocking about these cases? Why or why not?
3. Do you think that there could have been a way to prevent either of these crimes? Please explain your answer.

---

shows that some women intentionally choose a career so that they can embezzle later. For these women, the plan to embezzle is premeditated and often done in conjunction with others either inside or outside the business (Zeitz, 1981). (See Media Byte 4.4.) In these instances, however, men are usually the primary perpetrator, and women are in a supportive role, taking direction from the men.

Prostitution

European records of the act of **prostitution**, or the selling of sex or sex acts for money, date to ancient Greece (Sanders, O'Neil, and Pitcher, 2009). In medieval Europe, it was taxed and made part of the broader societal institution. However, as Protestantism grew within European society, public perception of prostitution shifted, by the Victorian era, to seeing it as a social evil and a source of disease. Today, the perception arguably remains the same: many view sex work and sex workers themselves as social pariahs (Day, 2007). However, it is essential to note that those who work in the commercial sex trade are individuals, and many are "ordinary" people with ordinary lives and families. For many individuals engaging in the commercial sex trade, this is just their occupation.

Throughout history, the majority of sex workers have been women, which relates to the barriers and challenges women encounter in securing legitimate financial employment. This pattern stems from constraints associated with gender and the roles we assign to men and women: women often lack marketable skills if they have only been homemakers, since that work is uncompensated. Moreover, the arrest process itself is shaped by gender. Sex workers, who are typically women, are arrested at a greater rate than those buying sex, who are typically men.

Women enter the sex work field in a variety of ways, but they are often driven by financial need. To underscore the last point: few girls dream of becoming a sex worker when they grow up. It is usually a crime that is committed out of economic necessity and a crime of survival. For underage girls, engaging in sex work is often the result of an older man's or pimp's efforts to coerce, entice, or otherwise manipulate them with a complicated grooming process. On the other hand, young girls who run away from home to escape abuse may enter sex work as a survival method. Unfortunately, these girls and women may develop (or already have developed) substance abuse problems, which can start as a strategy to cope with their situation but then serves to drive their continued involvement in prostitution.

Other sex workers may drift into prostitution because of friends already involved in this work; these friends act as a funneling system for those entering prostitution (O'Neill, 1997; O'Neill, 2001). Many women entering this field do a cost-benefit analysis in which they weigh their options to earn significant amounts of money quickly, which can be used to support themselves and their children, against working in a conventional job that would require significantly more time away from loved ones. In other words, for women lacking the skills and education to access higher-paid work, the sex work field is a route to make more money than lower-paid jobs that would require more of their time (O'Connell Davidson, 1998).

Prostitutes work in different types of spaces, which are often categorized in terms of "street-based" and "indoor-based." An individual who is street-based works outside on the streets of a city or town. Street-based sex work often involves walking the street or maintaining a specific area of the street from which interactions with clients occur and services are negotiated. This interaction can take place in the street or within the confines of a customer's automobile. Those that work on the street are more likely to have a drug problem, experience homelessness, encounter violence (O'Neill and Campbell, 2006), and they are more likely to have been coerced into prostitution at a young age (Pearce, Williams, and Galvin, 2002). Not all sex workers who work on the street share those characteristics though; some women choose to be street-based to obtain autonomy and financial security (Pitcher, 2006), and they are less likely to have "shift work" (scheduled working periods) than those who sell sex indoors. Put another way, street-based sex work allows women to choose when and where they work as well as for how long, which provides more flexibility (McKeganey and Barnard, 1996).

Indoor-based sex work can occur in a variety of locations. These can include the woman's own home, a rented apartment, or a hotel room that is rented individually or shared by multiple women involved in the business. Transactions can also be conducted in brothels, saunas, or massage parlors. There are other indoor locations in which prostitution occurs, but these transactions may be disguised as something other than sex work. For example, an individual who is an exotic dancer may also sell sex for money. This type of transaction may begin by presenting private shows at homes or businesses, but also providing "extras" in the form of sex or sex acts for money. Finally, indoor-based sex work can also take the form of a "hospitality" worker providing sex for money (Sanders, O'Neil, Pitcher, 2009).

Individuals may prefer working in indoor locations because of enhanced security and safety. There is often security and someone who runs the establishment to serve as the gatekeeper. Women also like having more control over the location where they work. Women working out of their homes may prefer the independence of being their own boss. In contrast, women who work in organized establishments, such as brothels or parlors, often report dissatisfaction with the fees they pay or the percentage that goes to the individual who owns or operates the brothel (Sanders, O'Neil, Pitcher, 2009).

While most prostitution research has focused on girls and women, as they are a majority of those arrested, new research directions seek to understand the experiences of other populations, like transgender people (Weitzer, 2005). For example, Dixon and Dixon (1998) researched the experiences of transgender women who sold sex and who still retained male anatomy. They found that most customers knew the situation and remained clients because of this. In terms of the sex workers, it was positive for them as well because they felt valued by their clients, and the experiences affirmed their sexuality. These feelings are especially important because engaging in sex work may help individuals save money for gender-affirming surgery (Kulick, 1998). While that surgery is often referred to as "gender reassignment surgery," a more accurate description from individuals who experience it is "gender affirmation surgery." That is the term that we shall use throughout the text.

Transnationally, the sex industry includes individuals from all walks of life who enter the field for various reasons. Terms, which are often conflated, used to describe these populations are commercial sex trade and migrant workers. Given that confusion, it is important to discuss the difference between the two. A **migrant worker** is an individual who migrates to a place for employment, such as sex work, of their own volition. For example, in Europe or the United States, individuals may migrate to a particular country, such as the United Kingdom, or an area of the country, such as the state of Nevada, where prostitution is legal. These individuals are making a rational choice to migrate to a location to engage in sex work as opposed to seeking lower-paying and more arduous work where they live (Sanders, O'Neil, and Pitcher, 2009).

In contrast to migrant workers, individuals who are **trafficked** into sex work are taken against their will by threat or coercion, and then they are forced to work in the sex industry. These individuals include adults as well as children. Estimates from the US State Department (2021) note that millions of people are sex-trafficked internationally each year: 80 percent are women and 50 percent are minors. These individuals are treated poorly, often raped, drugged, and beaten by their captors and others. They may die in the course of their confinement. They also travel from place to place, which makes locating them difficult.

Combatting Prostitution

There are many tactics designed to address sex work that the criminal-legal system has implemented throughout the years. Typically, police combat this offense by focusing on street-based prostitution, most often through patrols by frontline officers, which may involve undercover "sting" operations. However, while these initiatives are well intentioned, they often result merely in a relocation of the sex workers to a different area rather than a decrease of the activity itself. This relocation then puts sex workers in an area where they can meet new "johns," or the consumers of their services, and become familiar with new territory. Another policing strategy focuses on the consumers themselves, who are attempting to buy or buying sex, with the intention of spurring general and specific deterrence (Center for Problem-Oriented Policing, 2017).

In addition to arresting consumers of sex work, many jurisdictions have implemented what are called **john schools** as an attempt to deter recidivism among individuals who purchased sex. A goal is to encourage a different perspective among this group about how purchasing sex can have lifelong negative implications for their personal and professional objectives. Moreover, classes encourage attendees to think about the human toll their actions have on the women working in this industry. The classes can be one session for a few hours or

---

ACTIVE LEARNING ASSIGNMENT 4.2

Explore John Schools

Explore the following john schools and answer the following questions:
   http://www.loganinstitute.com/index.php
   http://www.demandforum.net/john-school/

  1. What is your opinion of these programs?
  2. Do you think that john schools will prevent prostitution? Why or why not?
  3. What do you think would be a better strategy to prevent prostitution?

---

regular sessions for a few weeks. The underlying idea for these courses is that deviance can be prevented through increased education. In other words, if men have been educated on the harm this behavior causes, they will not purchase sex. This drop in demand, in turn, would result in fewer instances of prostitution.

What is missing from these programs, however, is the recognition that gender and the lack of opportunities disproportionately affecting individuals of particular genders influence choices about criminal engagement. Indeed, while education is important for understanding the issues related to someone selling sex, these programs do not get at the root cause of prostitution: that women without choices or legitimate avenues for economic and financial success may choose crime. Therefore, to truly combat prostitution, programs need to be "gender-responsive" and address the broader systemic issues by creating opportunities for education, living-wage employment, and social support.

Another pathway to combatting prostitution is legalizing it or decriminalizing it. Activists, often including sex workers, argue for legalization as it would regulate the act and provide more safety for women. Indeed, sex workers are often at the mercy of the pimps or individuals that they work for, which affects the level of autonomy they can assert in their day-to-day decisions. If they are limited in the control that they can exercise, sex workers may be at risk of violence, including assault, rape, and murder. Moreover, they are also at risk of sexually transmitted diseases and unwanted pregnancies. If the practice were legalized, prostitutes could get regular health screenings, have greater control over the services they provide, and require clients to wear protection. (See Media Byte 4.5.)

Women and Violent Crime

Neonaticide and Infanticide

Neonaticide is the killing of a newborn within the first twenty-four hours of life (Liem and Koenraadt, 2008; Porter and Gavin, 2010; Resnick, 1969;

> ### MEDIA BYTE 4.5   Inside a Legal Brothel
>
> Please watch this brief clip about a legal brothel in Nevada: https://www.cnn.com/videos/tv/2016/10/14/lisa-ling-21st-century-brothels-orig.cnn. Answer the following questions:
>
> 1. Do you think that it is safer for women to work in an environment like this than on the streets? Why or why not?
> 2. Would you be in favor of legalizing prostitution in the United States? Please explain.

Resnick, 1970). **Infanticide** is the killing of a child who is less than a year old. The risk of extreme violence to children is high in the early stages of life because children are not capable of taking care of or protecting themselves from others (Finkelhor, 2008; Finkelhor and Ormrod, 2001). In examining these events and why they happen, studies have found very different reasons that prompt neonaticides versus infanticides. Women who kill infants within twenty-four hours of their birth may have concealed their pregnancy from others and may have denied it to themselves. These women are often teenagers or younger (usually under the age of 20), did not receive prenatal care, and are first-time mothers (Porter and Gavin, 2010).

In contrast, a woman who commits infanticide often suffers from mental health issues during her pregnancy, which plays a disastrous role after she gives birth and begins to care for the infant (Porter and Gavin, 2010; Resnick, 1970). In contrast to women who commit neonaticide, these women tend to be older (Porter and Gavin, 2010; Silverman and Kennedy, 1988). This is not to suggest that women involved in neonaticide do not struggle with mental health; indeed, women who commit either act are often classified as suffering from mental illness (Spinelli, 2004), emotional stress, bipolar disorder (Porter and Gavin, 2010), or postpartum depression (Pearlstein et al., 2009). Women with unstable partners are also more likely to harm their children (Daly and Wilson, 1988).

Although laypersons may believe these crimes are contemporary aberrations, neonaticide and infanticide have been practiced since prehistoric times. Anthropologists note that these actions occur in nearly all civilizations. For example, in some societies, if a child had a physical defect of some kind, it might be killed. Until the fourth century, Greek and Roman laws gave complete control over children to their father, who ultimately decided—sometimes before the birth itself—whether his offspring lived or died. In other words, the father could terminate the child's life at any point. These rights did not extend to the mother: if she killed her child, she could be executed (Jones, 1980).

History also reveals other reasons for engaging in neonaticide and infanticide. For instance, slaves and indentured servants in America committed infanticide. Women who were raped by slave owners, who did not want to have a child with the man who hurt them and their loved ones, often concealed their pregnancy and then committed infanticide after the baby was born. However, if they were discovered, those who killed infants were often executed themselves: the earliest record of this practice dates to 1648. Neonaticide and infanticide in early America was also a response to the lack of legalized or safe abortions and the absence of birth control. Women who had no reproductive control over their bodies, who did not want to be mothers, often found themselves without options. In England, the Infanticide Act of 1938 proclaimed a woman to be mentally ill if she killed her child within the first year of life. The most severe crime she could be charged with was manslaughter. Still, juries were often not likely to send to prison a woman who committed this crime as there was a recognized connection between mental illness and subsequent harm to a child. Fathers who committed infanticide, however, were often charged with murder (Jones, 1980).

Today in America, neonaticide and infanticide are often classified as a homicide, and women who engage in either action may qualify for the death penalty, depending upon the state. However, the sentencing for these crimes varies widely: from probation to jail, to prison, to being sent to a mental health facility. These variations are based on factors such as the system-involved individual's age, past trauma and victimization, postpartum depression, and current circumstances.

In examinations of neonaticide and infanticide globally, it has been found that those who commit these crimes in industrialized nations are often members of the child's family (Kauppi et al., 2010; Porter and Gavin, 2010). In Western countries, it is almost exclusively mothers who commit neonaticide, and boys are more likely to be killed. The reasons for these patterns are not apparent. In Asia, girls are more likely to be killed, which can be attributed to cultural ideals related to boys being seen as more "valuable" (Porter and Gavin, 2010) and to socioeconomic pressures related to gender: given the earning potential of men, boys are more desired (Vlachová and Biason, 2005). These pressures at the individual level have affected populations of children. For example, China has experienced a decrease in the number of girls within recent decades because of the neglect and infanticide of girls (Banister 2004).

In India, infanticide related to sex has been occurring since the 1870s, and girls are often killed as babies (Miller, 1997). The neglect and murder of baby girls continue in India and are thought to stem from the country's robust patriarchal model. There, boys are considered more desirable because they will eventually control the land and the wealth of their family. On the other hand, when girls are married, their family must supply a dowry to the husband. The dowry can consist of money, financial tokens, or other incentives for their daughter's husband to support the match. Because many families cannot afford more than one girl and more than one dowry, girls born into a family after the first girl have an increased chance of death (Gupta, 1987).

MEDIA BYTE 4.6   Trash Bin Babies and Baby Hatches

Please read the following article about attempts to save abandoned babies in India: https://www.theatlantic.com/international/archive/2012/05/trash-bin-babies-indias-female-infanticide-crisis/257672/. Answer the following questions:

1. Do you think that baby hatches or safe haven laws can prevent neonaticide and infanticide? Why or why not?

2. Do you think that baby hatches will increase the abandonment of infants? Please explain.

3. What are some other ways that neonaticide and infanticide might be prevented?

The actual number of neonaticides and infanticides that occur globally may not be reflected in the statistics. The main reason is that there may be no birth or death certificate filed for a newborn. For example, in France, 80 percent of neonaticides that are reported to the police are not reflected in the statistics because there was no birth or death certificate issued (Tursz and Cook, 2011). The cause of death is not always clear. Many infant deaths are ruled as due to sudden infant death syndrome and do not lead to an investigation. In Germany, it is estimated that nearly 90 percent of neonaticides are not discovered or reported to the authorities (Hoynck, Zahringer, and Behnsen, 2012). (See Media Byte 4.6.)

Maternal Filicide

Filicide occurs when a parent kills their child after they are older than a year. If it is committed by the mother, it is referred to as **maternal filicide**. If the father does it, it is referred to as **paternal filicide**. Mothers who commit filicide are often full-time caregivers and from lower socioeconomic backgrounds. They often have suffered relationship problems or intimate partner violence. They may have committed acts of child abuse previously, although some have not and have been devoted to their children (Oberman, 1996). Women who commit filicide often have mental health issues, depression, and suicidal thoughts. There may also be substance abuse at the time of the killing (Meyer and Oberman, 2001; Silverman and Kennedy, 1988).

The motives of women who commit maternal filicide vary. As a result of research conducted by Resnick (1969), five categories were created to explain why a woman would kill her child. The first category is **altruistic filicide**: a mother kills her child because she thinks that the child is dying and it is in the child's best interest. Her motive, from her perspective, is love. She believes that killing her child would be better than having the child live in this world, or if she is suicidal, she reasons that it is better to kill her child than to leave the child motherless. Sixteen to 29 percent of filicides are the result of a suicide-filicide (a mother killing herself and her children) (Nock and Marzuk, 1999). Research shows that 5 percent of mothers of young children who commit suicide kill at least one of their children along with themselves (Appleby, 1996). Women who committed suicide and filicide were more likely to kill older children than infants (Hatters-Friedman et al., 2005).

The second category is acutely psychotic filicide (Resnick, 1969). This occurs when a mother kills her child without any motive, or any motive that is understandable or discernable. It can be the result of delusions of hallucinations, or no motive can be determined from the preceding behavior of the woman.

The third category that Resnick created was fatal maltreatment filicide. In this situation, the mother did not try to kill the child, but rather, the child died as a result of the mother's actions, such as neglect or abuse. This type of filicide can be the result of abuse due to stress or strain. Research has shown that 70 percent of mothers with colicky infants had aggressive and violent thoughts regarding hurting their children, with 26 percent having thoughts of murdering their children (Levitzky and Cooper, 2000). The stress or strain of parenthood, particularly in challenging situations, may cause mothers to react violently or aggressively.

A woman will also fall into this category if she suffers from Munchausen syndrome by proxy (MSP). This is a disorder suffered almost exclusively by women. It occurs when a woman who is a caretaker of a child invents or causes injuries to the child, making them actually sick or presenting them as sick, with "imagined" stories. The woman may poison the child's food or put items in the food that would make the child sick, such as glass. She may create symptoms that are difficult to measure, such as an upset stomach, body aches and pains, trouble breathing, and trouble sleeping. Women who suffer from this disorder often thrive on the attention that they get from doctors, medical professionals, friends, family, and coworkers from having a sick child. Mothers suffering from MSP become addicted to the attention, consideration, kindness, and special treatment they receive. Many cases of MSP never come to the attention of medical professionals, so the exact number or extent is unknown. The gap in the information mainly occurs because women may use different names or identities and see multiple medical providers or visit different hospitals. Even though the real number is hard to determine, when considering motivations as to why a mother may murder her child, this disorder is not one that can be overlooked.

The fourth category is unwanted child filicide (Resnick, 1969). This occurs when a mother does not want her child, and she thinks of the child as a burden. This is seen many times when a mother is exhausted or overwhelmed with the workload that comes with being a mother. It could be the case that she already

ACTIVE LEARNING ASSIGNMENT 4.3

Make Your Own Case Study

Please find a case in the news of a woman who committed filicide. Provide the details of the crime and the outcome of the case, including the sentence (if she has been sentenced). If the motive was known, identify and justify how it fits into one of Resnick's five categories regarding motivation for a mother killing her children. If the motive was not identified in the case, please provide your justification for what category you think it fits into and why.

MEDIA BYTE 4.7   **Susan Smith**

In 1995, Susan Smith was in the headlines for killing her two young sons. For more on the case, read the following article and watch the video attached to it: http://people.com/crime/susan-smith-drowning-sons-inside-life-prison/. Then answer the following questions:

1. Which of the five categories identified by Resnick do you think best aligns with Susan Smith? Justify your answer.
2. What is your reaction to this case?
3. Do you think that the sentence that she received was appropriate? Why or why not?

---

has other children or that circumstances in her life make motherhood a challenge. Women may also commit this type of filicide if they experienced pregnancy as a result of rape or abuse. If they did not have access to abortion and any attempted remedies, they may kill the child who is a reminder of the harm they experienced.

The final category, and the rarest, is **spouse revenge filicide** (Resnick, 1969). In some instances, a mother will kill her child with the specific intent to cause emotional hurt and distress to the father of the child. She uses the murder of their child as a way to seek vengeance. This could be revenge for the abuse that the woman suffered or something that was done that caused pain, such as having an affair or leaving the family. (See Active Learning Assignment 4.3 and Media Byte 4.7.)

SUMMARY

While girls and women do not commit as many crimes as boys and men, the crimes they commit are often related to the experience of being a female within society. Girls and women are more likely to be victimized and less likely to have legitimate opportunities for success than boys and men. Most of the crimes committed by girls and women that have been examined and discussed in this chapter (embezzlement, shoplifting, being a drug mule, prostitution) result from not having many options for economic stability and success and/or are committed under duress. The same can be said about girls joining gangs. The offenses of neonaticide, infanticide, and filicide have many different motives associated with them. Still, they are tied to the gender of the person committing them and the unique experience of being a woman in a man-dominated system. Women have different needs, reasons for committing crime, and life experiences than men do. Understanding women and the issues related to crime are essential when considering treatment, punishment, and prevention.

At the Margins

Criminalization in the LGBTQIA+ Communities

Acts committed by LGBTQIA+ (lesbian, gay, bisexual, transgender, queer, intersex, asexual) individuals are often deemed crimes because of the differential laws that target those within these communities. If a heterosexual or cisgender individual commits one of these acts, it does not result in sanctions. This has been seen in the United States and globally. In this chapter, we will review the history of laws that criminalize LGBTQIA+ individuals and provide contemporary examples of the persistence of the problem: bathroom laws, HIV reporting laws, and laws affecting sex workers—laws that disproportionately affect LGBTQIA+ individuals. We will also review the inequitable treatment of LGBTQIA+ individuals who are system-involved (during case processing or state-supervision stages) in comparison to cisgender people. Finally, we will examine international laws that criminalize LGBTQIA+ individuals, such as those that make intimacy between same-sex couples illegal.

THE EARLY HISTORY OF LGBTQIA+ INDIVIDUALS AS "OFFENDERS" AND "DEVIANTS"

There has been a centuries-long history of treatment disparity, criminalization, and punishment of individuals considered "deviant" in what is now the United States. This disparity existed long before the labels of lesbian, gay, bisexual, transgender, queer, intersex, or asexual were established. The **colonialism** that is part of the history of the United States is very gendered, racialized, and sexualized. It reflects white cisgender male privilege and heteronormative culture. People who were different from the colonists in the United States and who lacked power and privilege were treated differently, which is evident from individual stories and research about that period.

During this early period, the colonizers promoted the "queering" of Indigenous cultures by depicting native people as committing acts of sexual deviance (according to the colonists) like **sodomy** (Smith, 2010a; 2010b). In 1513, Vasco Núñez de Balboa, in his journey to the Pacific Ocean, met the **Indigenous people** of the Quaraca. His recollections of these people were that they were men dressed as women and having sex with each other. He was outraged and disgusted, and he ordered them to be thrown to his hunting dogs to be dismembered and killed. This incident was captured in a painting and is believed to be the first colonial punishment of sodomy (Springdale, 2016).

Native people were portrayed for centuries as "sodomites" by Christian colonizers. By engaging in this labeling and "othering," colonists made native people seem inherently evil, different, and "sinners" (given that sodomy was a sin). This helped the colonizers to establish a sense of dominance and superiority in early American society. They were able to claim that their behavior was morally superior (Smith, 2015). (See Media Byte 5.1.)

The creation and promotion of the gender binary system, globally, was also important for the success of the colonies in terms of establishing and maintaining control. Many of the Indigenous people and groups did not have a hierarchical system, and their societies allowed for a wide range of gender identities, gender expressions, and gender fluidity. To subjugate Indigenous people,

---

MEDIA BYTE 5.1   **An Early Punishment of Sodomy**

Please examine the sixteenth-century engraving "Balboa Throws a Number of Indians, Who Committed the Sin of Sodomy, to the Hounds": https://commons.wikimedia.org/wiki/File:Balboamurder.jpg. In this picture, Vasco Núñez de Balboa has discovered that the Indigenous people of the Quaraca (now Panama) practice sodomy and has delivered punishment by dismembering their bodies and feeding them to his dogs.

1. What message does this painting send about sexual activity between people of the same sex?
2. How do you think people feel when they view this? Do you think that they know what the context of the painting is? Please explain.

establishing a gender binary and patriarchy was necessary. In this model imposed by colonists, men wielded power and were at the top of the hierarchy. Put another way, men engaged in activities that aligned with control and domination over others. Women were subservient to men and their role was to be of service and utility to men, especially concerning child-rearing and taking care of the home and the man's needs. Women who deviated from their prescribed role were often investigated and persecuted as deviants or "criminals." Men and women were to act and behave within the limits of their roles, and deviation from roles could lead to being the subject of an inquiry. The church was often the entity that conducted these investigations and doled out punishment, sometimes in conjunction with the state, for individuals who violated their roles (Smith, 2015). The establishment of this system, with men in control, served as a model that colonists implemented in all their settlements worldwide, and which we still see mostly in place today.

By the turn of the twentieth century in the United States, "Indian agents" were patrolling and policing Indigenous peoples' behaviors, including their sexual behavior and dress. If a person was dressing in clothing associated with the "wrong" gender, the agents (under authority from the colonial government) could legally punish them. For example, an Indian agent who was patrolling the Apsáalooke Nation (Crow Tribe) arrested and held an Indigenous man who was not conforming to the male gender, as prescribed by the colonists. The agent punished this man by making him cut his hair to an acceptable male length and wear traditionally male clothing (according to colonial standards). This act not only punished this man but served as an example to others that deviation from the gender-binary system would not be accepted under colonial rule. Agents were given authority and much autonomy to patrol and punish (often through physical brutality) individuals whom they felt deserved punishment for their dress or behavior (Eaklor, 2008).

Colonists viewed Indigenous people through their Christian Westernized lenses. They saw them as "queer" or "deviant" or "wrong" based on their own viewpoint and experiences. This, in turn, led to the perception that Indigenous people were "sinners" or "evil." However, that is not a fair or accurate assessment of the behavior of the Indigenous people. The behaviors of many Indigenous people that were not strictly heterosexual and would place them in the colonizers' categories of "deviant" or "queer" (such as dressing as a different gender or having fluid gender expression and sexual relations) were not deviant by the standards of their community. Indigenous people viewed gender expression and sexuality differently, not as something that was static or binary. Imposing the cultural ideals of one culture onto another—without context—is unfair to both given they are rarely comparable. For example, someone looking at old pictures and saying that the Indigenous people had drag queens because men were wearing skirts and makeup is not making an accurate comparison. Drag queens today in America are men who choose to work as entertainers while dressed as women. An Indigenous man may be wearing a dress and makeup for a religious or cultural reason or as part of a ceremony. Without understanding the reason or thought behind the dress or behavior, it is not appropriate to equate them (Duberman, 1986). This is the same sort of thinking that led colonists to deem what they were witnessing when they saw native peoples practicing different sexual or gender practices as wrong or deviant and then punishing them for it. Once colonization gained momentum, no one was safe from being labeled and persecuted for not adhering to a traditional patriarchal, heteronormative ideal.

Queering immigrants has a long history that can be traced to the Crusades and the Ottoman Empire. It is often related to fearing the unknown, or the "other," which means anyone different. Early immigrants to the United States faced stigma and unjust treatment based on myths related to sexuality, deviance, and disease. This often led to persecution and criminalization, including sodomy laws being excessively applied to immigrants, the poor, and people of color.

Sodomy laws were passed as the territories became states. To be clear, these laws did impact heterosexual individuals, but they disproportionately affected those who engaged in same-sex relationships because anal and oral sex were specifically outlawed (Eaklor, 2008). While sodomy laws remained in effect for hundreds of years, they were only selectively enforced and often served to reinforce systemic bias and hierarchies of race, gender, class, and citizenship. Throughout the seventeenth to nineteenth centuries, sodomy laws were often used to charge men who engaged in sex with other men but typically did not address sex between two women. Although many women were charged for performing oral sex on men, even that was selectively applied (Eskridge, 2008). Free Black women, poor white women, poor immigrant women, and Native American women who were caught and charged with sodomy could also face charges of vagrancy, disorderly conduct, fornication, and prostitution. The penalties varied but included public shaming, fines, corporal punishment, and incarceration.

As discussed on many pages of this text, the criminalization of "deviant" sexual activity was unevenly enforced across individuals of different backgrounds. Wealthier women who engaged in chargeable offenses rarely appeared in court, and their cases were usually not handled publicly. They were often dealt with by their community, church, or family and were not punished nearly as harshly as poorer women (Davis, 2003). During this period, in some states, the death penalty could be imposed for sodomy. Pennsylvania was the first state to repeal this as a sentence for white people. However, a separate law still provided the death penalty for Black people convicted of the same crime (Davis, 2003). Eventually, even though sodomy laws remained on the books in many states, they were not necessarily enforced. In 2003, the Supreme Court in *Lawrence v. Texas* ruled sodomy laws unconstitutional. At that time, thirteen states still had sodomy laws on their books.

In addition to Indigenous people, colonizers also took to painting a picture of Africans as "sexual deviants" and "sodomites," thus persecuting Black men and women before they even entered the country (Trexler, 1995). This disparaging treatment and othering were later reinforced by pseudoscience that perpetuated myths about physiological differences like Black people having larger penises and clitorises. For example, a mid-nineteenth century handbook on gynecology stated that an abnormal clitoris, such as those it claimed were seen in Black women, could lead to lesbianism. Medical journals as late as 1921 declared that lesbianism was the result of a large clitoris (Gilman, 1985). These reports, which made inappropriate and racist assumptions regarding physical differences, led to many believing that Black men and women were sexually deviant and stigmatizing them as a result.

Black people continued to suffer severe harm at the individual and societal level. They were often depicted as sexually insatiable and as sexual predators, justifying the killing of Black men and the raping of Black women. The lynching and torture of Black men, who were believed to have preyed upon and raped "pure" white women, continued to occur in the nineteenth century. However, lynching was also used to punish free or economically prosperous Black men as the ultimate instrument of hate (Mogul, Ritchie and Whitlock, 2011).

Aside from being demonized and harmed by broader society, enslaved Black women were raped by slave owners. Moreover, even as they were dehumanized at the individual level, inaccurate and racist notions continued to spread in broader society. For example, it was commonly believed that enslaved Black women were **jezebels,** or sexually aggressive and seductive women who lured slave owners into sex. Put another way, this "whitewashed" the responsibility for Black women's victimization away from slave owners and put the blame on the Black women themselves: a historical example of victim blaming. What is even more appalling about the stark reality that Black women survived is that slave owners often raped them to increase their wealth with additional slaves (Gilman, 1985). Indeed, the incorrect and racist notions about physical differences perpetuated by white people of privilege and power led to far-reaching systemic harm to Black men and women that many would argue continues today. A critical view of the history of the United States shows that those in power also harmed other minority groups.

Chinese men immigrating in the nineteenth century to the United States were accused of bringing disease and unnatural sexual practices like sodomy. Chinese women were thought to be promiscuous and prostitutes. All Chinese were thought to be lacking in morality. These beliefs led to the surveillance and taxing of Chinese men who were working in the United States and in 1882 their exclusion from the country with the **Chinese Exclusion Act.** This law prevented Chinese individuals from entering the United States and also prohibited Chinese nationals from obtaining US citizenship. This was the first law that excluded an entire ethnic group from entering the country or becoming a citizen.

In the mid-1800s, there had been an influx of Chinese immigrants into the United States, specifically to California for the gold rush. Chinese immigrants worked in the mines and building the railroads that would be used for trade and distribution across the United States. There was a great deal of violence against Chinese immigrants that was racially motivated and often based upon myths and biases held by whites. Chinese men and women in the United States were also often unfairly targeted by the police for arrest. The Supreme Court ruled in *People v. Hall* (1854) that Chinese people (like Black people and Native American people at the time) were not allowed to testify in court. This meant that they could not pursue any justice when they were victimized or discriminated against (Blakemore, 2019).

In the nineteenth century, British and French immigrants were accused of same-sex relations, but their punishments and treatment were not as severe as those of people of color or other minority status. Most notably, in New York City, the entry point for many immigrants, there was a **homosexual panic** related to the surge of immigrants and their misrepresentation in the media (Eaklor, 2008). People started to fear individuals who might be attracted to those of the same sex or who dressed differently than society deemed appropriate. This fear fueled hate as well as support for policies or actions against such people, and particularly immigrants.

Fear of individuals who were attracted to the same sex continued to grow. In Massachusetts, in 1868, a man claimed temporary insanity for murdering a friend. He justified the homicide by stating that his friend (a man) had attempted to have sex with him. While he was not successful in his defense and was convicted of manslaughter, the coverage of this story in the media fueled societal fear into a full-fledged homosexual panic. The term *homosexual panic* was coined by Edward Kempf in 1920 and was used to describe uncontrollable sexual urges for sex with someone of the same sex. This often occurred in prisons, the military, or wherever men were deprived of women. The symptoms of homosexual panic included catatonia and submitting to an assault or seeking to commit an act of sexual assault and could cause men to act out of character or commit crimes (Kempf, 1920). Homosexual panic was listed in the first edition of the American Psychiatric Association's *Diagnostic and Statistical Manual* (*DSM*) in 1952 as a treatable disorder. It has been used intermittently over the years in the criminal-legal system and in recent years as a defense for individuals accused of a crime as a sort of temporary insanity plea (the person did not know what they were doing because they were in a homosexual panic).

In the 1960s and 1970s, there was a movement to decriminalize sodomy. Homosexuality and homosexual panic were removed from the *DSM* in 1973, no longer making homosexuality a mental illness or disorder. However, homosexuality was replaced with "sexual disturbance disorder" and then "ego-dystonic homosexuality" until those terms were removed in 1987. Changing the name of the disorder on the surface may have conveyed publicly that the

ACTIVE LEARNING ASSIGNMENT 5.1

Understanding Sodomy Laws

Read the ACLU article "Why Sodomy Laws Matter": https://www.aclu.org/other/why-sodomy-laws-matter. Answer the following questions:

1. How were sodomy laws most commonly used in the nineteenth and twentieth centuries?
2. In the late 1960s, how were sodomy laws beginning to be used?
3. What are the three ways sodomy laws are used against gay people?
4. What was the impact of the *Lawrence* decision?
5. Are there parallels between sodomy laws and issues arising today? Which ones? Please explain the similarities.

mental health community no longer saw homosexuality as a mental disorder, but practitioners were still able to treat and diagnose individuals that did not meet the traditional heterosexual orientation. While the US Supreme Court ruled sodomy laws unconstitutional in 2003, other behaviors were outlawed in some jurisdictions and were selectively enforced, such as dressing in clothing that was not of one's sex assigned at birth. These laws target transgender and gender non-binary individuals, lesbian women, and gay men. A person could be cited, arrested, and subsequently punished for wearing "gender inappropriate clothing" as deemed by the officer, prosecutor, or judge (Spade, 2011). (See Active Learning Assignment 5.1.)

The idea that anything or anyone different or foreign may be dangerous has been pervasive in American culture, and it is reflected in past and current immigration policies. Most often this is done by denying legal access to this country, as was done with the Chinese Exclusion Act. Historically, US immigration law has excluded homosexuals. The concept of homosexual panic and the fear of individuals who were different influenced many of the views of policy makers. The **Immigration and Nationality Act** was amended in 1965 to specifically exclude individuals from receiving a visa and admission into the United States if they had "sexual deviation," which included homosexuality (INA § 212(a)(4)). This could potentially criminalize individuals who entered the United States without legal documentation or who were denied based on sexual orientation. In 1979, the US Public Health Service said it would no longer consider homosexuality a disease, but sexual deviation and homosexuality were not officially removed as possible exclusionary reasons from entrance or citizenship until the Immigration Act of 1990. In addition, immigrants wanting to enter the United States who were HIV positive were also prohibited from entering the country under federal immigration law until January 4, 2010. It is important to note that in both cases, preventing individuals from immigrating based on these reasons separates families, dividing parents, children, and spouses. It also discourages individuals from getting tested for HIV and seeking treatment for fear of being denied entry to the United States or deported (Mogul, Ritchie and Whitlock, 2011).

CRIMINALIZATION OF LGBTQIA+ INDIVIDUALS

The criminalization of individuals who identify as LGBTQIA+ began with police targeting and raiding bars where LGBTQIA+ individuals hung out, subsequently arresting them under clothing and sodomy laws. This became an even greater issue after urbanization and the women's suffrage movement. As women gained the right to vote in the 1920s and felt more empowered, there was an increase in women moving to as well as living and working in urban areas. Individuals who identified as LGBTQIA+ also began moving to urban areas and forming communities. These communities gave people a place where they felt that they belonged, which they may not have had previously living in a rural or suburban area with their family. However, the move to urban areas also gave the opportunity for additional laws to be passed that targeted people who identified as LGBTQIA+ and provided a cluster of places where police could target, harass, and arrest individuals (Stryker, 2008).

As more people flocked to cities, the societal concern about sexual predators and "sex maniacs" grew, which people often falsely associated with LGBTQIA+ individuals. A series of high-profile crimes led to the passage of **sexual psychopath laws** in twenty-six states and the District of Colombia between 1937 and 1967 (Swanson, 1960). By the 1990s states began passing laws against sexually violent predators, and most of the sexual psychopath laws had fallen out of use or were overturned. But in the decades while these laws were in place and at the height of their enforcement, LGBTQIA+ identifying individuals could be arrested and prosecuted for consensual sexual behavior and held indefinitely in custody, convicted and incarcerated. A provision of the sexual psychopath laws included homosexuality and sodomy, regardless of whether it was consensual. Individuals convicted of these offenses could be subsequently committed to mental institutions indefinitely, and only released if treatment was "successful." People in the LGBTQIA+ community who were convicted under these laws as sexual psychopaths were labeled as having committed sexual crimes. This gave them a criminal record and officially labeled them as outcasts. At the time, many believed that sexual psychopaths were unable to control their impulses and would commit the same crimes over and over, whether against children or adults and regardless of the types of punishment they received (Sutherland, 1950). This consequence was compounded by the fact that homosexuality was considered a mental illness or disorder that could lead to pervasive deviant sexual offending, which was included win the *Diagnostic and Statistical Man-*

ual at the time. The sexual psychopath laws meant that individuals from the LGBTQIA+ community could legally be treated and labeled the same as pedophiles, rapists, and child sexual murderers. These laws made individuals into criminals who were, in the majority of cases, having consensual sexual activity with another adult of the same sex.

Even if one was not convicted or the charges were eventually dropped, individuals who were initially arrested and charged under the sexual psychopath laws faced social stigma as a punishment. If a person's name was printed in the paper after an arrest or police raid of a known gay establishment, this could have a detrimental impact on the person's life. The printing of a person's name in association with homosexuality could damage a person professionally and personally. There was a great fear in post–World War II America of LGBTQIA+ individuals due to the perception, often falsely fueled by the media, of their subversive nature. Young gay, lesbian, and transgender individuals of color were often the hardest hit within the LGBTQIA+ community. While adults might be charged or detained under the sexual psychopath laws, they were often let go, but LGBTQIA+ youth were often sent to inpatient mental institutions to try to prevent their future sexual offending as homosexuals through different types of "therapy," and they experienced separation from their friends and families and isolation (Dodge, 2000).

During this same period, policing of urban gay and Black communities often became more aggressive, which led to arrests and criminalization of individuals who identified as LGBTQIA+, but principally gay men and transgender people. The **Compton's Cafeteria Riot** in San Francisco in 1966 is a pivotal event that influenced the activism of the coming years. Drag queens, transgender women, and individuals from the lesbian, gay, and bisexual communities were involved (Broverman, 2018).

Compton's Cafeteria, which was in the Tenderloin district in San Francisco, was a haven for people in the LGBTQIA+ communities. While many gay men had regular employment, many transgender women often struggled to make money and find legal employment. As a result, many turned to sex work and worked in the Tenderloin district. At the end of the night, the transgender women and drag queens who worked in clubs in the district would head to Compton's Cafeteria to eat but also to meet, talk, and find comfort in one another. It was one place that was open twenty-four hours a day and did not ban transgender women or drag queens. Many of the clubs and restaurants in the Tenderloin did not allow transgender individuals and drag queens to patronize their establishments. The LGBTQIA+ communities had been targeted for years by the San Francisco Police Department as individuals were often arrested under the anti-cross-dressing ordinance and laws outlawing loitering, solicitation, and sex work.

Transgender women and drag queens had been targeted for years by the San Francisco Police Department and individuals were often arrested under the

MEDIA BYTE 5.2   Compton's Cafeteria Riot

Please watch this video clip about Compton's Cafeteria and the riot there: https://youtu.be/hlt_ExhfGJM. Afterward, answer the following questions:

1. What is your reaction to the treatment of the transgender women in San Francisco during this time?
2. Do you think that a similar incident could happen today? Why or why not?

anti-cross-dressing ordinance, as well as for solicitation and sex work. The Compton's Cafeteria Riot erupted in August 1966. One of the women at the cafeteria was harassed by the police and she had enough. She threw a cup of coffee at the officer out of anger and frustration. He grabbed and arrested her. This led to an outbreak of violence among the other patrons, who were also exhausted and aggravated by the police behavior, harassment, and violence. People in the cafeteria threw things in protest, screamed, set a newsstand on fire, and smashed the windows of a police squad car, as well as the windows of the restaurant. This was the first active demonstration by people within the LGBTQIA+ community against police. It came about as a result of the fact that transgender women and drag queens were fed up with the open discrimination from the police that they had received over the years. While this riot was violent against police and rather large, it did not receive media attention because it was not something that the city or police wanted attention drawn to (Broverman, 2018). (See Media Byte 5.2.)

The more widely known **Stonewall Riot** in 1969 in New York City did receive media coverage and drew attention to the issues within the queer community. As had been the case in San Francisco, police in New York were harassing and targeting individuals in gay clubs and on streets where transgender individuals often sold sex. Preceding the Stonewall Riot, the police raided queer spaces to humiliate and criminalize the community. This united and mobilized individuals within the community to act. This particular event served as a catalyst for the gay rights movement and a fight for change in how the LGBTQIA+ population was being treated (see Case Study 5.1 more details).

In 1970, the first gay pride parades were held in New York City, San Francisco, and Los Angeles. Organizations were formed to fight the criminalization and persecution of those who identified as LGBTQIA+, such as the Gay Liberation Front, the Human Rights Campaign, GLAAD (Gay and Lesbian Alliance Against Defamation), and PFLAG (Parents, Families, and Friends of Lesbians and Gays). Police harassment and targeting of LGBTQIA+ still occurred, but there was a decline in certain areas as there was a push to recruit and hire gay police officers and to have them advise curriculum in police academies to train

CASE STUDY 5.1

Stonewall Inn, New York City, 1969

The 1960s in New York City was not an easy time and place to be part of LGBTQIA+ communities. There were laws against solicitation of homosexual sex, and people who were wearing fewer than three gender-appropriate articles of clothing could be arrested. LGBTQIA+ individuals were often targeted for arrest and prosecuted. One of the few places where people could feel safe to be themselves was in gay bars and clubs. However, the New York State Liquor Authority closed bars that were serving alcohol to known or suspected LGBTQIA+ individuals. The rationale was that the gathering of too many individuals from this population was dangerous and could cause disorder. This policy was overturned in 1966, and LGBTQIA+ patrons could be served alcohol in bars, but holding hands, kissing, or dancing with someone of the same sex was still illegal. This meant that police often raided known gay bars to make arrests.

On June 28, 1969, the New York City police raided the Stonewall Inn, a known gay bar in Greenwich Village. It was run by a local mafia, which paid a local police precinct to ignore the activities going on there. It was a bar that did not require a liquor license because people could bring their own alcohol. It was a popular LGBTQIA+ spot because it was one of the few such establishments that allowed dancing. Before raids at Stonewall, the corrupt police paid by the mafia would tip them off, so that they could take precautions not to get cited or have their patrons arrested. Previous raids had occurred without problems due to these warnings.

On June 28, 1969, a raid occurred at the Stonewall Inn without a warning. Police entered the club with a warrant. They found bootlegged alcohol and LGBTQIA+ individuals dancing, kissing, and hugging. The police roughed up and arrested thirteen individuals. Officers took people into the bathroom to check their sex if they were suspected of cross-dressing. Some people were physically abused by police while being put into a police vehicle. This, along with the pervasive harassment and discrimination against LGBTQIA+ communities, caused onlookers to act. People began throwing things at police and became violent, leading to a riot between those in the neighborhood and law enforcement. The riots and protests went on for six days. Many LGBTQIA+ individuals were arrested, and some were injured.

In 2016, President Barack Obama designated the site of the Stonewall riots in Christopher Park and the surrounding streets a national monument to commemorate the struggle as well as its impact on human rights.

1. What is your opinion about what happened at the Stonewall riot?
2. Do you think that the police anticipated that this raid would lead to such a long time of riots and spark a movement? Please explain.

officers to be more sensitive to people in the LGBTQIA+ communities (Stewart-Winter, 2015). The hope was that understanding this population would lead to fewer arrests and less criminalization. Decades later, there are still issues and police still often target those who identify as LGTBQIA+, especially people of color, immigrants, homeless and sex workers. (See Active Learning Assignment 5.2.)

A Timeline of the LGBTQ Movement

Please examine the "American Gay Rights Movement: A Timeline" at https://www.infoplease.com/history/pride-month/the-american-gay-rights-movement-a-timeline. Use it to answer the following questions:

1. When was the first gay rights organization in the United States founded? Were you surprised by this date?
2. When was the first US lesbian organization founded?
3. What state becomes the first to decriminalize same-sex sexual acts between consenting adults?
4. Who was Harvey Milk? Why is he important?
5. When was homosexuality removed from the American Psychiatric Association's list of mental disorders? Why is this important?
6. What did Supreme Court ruling in the *Lawrence v. Texas* case do?
7. What did the Supreme Court ruling in the *Obergefell v. Hodges* case do?
8. In examining the timeline, what decision, law, act or issue do you think was the most important for LGBTQ communities in terms of no longer criminalizing individuals? Please explain your answer.
9. What do you think is still left to be done or passed into law? Please explain.

CURRENT LAWS THAT CRIMINALIZE LGBTQIA+ INDIVIDUALS

While there have been attempts to improve law enforcement's treatment of those who identify as LGBTQIA+, as well as to repeal laws aimed at criminalizing and discriminating against people in these communities, there are still laws today that disproportionately affect and criminalize LGBTQIA+ individuals.

Bathroom Laws

One of the most heated national debates in the past few years is about gender and **bathroom laws.** Advocates for these laws often argue privacy and safety concerns, claiming that allowing a transgender individual to use a bathroom that is different from the one for their sex assigned at birth will lead to sex crimes. Support for these laws comes from the belief that transgender individuals are deviant, criminal, and out to assault people in bathrooms. At the time of this writing only one state, North Carolina, has successfully passed, and subsequently repealed, a transgender bathroom law that restricted the use of restrooms, locker rooms, and other same-sex facilities based on one's sex assigned at birth. However, politicians in other states have proposed laws to require individuals to use the bathrooms for their sex assigned at birth. In the spring of 2018, voters in Anchorage, Alaska, turned down Proposition 1, which would have required individuals to use the bathroom for their sex assigned at birth. It was a close election, with 53 percent voting against it, and 47 percent voting in favor (Axelrod, 2018).

Although states have not been successful, cities and towns have enacted bathroom laws. Research has revealed that there is no danger or public safety problem associated with public transgender bathroom use. The Williams Institute (Human Rights Campaign, 2018) assessed restroom crime reported in Massachusetts cities of similar size and demographics. It found no increase in crime for the cities that adopted the public transgender bathroom policy. Many states have taken to passing laws for gender-neutral restrooms. Washington, DC, has a law that single-stall restrooms must have gender neutral signs. New York City has a law that single-stall restrooms must replace "Men" and "Women" in the signs with gender-neutral language. Philadelphia has a law that an individual can use whatever restroom the person feels most comfortable in, as well as that businesses must replace the signs for men and women with gender-neutral signs or face a fine of $75 to $2,000 (GLAAD, 2017a).

Laws that prohibit individuals from using a restroom unless they were assigned that sex at birth create a whole new category of system-involved individuals in transgender individuals who could be criminalized for using the bathroom. This may not seem like a pertinent issue to the cisgender population, but for transgender individuals, not having the freedom to use the bathroom of the gender they identify with is persecution and discrimination, and being labeled "criminal" could have a detrimental effect on them and their family. (See Case Study 5.2.)

HIV Reporting Laws

Gay men and transgender women suffer from HIV at a disproportionately high rate (Centers for Disease Control and Prevention, 2019). **HIV reporting laws** have been passed that can punish people with HIV and label them as criminals if they fail to meet reporting requirements. If a person is HIV positive, the testing site must report the results to the local health department, which sends it to the Centers for Disease Control and Prevention (CDC) after removing the identifying information. The CDC keeps this information private and does not share it. However, many states and cities have partner-notification laws. This means that a person must notify partners that they are HIV positive before engaging in sexual intercourse or sharing a needle, or they can be charged with a criminal act. Some states also have legislation that requires those administering the test to notify the significant other of the person who has tested positive for HIV. The Ryan White HIV/AIDS Program requires that any health department that receives funding from it must show that it made an effort to contact

CASE STUDY 5.2

Gavin Grimm

The recent ruling in *Grimm v. Gloucester Country School Board* is important for the controversy over bathrooms. Gavin Grimm, who was transitioning to living as a boy, began using the boys' restroom at school until parents complained. After meetings and debate, the school issued a policy that students must use the restroom of their sex assigned at birth, and that if a student had a sincere gender identity issue, they would be provided an alternative facility that would be private. The American Civil Liberties Union (ACLU) sued the school on the behalf of Grimm, saying that policy violated Title IX, which states that there can be no discrimination against an individual on the basis of sex for educational programs that receive funding from the federal government. The school allowed Gavin to use the restroom while the lawsuit was ongoing.

Initially, the district court for the Eastern District of Virginia dismissed the claim and denied the request for an injunction. But the Fourth Court of Appeals reversed and remanded the decision, finding that the claim about Title IX was valid. This set precedent that schools, which receive funding under Title IX, need to treat transgender students equally and allow them to use the restroom of their gender identity.

1. What is your opinion of this case?
2. Do you think that children of all ages should be able to select which restroom they use? Why or why not?

the significant other or sexual partner of the person diagnosed with HIV (Health Resources and Services Administration, 2020).

Thirty-three states criminalize various behaviors if they are committed by those who are HIV positive, with twenty-five states criminalizing behaviors that pose a low risk for transmission of HIV. In two states, it is illegal to marry someone who has been diagnosed as HIV positive: in Vermont, an individual can be charged with a misdemeanor, and in Oklahoma, a felony. Twenty-four states have laws that require a person to tell their partner that they are infected and disclose who they would share a needle with when using drugs intravenously. Research examining the prosecution of HIV laws found that in California, 99 percent of individuals charged were convicted and almost all served time (Hasenbush, Miyashita, and Wilson, 2015).

HIV legislation has supporters and opponents. Those who are in favor of such legislation cite public safety and disease prevention. Those who are against it argue that it unfairly discriminates and targets individuals with HIV, who are disproportionately gay men and transgender women. It has also been argued that the laws are too strict and that criminalizing those who are HIV positive is a waste of criminal-legal system resources. For example, a man in Texas is serving a thirty-five-year sentence as a result of being HIV positive and spitting on a police officer, although saliva is not a way to transmit HIV. There was also an HIV-positive man in Michigan who was charged with possessing a

---

ACTIVE LEARNING ASSIGNMENT 5.3

Pick a Side

There is a lot of debate about regulating HIV-positive notifications and laws. Please pick a side of the argument and research support either for or against your position. Use resources and facts to back up your position. Write a one- to two-page double-spaced argument for your side. Be sure to cite your sources!

---

biological weapon under the anti-terrorism statute for biting a neighbor, although biting also poses a low likelihood of transmission (Centers for Disease Control and Prevention, 2019). (See Active Learning Assignment 5.3.)

LGBTQIA+ SEX WORKERS AND SEX OFFENSES

When considering LGBTQIA+ individuals who classified by the criminal-legal system as sex offenders, it is important to note that many enter into sex work after experiencing systematic, institutional, and interpersonal discrimination and bias. Transgendered individuals often turn to sex work as a last resort to support themselves because they have experienced discrimination and harassment elsewhere and sex work is their only way to survive (Nadal et al., 2012). A disproportionate number of the transgender individuals who engage in sex work are people of color; in one study, 33 percent of Latinx and 40 percent Black transgender respondents reporting working in the sex trade (Dank et al., 2012). The same study showed that homeless LGBTQIA+ youth trade sex for a place to stay at seven times the rate of homeless heterosexual youth. However, it is important to note that more national and international research is needed to know the true number of sex workers who are transgender.

LGBTQIA+ individuals often experience higher levels of targeted policing, with a part of the policing strategy being to crack down on prostitution by individuals who identify as transgender or gay. LGB female youth are twice as likely and LGB males ten times more likely to be in a juvenile detention center for prostitution convictions than heterosexual youth (Irvine, 2010). There are laws in certain jurisdictions against loitering for the purposes of prostitution. Individuals can be arrested under these laws if they are walking outside or loitering in an area known for prostitution, waving at cars, wearing clothing that "suggests" prostitution, or have been arrested before for prostitution. Transgender women are especially targeted by such laws, and the term "walking while trans" has become a common colloquialism, because they are stopped so frequently by the police. Individuals have also been arrested for carrying condoms, and police making such arrests have been documented worldwide. This has led sex workers to stop carrying condoms for fear of arrest and prosecution. The targeted policing of prostitution of LGBTQIA+ individuals has led to high rates of arrest for individuals from these communities (Amnesty International, 2019).

While many turn to sex work as a survival tactic, being arrested can make life even more difficult economically and personally. For example, individuals arrested and convicted for prostitution may be disqualified from public housing (Curtis, Garlington, and Schottenfeld, 2013), which may be one of the few options for secure housing and not becoming homeless. An arrest and conviction for prostitution can also mean deportation depending on the person's immigrant and residency status. Or they can be expelled from higher education and denied financial aid. Eviction as well as having one' children removed from their home are other possible consequences.

INCARCERATED INDIVIDUALS WHO IDENTIFY AS LGBTQIA+

Prevalence

The National Inmate Survey 2011–2012 revealed that 7.9 percent of incarcerated individuals in state and federal prison and 7.1 percent of incarcerated individuals in city and county jails identified as lesbian, gay, or bisexual; the survey did not ask about transgender, queer, intersex, or asexual people (US Department of Justice, 2015). The National Transgender Discrimination Survey revealed that 16 percent of the respondents who identified as transgender or gender-nonconforming had spent time in prison or jail: 21 percent of the transgender women, and 10 percent of the transgender men in the survey. In contrast, 5 percent of Americans overall will spend time in jail or prison (Grant et al., 2011). As for juveniles, research indicates that 20 percent of those in juvenile detention facilities identify as LGBTQIA+ or are gender-nonconforming, which includes 40 percent of girls and 14 percent of boys. These rates are higher than the percentage of juveniles who would identify as such in the general population. There is a growing number of individuals who identify as LGBTQIA+ within the criminal-legal system and their issues are different from the issues of those who are cisgender (Irvine, 2015).

When examining why there are so many individuals who identify as LGBTQIA+ in correctional facilities, it is important to understand some of the reasons why they may end up in the system. Individuals who identify as LGBTQIA+ often face discrimination and stigma in society (see chapter 8 for further discussion)—at home from their family and friends, at work, at school, and in the community. Young people can be pushed out of their home by a family that does not approve or understand them or to leave school because of misperceptions and stigma. This maltreatment often leads LGBTQIA+ youth to run away, ending up homeless or having difficulty gaining assistance in shelters or through social services. To survive, they may turn to tactics that are illegal, such as selling drugs or working in prostitution, which may lead to encounters law enforcement resulting in arrest and incarceration.

Laws that are discriminatory and affect those that identify as LBGTQIA+ but not cisgender individuals also contribute to the criminalization of these communities. As discussed earlier in this chapter, people's biases affect the passage and enforcement of these laws. When examining the enforcement of laws, individuals who identify as LGBTQIA+, along with people of color and low-income individuals, are often disproportionately targeted in, for example, the enforcement of drug laws or laws against behaviors labeled "undesirable" (Movement Advancement Program, 2016).

Issues while Incarcerated

After LGBTQIA+ individuals who violate the law have been arrested, tried, and sentenced, they must be monitored in the community or incarcerated. There are issues unique to this population regarding intake procedures, classification, and housing. (See Active Learning Assignment 5.4.) There are also considerations that need to be made in terms of suicide prevention and victimization risks. The way that the law categorizes someone as male and female is very rigid, and the courts often rely upon medical records or experts to determine the definition of "male" and "female," but no one definition is universally used when it comes to classification. LGBTQIA+ incarcerated individuals are often assigned to a facility based on their sex assigned at birth if they have not had gender-affirming surgery. If a male transgender incarcerated individual has not had surgery, they will be assigned to a women's prison, and a female transgender incarcerated individual will be sent to a men's prison (Broadus, 2009; Buist and Stone, 2014). Individuals who have had gender-affirming surgery often do receive assignment to the facility associated with their current gender identity. The current mode that most state and federal correctional facilities use to assess placement lacks an understanding of transgender individuals and the gender transition processes. A gender transition is often a very personal and difficult process to undergo. It can also be very long and very expensive. There are many transgender individuals who are not able to afford surgery, but that does not mean that they should not be placed in a facility based on the gender they identify with.

When considering the rationale behind assigning a person who is transgender to a facility that is not reflective of their current gender identity, it is important to note that while the official reason of "safety" is used to justify such a placement, other reasons may be given. Individuals within the criminal-legal system who make decisions about incarcerated individuals' housing assignment have biases like anyone else. Personal and cultural beliefs may affect legal

---

ACTIVE LEARNING ASSIGNMENT 5.4

Demographics of Your State

Go to the Prison Policy Initiative's map at https://www.prisonpolicy.org/profiles/. Answer the following question about your state:

1. What demographic information did you notice was missing? Why do think that is the case?
2. What are your thoughts on the racial/ethnic breakdown shown for your state?
3. What information would you like to see added to this site?
4. How does your state's incarceration rate compare to that of the United States as a whole?
5. In examining the incarceration rate, how you think this will impact the LGBTQ population? Do you think that there will be more individuals from these communities incarcerated? Why or why not?

---

decisions that are made in transgender incarcerated individuals' cases. Some decision-makers may not fully understand transgender people and may think that individuals who are living and dressing as another gender are trying to trick or deceive people. Such assumptions are deeply rooted in gender norms or cultural biases that those with a penis are males and masculine and those with a vagina are females and feminine. There is also the societal belief that one's genitalia dictates who they are sexually attracted to (Buist and Stone, 2014). When someone goes against these highly internalized gender norms, especially in relation to gender identity, it often upsets people and there can be negative consequences (Buist and Stone, 2014; Butler, 1990; Bettcher, 2007). This can translate into not having sympathy or empathy for an incarcerated individual who identifies as a different gender than the one they were assigned at birth, and deciding to put them in an institution where they may be at risk for harassment, physical violence, and even death.

Incarceration for LGBTQIA+ individuals, particularly transgender individuals, is often much different than for those who are straight or cisgender. LGBTQIA+ individuals often experience physical and sexual abuse by fellow incarcerated individuals and staff. Transgender individuals in custody have higher rates of physical and sexual victimization than cisgender individuals in both adult and juvenile facilities. Transgender incarcerated individuals are ten times more likely to be sexually assaulted by a fellow incarcerated individual and five times more likely to be assaulted by a staff member (James et al., 2016). Black transgender incarcerated individuals are even more likely to be assaulted (Grant et al., 2011; National Center for Lesbian Rights, 2006; US Transgender Survey, 2015). Because safety is often an issue for transgender prisoners, they may be placed in protective custody, often against their will (Leach, 2007). "Protective custody" usually means solitary confinement, or being locked in a cell alone for twenty-three hours a day without human contact or interaction. Solitary

---

MEDIA BYTE 5.3   **Transgender Woman's Request for Transfer Denied**

Please read the 2015 article "Judge Denies Transgender Inmate's Request for Transfer": https://www.nytimes.com/2015/04/21/us/judge-denies-ashley-diamonds-a-transgender-inmate-request-for-transfer.html. Then answer the following questions:

1. Do you think that this incarcerated individual should be moved to a female facility? Why or why not?
2. Do you believe that the reasoning for denying the transfer is sound? Please explain your answer.
3. Do you think that the incarcerated individual's fear of victimization by the male incarcerated individuals is valid? Why or why not?

---

confinement is often what correctional facilities use to punish incarcerated individuals who commit acts of physical or sexual violence (Shah, 2010). One could argue that incarcerated transgender individuals are being punished for just being a transgender person in a facility where they are targeted or victimized. (See Media Byte 5.3.)

Reintegration into Society

For any person convicted of a crime, reintegration back into society can be a challenge. However, LGBTQIA+ people often face additional challenges in their probation and parole as there is a lack of reentry programs that address their specific needs in terms of housing, jobs, and services. Individuals in this community often experience discrimination at a high rate, which can decrease their ability to obtain housing and employment. They also commonly do not have family support. Transgender individuals may also need additional specific health care services that may not be easy to come by during their reintegration. LGBTQIA+ individuals of color face the additional challenges of racism, as well as bigotry related to their gender identity and sexual identity and/or orientation and being a person convicted of a crime. For LGBTQIA+ individuals who are immigrants, a criminal record can lead to deportation, often back into a place where they may be in danger or at risk for violence or death as a result of their identity (Amnesty International, 2019).

In order to better address these issues, reintegration services should be tailored to LGBTQIA+ individuals. They may need resources and care other than the typical aftercare of parole or release. In addition, to help an LGBTQIA+ individual succeed post-release, it would be useful if the supervising parole officer were familiar with LGBTQIA+ populations and their needs.

INTERNATIONAL LAWS CRIMINALIZING SAME-SEX RELATIONSHIPS AND ACTIVITY

Internationally, there have been strides in recognizing same-sex relationships as equal under the law to heterosexual relationships, with twenty-six countries passing same-sex marriage laws. However, sexual activity between consenting adults of the same sex is currently illegal in seventy-three countries and across continents (Equaldex, 2021), thus making individuals criminals who engage in same-sex relationships and consensual sex. Some countries criminalize sex only between men, and not women. Many laws prohibit any type of sexual intimacy between people of the same sex, and bisexual individuals can be charged and prosecuted as well as those who identify as gay or lesbian.

Globally, there are also eight countries where engaging in sex with someone of the same sex can be punished by death: Iran, Sudan, Arabia, Yemen, part of Somalia, northern Nigeria, Syria, and Iraq. Other countries that abide by sharia law could theoretically impose the death penalty on individuals who engage in sex with someone of the same sex; these include Mauritania, Afghanistan, United Arab Emirates, Qatar, and Pakistan (Carroll and Mendos, 2017). In these countries, sexual relations with someone of the same sex is seen as serious or heinous an offense as murder.

While not all countries have such extreme penalties as death sentences for same-sex relationships and sexual relationships, some countries criminalize LGBTQ populations in other ways. In 2013, for example, Russia passed gay propaganda laws. This legislation prohibits individuals from endorsing or encouraging minors to identify as lesbian or gay, even if the minors want to identify as such. An individual who is judged to be promoting being gay or lesbian can be fined. Businesses and schools can also be fined under this law if they are deemed to be promoting this "lifestyle" or saying positive things about being gay or lesbian. Same-sex activity was decriminalized in Russia in 1993, but the gay propaganda laws have created a lasting stigma and send a message that those within the gay and lesbian community that they are not as valued as those in the heterosexual community. Russia has legally prevented pride marches under these laws and allowed LGBTQIA+ individuals participating in pride marches to be detained and arrested. Russia is not alone in these laws. Eighteen other countries have similar laws on the books that criminalize the promotion of identifying as gay or lesbian. However, the enforcement of these laws is less common than in Russia (Carroll and Mendos, 2017).

In order to escape the persecution and criminalization of their sexual identity or sexual orientation, there is an international movement for LGBTQIA+ identifying individuals called the **Rainbow Railroad**. (See Active Learning Assignment 5.5.) This group works to legally assist individuals who are trying to escape a country that has laws that would criminalize them for being who they are. The Rainbow Railroad helps LGBTQIA+ individuals by providing

ACTIVE LEARNING ASSIGNMENT 5.5

Explore the Rainbow Railroad

Explore the website of the Rainbow Railroad, https://www.rainbowrailroad.org/. Then answer the following questions:

1. What is the mission of the Rainbow Railroad?
2. Under "Profiles," pick one of the individuals whom this organization has helped and summarize how this organization has assisted them.
3. What is the process that someone who needed help would need to go through?
4. How many requests did Rainbow Railroad have for assistance last year?
5. How many cases could it fund?
6. How many cases are waiting for funding?
7. What is your opinion of this program? Do you think that it will help LGBTQ individuals seeking asylum? Why or why not?

information on safety and how to seek asylum, as well as providing moral and financial support (when available) to assist people to live in hiding and then travel to safer places, often in North America or in Europe. This organization also puts individuals in touch with settlement agencies once they arrive. Leaving a country where one can be charged, imprisoned, or executed for being gay, lesbian, or transgendered to seek asylum can be a way to escape suffering, criminalization, and death.

SUMMARY

Those within LGBTQIA+ communities have historically been a targeted population for laws that would criminalize them, as was demonstrated in this chapter. Colonial rule's imposition of a heteronormative gender-binary system and laws to punish Indigenous people who violated colonial norms shows that oppression and persecution of LGBTQIA+ identifying individuals has deep roots in American, as well as global, history. Early laws that criminalized sodomy, dressing in clothing that was not "gender inappropriate," as well as sexual activity with those of the same sex led to LGBTQIA+ individuals being officially charged and sentenced, as well as institutionalized.

Research has also shown that there has been unfair treatment of these communities by the criminal-legal system, especially in the harassment and raids by police of gay clubs and police brutality against LGBTQIA+ individuals. The most notable examples of opposition were the riots at Compton's Cafeteria and the Stonewall Inn. While many strides have been made, there are still laws that target LGBTQIA+ individuals domestically and globally. In the United States, bathroom laws and HIV reporting laws disproportionately affect people in LGBTQIA+ communities. Worldwide, there are countries where individuals can be punished or sentenced to death for identifying as LGBTQIA+.

The incarceration of LGBTQIA+ individuals merits attention because of the special needs that they often have, as well as housing and security issues often related to being placed in a prison related to their sex assigned at birth and not the gender to which they identify with. Reintegration can be difficult because of anti-LQBTQIA+ bias and bigotry in addition to having been labeled as criminal. What is needed are changes in policies, public awareness, and treatment of LGBTQIA+ individuals in the criminal-legal system.

Gender-Based Online Victimization

KEY TERMS

- child sexual abuse material
- coercive control
- cyber dating abuse
- cyber intimate-partner abuse
- cyberbullying
- cyberfraud
- cybersextortion
- cybersexual abuse
- cyberstalking
- digital piracy
- emphasized femininity
- hacking
- identity theft
- interpersonal cybercrime
- romance scams
- work-at-home scams

LEARNING OBJECTIVES

- Understand cybercrime and victimizations.
- Be able to identify different types of cybervictimizations.
- Recognize issues pertaining to gender that exist in online environments.

Since the early 2000s, technology has increasingly permeated social life. It has led to considerable benefits such as greater accessibility to information and increased connectivity to others regardless of geographic distance (Lenhart, 2015). However, these gains are not without cost. Unfortunately, as social life has moved online, so has crime. In other words, bullying has morphed into cyberbullying, domestic abuse has morphed into cyber dating abuse and cyber domestic abuse, sexual abuse has morphed into cybersexual abuse, and stalking has morphed into cyberstalking. Even more horrific, homicide perpetrators have now started to leverage cyberspace to facilitate and stream murderous events. As time has passed, it has become painfully clear that even non-tech-savvy perpetrators have learned how to exploit technology to injure others.

In this chapter, we explore the connection between gender and online victimization. Our discussion will focus on cyberbullying and cyberharassment, cyber dating and domestic abuse, cybersexual exploitation, and cyberstalking. However, before analyzing each of these offenses, we will explore the gendered development of the internet and technology overall. We will also briefly discuss the role of gender in offending, which can subsequently open one up to victimization—known as the "offender-victim overlap." As readers will quickly see, the utopian idea that the internet could free individuals of identities linked to various systems of oppression (such as ableism, ethnocentrism, racism, sexism) never materialized (Plant, 1997). Rather, our social identities, particularly gender, shape our experiences on the internet.

DEVELOPMENT OF THE INTERNET

The origin of the internet traces back to the halls of higher education in the 1960s and includes scholars involved in a US Department of Defense agency, the Defense Advanced Research Projects (DARPA). At this point in time, J. C. R. Licklider, a faculty member at the Massachusetts Institute of Technology, proposed a method of communication through connected computers that would make information freely accessible despite geographic distances. Although he referred to this system as the "Galactic Network," its form mirrors what is know today as the internet (Leiner et al., 2009).

After Licklider proposed this network of interconnected computers, DARPA employees worked toward that vision and the project eventually became known as ARPANET, or Advanced Research Projects Agency Network (Featherly, 2016; Leiner et al., 2009). By the end of the 1960s, this internet connected a small number of universities around the United States, which proved the power of this new frontier. In the years following, more organizations became involved, and programs that we now take for granted (such as email) were introduced. As time passed, ARPANET continued to improve and expand, particularly after Bob Kahn developed the transmission control protocol/internet protocol (TCP/IP) that still is critical to cyberspace traffic today. Years later, the Federal Networking Council formally recognized the "internet" as defined below and ARPANET was decommissioned (Leiner et al., 2009):

> Internet refers to the global information system that (i) is logically linked together by a globally unique address space based on the Internet Protocol (IP), . . . (ii) is able to support communications using the Transmission Control Protocol/Internet Protocol (TCP/IP) suite, . . . and (iii) provides, uses or makes accessible, either publicly or privately, high level services layered on the communications and related infrastructure described herein. (14–15)

While the development of the internet led some to imagine the possibility of existing within a realm not bounded by social constructs associated with power, that utopian vision has yet to materialize. Indeed, those holding more skeptical views of technology point to the development of the internet within two deeply gendered environments, academia and the military, as evidence that it is unlikely to ever be free of offline power differentials (Wajcman, 2006).

As this chapter shows, there are good reasons to consider these skeptical viewpoints. Cybertechnology has become a frequent tool for gender-based cybervictimization like cyber dating abuse, cyber domestic abuse, and cybersexual violence. The internet has provided a place for those holding misogynistic and toxic viewpoints to congregate and spread their harmful messages across time and space. Aside from shaping victimization risks online, these viewpoints also influence individuals' experiences. While not the focus of this chapter, it is worth noting that gender shapes all roles in a criminal event: the person committing the crime, the person against whom the crime is committed, and even the setting itself.

THE ROLE OF GENDER IN ONLINE OFFENDING

In the cult classic film *Hackers,* the young Angelina Jolie plays the role of Acid Burn, a very intelligent woman hacker who plays a pivotal role in preventing an environmental disaster, which is in contrast to how women are often portrayed in mass media or treated within the hacking community (Softley, 1995). In the film, Jolie is respected by her peers and functions as co-leader of a small peer network (along with a man hacker named Dade Murphy, also known as Crash Override). While other hackers in the film respect both characters, research on actual women hackers points to a vastly different dynamic online.

Hacking, like most activities associated with cyber technology, developed in a man-centric environment; it was viewed as a harmless pastime among college students at the Massachusetts Institute of Technology (MIT). During the 1950s and 1960s, students sought to manipulate technology to perform actions not otherwise intended—that is, to "hack" (Marcum, 2015). Eventually, the desire to manipulate technology expanded and hacking now encompasses a wide spectrum of activities that are both legal (such as ethical hackers conducting penetration testing) and illegal (such as cyberterrorism), including the manipulation of people to compromise their own technology (that is, social engineering). While research about the role of gender in cybervictimization has slowly expanded through the years, the impact of gender on risk of offending is understudied. One exception, however, is within the hacker subfield.

Overall, studies continue to show that women hackers experience great hostility and resistance when engaging in exploits (Steinmetz, Holt, and Holt, 2019). The suspicion among scholars is that this hostility and resistance stems from the wider socialization process of steering boys but not girls toward technological pursuits (Holt, Navarro, and Clevenger, 2019). This socialization has resulted in technologically driven online and offline environments that are made up of mostly men who are largely resistant to addressing obvious inequalities and instead emphasize that access is driven by accomplishments. Thus, when girls engage in hacking, research shows they have traveled on a different pathway than boys.

In one of the few studies exploring the role of gender in pathways toward engagement in hacking, scholars found that peer association increased the chances of girls hacking, but did not function in a similar manner for boys (Holt, Navarro, and Clevenger, 2019). Surprisingly, the significance of peer association among girls dwarfed the importance of access to and ownership of technology, which was important for only boys. This aligns with fantastical stories of early woman hackers, like Susan Thunder, who learned to "hack" via social engineering through her associations with others (Holt and Schell, 2013). Despite the significance related to association, however, other work in the field shows that girls are marginalized at networking events frequented by hackers like the Chaos Computer Club (CCC) (Kinkade, Bachmann, and Smith-Bachmann, 2013). Indeed, at the CCC, the researchers found that women who attended the conference with male partners were assigned the term "groupies." Given deeply entrenched beliefs about the ineffectiveness of women in engaging cybercrime, it is not surprising that research has shown that girls traveling down this pathway are victimized by the very networks they seek access too. For example, scholars have referred to interviews from Gigabyte (a woman hacker) in which she discusses the open hostility she faced as she operated within the very man-dominated hacking community (Holt and Schell, 2013). (See Active Learning Assignment 6.1.)

ACTIVE LEARNING ASSIGNMENT 6.1

Negotiating Gender in Cybercrime Offending

Watch the film *Hackers*, which is mentioned in the chapter section "The Role of Gender in Online Offending." As the film plays, critically examine how characters of different genders interact with each other—particularly how the male hackers (like Crash Override, Cereal Killer, and Lord Nikon) interact with the lone female hacker (Acid Burn). Pay attention to both verbal and nonverbal communication as well as how each character is dressed, which communicates implicit messages about importance and roles. For example, during the scene where Dade Murphy learns that Kate Libby (Angelina Jolie) is Acid Burn, the hacker who "bested" him at the start of the movie, he appears not to believe what he has just been told—as if it is not possible that a female hacker outwitted him.

After watching the film, write up your analysis in a formal paper that addresses the following questions:

1. What patterns were depicted in terms of communication, intelligence, hacking craft (if applicable), and styles across men?
2. What patterns were depicted in terms of communication, intelligence, hacking craft (if applicable), and styles across women? Broaden your analysis to other female hackers beyond Kate Libby, since she is the only female hacker.
3. Do these depictions align with the dominant gender norms in the United States associated with men and women? Please explain your answer.
4. Discuss the implicit messages that *Hackers* communicates about female and male hackers, both as separate groups involved in hacking and in terms of the dynamics between the two.

THE ROLE OF GENDER IN ONLINE VICTIMIZATION

While the literature examining gender as a risk factor for cybervictimization is more developed compared than that for offending, both subjects remained understudied overall. Yet, both are important because gender shapes cyberoffending, which in turn affects victimization risk. Given that relationship, we now turn to examining various cybervictimization areas. The first topic we will examine is cyberoffenses targeted at property rather than people, as in cases of digital piracy and identity theft. In these offense types, the role of gender is less clear with a few exceptions (such as identity theft and romance fraud), but all variations are vital to address for foundational knowledge about cybercrime victimization. Following this section, we will turn to exploring the pronounced connection between gender and interpersonal cybervictimization like cyberbullying, cyber dating abuse and cyber domestic abuse, cybersexual abuse, and cyberstalking.

CYBERCRIME TARGETING PROPERTY

Cyberfraud is a broad term that refers to deceptive activities that involve cyber technology to gain access to something of value (Wall, 2001). To be clear, while this offense (and similar offenses, like cybertheft) is grouped in the "Cybercrime Targeting Property" section, it not always motivated by the desire to simply obtain something of value from a target. As discussed shortly, the most pronounced relationship between gender and these cyberoffenses is in when the motivation is a desire to inflict emotional harm. Unsurprisingly, when cyberfraud does occur, it also often involves cybertheft because the initial deception leads to the loss (by theft) of something of value.

A few cyberfraud examples, and corresponding cyberthefts, are work-at-home scams, digital piracy, and identity theft. Overall, cyberfraud and cybertheft result in millions of dollars lost every year (Marchini and Pascual, 2019). On an individual level, people who have these cybercrimes committed against them lose countless hours in potential productivity time and suffer various financial, physiological, and psychological consequences (Navarro and Jasinski, 2014). While the role of gender is not clear in these cybercrimes, there are studies that point to a probable relationship.

Before discussing the research on gender and these types of cybercrimes, however, we will briefly define each offense. **Work-at-home scams** encompass various cons that many laypersons have experienced. In terms of cyberfraud, the deception may begin with receiving an email about an opportunity that is too good to be true. For example, "Make $5,000 each month from your couch!" To take advantage of this opportunity, the individual must divulge sensitive personal information or pay an up-front membership fee, or both (Turner et al.,

CASE STUDY 6.1

Meri Brown and Catfishing

In 2015, news broke that Meri Brown from TLC's *My Sister Wives* had experienced an invasive catfishing scandal. As reported by multiple news outlets, Meri fell victim to an online scammer who assumed a male persona named "Sam." After meeting on Twitter, Sam and Meri developed a relationship using multiple lines of communication as well as exchanging risqué photos. At some point, the relationship dissolved, and Sam began blackmailing Meri.

Even several years later, occasional articles about Meri's catfishing victimization continue to be published. Conduct further research on Meri's catfishing victimization, and answer the following questions:

1. Discuss how Meri's experience aligns with cyberdeception, cybertheft, or both.
2. Discuss how gender norms may have influenced the reporting on Meri's catfishing victimization.

2013). After the individual does that, the job opportunity never materializes and the membership fee is lost, or there is a risk of the "employed" target engaging in actions that amount to money laundering (e.g., by cashing checks provided by the fraudsters).

Romance scams, or catfishing, and scams like the "I'm trapped in London" fraud revolve around an interpersonal relationship and a request for help (Lamphere and Pikciunas, 2016; Shadel and Dudley, n.d.). The latter con can occur when someone receives a panicked email from a traveling "relative" saying that they have lost their money and need help escaping an area (e.g., London). On the other hand, romance scams can also take months to take shape, with the individual setting up a virtual romantic relationship with their target, which can include photos and videos. After the relationship is established, the scammer will begin asking for money for various unfortunate events (such as job loss, medical emergency) until the deception is revealed. At that point, the person being scammed may have suffered serious financial losses in addition to emotional shocks. It is important to note, however, that catfishing is not always motivated by money and, like other types of cybercrimes, it could be motivated by revenge or other personal reasons. (See Case Study 6.1.)

Digital piracy involves acquiring, using, or distributing copyright-protected material without supplying the required acknowledgment to the copyright holder—whether that be crediting the source (as in an academic paper) or monetary payment (Higgins, Fell, and Wilson, 2007). As with the other examples in this section, this cybercrime can begin with a cyberfraud and often also includes cybertheft. For example, Aaron Swartz used a false guest email account to hide his identity (cyberfraud) and a software program to rapidly download thousands of JSTOR academic articles (cybertheft) (*United*

States v. Swartz). Swartz was not authorized to circumvent the articles' copyright protections. The estimated loss to JSTOR totaled thousands of dollars and Swartz's actions caused a considerable slowing of MIT's network.

Identity theft, or the acquiring and using of personal identity information to obtain some benefit (such as criminal sanction avoidance, financial payments, or medical benefits), is another widespread cybercrime that involves both cyberfraud and cybertheft (Navarro and Jasinski, 2014). While this cybercrime can be very high-tech and involve the use of malicious software that facilitates or performs a criminal action (crimeware), it is also possible to use public information available online. The case of Sarah Palin's stolen identity is an excellent example. A young individual simply guessed Palin's Yahoo! password using information found online (Zetter, 2008). After guessing the password, the individual gained access to Palin's personal email (cybertheft), which was undoubtedly valuable during her vice-presidential campaign, and he could masquerade as her online (cyberfraud).

While the relationship between gender and property-driven cybercrime is less pronounced than in interpersonal cybercrime like cyberbullying and cyber domestic abuse, gender is a risk factor for victimization via romance scams. For example, one novel study found that several factors increased the risk of victimization: age (middle age is the most vulnerable), gender (women are the most vulnerable), and traits aligning with low self-control (such as addiction disposition, sensation seeking, and urgency) (Whitty, 2018). These factors may point to the desire among women, particularly middle-aged women, to find romantic partners. This desire stems from the societal prioritizing of women's worth based on domestic lifestyle, including partners, rather than professional pursuits.

Another study examining how gender norms structure individual strategies in perpetrating romance swindles found that individuals emphasized gender-congruent activities and characteristics in their false profiles (Kopp et al., 2015). For example, date-seeking "men" emphasized masculine traits like loyalty, respect, and strong adherence to religion. On the other hand, date-seeking "women" emphasized their attractiveness in terms of confidence and sexual appeal. Perpetrators of these scams are cognizant of the dominant social scripts surrounding romantic relationships, as well as societal gender norms, and craft fictitious profiles that align with them to maximize the chance of success.

In examinations of identity theft, findings about gender as a risk factor are inconsistent. For instance, Reyns's (2013) investigation into identity theft yielded several interesting findings about risk factors affecting odds of victimization. In a full model assessing individual characteristics and routines, women were less likely to experience identity theft victimization than men. Reyns suggested that the lower risk associated with women may be due to differences in browsing and internet activities compared to men. For example, as discussed elsewhere in this chapter, certain online activities, like hacking and digital piracy, are dominated by men. Therefore, the lower identity theft victimization risk for women may stem from differences in how often they are downloading or using the internet. This finding, however, was contradicted in a later analysis by Reyns and Henson (2016), which found there was no difference in risk of experiencing identity theft between men and women.

These studies show that while gender may have a less pronounced role in understanding property-driven cybercrime, it still is an important consideration for certain offense types like identity theft and romance frauds. A cursory review of the literature indicates that individuals who engage in these offenses are aware of cultural scripts, gender norms, and internet activities that—when leveraged—can increase the odds of the success of their crimes. Thus, cyber-criminologists must remain vigilant about the role of gender across all types of cybervictimizations—both offenses targeting property and those targeting people, known as interpersonal cybercrime.

INTERPERSONAL CYBERCRIME

Interpersonal cybercrime is a broad term that describes offenses aimed at people rather than their property. The most common offenses in this category are cyberbullying, cyber dating or cyber intimate-partner abuse, cybersexual offenses, and cyberstalking. To be clear, these offenses may also include behaviors targeted at property—as in the case of cyber intimate-partner abuse. However, even in this case, the main goal is to harm the intimate partner rather than simply stealing money or other financial resources.

Cyberbullying

Cyberbullying entered the national discourse in the early 2000s following the tragic suicide of several youth who were victimized (Navarro and Jasinski, 2012). Since that time, concern about cyberbullying has expanded rapidly, which has considerably increased knowledge about victimization. Challenges still confront the field, however. One of the most significant is the lack of a consistent definition (Patchin and Hinduja, 2012). Definitions vary widely in terms of what actions constitute this cyberoffense, whether intent is a necessary consideration, and whether people must suffer repeated actions. To address this inconsistency, Tokunaga (2010) proposed the following definition that accounted for variations across studies: "Cyberbullying is any behavior performed through electronic or digital media by individuals or groups that repeatedly communicates hostile or aggressive messages intended to inflict harm or discomfort on others" (278).

Although bullying existed long before the technological age, cyberbullying presents new challenges for individuals who are victimized (Slonje and Smith,

---

ACTIVE LEARNING ASSIGNMENT 6.2

Cyberbullying Prevention

Seek out your institution's policy on cyberbullying and cyberharassment. If a policy exists, critically examine how those offenses are defined and whether the definition reflects conceptions in the field. Also, note whether there are weaknesses in the policy and consider potential improvements.

After comparing your institution's policy to definitions of these cyberoffenses, create a plan to raise awareness about them. This plan should include activities with a schedule and a projected budget. The plan should also address any weaknesses in the current policy or ongoing activities. If there is no policy, create an awareness plan guided by *your* definitions based on *your* knowledge from this chapter.

2008). First, unlike offline bullying, cyberbullying can be a 24/7 event. For young people, there is no respite after the school day. Secondly, unlike offline bullying, cyberbullying can involve an infinite number of witnesses. Third, unlike offline bullying, cyberbullying can include multiple avenues of *anonymous* attack. Put another way, individuals bullying others offline cannot hide their identity, particularly from capable guardians within confined school settings. In contrast, individuals bullying others online can exploit the lax safeguards in that environment to both shield their identity and to confront their targets in multiple ways regardless of guardianship (Navarro and Jasinski, 2012; Navarro and Jasinski, 2013). (See Active Learning Assignment 6.2.)

The variations in cyberbullying definitions across studies have led to a wide range of offense and victimization rates. In studies using broad definitions, scholars have found that upward of 70 percent of sampled youth had experienced cyberbullying (Juvonen and Gross, 2008). In contrast, those using narrower definitions have found cyberbullying victimization rates between 20 percent and 30 percent (Patchin and Hinduja, 2006; Smith et al., 2008). Similarly, definition inconsistencies have led to a wide range of cyberbullying perpetration rates across studies, from 1 percent to 44 percent (Akbulut and Eristi, 2011; Allen, 2012; Aricak et al., 2008; Beran and Li, 2007; Beran et al., 2012; Calvete et al., 2010; Dilmac, 2009).

As the cyberbullying research field has grown, scholars have uncovered several demographic and background factors that affect the risks of experiencing and perpetrating this cyberoffense. In terms of basic demographics, some studies have found a relationship between age and involvement in cyberbullying (Navarro et al., 2017; Seiler and Navarro, 2014; Navarro and Jasinski, 2013). However, there are contradictory findings about the nature of that relationship: some evidence suggests that the risk of experiencing cyberbullying increases with age, while other findings note the opposite, that cyberbullying decreases with age. To add to this confusion, some studies have failed to support the presence of a relationship at all (Didden et al., 2009; Juvonen and Gross, 2008). In addition to age and gender (discussed in the upcoming section), scholars have also investigated the relationship between race and involvement in cyberbullying. While follow-up is necessary before making firm conclusions, results derived in many studies have not supported the existence of a relationship between race and cyberbullying (Bauman, Toomey, and Walker, 2013; Hinduja and Patchin, 2008; Kwan and Skoric, 2013; Schneider et al., 2012). Finally, and most disturbingly, findings show that youth with disabilities are more likely to experience cyberbullying (Kowalski et al., 2016).

In addition to these factors, scholars have also investigated the role of online behavior in cyberbullying. Broadly speaking, as involvement in online activity increases, so does risk of experiencing cyberbullying (Navarro et al., 2017; Navarro and Jasinski, 2012; Seiler and Navarro, 2014). Moreover, activities that place individuals within online proximity to others, particularly individuals who may be motivated to commit crime, to use a routine activities theory term, tend to increase the risk of experiencing cyberbullying. These activities include using chatrooms, instant messaging programs, and social networking sites. Studies have also emphasized the relationship between engaging in risky behavior, such as posting explicit photos or victimizing others, and experiencing cyberbullying (Navarro et al.; Navarro and Jasinski, 2013; Seiler and Navarro, 2014). Finally, a few other areas of vulnerability stem from offline social constructs like gender.

Although there is an ongoing debate within the field on the role of gender in cyberbullying, there is some evidence that women and youth who do not conform to gender expectations are at increased risk of experiencing this cyberoffense. For instance, evidence from several studies shows that women are more likely than men to experience cyberbullying when engaging in similar online behaviors (Mesch, 2009; Navarro et al., 2017; Navarro and Jasinski, 2012; Navarro and Jasinski, 2013; Seiler and Navarro, 2014). While some studies have found that women may be at more risk because they are more likely to perpetrate cyberbullying than men are (Barlett and Coyne, 2014; Görzig and Ólafsson, 2013), other studies have found that men are more likely to cyberharass others (Lee and Shin, 2017; Wong, Cheung, and Xiao, 2018; Zsila et al., 2018). These studies only suggest the presence of a relationship, however, and not necessarily *why* particular youth are at increased risk.

To answer the question of why, qualitative studies have gathered considerable information from youth who were victimized that supports the idea that gender affects cyberbullying experiences. For example, in a study conducted by Berne, Frisén, and Kling in 2014, young women reported being cyberbullied because of their weight, while young men reported being cyberbullied because of their physical stature or perceived lack of masculinity. (See Active Learning Assignment 6.3.)

ACTIVE LEARNING ASSIGNMENT 6.3

Deviating from Gender Ideals

This activity builds upon classic sociological exercises about judging and scoring "deviance" (for example, see Ulrich, 2010). Create a three-by-four table as shown below and list behaviors that you believe conform to and challenge societal conceptions associated with men and women. Given the nature of these concepts, genders other than the binary are not listed in column 1 but should be represented in the chart. After listing both normative and deviant behaviors, score how severe each "deviation" is on a scale of (least likely to result in negative reaction) to 10 (most likely to result in negative reaction).

	Normative behaviors	Deviant behaviors	Deviant behavior score 1 (least severe) to 10 (extremely severe)
Male			
Female			

Once this chart is complete, reflect on how these columns shape your own behavior. Specifically, write brief responses to each of the following questions and be prepared to share them with the class:

1. Do you engage in certain behaviors because they seem to be expected? Give one example to support your answer. If your answer is "no," explain your reasoning.
2. Do you avoid engaging in certain behaviors because you are worried about the reaction from others? Again, give one example to support your answer. If your answer is "no," explain your reasoning.
3. Could these feelings lead to criminal offending or victimization? Give an example to support your answer. Given the material covered in earlier chapters, "no" is not a valid answer for this question.

Relatedly, studies show that youth who identify as LGBTQIA+ are also at increased risk of cyberbullying. A study conducted by the Gay, Lesbian, and Straight Education Network (GLSEN) revealed that cyberbullying is a reality for youth who identify as LGBTQ IA+, particularly those that identify as transgender (Kosciw et al., 2016). The results showed that non-cisgender youth experienced harmful speech as well as various forms of bullying offline and online. This targeting of youth who do not conform to societal expectations of their perceived gender aligns with prior discussion of the concepts of emphasized femininity and hegemonic masculinity (Connell, 1987).

These two concepts refer to sociocultural normative traits and roles associated with men and women. While hegemonic masculinity varies across cultures and time, in current Western culture, this concept often refers to the fol-

---

ACTIVE LEARNING ASSIGNMENT 6.4

Bronies and Cyberbullying

In 2014, Michael Morones, an eleven year old, attempted suicide but was saved by his family and rushed to the hospital. He suffered from various complications because of the failed attempt and died in 2021. The cause of the suicide attempt, according to his family, was the incessant bullying Michael experienced because of his love for the *My Little Pony* show (Satchell, 2014). Men and boys who are fans of this show are often referred to as "bronies," and although they have a community among themselves, they often are harassed and bullied online.

Do a Google search for "Michael Morones." After conducting research on Michael, discuss the connection between hegemonic masculinity and the cyberbullying in this case in a one- to two-page double-spaced response paper. In other words, explain how societal conceptions of masculinity shaped this case of cyberbullying from both a perpetration and a victimization standpoint.

---

lowing set of traits: attractiveness, heterosexuality, independence, sexual prowess, and emotional and physical strength (Connell, 1987; Kupers, 2005; Pemberton, 2013). In other words, within Western culture, masculinity aligns with a man's independence, both in the financial and physical sense, as well as his ability to protect and support his loved ones. Masculine status is not permanent, however, and is always shifting as one navigates social life (Connell and Messerschmidt, 2005). For example, a challenge to one's masculinity can occur through an insults at a local bar or through the loss of a job, which can then spur potentially devastating actions (see chapter 3). Because hegemonic masculinity works in tandem with Western patriarchal culture, all other forms of gender expression are inherently subordinated to it (Connell and Messerschmidt, 2005). Thus, men who do not conform to dominant ideals face criticism and scorn. (See Active Learning Assignment 6.4.)

Emphasized femininity is the complement to hegemonic masculinity and refers to a set of sociocultural normative traits and roles associated with women (Connell and Messerschmidt, 2005). Again, while it can vary across cultures and time, in current Western culture, this concept refers to the following traits: attractiveness, compliance, dependence, nurturance, and passivity (Connell, 1987). In other words, within this culture, femininity aligns with physical attractiveness as well as with how a woman conducts herself in relation to her partner and children. Because emphasized femininity complements hegemonic masculinity, dominant societal conceptions associate ideal women as beautiful and always sexually available to their partners. The ideal woman is also passive, particularly within the family, and exists to support the head of the household. Finally, given the role of the hegemonic man as protector and provider, the ideal woman cares for children and the family. Any deviation

---

CASE STUDY 6.2

Brandy Vela, Cyberbullied to Death

Research the bullycide, or suicide with a connection to bullying, of Brandy Vela, which occurred in December 2016. After suffering relentless weight-based cyberbullying, Brandy tragically took her own life (Hassan, 2016).

1. After conducting research on this case, analyze it through a gendered lens and address the connection between emphasized femininity and this bullycide.
2. Explain how societal conceptions of femininity affected this case in terms of perpetration and victimization.

---

from these traits, particularly any that directly challenge hegemonic masculinity, is likely to result in negative sanctions.

As the prior passages demonstrate, the concepts of hegemonic masculinity and emphasized femininity are extremely relevant in understanding cyberbullying victimization. In terms of men, the prior research underscores the reality that young men who act in ways counter to dominant hegemonic masculine ideals, such as by watching a show socially constructed as "feminine," are at increased risk of experiencing cyberbullying. The influence of gender is also readily seen in research exploring the experiences of youth identifying as LGBTQIA+. Given that hegemonic masculine ideals include aggressiveness, dominance, and heterosexuality, men identifying as LGBTQIA+ are inherently considered inferior.

Likewise, women who act in ways counter to emphasized femininity, such as being unattractive or sexually unpleasing to others, are at increased risk of experiencing cyberbullying (Berne, Frisén, and Kling, 2014). Women can also be cyberbullied if they engage in behavior that directly challenges hegemonic men: asserting independence, behaving aggressively, exerting sexual agency, or rejecting sexual advances. Support for these statements appears within cyberspace through the derogatory treatment of female hackers by male hackers who consider them to be "inferior" and "outsiders" until they have "proven" otherwise (Segan, 2000).

Cyber Dating Abuse and Cyber Intimate-Partner Abuse

As discussed in prior chapters, gender is a strong undercurrent in the perpetration of dating abuse and intimate partner abuse (World Health Organization, 2017). It plays a role in assaults on both the physical and psychological states of those who experience intimate partner abuse, including financial abuse, physical abuse, psychological abuse, sexual abuse, social abuse, and spiritual abuse. While these behaviors typically occur offline, evidence shows that individuals abusing others exploit technology to further their coercive control (Draucker and Martsolf, 2010; Woodlock, 2017). Unfortunately, there are ample routes available in cyberspace. Studies have found that individuals engaging in abuse have harmed others by perpetrating cyber financial theft (e.g., via account takeovers), cyberfraud (e.g., via identity theft), cybersexual abuse, and cyber-stalking (Reed, Tolman, and Ward, 2016; Wolford-Clevenger et al., 2016). Before discussing the connection between gender and cyberabuse, however, we present information on the current state of knowledge within this field.

Although we use the term *cyberabuse* to describe both cyber dating abuse and cyber intimate-partner abuse, one should not assume these kinds of abuse are identical. Although **cyber dating abuse** (C/DA) is like **cyber intimate-partner abuse** (C/IPA), scholars use the former term to refer to informal relationships that are more common among youth and young adults, and the latter term to refer to formalized relationships that may involve shared assets and children. This distinction matters because individuals in dating relationships, where those who experience it may live with parents or roommates, are more difficult for abusers to control. Moreover, it is far easier to dissolve dating relationships, where shared assets and children are unlikely, than formalized unions, where the person perpetrating the abuse may use those connections as leverage. Thus, while we present discussion on both these offenses, it is important to remember that while they are related, they are also different.

Though the definition of IPA varies slightly across studies, the offense consists of abusive actions by one individual to exert coercive control over others (Stark, 2009). **Coercive control** is a key factor in abusive relationships and refers to an individual's ability to control the behaviors of children and the partner through *covert* means (such as a look that might not be noticed by others) or overt means (physical violence). (See Active Learning Assignment 6.5.) Similarly, the definition of DA also varies across studies, but it consists of abusive actions by one individual (18 years old or younger) toward another of approximately the same age to control their behavior (Centers for Disease Control and Prevention, 2021). Unfortunately, while research in these fields has expanded since the battered women's movement in the 1970s, there are significant challenges to understanding the prevalence of the problem (Navarro, Jasinski, and Wick, 2014).

It is common knowledge that partner abuse, whether DA or IPA, is notoriously underreported. Consequently, prevalence rates give only a snippet of the actual scope of the problem. Yet even these rates show that partner abuse occurs with alarming frequency in relationships across the country. For example, findings from a recent National Intimate Partner and Sexual Violence Survey (NISVS) showed that injurious abuse was a reality across age and gender but disproportionally affected women (24.4%) compared to men (10.6%) (Smith et al., 2018). Although there were few technological abuse questions in the survey, the number of women who reported experiencing stalking, offline and

---

ACTIVE LEARNING ASSIGNMENT 6.5

Technology and Coercive Control

Imagine that you are in an abusive relationship and your partner watches your every move via technology. In other words, your partner keeps track of your location via apps like Where's My iPhone and through social media. Although you have access to a car, it is for emergency situations and has a GPS locator installed on it. Your partner has the car geofenced as well, meaning an alert is sent if it leaves the home. Moreover, it is registered under your partner's name with no mention of you. In terms of money, your partner watches the bank accounts, which you do not have access to. In fact, you are not even sure if your name is attached to the accounts. To increase control, your partner has isolated you from everyone you know and gives you only $25 in cash to spend daily, which is all you have at this moment. A few weeks ago, you did manage to take a rarely used credit card from your partner's wallet.

Now imagine that you have decided to flee the relationship. Describe your plan for escaping given your partner's "technological leash." Ensure you that you address each form of technological monitoring described above. For example, consider how you would mitigate the monitoring by phone when simply turning it off would alert your abuser. How would you access the car, given the monitoring? If you could, how would you access money in the bank accounts? And, finally, if you could, how would you use the credit card? After noting how you would neutralize the technological leash, describe where you would go and how you would get there. Finally, create a long-term plan of how and what you need to do to ensure your safety, given the power of technology.

---

online, by an intimate partner greatly outnumbered the number of men (about 12.5 million and about 2.5 million, respectively). Results from smaller studies support these findings and show how individuals who engage in abuse use technology to terrorize intimate partners. In one notable example, individuals who abused their partners used landline telephones to block help-seeking and to send threatening messages (Belknap, Chu, and DePrince, 2012). Again, as technology has advanced, individuals who abuse others have exploited new tools like GPS to further their coercive control (Woodlock, 2017).

These results are in line with studies on DA among youth and young adults. Many individuals who abuse others reported using technology to extend their control over their partners (Draucker and Martsolf, 2010). The individuals who abused others used the gamut of technology, from ubiquitous tools like email to sophisticated surveillance like keyloggers. In terms of prevalence rates across studies, reported DA perpetration and victimization rates have exceeded 50 percent (Stonard et al., 2014). Like IPA, while DA crosses genders, findings show most people who experience it are women (Dick et al., 2014).

Before discussing the role of gender as a risk factor for cyberabuse, it is important to note other risk factors that research has established. As in cyberbullying literature, as individuals increase their online presence, their risk of cyberabuse also increases (Wick et al., 2017). For individuals entangled in DA or IPA, the types of activities they engage in online also matter. For example, individuals who used social networking sites were more likely to perpetrate cyberabuse (Van Ouytsel et al., 2017). Research has also found that vulnerability increases if individuals engage in risky behaviors offline. For example, youth who engaged in activities that deviated from social norms but that were not necessarily classified as crimes or who were sexually active were more likely to experience cyberabuse (Zweig et al., 2013).

Abuse affects individuals with various characteristics, but one of the most salient risk factors is gender. In terms of understanding cyberabuse, studies continue to show that cyberDA and IPA disproportionately affect women—especially in terms of cyberstalking (Smith et al., 2018) and cybersexual abuse (Zweig et al., 2013). While not all abuse is gender-based, according to Johnson's (1995) foundational work, this "gender divide" likely indicates that the concept of "patriarchal terrorism" is a reality even in cyberspace.

We introduced Johnson's typology in chapter 3 but stopped short of discussing its applicability in cyberspace. However, research has shown that Johnson's framework for understanding behavior in abusive relationships applies to cyberspace (Melander, 2010). For example, in relationships not grounded in power and control, where men and women use violence at comparable levels, technology triggered altercations. However, Melander discovered that technology served a vastly different purpose in relationships marked by intimate partner terrorism. In these cases, technology was a tool used by one partner to constantly check on and watch the other. Unlike common couple violence, this behavior is gender-based and grounded in the desire for power and control.

Johnson's two other relationship behaviors, mutual violent control and violent resistance, are also applicable to understanding interactions in cyberspace. In relationships of mutual violent control, where two individuals are jockeying for power and control over each other, both partners used technology to check on and watch the other. Finally, in relationships that displayed violent resistance, the partner experiencing the abuse used technology to force the end of abusive relationships quite literally (Melander, 2010). Given that research has supported the connection between certain relationship behaviors, particularly intimate partner terrorism, and gender, it makes intuitive sense that these connections exist in cyberspace.

As of this writing, there are no studies (to the best of our knowledge) that examine the applicability of emphasized femininity and/or hegemonic masculinity to the understanding of cyberDA or IPA. However, research about offline DA and IPA points to a connection between these important concepts in gender studies and cyberabuse. For example, research shows that men use violence both within and outside of the home as a resource to assert and reestablish their masculinity (Dobash and Dobash, 1998; Little, 2017; Messerschmidt, 1997). While violence tends to be associated with large, urban areas, these events occur in rural communities as well—particularly those characterized by an adherence to traditional gender norms and strong community relations (Little, 2017). Thus, if these gender concepts apply to offline DA and IPA, they are applicable to cyberabuse.

Cybersexual Abuse

Cybersexual abuse is a broad term that includes various online offenses involving both adolescents and adults. For example, in terms of children, cybersexual abuse includes **child sexual abuse material** (CSAM) as well as online sexual solicitation or exploitation of children. Broadly speaking, CSAM includes the acquiring, dissemination, and production of explicit material involving minors—whether it involves actual children or digital content that is indistinguishable from real children. Sexual solicitation, on the other hand, is a request by the individual engaging in the offense to the minor to engage in explicit activity. Relatedly, another form of cybersexual abuse is **cybersextortion,** a form of exploitation, which is the coercing of an individual into undesirable behavior out of fear of some negative consequence brought on by the perpetrator (such as the release of compromising information, photos, or videos). Thus, cybersextortion is akin to blackmail in cyberspace. A final form of cybersexual abuse is the dissemination of explicit content without the approval of all depicted individuals, such as non-consensual distribution of pornography (NCDP). The common thread to all these offenses is that they are grounded in a desire to remove the agency of the person who is victimized over a deeply personal area of their life. Before discussing the connection between gender and these cyberoffenses, we present an overview of the current state of knowledge within the field.

Like DA and IPA, sexual offenses, offline and online, are notoriously underreported. In terms of child sexual abuse, which includes offenses like CSAM, recent meta-analysis findings show that the problem spans the globe (Stoltenborgh et al., 2015). For instance, the combined prevalence rates for women who are sexually abused across the major continents ranged from about 11 percent (Asia) to nearly 22 percent (Australia). Men were not immune as the prevalence rates associated with the sexual abuse of boys ranged from about 4 percent (Asia) to about 19 percent (Africa). The prevalence rates for sexual abuse of girls and boys in the United States was 20.1 percent and 8 percent, respectively.

In studies about cybersexual abuse and specifically cybersexual solicitation, findings showed that there was great variation in how youth received and responded to threatening situations. For example, Wolak, Finkelhor, and Mitchell (2007) found that only a small minority of youth received "aggressive sexual solicitations" via cyberspace, but that these events were the most likely to result in victimization. Less than 5 percent of youth reported that

---

ACTIVE LEARNING ASSIGNMENT 6.6

Amanda Todd

Research the story of Amanda Todd via a Google search. Be sure to watch the video she posted to YouTube shortly before committing suicide: https://youtu.be/wjvq23sPrHA.

1. Identify the forms of interpersonal cybervictimization she endured. As you identify these cyberoffenses, justify your answers based on information from this chapter.
2. Theorize about and explain the role of gender in these events. In other words, discuss whether Amanda's behavior conformed to the emphasized feminine ideals. If so, how? If not, how?
3. Discuss whether this alignment could (or could not) have increased her vulnerability to abuse. Again, justify your answer.

As a word of caution, be careful not tread into victim blaming. This assignment is about critically analyzing the role of gender in what Amanda experienced and not about what she should have or could have done differently. The former is an academic endeavor while the latter is victim blaming.

---

they had received an online sexual solicitation and felt distressed because of it. These statistics are not meant to minimize the harm of cybersexual solicitation, as it can lead to victimization, but to show that this form of cybersexual abuse is not at epidemic proportions. Indeed, Wolak, Finkelhor, and Mitchell found that most youth reacted swiftly and securely to cybersexual solicitations (by blocking the requester, for example). (See Active Learning Assignment 6.6.)

Research on new areas of cybersexual abuse, like cybersexual exploitation, is increasing rapidly, but the field is still in a nascent stage. Existing research shows that this problem is widespread and cuts across various boundaries. For example, in one report on the matter, Wittes, Poplin, Jurecic, and Spera (2016) note their research shows potentially thousands of people could be victimized by cybersextortion and that this is only a fraction of the actual prevalence. This finding is disturbing because their research also suggests that many justice-involved individuals have long histories of victimizing others before coming to the attention of authorities. In terms of system-involved people and people against whom crimes are committed, men dominated among the first group, and women dominated among the second.

Another area that is rapidly growing in terms of research is the use of technology to produce and distribute explicit content without the consent of all parties depicted. This offense is referred to as the non-consensual distribution of pornography (NCDP), which sometimes occurs against the backdrop of a failed relationship (Lamphere and Pikciunas, 2016). In terms of prevalence, research shows that thousands of websites advertise NCDP content for viewers. A study by the Cyber Civil Rights Initiative revealed disturbing trends (Eaton, Jacobs, and Ruvalcaba, 2017). For example, nearly 13 percent of respondents had experienced an attempted NCDP situation or had actually had the material distributed without their consent. In terms of demographics of those involved, a greater proportion of women than men reported victimization (attempted or completed). In contrast, a greater proportion of men than women reported victimizing others. While most perpetrators reported that they never intended to hurt anyone (79%), a large number (11%) noted that they had been motivated by their anger toward the person they victimized.

Scholars have long called attention to the notion that gender is a strong undercurrent in the perpetration of sexual violence, whether offline or online. The relationship is visible in research surrounding various rapist typologies, which emphasize the need for power and control, as well as in data from individuals who rape, who voice similar motivations (Groth and Birnbaum, 1979). These motivations are salient to understanding sexual violence and are strongly associated with hegemonic masculinity.

In a broader example, scholars have also found that during armed conflict opposing sides use sexual violence to inflict actual as well as symbolic harm on each other (Skjelsbaek, 2001). While the actual harm inflicted is important, the symbolic harm is vital to take note of because it is also deeply associated with conceptions of femininity and masculinity. Indeed, if we reflect on prior discussions of hegemonic masculinity and emphasized femininity, men are conceptualized to be pillars of strength, while women are conceptualized to be the heart of the family. Taken to a macro level, men are the protectors of society at large, while women are the heart of a nation. Thus, it makes intuitive sense, from an enemy-combatant standpoint, why sexual violence would be a powerful weapon of war. Sexually violating women affiliated with the enemy not only shows the ineffectiveness of the "protectors" to prevent the violence, but also drives a figurative stake through the heart of the nation itself (Skjelsbaek, 2001). Considering these connections between gender and sexual violence offline both at the micro and macro levels, it should be unsurprising that gender also underscores cybersexual violence. (See Active Learning Assignment 6.7.)

Given the nascent status of this line of research within cybercriminology, there is sparse information on the role of gender in cybersexual abuse. However, again, given the relationship between gender and offline sexual violence, the clear gender divide in terms of likely individuals involved in cybersexual abuse, and the role of gender in other forms of interpersonal cybervictimization, there are multiple reasons to believe this relationship exists. If existing offline information holds within an online context, cybersexual violence is likely to arise from the following multiple sources.

First, sexual prowess is strongly associated with societal conceptions of masculinity: hegemonic masculinity. Given that connection, a rejection of

---

ACTIVE LEARNING ASSIGNMENT 6.7

In the Land of Blood and Honey

In the Land of Blood and Honey is an extremely graphic portrayal of sexual violence during the Bosnian War. (NOTE: This film is graphic in its depiction of sexual violence. People who have experienced sexual violence should speak with their instructor if they expect difficulty in completing this assignment.) As you watch it, critically analyze it from a gender perspective. In other words, provide thoughtful answers to the following questions, justifying your answers with material from this class and this book:

1. How is masculinity is performed in the film? Do these performances mirror any characteristics associated with hegemonic masculinity?
2. How is femininity is portrayed in the film? Do these performances mirror any characteristics associated with emphasized femininity?
3. How do female and male characters interact with each other? Do their interactions mirror the gender hierarchy discussed throughout this text?
4. Evaluate sexual violence within the film from a gender perspective. In other words, is sexual violence associated with masculinity? Is sexual violence used as a weapon of war?

---

masculine advances or any sign of sexual inferiority is socially construed as tantamount to questioning one's masculinity. For men with few other resources available to them, we have already documented ample research that shows they are the most likely to resort to violence as they look to reassert their status within the gender hierarchy (Messerschmidt, 1997). In this situation, given that masculinity and sexual prowess are conflated, it makes intuitive sense that aggrieved men may weaponize cyberspace to engage in cybersexual violence toward others perceived to be inferior.

Secondly, cyberspace allows toxic masculinity to flourish within dark places of the "manosphere" (Ging, 2019). These cyberspace congregations are distressing because not only do they give fertile ground to antisocial ideas to flourish, but also they provide an audience for aggrieved men to reassert their masculinity. Again, as we have shown in this text, masculinity is fluid and is performed in relation to others. Thus, when a man's sexuality is challenged, it is likely that it will be rectified by engaging in a performance strongly associated with that perceived harm (such as sexual violence). Men who adhere to toxic masculine principles within the manosphere not only provide the necessary audience to confirm status but also likely encourage and reinforce cybersexual abuse. Indeed, one only needs to look at the case study (3.1) of Elliot Rodger to see evidence of the dangers outlined here.

While research shows that the principal target of cybersexual abuse is women, this cybercrime cuts across all gender lines. And, unfortunately, these same societal gender conceptions can silence the victimization of others not believed to be "real victims." For example, given that masculinity is strongly associated with sexual prowess and strength (in all forms), sexually victimized heterosexual men often hesitate to disclose their victimization to others out of fear of not being believed or, even worse, ridiculed (Navarro and Clevenger, 2017). This fear stems from the ingrained (but inaccurate) belief that men cannot be sexually assaulted or that men are always open to sexual relations in any circumstances (Rentoul and Applebloom, 1997). This fear is palpable among gay men, who must also contend with dominant hegemonic masculine ideals that subordinate their identities from the start. Thus, if they are victimized, not only do they fear not being believed, but they also must face the possibility of being criticized by other men who perceive them as inferior. Given these considerations, the connection between gender and sexual violence, both offline and online, cannot be ignored. Not only can dominant gender conceptions fuel cybersexual abuse, particularly upon rejection, but they also can silence those who do not conform to dominant beliefs about "real victims."

Cyberstalking

Cyberstalking, much like cyberabuse, often occurs within the context of a failed or ongoing abusive relationship. Although definitions slightly vary across studies, cyberstalking refers to online behaviors where an individual repeatedly engages in unwanted and threatening behaviors toward another (Navarro et al., 2016). These behaviors can range from very high-tech methods like GPS (global positioning system) monitoring and spyware to low-tech methods like aggregating publicly available data or constantly watching public social media sites (Navarro and Jasinski, 2014). Before discussing the relationship between gender and cyberstalking, we present an overview of the extent and nature of the problem.

Studies show that unwanted intrusion and monitoring is a reality for many adult and young women in the United States (Smith et al., 2018; Zweig et al., 2013). Although studies do not always examine cyberstalking per se, findings continue to show an alarming number of individuals experience stalking every year. For example, a greater percentage of women (10.4%) than men (2.2%) have reported partner-perpetrated stalking across their lifetime (Smith et al., 2018). (See Case Study 6.3.) This disparity appears in studies across age ranges. For instance, in a cyberDA study conducted by Draucker and Martsolf (2010), many respondents admitted to cyberstalking their partner to watch their behavior. Disturbingly, individuals can now be stalked from afar without ever having crossed their perpetrator's path. For example, in the 2006 National Crime Victimization Survey (NCVS) supplement, over 10 percent of those who experienced this abuse could not name their stalker (Catalano, 2012). In other studies, the percentage of those who were cyberstalked by unknown persons exceeded 20 percent (Finn, 2004; Short et al., 2015).

CASE STUDY 6.3

David Matusiewicz, Cyberstalker

David Matusiewicz will never step outside of prison. He is currently serving a sentence of life without parole for cyberstalking his ex-wife, Christine Belford, for years before she was killed (Wilson, 2018). In 2013, David's father, Thomas Matusiewicz, shot Christine following several days in court where disparaging information about David was presented during a custody proceeding

(Wilson, 2018). Although this was a tragic end to Christine's years of cyberharassment, her story is not unique. Many individuals are cyberstalked annually, some by people they know, and some by strangers.

1. What is your opinion of this case?
2. What do you think of the fact that David was given a life sentence?

Despite the recognition of cyberstalking as a serious social problem, this area of cybercriminology is still under-researched. In terms of victimization, studies continue to show that while the risk of stalking crosses all demographic boundaries, the social problem continues to primarily affect women (Dreßing et al., 2014). Additionally, research shows that individuals involved in cyberstalking, either as the person committing it or the person having it committed against them, are likely to be white, educated, employed, and unattached (McFarlane and Bocij, 2003). Considering the nature of this offense, it is not surprising that many are at least moderately skilled with technology. While the area of research is still controversial, scholars have also found a relationship between internet addiction and engagement in cyberstalking. More specifically, individuals who engaged in problematic internet use were more likely to also engage in cyberstalking (Navarro et al., 2016). Aside from these factors, scholars have examined various other potential background factors to determine their importance for assessing cyberstalking risk. For instance, Ménard and Pincus (2012) found that engagement in cyberstalking increased if individuals had experienced childhood sexual trauma. Moreover, narcissistic men who were unable to emotionally recover from their perceived failures were also more likely to cyberstalk; in contrast, it was unhealthy attachments that increased that risk among women.

Cyberstalking, much like the other forms of cybervictimization discussed in this chapter, is thought to stem from the perpetrator's desire for power and control over another. Indeed, there is no greater power, from the perspective of those engaging in this offense, than controlling the actions and behaviors of another person remotely. Again, while information on the role of gender ideals in cyberstalking is sparse, there are a couple reasons to believe a relationship exists. First, cyberstalking typically occurs within the context of domestic violence—either after a dissolved relationship or within an ongoing one. Given that gender underscores domestic violence, it would be a mistake to not appreciate its significance in the analysis of cyberstalking. Second, much like other forms of interpersonal cybervictimization, there is a clear gender divide in cyberstalking. In other words, men are overrepresented among those who commit cyberstalking, and women are overrepresented among those who are cyberstalked. This statement should not be understood to mean that men are never cyberstalked, but only that there is a clear relationship between gender and this cyberoffense.

Although this area of cybercriminology is still understudied, prior discussion of how hegemonic masculinity and emphasized femininity structures social action can inform us on the relationship between gender and cyberstalking. First, as we have noted at multiple points throughout this text, the ideal hegemonic masculine male is an individual who is successful in all aspects of life, both interpersonal and professional. Men strongly adhering to these gender norms are likely to see themselves as the "head of the household," and the partner and the children are subordinated within the home. Consequently, any threat to that status is likely to be understood as a challenge to their very masculinity, which can then lead to violence to resolve those feelings of anger. This application not only explains cyberstalking within an ongoing violent relationship but also within a dissolved relationship. In the former, the individual engaging in the cyberstalking is attempting to keep control over their partner. In the latter case, the individual engaging in the abuse cannot reconcile the loss of someone so deeply intertwined with their own conception of self; therefore, they cyberstalk out of anger and a misguided sense of entitlement to remain present within the lives of their ex-partner.

The idea of entitlement and, specifically, the notion that females should always be available and are inferior to hegemonic masculine men, gives exceptional framing to cyberstalking by strangers. Again, a central theme to gender-based cyber violence is the idea of aggrieved entitlement or the anger directed at an inferior other by someone (typically male) who views themself as superior.

Strong adherence to these ideals not only explains the gender divide in cyberstalking, but also gives insight into why men may hesitate to disclose their victimization. As with cyberabuse, men likely hesitate coming forward out of fear of not being believed or even having their masculinity challenged by others. Likewise, men who are already subordinated by other ways of being confront two significant barriers to reporting. First, they do not conform to societal conceptions of "real victims." Second, they do not conform to hegemonic masculine notions of strength. Thus, the recourse they may feel the most comfortable with is not formally disclosing the event, which unfortunately leaves them suffering in silence.

SUMMARY

This chapter provided an overview of cybervictimization through a gendered lens. As we have asserted throughout this text, given that gender underscores all social action offline, it is likely to also affect interactions in cyberspace. Indeed, this chapter shows that gender underscores several types of interpersonal cyberviolence. Thus, if we ever hope to completely prevent or effectively intervene in cyberoffenses, the role of gender cannot be ignored.

7

"Boys Will Be Boys" and "Sugar and Spice"

The Relationship between Gender and Victimization

KEY TERMS
► crime pattern theory
► emphasized femininity
► general theory of crime
► hegemonic masculinity
► liberation thesis
► power-control theory
► routine activities theory
► toxic masculinity

LEARNING OBJECTIVES
► Understand the relationship between masculinity and crime.
► Be able to apply theories to perpetration of crime and victimization.
► Recognize the impact of gender on perpetrating crime and victimization.

A singular mission dominated early criminology: to understand the origins of criminal activity through investigating the actions and backgrounds of system-involved individuals (Schneider, 2001). This goal is most visible through the debunked work of Cesare Lombroso (1911), who alleged that criminality stemmed from biology. During his time, scholars did not overtly ignore women who perpetrated crime, but because men dominated as perpetrators of crime, women were simply rarely the focus of early research. Similarly, investigating the role of the person who had the crime committed against them in the genesis of crime was a tertiary concern. Women have been ignored for decades in terms of committing crime and being victimized by it.

In the post–World War II world of the 1950s, scholars increasingly recognized the importance of understanding individuals who were victimized through a broader investigative lens. This shift in focus led to the rapid growth of a subfield of criminology called victimology, or "the science of victims and victimity" (Mendelsohn, 1976, 9). Since that time, criminologists and victimologists have contributed to wider understandings about the origins and ramifications of crime. It is through these efforts that scholars showed there were two dominant gender patterns to criminal activity that continue to exist. The first pattern is that men are most of the perpetrators of crime across all offense types. As displayed in table 7.1, over 50 percent of the perpetrators in crimes against persons, crimes against property, and crimes against society in 2017 were men. The only two crimes that are remotely close in terms of "equal engagement" between men and women are embezzlement and prostitution.

The second pattern is that victimization risk varies across genders. For instance, victimization experienced by women is typically predatory in nature and the individual engaging in the action is often known and is a close intimate partner (as in intimate partner abuse or sexual violence). In contrast, the victimization of men often involves other men who do not share close ties with them. Table 7.2 displays these patterns using National Crime Victimization Survey (NCVS) data from 2012–2016 from the Bureau of Justice Statistics (BJS). As shown by the table, a greater percentage of women than men were victimized by intimates, other relatives, and acquaintances (except for 2012). In contrast, a greater percentage of men than women were victimized by strangers (except for 2015) and unknown assailants during that same time.

These broad relationships have led scholars to spend considerable effort in understanding the role of gender in criminal events. Within this text, we have devoted much discussion to the role of gender in shaping criminal engagement (see chapters 3, 4, and 5), which now shifts to an emphasis on how gender affects the risk of victimization. In this chapter, we will focus on cisgender men and women. (Chapter 8 will discuss the risk of victimization for individuals in the LGBTQIA+ communities.) We begin by discussing overall socialization practices for boys and girls in the United States, which have implications for performing gender and navigating social spaces as adults. Following that discussion, we present an overview of theoretical perspectives specific to understanding victimization across genders. Finally, we examine the role of gender across specific crimes: violent crime (assault, homicide, robbery, sexual violence) and societal offenses (drug offenses, prostitution). Given the strong connection between those that commit crime and victimization, we discuss crimes from both angles throughout this chapter. Our aim is to show that gender shapes everyday experiences that affect decisions about offending and later risks of victimization.

GENDER SOCIALIZATION AND VICTIMIZATION

As earlier chapters have shown, there are obvious gender patterns in crime statistics that have existed for years. The pathway to these patterns starts early in life through childhood socialization practices. To begin this discussion, it is important to reiterate two key concepts: emphasized femininity and hegemonic masculinity (Connell, 1987). Readers will recall that emphasized femininity is a term used to refer to how society broadly conceptualizes ideal

Table 7.1 System-Involved Individuals' Sex across Offense Types, 2017

Offense category	Total individuals	Male	% of Total	Female	% of Total	Unknown	% of Total
				Sex			
Crimes against persons	1,382,797	976,947	71	377,823	27	28,027	2
Assault	1,262,885	870,282	69	368,044	29	24,559	2
Homicide	6,561	5,110	78	889	14	562	9
Human trafficking	462	345	75	96	21	21	5
Kidnapping/abduction	20,475	16,716	82	3,391	17	368	2
Sex offenses	86,970	79,635	92	4,887	6	2,448	3
Sex offenses, nonforcible	5,444	4,859	89	516	9	69	1
Crimes against property	2,600,568	1,382,487	53	623,039	24	595,042	23
Arson	10,236	6,558	64	1,537	15	2,141	21
Bribery	446	317	71	114	26	15	3
Burglary/breaking and entering	279,790	152,436	54	35,923	13	91,431	33
Counterfeiting/forgery	81,880	44,891	55	27,164	33	9,825	12
Destruction/damage/vandalism	456,273	253,629	56	84,304	18	118,340	26
Embezzlement	21,657	10,685	49	10,628	49	344	2
Extortion/blackmail	2,697	1,403	52	796	30	498	18
Fraud offenses	237,564	113,744	48	71,441	30	52,379	22
Larceny/theft offenses	1,197,252	591,479	49	340,170	28	265,603	22
Motor vehicle theft	147,882	76,353	52	24,441	17	47,088	32
Robbery	101,021	84,307	83	11,427	11	5,287	5
Stolen property offenses	63,870	46,685	73	15,094	24	2,091	3
Crimes against society	1,282,810	926,380	72	342,441	27	13,989	1
Animal cruelty	3,115	1,758	56	1,113	3	244	8
Drug/narcotic offenses	1,122,416	800,877	7	314,909	28	6,630	1
Gambling offenses	1,237	972	79	207	17	58	5
Pornography/obscene material	13,399	9,617	72	3,073	23	709	5
Prostitution offenses	12,515	6,271	50	6,148	49	96	1
Weapons law violations	130,128	106,885	82	16,991	13%	6,252	5
Total	5,266,175	3,285,814	62	1,343,303	26%	637,058	12

SOURCE: FBI, 2017b, National Incident-Based Reporting System Data Tables, https://ucr.fbi.gov/nibrs/2017/tables/data-tables.

NOTES: Individuals are counted once for each offense type to which they are connected. Neither the individual data nor the offense data for the 1,665,707 incidents reported with unknown individuals were used in constructing this table.

Table 7.2 Victim-Offender Relationships in Violent Victimizations, 2012–2016

	2012		2013		2014		2015		2016	
	Count	%	Count	%	Count	%	Count	%	Count	%
Intimate Partners										
Male	128,378	16	129,438	17	133,692	21	64,403	8	78,487	13
Female	682,417	84	619,357	83	500,920	79	741,645	92	519,251	87
Subtotal	810,795	100	748,795	100	634,612	100	806,048	100	597,738	100
Other relatives										
Male	167,638	37	124,079	34	192,039	40	129,785	45	126,979	25
Female	280,960	63	243,212	66	283,227	60	158,826	55	384,894	75
Subtotal	448,598	100	367,291	100	475,266	100	288,611	100	511,873	100
Acquaintances										
Male	1,197,927	53	1,166,903	48	717,381	42	708,047	41	868,366	47
Female	1,074,590	47	1,278,196	52	991,985	58	1,013,355	59	989,030	53
Subtotal	2,272,517	100	2,445,099	100	1,709,366	100	1,721,402	100	1,857,396	100
Strangers*										
Male	1,774,501	65	1,273,201	61	1,470,820	68	913,408	50	1,420,090	64
Female	935,613	35	824,969	39	695,309	32	907,901	50	812,172	36
Subtotal	2,710,114	100	2,098,170	100	2,166,129	100	1,821,309	100	2,232,262	100
Unknown relationship*										
Male	300,574	81	198,671	69	137,087	61	98,395	64	174,283	58
Female	71,335	19	90,124	31	86,760	39	55,814	36	123,637	42
Subtotal	371,909	100	288,795	100	223,847	100	154,209	100	297,920	100
Unknown offender*										
Male	139,415	61	153,676	86	90,535	60	173,365	81	173,425	69
Female	89,246	39	24,597	14	59,816	40	41,672	19	78,716	31
Subtotal	228,661	100	178,273	100	150,351	100	215,037	100	252,141	100

* In these data, "strangers" is used when the victim did not know the offender, "unknown relationship" is used when the relationship between the victim and offender was not identified in the original crime report, and "unknown offender" is used when the offender information was unknown.

SOURCE: Bureau of Justice Statistics, 2012–2016a, National Crime Victimization Survey Analysis Tool, generated with NCVS Victimization Analysis Tool at www.bjs.gov.

qualities in women, to complement and support men. These qualities include beauty, caring, passivity, nurturance, and sexual availability to men. Because these qualities are subordinate to hegemonic masculinity, women must negotiate "doing gender" in their personal (Kelly, Pomerantz, and Currie, 2005) and professional lives (Morash and Haarr, 2012; West and Zimmerman, 1987).

The corollary to emphasized femininity is hegemonic masculinity. Readers will recall that **hegemonic masculinity** is a term that refers to how society broadly conceptualizes ideal masculinity. In the United States, one could argue this equates to attractiveness, financial independence and success, emotional and physical strength, and heterosexual prowess (Connell, 1987; Kupers, 2005). Hegemonic masculinity dominates all other identities or ways of being and, thus, those who merely "do [this] gender" are afforded significant social capital (West and Zimmerman, 1987).

To understand the formation of these deeply ingrained gender conceptions in men and women, it is important to reflect on common socialization practices in the United States. Parents begin socializing boys and girls toward these ideals before they even exit the womb. From the names assigned to females (e.g., Clementine, Gigi, Sabine) and males (e.g., Bryce, Colton, Hunter, Jackson, Silas, Spencer) to how parents manage behavior ("boys will be boys" versus "sugar and spice") to the superheroes they idolize (Pecora, 1992), children receive constant messages about gender across all aspects of life. Boys learn to be strong for others and themselves. Girls learn to be nurturing and supportive of their families. (See Active Learning Assignment 7.1.)

These messages exist across cultures as shown in a recent mixed-methods review conducted by Kågesten and colleagues (2016). In that review, the scholars found that parents and peers shaped an individual's beliefs about gender roles. Specifically, girls were socialized toward behaviors and duties aligned with dominant conceptions of femininity (e.g., childcare, passivity) while boys

---

ACTIVE LEARNING ASSIGNMENT 7.1

Doing Gender in Film

Watch the first *Twilight* film. After watching the film, answer the following questions:

1. How do Edward and Jacob perform masculinity?
2. How does Bella perform emphasized femininity?
3. Describe the relationship between Edward and Bella. Is this a healthy relationship? If so, explain how and why. If not, explain how and why.
4. Describe the relationship between Jacob and Bella. Is this a healthy relationship? If so, explain how and why. If not, explain how and why.
5. Describe how gender roles influence healthy and potentially unhealthy relationship behavior.

ACTIVE LEARNING ASSIGNMENT 7.2

Gendering Comics

Read at least three *Superman* comics either from the library or through public domain online. AS you read, consider the following questions in reference to the main characters in the story:

1. What are the roles of the male characters?
2. Are these roles essential to the story or secondary?
3. Are there patterns in the physical characteristics of the male characters? Do these patterns change depending on whether the character is good or evil?
4. Are there patterns in terms of the emotion displayed by the male characters? Do these patterns change depending on whether the character is good or evil?
5. Consider the same four questions about the female characters.
6. Discuss whether the comic book characters align with hegemonic masculinity and emphasized femininity. Fully justify your answer.

---

were socialized toward behaviors and duties that aligned with dominant conceptions of masculinity (e.g., strength). As children grow, these messages are reinforced through educational settings and interactions with peer networks where youth establish their identities. (See Active Learning Assignment 7.2.)

Upon reflection about the above information and prior chapters in this text, the role of gender in shaping criminal engagement and victimization becomes clear. Because masculinity is strongly associated with financial and personal independence and strength, engaging in violence is a constantly available route to perform gender identity in the absence of other social capital (Messerschmidt, 1997). However, using violence does not align with dominant conceptions of femininity (Connell, 1987). Therefore, violence is *normally* not an available route to perform femininity in the absence of other social capital; however, exceptions do exist (such as gangs). This does not mean women are absent from criminal engagement statistics, but that they are more represented in crimes such as prostitution that align with (or at least do not directly conflict with) dominant gender conceptions. For example, as Messerschmidt discusses, despite the deviancy attached to prostitution, it still aligns with emphasized femininity as women are sexually serving men.

In terms of victimization, because masculinity is intertwined with independence and strength, it makes intuitive sense that men who were victimized are less likely to engage in formal help-seeking (Depraetere et al., 2018) or may even resort to engaging in retaliatory violence to reassert their self-identity (Messerschmidt and Tomsen, 2018). In This cyclical "tit for tat" involving individuals who both commit crime and have crime committed against them, this pattern is specifically visible in gang violence as well as retaliatory hate crimes

(Fox, Levin, and Quinet, 2018) but is applicable to other offense types. In contrast to men's perpetration of crime and victimization, because society conceptualizes ideal femininity as passive and weak in comparison to hegemonic masculinity, it also makes intuitive sense that women are more represented in crime statistics as having crimes committed against them rather than as committing crime. Again, this is not to suggest that men are immune from victimization, but that those perpetrating crime, regardless of gender, consider women to be easier targets.

The above paragraphs have broadly presented our argument for how gender shapes both criminal engagement and victimization. We argue, in line with other scholars, that gender provides insight into why men and women are overrepresented in certain crimes aligning with hegemonic masculinity (assaults, homicide) or emphasized femininity (prostitution). Additionally, gender also shapes decisions on suitable targets, which bears on crime statistics. Now, after presenting this broad argument, we will revisit important criminological perspectives.

Victimization as a Gendered Opportunity

The opportunity perspective frames crime as resulting from a person who commits crime consciously (and by choice) meeting a prospective target in opportune circumstances in time and space. This broad perspective houses three important frameworks: crime pattern theory (Brantingham and Brantingham, 2013), routine activities theory (Cohen and Felson, 1979), and situational crime prevention (Clarke, 1997), among others. This theoretical branch is especially flexible as it explains both personal and property victimization. Moreover, these perspectives apply to both offline and online crime. Given the nature of the topic considered in this chapter, we will focus on routine activities theory and lifestyle exposure theory (Hindelang, Gottfredson, and Garofalo, 1978).

From a **routine activities theory** perspective, crime results from the convergence of a person who is motivated to commit crime, a suitable target, and the lack of a capable guardian in time and space (Cohen and Felson, 1979). For example, an individual contemplating engaging in a sexual offense (that is, a person who is motivated to commit crime) lives in a densely populated neighborhood. The person he prefers to victimize is a young woman with long brown hair, and he quickly notices a new arrival in the area who meets that description. He watches his new neighbor closely for several weeks: her arrivals, departures, and visitors. During this time, he notices that her garage opener is easily accessible in her often-unlocked car. After watching her for a few weeks, he is confident that she is often alone at night (and therefore a suitable target and lacking a guardian). One night, he breaks into her home through the garage and sexually assaults her. In short, the person motivated to commit crime and a suitable target (the neighbor) converged in time and space without a guardian to stop the crime from happening.

It is impossible to understate the applicability of routine activities theory to understanding the gendered risk of victimization. In terms of the potential system-involved person, Cohen and Felson allege that someone who wants to commit crime will weigh the benefits and consequences of their actions before engaging in an offense. To relate this to gender, men and women are constantly making rational choices in their performances every day. For men and women with limited access to other means of social capital, crime may be a practical path to both perform gender and secure resources. Secondly, by considering gender ideals, it becomes plain that this factor also shapes risk of crime. For example, since gender ideals for men emphasize independence and strength, it makes intuitive sense they dominate as system-involved individuals and as those who have offenses committed against them across confrontational offenses (e.g., aggravated assaults, homicides, robbery). On the other hand, since gender ideals for women emphasize passivity and sexual availability, it makes intuitive sense that women are overrepresented among those who have sexually motivated crimes committed against them.

Lifestyle exposure theory developed at the same time as routine activities theory. However, lifestyle exposure theory emphasizes the risk of crime stemming from certain lifestyles rather than a convergence of factors in time and space. Put simply, victimization risk increases if one engages in risky activities (e.g., criminal engagement) or if one is routinely within risky environments (e.g., lives in a crime-ridden neighborhood). Thus, from a gender perspective, men who engage in crimes to perform masculinity also elevate their own odds of victimization. Likewise, women who engage in crimes like sex work also elevate their own odds of victimization. Because these two theories overlap at the point of routine activities, they are often used together to supply a holistic explanation of victimization. (See Case Study 7.1.)

CASE STUDY 7.1

Aileen Wuornos

Research the case of Aileen Wuornos, a notorious serial killer who operated in Florida. During her trial, Wuornos claimed that she had killed her clients in self-defense. She also claimed that she had experienced repeated sexual assaults on and off throughout her life. These statements did not influence the jury, and she received the death penalty.

1. From a lifestyle/routine activities theory perspective, please explain why Wuornos experienced repeated victimizations throughout her life.
2. Theorize whether gender influenced Wuornos's criminal engagement.

Victimization as an Outcome of Gendered Socialization

In contrast to the opportunity perspective, Gottfredson and Hirschi (1990) allege that the **general theory of crime** is applicable across context and cultures. Their explanation emphasizes that failings during childhood, specifically the lack of parental management, "sets the stage" for the development of adults who are unable to restrain destructive impulses. In other words, if left unchecked by parents, children do not develop self-control and are unable to restrain themselves from rewarding opportunities like crime as adults. Relatedly, by being susceptible to criminal engagement, low-self-control adults are at an increased risk victimization (Schreck, 1999). Therefore, while this perspective centers on criminal engagement, it is also applicable in understanding victimization.

Although the role of gender is not a central tenet in the general theory of crime, it is impossible not the see its applicability in terms of criminal engagement or victimization. As we have seen, research has shown that parents socialize their children differently depending on gender (Kågesten et al., 2016). Specifically, parents watch the behavior of girls much more closely than that of boys (Raffaelli and Ontai, 2004). Moreover, adults are more accepting of aggressive behavior from boys than girls (Bowie, 2007). In contrast, displaying emotion is more accepted coming from girls than from boys (Chaplin, Cole, and Zahn-Waxler, 2005). As discussed earlier, during childhood, children are socialized toward behaviors that align with dominant gender ideals. For boys, since masculine gender ideals rationalize aggressiveness as "boys being boys" and there is less policing of boys' behavior, it makes sense that some studies find that young men are more likely to display low self-control (Botchkovar et al., 2015; Chapple, Vaske, and Hope, 2010). However, boys are also socialized to not display vulnerability, which supplies context as to why some studies find that young men do not want to report serious victimization like sexual assault (Navarro and Clevenger, 2017).

In terms of the criminal engagement and victimization of women, the general theory of crime supplies multiple insights. First, given the over-policing of women's' behavior, to combat the potential of low self-control among other behaviors, young women may meet the criminal-legal system early in life and unintentionally be "set on a path" toward deviance and victimization (Chesney-Lind and Pasko, 2013). Secondly, given the dominant gender ideals prescribe "appropriate" behavior for women, women may feel shame and hesitate to seek help after they have engaged in actions indicative of what laypersons would describe as low self-control (Branch et al., 2017). One example is a woman who declines to report experiencing nonconsensual distribution of pornography, because she is ashamed for sending the pictures in the first place and fears law enforcement will blame her. It is important to state that this perspective does not assign *blame* for offenses. Indeed, the only individual making a choice to violate another's agency is the person engaging in the offense. However, this perspective highlights potential vulnerabilities that contribute to someone's engagement in or victimization from crime. Additionally, these perspectives are applicable across demographic boundaries, which is extremely useful for examining risks within the gender binary.

Victimization as an Outcome of Structural Gender Inequality

As discussed later in this chapter, one critical factor that contributes to the risk of victimization is engaging in risky behavior, which includes criminal behavior. Therefore, theoretical perspectives that purport to explain risk of criminal engagement are also important for understanding any later risk of victimization. In this section of the chapter, we will examine a few perspectives that are particularly crucial for understanding the role of gender in one's life course: power-control theory (Hagan, Gillis, and Simpson, 1990), the liberation thesis (Giordano and Cernkovich, 1979), and the economic marginality hypothesis.

According to the **power-control theory** (PCT) perspective, patriarchal families, and especially mothers within them, exert less instrumental and relational control over sons than over daughters. As a result, sons in patriarchal families grow up to be more accepting of risk taking, such as engaging in crime, than daughters do. On the other hand, in more egalitarian families where parental control does not vary by children's gender, willingness to engage in risk-taking behavior like crime also does not vary between boys and girls. Consequently, PCT asserts that men's dominance in criminal activity is a function of wider gendered socialization practices, largely the mother's child-rearing practices, that constrain girls' risk-taking both in terms of attitude and overt behavior. Likewise, as society lurches toward a more egalitarian framework, like equal participation in the workforce, these "controls" have loosened within homes mirroring that dynamic, and young women's acceptance of engaging in risky behavior (like crime) has increased.

After PCT was proposed, there was considerable discussion among academics about its utility in explaining women's increasing involvement in crime. To reassess the perspective, scholars examined data from an upper-socioeconomic neighborhood in Toronto (Hagan, Gillis, and Simpson, 1990). To reassess PCT, the study included variables designed to determine marital power, such as decisions on wife's employment, where the family should live, and so on. The scholars found that a substantial percentage of sampled families aligned more closely with an egalitarian dynamic than a patriarchal one. In terms of PCT, the scholars found support for the perspective that boys and girls of egalitarian families are equally likely to engage in risk-taking behavior like crime.

Scholars have also examined the influential power of patriarchal systems on life pathways via involvement in the criminal-legal system (Schulze and Bryan,

2017). To support the importance of this line of research, the scholars note several considerations:

1. The criminal-legal system itself remains very patriarchal and, by its nature, is designed to correct "deviant" behavior (akin to the role of parents within family units).
2. Scholarly work continues to indicate that the gender of the system-involved person matters for system involvement and sentencing.
3. The formation of the juvenile justice system in particular was meant to steer "incorrigible" youth toward gender-congruent behavior.

As a result, the authors assert that PCT is a practical framework to apply in their investigation of juvenile delinquents.

Ultimately, Schulze and Bryan's research yielded important findings, but there was marginal support for the central tenets of PCT. In terms of status offenses, while gender was a crucial factor, it was important only in terms of its coupling with race. In other words, status offense charges were less likely among white boys, boys of color, and white girls than among Black girls. In considering overall offenses, gender and mother-headed households were important factors, but they behaved counter to the tenets of PCT. Put another way, charges (not the behaviors themselves) were more likely for boys than for girls, where one might expect the opposite result given the patriarchal nature of the home, and this finding did not fluctuate based on who was the head of the household.

In a similar investigation about PCT and Native American youth, scholars found more direct support for PCT (Eitle, Niedrist, and Eitle, 2014). They found that several factors aggravated the risk of young girls engaging in general, property, and delinquent offenses. These aggravating factors included growing up in a home environment with weak parental control, growing up in a home environment that was more egalitarian than patriarchal, and engaging in risk-taking behavior. Thus, the scholars found that stronger control over daughters in terms of general family structure (that is, patriarchal structure), and by fathers directly, decreased the risk of girls engaging in delinquent acts.

The liberation thesis and the economic marginality hypothesis assume an even broader perspective when examining deviance at the micro level. The **liberation thesis** is grounded in the work of Adler (1975) and Simon (1975), who theorized that women's increasing participation in deviance stemmed from their greater freedom to navigate social life vis-à-vis access to divorce, workforce participation, and so on. The thinking was that women, given their increasing liberation and improving social positions, would be emboldened to become involved in all aspects of life, including deviant networks. However, as Hunnicutt and Broidy (2004) note, there is mixed support for this perspective in view of statistics that show women are overrepresented among low socioeconomic strata. Moreover, research continues to show that one of the reasons women engage in deviance is to combat a depressed economic situation, and this finding led to the development of the economic marginality hypothesis.

The **economic marginality hypothesis** challenges the notion that women engage in crime because of an improved social position, and instead alleges their involvement in crime is the result of a *worse* social position (Hunnicutt and Broidy, 2004). The viability of this perspective is supported by the difficulty of accurately assessing the liberation thesis and statistics that continue to show that women significantly suffer during "liberating" events like divorce. In fact, the term *feminization of poverty* points to the fact that women, especially women with children, are overrepresented among those struggling in poverty (Fontenot, Semega, and Kollar, 2018). For this reason, among others, many women stay trapped in abusive relationships: they fear living in poverty and not being able to support their children (Postmus et al., 2011). Thus, unlike the liberation thesis, the economic marginality hypothesis asserts that women relegated to the outskirts of social life engage in deviance to overcome increasing dire social conditions.

In an innovative study that assessed both perspectives, Hunnicutt and Broidy (2004) found that each framework contributed to the understanding of women's deviance. In terms of the liberation thesis, the scholars found the following factors decreased the risk of conviction for women: increasing number of dependents and greater public spending on education. However, divorce and greater involvement in the industrial sector increased the risk of conviction. These results broadly align with the liberation thesis in that women with few or no child-rearing responsibilities (that is, few or no dependents), who are not in a marriage with other joint responsibilities, and who are actively involved in the workforce may engage in deviance as a result of their "liberated" position.

Regarding the economic marginality hypothesis, Hunnicutt and Broidy found support for this framework as well. According to their results, as women's involvement in the service industry increased, their conviction rates also increased. Interestingly, women's conviction rates also increased as men's unemployment increased. The only factors that were correlated with lower conviction rates of women were increases in use of government services and men's employment in service industries. Taking these factors into account, depressed economic conditions (that is, women's service work, which typically pays less, and men's unemployment) are associated with criminal engagement. To reiterate, these findings are important given the known relationship between offending and victimization. By understanding what leads individuals to engage in crime, scholars can also understand increases in risk of victimization.

The above paragraphs have presented a broad overview of key gender concepts and theoretical perspectives used to understand offending and victimization. We will now shift to several specific offenses where the role of gender is important within violent crime: assaults, homicide, robbery, and sexual violence. To supply a robust explanation, the following paragraphs revisit how gender influences choices about *who* is targeted and *why*. As you consider the following, remember the role of opportunity theory and the general theory of crime in framing these events.

GENDER AND VIOLENT CRIME VICTIMIZATION

The FBI's four violent crime offense types are murder/nonnegligent manslaughter, aggravated assault (an attempted or completed attack that results in extreme injury), forcible rape, and robbery; see chapter 3 for more information. In each of these offense types, except for forcible rape, men dominate among system-involved individuals and those against whom crimes are committed (see table 7.3). In terms of murder and nonnegligent manslaughter, 87 percent of incidents included a man who committed the crime against another man. For 2011–2014 and 2016, most people who experienced aggravated assault and robbery were also men (BJS, 2011–2016b). The only crime where the pattern flipped was rape and sexual violence (BJS, 2011–2016b).

Aggravated Assault and Murder/Nonnegligent Manslaughter

The overrepresentation of men among those who commit aggravated assault and murder/nonnegligent manslaughter as well as their targets aligns with

Table 7.3   Number of Violent Victimizations by Sex, 2011–2016

	2011 total	% of total	2012 total	% of total	2013 total	% of total	2014 total	% of total	2015 total	% of total	2016 total	% of total
Aggravated assault												
Male	600,274	57	573,113	58	605,573	61	660,072	60	358,483	44	548,817	51
Female	453,117	43	422,993	42	388,647	39	432,019	40	458,274	56	535,525	49
Total	1,053,391	100	996,106	100	994,220	100	1,092,091	100	816,757	100	1,084,342	100
Rape and sexual assault												
Male	34,804	14	131,259	38	34,057	11	28,032	10	62,916	15	51,408	16
Female	209,384	86	215,570	62	266,107	89	256,313	90	368,921	85	272,040	84
Total	244,188	100	346,830	100	300,165	100	284,345	100	431,837	100	323,449	100
Robbery												
Male	339,509	61	497,662	67	349,239	54	395,544	60	282,411	49	262,324	52
Female	217,749	39	244,094	33	296,406	46	268,668	40	296,166	51	238,359	48
Total	557,258	100	741,756	100	645,645	100	664,211	100	578,578	100	500,682	100

SOURCE: Bureau of Justice Statistics, 2011–2016b, generated with NCVS Victimization Analysis Tool at www.bjs.gov.

prior discussions on the role of gender in shaping criminal engagement and victimization. Violence, as discussed, is a resource that men can use to assert their masculinity in the absence of other available resources (Messerschmidt, 1997). Since dominant gender ideals associate masculinity with strength, it is not unusual for men against whom crimes are committed to resort to violence to reestablish their identity (Anderson, 1999; Mullins, Wright, and Jacobs, 2004). In some situations, this can appear as a cyclical tit for tat, where men alternate between committing crime and having crime committed against them, as in gang violence. In other situations, this can appear an outburst of violence where men who are victimized target individuals they perceive to be at fault for their harm (real or imagined), as in intimate partner abuse, retaliatory hate crimes, and mass shootings (Fox, Levin, and Quinet, 2018; Kimmel, 2017), which will be discussed in the following pages.

Gangs

Gangs are typically hypermasculine organizations (Beesley and McGuire, 2009), aligning more with the extreme form of hegemonic masculinity called **toxic masculinity** (Kupers, 2005) since status is accumulated through the flouting of conventional rules and the willingness to use violence (Messerschmidt, 1997; Thornberry et al., 1993). Not only is status achieved through violence, but it is supported through the fear of more violence (Mullins, Wright, and Jacobs, 2004). The omnipresence of fear and the willingness to use violence are particularly important to ward off challenges from others who seek status themselves (). As a result, this destructive culture leads to an increased risk of criminal engagement and victimization for all involved. Indeed, given the toxic masculinity culture, it is impermissible to contact formal entities of social control after one has been victimized; instead, victimized men must use violence to rectify slights. Should a man fail to reclaim his status, he exposes himself to further victimization by his own gang and outsiders (Anderson, 1999).

Realizing that hypermasculinity typically predominates among gangs, women must negotiate their roles very carefully in these organizations. On one hand, while engaging in deviance itself is counter to notions of emphasized femininity (Connell, 1987) and thus provides space for women to establish alternate versions of femininity, they still experience pressure to conform to cultural norms that generally do not place them on equal footing with men gang members (Mullins, 2006). This pressure leads to women engaging in conventional activities associated with femininity like managing their physical appearance, caring for children, and showing loyalty to their partner lest they risk being outcast and exposed to violence (Laidler and Hunt, 2001). When they are directly involved in deviant activities, they typically fulfill supportive roles (e.g., decoys to distract targets through sexual encounters), which again underscores their subservient position. Thus, as it does for men, gender shapes women's behaviors and involvement in gangs. However, in contrast to men, the subordinate role assigned to women puts them at an increased risk of experiencing general violence as well as sexual violence both as a retaliatory action and in service to the organization.

Intimate Partner Abuse

Another arena where gender shapes violent encounters is within the home in intimate partner abuse situations. Since the 1970s, scholars have increasingly called attention to how prevalent, yet underreported, intimate partner abuse is in the United States. Although national studies continue to show that most individuals who commit domestic violence are men and most individuals who experience domestic violence are women, intimate partner abuse crosses all demographic boundaries (Smith et al., 2017). The challenge with addressing intimate partner abuse, however, is that it is a multifaceted social problem (World Health Organization, 2018). Unfortunately, a strong, even toxic, adherence to societal gender ideals of hegemonic masculinity and emphasized femininity is simply one part of the problem (Dobash and Dobash, 1998). Yet, if the problem is ever going to be truly halted, we must understand this vantage point.

In terms of understanding patterns related to men, studies continue to show that most intimate partner abuse is man to woman. For example, NISVS data from 2010–2012 shows most perpetrators of sexual violence against women (through contact sexual violence, forced penetration, rape, and sexual coercion) and stalking were men who were current or former intimate partners. Additionally, more than 37 percent of surveyed women, or about 45 million, had been victimized at some time by intimate partners (Smith et al., 2017).

Scholars within the field have long asserted that the most insidious types of intimate partner abuse are grounded in men's desires to control their partners (Dobash and Dobash, 1998; Johnson, 2008), which is particularly clear in couples where there is a strong adherence to traditional gender norms that subordinate women to men (Connell, 1987). In these families, gender shapes male performance of masculinity and femininity in two important ways. First, due to the strong association between familial control and self-identity, hegemonic men may perceive any rupture to the family unit as a seismic threat to their own identity (Websdale, 2010). Following a divorce or a shameful event, hegemonic masculine men may resort to extreme violence to reassert their identity. Second, due to the strong adherence between emphasized femininity and family caretaker roles, individuals fleeing violence—particularly those who adhere to religious backgrounds discouraging of divorce—may meet societal barriers (Jankowski et al., 2018).

According to Websdale (2010), there are two types of family annihilators: *livid coercive hearts* and *civil reputable hearts*. The former "heart" is an individual who is typically already abusive within the home, and the homicide is

ACTIVE LEARNING ASSIGNMENT 7.3

Spotting Gender Dynamics in Popular Music

Please watch two music videos that depict intimate partner abuse: one from the vantage point of male-to-female abuse and one from the vantage point of female-to-male abuse. For example, Eminem and Rihanna's *Love the Way You Lie* and the Dixie Chicks *Goodbye, Earl* work well for this assignment. As the videos are playing, consider how the men and women are depicted in each song in terms of gender roles. Also, look for any behaviors that are supportive of myths about intimate partner abuse and rape. Finally, and most importantly, consider the whole framing of the video and whether it minimizes the violence discussed in the song. After watching both videos, consider whether there are implicit or overt messages in the songs that align with class material. If so, identify those messages and relate it to the material. If not, please discuss the areas of disagreement with the material.

the ultimate escalation of that violence. These cases often involve men who feel a sense of control and ownership over the partner and children, which aligns with dominant gender ideals already discussed, but on rare occasions the homicide will be committed by a woman. In contrast, the civil reputable heart engages in homicide to avoid embarrassment and shame. In this case, the sense of ownership over the partner and children is still present, but there is also a twisted desire to protect them from future harm. Again, while most civil reputable hearts in Websdale's (2010) analysis were men, a greater number were women compared to the livid coercive category. This makes sense given dominant gender ideals that assign women as the primary caretakers of their families.

As showed by Websdale's (2010) study, a strong adherence to hegemonic masculinity and emphasized femininity within the home sets the stage for extreme violence against women and children. However, these same gender ideals also influence and shape women's violence toward men, which, despite underreporting, studies continue to show exists. For example, according to the NISVS for 2010–2012, most individuals who committed forced penetration of men (50.5%) and sexual coercion of men (66.3%) were current or former intimate partners (lifetime reports; Smith et al., 2017). In each of those categories, most individuals who committed the crime were women: 78.5 percent and 81.6, percent respectively. Most individuals who committed incidents of stalking men were current or former intimate partners (42.8%; relative to four other categories) and women (45.7%; relative to men [43%] and multiple individuals [8.3%]). Finally, about 31 percent of sampled men reported experiencing intimate partner abuse during their lifetime.

One of the most troubling aspects of the role of gender in shaping engagement in and victimization from intimate partner abuse is that these dominant conceptions act as unique barriers to help-seeking among men who were victimized. The most obvious barrier is overcoming the common misconception that "real" men are *incapable* of suffering abuse, especially physical abuse, and manipulation at the hands of women due to their strength (Bates, 2019). Thus, if men are abused, they must be to blame for the violence (Taylor and Sorenson, 2005) or they "secretly wanted" the event to happen, as in the case of men who experience sexual assault (Rumney, 2008). These misconceptions limit the ability of men to escape violence and seek help from formal entities of social control, because they may fear encountering skepticism (Drijber, Reijnders, and Ceelen, 2013). Thus, while gender frames engagement in intimate partner abuse, it also affects those who experience it as well.

Retaliatory Hate Crimes

Toxic adherence to gender ideals also underscores what Fox, Levin, and Quinet (2018) refer to as retaliatory hate crimes. As described by Fox, Levin, and Quinet, a retaliatory hate crime occurs when an individual enacts revenge for a real or imagined slight (such as a crime, insult, job loss, or rejection of sexual advances) against an individual or group perceived to be "at fault" for that slight. Again, although this is not explicitly related to gender, the connection to dominant ideals about masculinity is readily visible. As previously discussed, given that hegemonic masculinity prescribes ideal routes to perform gender, all other identities are inherently subordinated to that dominant conception, such as gay men and men of color, as well as women (Connell, 1987). Thus, a hegemonic male who perceives a slight from an "inferior" other may react violently to combat feeling emasculated—particularly if the event occurs in front of witnesses (Messerschmidt, 1997). This need for revenge can also be set off by an actual criminal victimization (Fox, Levin, and Quinet, 2018). In either event, this type of offense can result in horrific violence (as in the murder of Matthew Shepard; see Case Study 7.2) or set off a cyclical tit for tat between those that commit crime and those who have crime committed against them.

Retaliatory hate crimes can manifest as crimes against persons (such as assault, murder, rape), crimes against property (such as arson, burglary, larceny-theft), or even crimes against society. According to statistics published by the FBI there were more than 7,000 hate crimes in 2017 across those categories, but this is likely an undercount because agencies voluntarily report these data, and assessing whether something qualifies as a hate crime can be difficult if evidence is lacking (Fox, Levin, and Quinet, 2018). Regardless of those limitations, these data show that hate crimes span the gamut of offenses, with most consisting of assault (54%), intimidation (44.2%), and destruction to property (75%) (see table 7.4).

The FBI data shows that most of these hate crimes were motivated by an individual biases against the targeted person's race/ethnicity (about 60%),

Table 7.4 FBI Hate Crime Incidents by Offense Type, 2017

Offense type	Incidents*	%
Hate crimes against persons	**4,090**	
Murder and nonnegligent manslaughter	12	0.29
Rape	23	0.56
Aggravated assault	788	19.3
Simple assault	1,433	35.
Intimidation	1,807	44.2
Human trafficking, commercial sex acts	1	0.02
Other	26	0.64
Hate crimes against property	**3,115**	
Robbery	157	5
Burglary	145	5
Larceny-theft	326	10
Motor vehicle theft	41	1
Arson	42	1
Destruction/damage/vandalism	2,325	75
Other	79	3
Hate crimes against society	**238**	
Total	**7,175**	

SOURCE: FBI, 2017b, National Incident-Based Reporting System Data Tables, https://ucr.fbi.gov/nibrs/2017/tables/data-tables.

NOTE: *The actual number of incidents is 7,175. However, the column figures do not add to the total because some incidents include more than one offense type, and these are counted in each appropriate offense type category.

religion (about 21%), or sexual orientation (about 16%). However, individuals also targeted people based on gender bias as well: gender-identity bias (about 2%) and gender bias (about 1%). Even though these percentages are a small part of the total number of hate crimes, there were still 28 women victimized simply for being women. Likewise, there were 26 men victimized simply for being men. Again, these are incomplete figures. Aside from the case of Matthew Shepard, there are several recent examples of retaliatory hate crimes grounded in gender that illustrate the role of societal ideals in shaping engagement and victimization.

In terms of man-to-woman violence, Elliot Rodger's specific targeting of women whom he felt "wrongly" rejected his advances is an example of how adherence to toxic masculinity can propel a retaliatory hate crime. As discussed in chapter 3, before Rodger engaged in a mass shooting at the University of California Santa Barbara, he uploaded a lengthy video in which he described his anger at women for preferring "inferior" men to him (SyndicatedNews, 2014). He could not understand why women did not pursue him, because he was the "supreme gentlemen" he says in video, signaling the ideal notions of masculinity as the chivalrous complement to women. He notes further in the video that he intends to "punish" these women as he seeks revenge for the years of denial he "unjustly" experienced, which again relates back to notions of masculinity and perceived entitlements to a woman's affections (Connell, 1987). Rodger carried out his murderous intentions, killing seven people including two women (CBS News, 2014). Misogynistic subcultures continue to glorify the shooting (BBC News, 2018).

Woman-to-man retaliatory hate crimes are exceedingly rare. However, one could use the case of Amy Bishop as a loosely related example. She was a faculty member at the University of Alabama in Huntsville who did not obtain tenure within her department (Keefe, 2013). As any academic will tell you, not obtaining tenure is an earth-shattering event as tenure is essentially job security for life, barring any major crimes or grievances. After learning of the vote, Bishop sat through an entire faculty meeting with her colleagues. As the meeting was ending, Bishop stood up and began to shoot her colleagues one by one. If Bishop had targeted colleagues of a specific group out of bias (such as only the men as an act of misandry) and as an act of revenge for voting against her, it would qualify as a retaliatory hate crime (Fox, Levin, and Quinet, 2018). However, there is no sign that bias motivated Bishop.

The rarity of woman-to-man retaliatory hate crimes does not mean that women do not perpetrate these offenses across the gender binary. According to NCVS data from 2011–2015, about 61 percent of those that committed hate crimes were men and 17 percent were women (Masucci and Langton, 2017). Men also experience these offenses. NCVS data from 2011–2015 shows that about 52 percent of those two experienced hate crimes were men and 48 percent were women (Masucci and Langton, 2017). These data show that men, as well as women, are targeted by other men.

Mass Murder

There is growing awareness that gender underscores mass murder not only within the home, but outside it as well. However, unlike domestic homicides, women are rarely mass murderers (Fox, Levin, and Quinet, 2018). Indeed, according to a comprehensive mass-shooting database that tallies incidents from 1982 to 2019, a woman was the perpetrator in only 3 out of 109 incidents (Follman, Aronsen, and Pan, 2019). There is also growing awareness that women may be particularly vulnerable to victimization through mass murder.

Despite the change in setting from domestic to public mass murder, the argument about the role of gender in shaping engagement in and victimization from crime stays the same in terms of men. In other words, there is growing awareness that a strong adherence to hegemonic masculine ideals, or even toxic masculinity, sets the stage for men to feel entitled to various forms of social capital (e.g., financial wealth, prestige) and social achievements (e.g., successful family, successful job). For some men that do not achieve these entitlements, their anger can turn outward toward "inferior others" in the form of what Kimmel (2017) refers to as aggrieved entitlement. This violence serves both as a method of retribution and as a route to reassert their masculinity in the most extreme manner possible: through mass murder. Because all other ways of being are inherently subordinated to hegemonic masculinity, those with alternative forms of masculinity (such as gay men, men of color) as well as women are at a heightened risk of victimization.

By again revisiting the mass murder perpetrated by Elliot Rodger, one can easily see how hegemonic men who feel they have been denied their "entitled" female affections, according to emphasized femininity, may use extreme violence as the ultimate expression of power. Unfortunately, Rodger's mass murder is not the only example. In yet another example, a man tried to kill seven people in a yoga studio in Tallahassee, Florida, and was successful in taking the lives of two of them (McLaughlin, 2018). The individual had a history of engaging in sexual violence against women, and the details of the events clearly show that he felt entitled to women's bodies. A criminologist attuned to the role of gender in extreme violence would argue that these events stemmed from a toxic adherence to hegemonic masculinity in which these men felt dejected and infuriated at rejection from women. As a result, these men asserted their power in the most extreme manner possible: by shooting those who "wronged" them (Kimmel, 2017).

Robbery

As outlined in tables 7.1 and 7.3, most people who commit robberies and most people against whom robberies are committed are men. Although there is less research on the role of gender in shaping robbery, we argue that the patterns outlined in the prior sections are just as applicable in this offense type. In other words, while there are some similarities driving the involvement of men and women in robbery (such as deviant pursuit of resources; Brookman et al., 2007), as in aggravated assault or homicide (Websdale, 2010), there are important gender considerations as well. Likewise, while the involvement in robbery increases the risk of victimization for both men and women, gender also bears on this risk.

Brookman and colleagues (2007) conducted one of the most recent studies on the role of gender in shaping robbery perpetration and victimization in the United Kingdom. Despite the difference in geography, the scholars found that the reasons that drive men and women to engage in this offense are applicable across cultures: (1) to assert strength, (2) to build social capital within their network, (3) to secure resources, and (4) to subvert potential challenges from others. Although their study found several areas of overlap in terms of perpetration, one area where gender difference appeared was in preferences about targeted people. More specifically, men rarely targeted women in robberies, which relates back to dominant gender ideals of hegemonic masculinity and the idea that using force against women is undesirable because, according to emphasized femininity, they are more vulnerable and weaker (Mullins, Wright, and Jacobs, 2006). This tendency, in of itself, adds context why most individuals who commit the crime and most who experience this offense are men.

The prior gender dynamic was not as plain among women who robbed, who reported targeting men and women both as crimes of opportunity and to enact revenge for offenses (Brookman et al., 2007). Yet, what is interesting is that women who engaged in robbery, like their male counterparts, were aware of dominant gender ideals and were skillful at using them in their victimization of others. For example, some women who robbed were less concerned about law enforcement intervention upon targeting a man, because "they [men] won't be able to go to the police and say some girl's just robbed me. Especially if they got a bit of street cred" (875). In another example, some women robbed during other offenses (e.g., sex work) where the "mark" was off guard and inherently vulnerable to the attack. Finally, women who robbed were selective in their reliance on weapons and used these tools more when targeting men, who posed greater physical threats, than when targeting women. Considering these findings, while there was great similarity in the motivations underscoring robbery, the method by which robbers selected and victimized others does point to a wider recognition of the unwritten characteristics associated with femininity and masculinity that extend across geographic boundaries.

Sexual Violence

Like intimate partner abuse, rape and sexual violence tend to cross genders in terms of those who commit crimes and who are victimized by them. In other words, while most perpetrators are men, most people who experience rape or sexual violence are women who know their attacker (BJS, 2012–2016b; FBI, 2017b). For instance, according to NISVS data from 2010–2012, 36.3 percent of women reported experiencing contact sexual violence within their lifetime, which amounts to over 43 million women (Smith et al., 2017). Looking across offense categories, most offenses were committed by acquaintances or current or former intimate partners: forced penetration (acquaintance = 26.8%; intimate partner = 48.6%), rape (acquaintance = 44.9%; intimate partner = 47.1%), sexual coercion (acquaintance = 23.5%; intimate partner = 74.7%), and unwanted sexual contact (acquaintance = 47.6%; intimate partner = 23.1%). Across each category, over 90 percent of perpetrators were men.

The above statistics are not meant to suggest that women never perpetrate crimes toward men, or that men do not experience rape regardless of perpetrator gender. According to the NISVS data from 2010–2012, across lifetime reports of rape of men, almost 10 percent of perpetrators were women (affecting 160,000 men) and 86.5 percent of perpetrators were men (affecting 1.4 million men). In terms of other sexual offenses against men aside from rape, women who perpetrated outnumbered men who perpetrated in terms of forced penetration of someone else (78.5% were female perpetrators), sexual coercion (about 82% were female perpetrators), and unwanted sexual contact (53% were female perpetrators). However, men who perpetrated crimes against men outnumbered women in terms of noncontact unwanted sexual experiences (48.3% versus 37.6%). Given that sexual violence among men is heavily underreported, it is extremely likely these figures are not representative of full scope of the problem (Stemple and Meyer, 2014). To understand the role of gender in shaping perpetration and victimization, we will revisit key concepts reiterated throughout this chapter.

Women's experiences with sexual violence outside and within families, despite years of progress toward achieving a more egalitarian society, can be framed through extreme adherence to the gender ideals that continue to dominate the wider culture (Murnen, Wright, and Kaluzny, 2002). As we discussed earlier in this chapter, dominant gender ideals associate masculinity with independence, sexual prowess, and strength, with extreme forms of these ideals treading into toxic masculinity. Given these ideals, sexual intimacy is deeply connected with masculinity. Additionally, because all other ways of being are subordinate to that dominant conception, emphasized femininity stresses passivity and sexual responsiveness to hegemonic men. In other words, emphasized femininity supports the broader patriarchal structure and calls for yielding to men's desires. This framing, which prior research supports, adds context to why sexual violence toward women persists within and outside of family.

Adherence to traditional gender ideals, particularly an extreme adherence, also frames why men who are sexually victimized do not report these events. Because laypersons within the United States associate masculinity with sexual prowess and strength, myths abound about rape of men being physically impossible because of biology, physical strength, and sexual desires that are universal, which act as barriers to help-seeking and official reporting. The prior barrier becomes even more complicated in offenses in which both the person committing the assault and the person who has the assault committed against them are men. In that case, dominant misunderstandings and myths about sexual violence can lead the man who was victimized to feel that their sexuality will be questioned if they report the assault (Aosved, Long and Voller, 2011). Thus, not only must men who were sexually victimized contend with locating resources and services specific to their unique needs, but they also must process the palpable fear that others will dismiss their assault as "not possible" because of conceptions associated with masculinity.

Dominant gender ideals shape engagement in and victimization from sexual violence. We argue that men are overrepresented among those who commit crime and are justice-involved, regardless of the gender of the person sexually assaulted, because sexuality is intimately associated with masculinity. Therefore, in the absence of other social capital, showing sexual dominance is a method to perform masculinity. Because these dominant gender ideals assign women as the complement to masculinity, they are vulnerable to this victimization. On the other hand, if men experience sexual assault, these same ideals pose unique barriers in their help-seeking and reporting, which adds context as to why this offense is still underreported—especially among men.

SUMMARY

In this chapter, we argue that widely held gender conceptions shape engagement in crimes as well as why certain people are targeted. This process starts early in life through parental socialization practices that excuse aggressive behavior from young men as "boys will be boys" while encouraging passivity in young women as "sugar and spice." Considering these practices, it should not be surprising that masculinity continues to be defined in terms of aggressiveness, sexual prowess, and strength into adulthood, which can have destructive consequences. Men with limited access to social capital may resort to violence as a method to "do gender." Put another way, when an interpersonal problem occurs, emasculated men may resort to performing gender by engaging in violence to reassert their identity. Unfortunately, the targets of the violence are often individuals considered "inferior" to the hegemonic male (such as those with alternative masculinities and women); the instigator may also expose himself to victimization. From any of these vantage points, it is impossible to ignore the role of gender in shaping both criminal engagement and victimization.

The Victimization of Individuals Who Identify as LGBTQIA+

KEY TERMS
- Affordable Care Act
- Black Lives Matter
- Black Trans Lives Matter
- internalized homophobia
- Matthew Shepard and James Byrd Jr. Hate Crimes Prevention Act
- minority stress
- misgendered
- National Coalition of Anti-Violence Programs
- *Obergefell v. Hodges*
- religious exemption laws
- Trevor Project

LEARNING OBJECTIVES
- Understand how discrimination and harassment of LGBTQIA+ individuals can translate into different types of victimization.
- Be able to identify systematic ways that LGBTQIA+ individuals experience victimization.
- Recognize the issues that LGBTQIA+ individuals face when seeking help with victimization.

Individuals who identify as LGBTQIA+ face higher victimization rates than heterosexual and cisgender men and women face, and the circumstances surrounding their victimization can differ. This is often a result of bias, bigotry, or misunderstanding of LGBTQIA+ individuals by law enforcement, criminal-legal personnel, and the public. In this chapter, discrimination, bullying and harassment victimizations of individuals within these communities will be covered. Specific crimes committed against these communities in the form of cybercrimes and hate crimes will also be presented, along with how specific victimizations such as intimate partner violence and sexual assault differ for this population. LGBTQIA+ people have endured many hardships when it comes to their treatment in the criminal-legal system (as discussed in chapter 5). This chapter will also examine the interactions with the criminal-legal system but from the perspective of LGBTQIA+ individuals who have had offenses committed against them. The victimization of and discrimination against LGBTQIA+ people is not limited to the United States. Global victimization, such as the persecution of and violence and abuse committed against individuals who identify as LGBTQIA+ in other countries will also be discussed.

DISCRIMINATION

Discrimination has been a pervasive issue for those within the LGBTQIA+ communities. Discrimination can make them more vulnerable to victimization. Legal battles to end discrimination and improve the treatment of individuals within these communities have been won, but there are still battles to be fought. Currently, nineteen states (and the District of Columbia) have laws to prohibit discrimination based on sexual orientation and gender identity in employment, housing, and/or public accommodations. However, the remaining thirty-one states lack laws that *explicitly* prohibit discrimination against people who identify as LGBTQIA+ (American Civil Liberties Union, 2019). Without explicit language barring discrimination based on sexual orientation or gender identity, there are ways in which discrimination can still legally exist and be harmful.

Individuals who are part of the LGBTQIA+ communities who are denied employment, housing, and public spaces may be criminalized, as they can be arrested and find themselves with little or no legal recourse. In addition, there are consequences for individuals without the legal protection of the law that can cause victimization, as sanctioned by the government. The US Department of Health and Human Services (HHS) provides over $500 billion in grants each year for food, healthcare, homeless shelters, elder care, and violence prevention as well as other life-saving programs. The Trump administration in August 2020 successfully pushed for modifications to the nondiscrimination protections laid out by Section 1557 of the **Affordable Care Act.** This law, proposed by President Obama in 2010, prohibited discrimination against individuals based on race, color, national origin, age, disability, and sex, including gender identity, which it defined as "male, female, neither or a combination of male and female." But the 2020 modifications allowed discrimination against individuals based on who they are. The Civil Rights Act and other federal laws prohibit the HHS from discrimination based on race, color, national origin, disability, and age. However, the new rule allowed service providers that receive HHS federal grant funding to discriminate based on sexual orientation, gender identity, sex, and/or religion (Movement Advancement Project, 2020); the Trump-era changes were struck down by the US Supreme Court in 2021 (Office for Civil Rights, 2021)

This rule went into effect during a global pandemic when individuals within the LGBTQIA+ communities were in dire need of healthcare. The alteration to the Affordable Care Act allowed individuals to be refused treatment and could prevent them from seeking treatment, which could be life threatening. It was particularly dangerous for individuals of color because research has shown that Black Americans who contract COVID-19 are more likely to die from the disease than are white Americans (Godoy and Wood, 2020.

Other government decisions have also affected those within the LGBTQIA+ communities. In 2015, a Supreme Court ruling, *Obergefell v. Hodges*, in favor of marriage equality was a major victory for same-sex couples, granting them the same rights and privileges as heterosexual couples. However, there still ways in which states have been able to keep or enact laws that are discriminatory in regard to services that can be rendered. One of the main ways that LGBTQIA+ can be discriminated against is through religious exemption laws. **Religious exemption laws** give businesses and organizations the right to not serve LGBTQIA+ people or to not allow them access to certain services if doing so would go against their religion or beliefs. Privately owned and operated transportation and personal services businesses as well as adoption and health-care agencies can withhold services from LGBTQIA+ people if the owners deem it to be against their religion or beliefs to serve them. Those who persist in trying to obtain these services can be arrested for such things as trespassing, loitering, or disturbing the peace and have no legal recourse to receive these services or benefits.

Most notably, in 2018, a Supreme Court case upheld religious exemption laws, setting a nationwide precedent that business owners can discriminate against individuals based on their own personal religious beliefs. In this case, a Colorado baker, Jack Phillips, refused to make a wedding cake for a same-sex couple. Initially, Phillips was found to be in violation of the Colorado law that bars discrimination based on race, sex, marital status, or sexual orientation. However, the Supreme Court ruled that Phillips was within his legal rights to decline service to the couple based on the First Amendment. This ruling allows businesses to refuse services to customers whose sexual orientation or gender identity violates the owners' personal religious beliefs. (See Active Learning Assignment 8.1.)

[handwritten margin note: Masterpiece Cake Shop v. Colorado]

These policies can be detrimental to individuals within LGBTQIA+ communities, especially those living in small town or rural areas, where there may not be many businesses or agencies to serve their needs. For example, religious exemption laws can pose difficulties in terms of elder care, hospice, and funerals. If a private run agency can refuse service based on religious beliefs, an elderly LGBTQIA+ individual who needs home care or hospice may not be able to receive it. Or an individual is seeking to bury their same-sex or transgender partner may be refused service at the only local funeral home. This is of particular concern as the United States has an aging population. By the year 2050, there will be an estimated 83.7 million people over the age of 65, among them an estimated 2.7 million people who identify as LGBTQIA+ adults (Movement Advancement Project, 2020).

A federal court decision allowed openly transgender individuals to serve in the military as of January 1, 2018. However, in January 2019, the Supreme Court ruled that openly transgender individuals should be banned or disqualified from service in the military, with the following exceptions:

ACTIVE LEARNING ASSIGNMENT 8.1

Colorado Cake Baker: Another Allegation of Discrimination

Read the following article in *USA Today* and watch the video in it about the second allegation against Jack Phillips for discrimination against LGBTQIA+ people: https://www.usatoday.com/story/news/nation/2018/12/19/colorado-cake-baker-jack-phillips-faces-another-lgbtq-bias-allegation/2362740002/.
   Answer the following questions:

1. Do you believe that Jack Phillips should have the right to deny service to an individual who is transgender? Why or why not?
2. What is your opinion of the assertion by Jack Phillips and his attorney that Jack is being targeted and bullied by the Division of Civil Rights and the Colorado Rights Commission?
3. Do you think that Jack Phillips's refusal to serve the LGBTQIA+ community will help or hurt his business? Please explain.
4. Do you believe that businesses should be able to choose who they serve based on religion or religious beliefs? Why not?
5. How do you think you would feel if a business refused to serve you based on your sexual orientation or gender identity?

---

1. Individuals who will serve as the sex they were assigned at birth;
2. Individuals who have been stable in their sex for three years (after surgery and hormone treatments);
3. Individuals who were diagnosed with gender dysphoria after entering the military but do not require a change of gender and remain deployable for duty;
4. Individuals who were diagnosed before the date of the policy change and are able to serve while receiving treatment;
5. Individuals who receive a waiver from the Department of Defense on a case-by-case basis.

The policy also prohibits individuals who have had gender-affirming surgery or hormonal treatments from being deployed for longer than twelve months. This planned policy change was first announced via Twitter by President Trump in 2017, and a 2019 opinion of the Supreme Court made it policy a reality (de Vogue and Cohen, 2019) until President Biden reversed the policy in 2021 (Detrow, 2021). While this policy change was not a complete ban of transgender individuals being able to serve in the military, it was discrimination. And, although the policy was eventually reversed, the attempt at enactment shows that transgender individuals are being singled out and treated differently from others in the same organization. There were 8,980 transgender

---

MEDIA BYTE 8.1   **Ban of Transgender Service Members**

Read the 2019 article "Supreme Court Allows Transgender Military Ban to Go into Effect": https://www.cnn.com/2019/01/22/politics/scotus-transgender-ban/index.html, about a ban in place from 2019 to 2021. Then answer the following questions:

1. What is your opinion of this ban?
2. Do you think that this qualifies as discrimination?
3. How you feel about the fact that this ban was initially announced via Twitter?

---

service members in 2016 (the most recent year available) (US Department of Defense, 2019). This ruling can impact current as well as future transgender service members' ability to serve as well as to stay active within the military. (See Media Byte 8.1.) Individuals who are currently serving may be forced to leave, which could put them and their families in jeopardy financially and in terms of health insurance and benefits.

HARASSMENT AND BULLYING

One of the most common types of victimizations that LGBTQIA+ experience is harassment and bullying both as children and adults. Research has found that middle and high school LGBTQIA+ identified individuals are more prone to suicidal thoughts and behaviors, as well as bullying and harassment victimizations (Robinson and Espelage, 2013). In research involving high school students, Birkett, Espelage and Koening (2009) and Espelage and colleagues (2008) found that questioning (Q) individuals reported significantly more victimization, depression, drug and alcohol use, and suicidal thoughts than LGB individuals. The research presented on the following pages does not explicitly include individuals who identify as intersex (I) or asexual (A), so they are not included.

LGBTQ youth are also more likely to be bullied online. The Youth Risk Behavior Study (Centers for Disease Control, 2015) found that LGBTQ students were three times more likely to be cyberbullied than students who identified as heterosexual. Cooper and Blumenfeld (2012) found that of the youth surveyed who identified as LGBTQ between the ages of 11 and 22, 52 percent reported having been cyberbullied several times. They also discovered that 54 percent reported being bullied about their sexual identity and 37 percent being bullied about their gender expression within the last thirty days. Cyberbullying

CASE STUDY 8.1

The Suicide of Jamel Myles

Jamel Myles was a 9-year-old fourth grader in Denver, Colorado, who hanged himself in his room in 2018 on the fourth day of school. Jamel and his sister had experienced a year of intense bullying the prior school year and it had continued and gotten worse in the new year. Jamel had come out to his mother over the summer and to his classmates that fall. Jamel was bullied in school for being gay. His mother had contacted the school about the bullying, and she felt that the school did not do enough (Turkewitz, 2018). Read this article about suicides among LGBTQ youth and answer the following questions:

http://time.com/5380203/lgbtq-youth-suicide/

1. What are your thoughts on this case?
2. How do you think this should have been handled?
3. Do you think that anything could have changed the outcome?

of LGBTQ youth can cause immense emotional pain, anxiety, and depression as well as suicidal thoughts, attempts, and acts. (See Case Study 8.1.)

Research into college populations has found that LGBTQ individuals also experience higher rates of bullying and harassment, as well as depression and suicidal thoughts (Espelage and Merrin, 2016; Hawker and Boulton, 2000; Hawton et al., 2013). LGBTQ college students experience verbal threats more often than physical violence (Moran, Chen, and Tryon, 2018). Transgender college students, in particular, report physical and verbal bullying both before and during their time in college (Effrig, Bieschke, and Locke, 2011; Hightow-Weidman et al., 2011). Questioning students report similar verbal and cyber bullying (Moran, Chen, and Tryon, 2018). As with high school students, having a support network of family and peers along with institutional support helped college students deal with some of the negative mental health outcomes due to bullying (Furman and Buhrmester, 1992; Moran, Chen and Tryon, 2018). Other studies have found that positive religious experiences assisted with psychological well-being as well as self-acceptance in those who were bullied (Woodford et al., 2014).

While bullying of LGBTQIA+ individuals is often thought of as being perpetrated by heterosexual and cisgender individuals, some research shows that members of LGBTQIA+ communities may also bully and ostracize each other (Weiss, 2003). Transgender individuals reported that they experience discrimination, prejudice, bullying and harassment not only from heterosexuals but also from LGBTQIA+ individuals. Research underscores that some within LGBTQIA+ communities experience isolation and harassment even from seemingly welcoming places (McCormick and Barthelemy, 2020).

In addition to the bullying that LGBTQIA+ students face from peers, transgender students often face an additional layer of harassment and abuse at the institutional level. Many schools are not supportive of transgender children. In the 2015 National School Climate Survey, 50.9 percent of transgender students reported that the school they attended refused to use the name and pronouns for the gender they identify with (Movement Advancement Project and GLSEN, 2018). The same survey also revealed that 69.5 percent of transgender students ere fearful to use the bathroom at school because they feel unsafe and worry about victimization (Kosciw et al., 2016). Schools also may have policies about which bathrooms the students can use, the sports that they can participate in, and activities they can participate in based on their sex assigned at birth. As a result of this institutional-level discrimination, transgender students are stigmatized and face verbal abuse and harassment not only from students but also from faculty, staff, and parents of other children.

Social media sites have been a source of support for LGBTQIA+ youth as they can be a safe way to connect with others and obtain advice or guidance. However, social media sites can also be sources of bullying and harassment for LGBTQIA+ youth and adults. LGBTQIA+ individuals are three times more likely to experience cyberbullying (Centers for Disease Control, 2015). Online perpetrators are more likely to express themselves more freely, as well as increase the duration, frequency and severity with which they bully LGBTQIA+ individuals (Shelton and Skalski, 2013; Sticca and Perren, 2012). Also, the online bullying and victimization can progress to in-person victimization in which individuals are physically harmed.

As a result of the risk of online victimization, LGBTQIA+ individuals may hide their identity or their sexual orientation or gender identity on social media sites, particularly sites that are widely used by a general audience and possibly their family, friends, and peers. Individuals may have different levels of "outness" among family, friends, and coworkers and may fear discrimination or victimization if they are open on social media about their sexual orientation or gender identity (Fox and Warber, 2015). As a result, LGBTQIA+ individuals may gravitate toward or frequent specialty sites that relate to their sexual orientation or gender identity rather more mainstream sites (Gudelunas, 2012).

LGBTQIA+ individuals often face issues with victimization in their workplace, such as illegal workplace harassment (see chapter 11 for further discussion). They often experience bullying (Cowan, 2007; Hunt and Dick, 2008), harassment (Bedgett et al., 2007; Das, 2009), and discrimination (Bedgett et al., 2007; Lewis, 2006; Lewis, 2009; Sears and Mallory, 2011) at higher rate than those who do not identify as LGBTQIA+. This can include hurtful, degrading, and bigoted commentary, jokes, and mocking (Baker, 2010; Silverschanz et al., 2008), as well ostracism from the group and work opportunities (Embrick, Walther, and Wickens, 2007). These types of victimization within the workplace are often a result of a lack of formal policies regarding LGBTQIA+ individuals, as well informal and prejudiced treatments that are tolerated, and even encouraged by acts or lack of action by leadership, in terms of hiring, firing, assignment of jobs and duties, promotion, and benefits (Lewis, 2009).

Another form of workplace victimization that LGBTQIA+ individuals experience is disrespectful language, such as slurs and using the word *gay* as a synonym for *bad* or as an insult. LGBTQIA+ people who have confided their sexuality or gender identity to others at work may also experience threats or coercion from subordinates or superiors to "out" themselves to other coworkers or publicly. This can cause a great deal of stress and anxiety as well as force individuals to do things that they do not want to do at work in order to protect themselves from being exposed. An individual may fear reprisals, harassment, physical harm, or job loss so the threats that are wielded can be very real and upsetting. For example, being as a gay police officer in a town that is largely homophobic can present a real threat of physical harm for that individual (Baker and Lucas, 2017).

Organizations have been established to help LGBTQIA+ individuals cope with the discrimination, abuse, bullying and harassment in schools and workplaces. The **Trevor Project** was one of the first. It provides a twenty-four-hour national hotline as well as free, confidential, protected instant messaging and text services for individuals in of help. The Trevor Project also offers suicide prevention services and crisis intervention services for individuals and communities. Another organization is PFLAG (Parents, Families and Friends of Lesbians and Gays). It offers education and programs aimed at preventing cyberbullying and assisting those who have experienced offenses against them and their families. While not specifically for LGBTQIA+ communities, the Cyberbullying Research Center provides information and resources for individuals who experience online harassment or bullying based on gender, sexual orientation, or sexual identity.

LGBTQIA+ INDIVIDUALS WHO EXPERIENCE CYBERCRIME

In addition to cyberbullying and harassment, other online crimes target this population. Some hackers target individuals who identify as LGBTQIA+. In December 2015, hackers dispersed information from 4,926 individuals using a dating app used by HIV-positive singles. The hackers released the name, sexual orientation, email address, and date of birth of these HIV-positive individuals. The spreading of such information could be detrimental to people on the list who were not out in terms of their sexual orientation or HIV status (Hamill, 2015). Also in some jurisdictions, HIV-positive people are required to tell their partner or partners about their status. If it were discovered that a person failed to do this, they could face criminal charges and penalties (see chapter 5).

Hackers also targeted individuals searching for same-sex partners on websites called We Know Down Low and ManCrunch. We Know Down Low's main demographic was married men who publicly identified as heterosexual but secretly used this app to find men to have sex with (Gallagher, 2015). Man-Crunch was a site dedicated to men trying to find other men to have sex with. One man in Saudi Arabia who was outed as a result of this hacking event fled left the country because he feared he would be stoned to death, the punishment there for same-sex activity. The hackers, known as the Impact Team, believed the acts of those using these websites to be morally wrong and cited this as their motivation. They saw their actions as part of the "greater good" because they believed that they were exposing the evils of infidelity and secrecy.

There have also been incidents of individuals posing online as interested in same-sex relationships or sexual encounters, only to use the information obtained from potential partners for personal or professional gain. Nico Hines victimized people in this way. Hines was a heterosexual male journalist who set up a profile on the app Grindr indicating that he was interested in men. He used the app to talk to Olympic athletes in 2016 and obtain information about them and set up dates. He did not disclose that he was a journalist or that he would use the information that they gave him as part of a story. Many of the athletes that he described in his story were from countries where it is either very stigmatized or illegal to be gay. These athletes could face criminal charges, punishment, or even death as a consequence for their sexual orientation or identity in their home country. Hines apologized in 2017 for his story, as did the *Daily Beast*, the publication that initially ran the story. But the damage was done and these men had their sexual orientation outed to the world. This case is a dramatic example of how interactions on the internet can lead to potential victimization in person or at the institutional level from governments in countries where same-sex relationships or sexual encounters are illegal (see chapter 5).

HATE CRIMES

In the past, the FBI investigated only hate crimes in which the crimes were perpetrated due to bias against a person's race, color, national origin, or religion. However, after the passage of the **Matthew Shepard and James Byrd Jr. Hate Crimes Prevention Act** (HCPA) in 2009, the FBI now can investigate hate crimes perpetrated on the basis of a person's actual or perceived sexual orientation, gender, gender identity, or disability. Sexual-orientation bias is the third most common reason for hate crimes. The most common is race, followed by religion. The most common location of sexual-orientation-bias crimes is a residence or private home (FBI, 2019a), followed by streets, highways, and roads. The third most common location is schools, then parking lots and garages, and finally, nightclubs or bars.

In 2017 (the most recent year available) 1,130 incidents of hate crimes were reported based on sexual orientation and 119 on gender identity. This is a 5 percent increase from the previous year. Also, in 2017, 29 transgender individuals were murdered, the highest number ever recorded. The Human Rights Campaign (Marzullo and Libman, 2019) tracked those 29 deaths and found that most were transgender women of color. They had been killed by acquaintances, partners, and strangers. Some of the perpetrators have been arrested and charged, but some have not yet been identified. Some cases clearly show the perpetrator's transgender bias. Other cases reflect the larger issues of bias against transgender individuals in the world. An example is a transgender person being homeless and jobless due to their identity and being murdered while living on the street. The investigation of such murders by the Human Rights Campaign (Marzullo and Libman, 2009) found that racism, homophobia, transphobia, and sexism intersect and lead to the victimization of these individuals, including murder.

Because reporting hate crimes to the FBI is not mandatory, the statistics provided by the FBI represent only a portion of the actual hate crimes occurring. The most current report of the FBI (2019a) indicates that there were 16,149 agencies reporting, but thousands of agencies did not report any data. And 87 percent of the reporting agencies reported no hate crimes. This does not necessarily mean that none occurred in their jurisdiction. The jurisdiction may not have classified a crime as a hate crime or did not investigate it as such. The responsibility of bias crime reporting falls on the responding officer and the report made by the person who had the offense committed against them. Thus, a crime may not be categorized as a hate crime if the officer does not deem it to be one or the person who experienced the offense is too upset or is incapable of giving such a statement to inform the officer. In addition, if the person who experienced the crime is **misgendered** (identified as a different gender than the one the individual identifies with) in the local police statements and official reports, the crime may not be investigated or classified as a hate crime or a crime committed against a transgender person (Marzullo and Libman, 2019).

In response, programs have been created to assist those who experience hate crimes against them and raise awareness about the prevalence of hate crimes against LGBTQIA+ individuals. The **National Coalition of Anti-Violence Programs** (NCAVP) is dedicated to prevention of violence, including that which targets LGBTQIA+ individuals specifically. This group also gives individuals advice about how to accurately report hate crimes and how to obtain services. The 2009 HCPA is another effort to assist those who experience hate crimes against them and their families and prevent crimes against people within LGBTQIA+ communities. This act encourages the FBI to update the reporting procedures to better track hate crimes against LGBTQIA+ individuals, as well as to provide training for law enforcement regarding hate crimes against these communities. However, in examining the most recent FBI (2019a) statistics, even twenty years after Matthew Shepard's brutal murder and almost ten years after the passage of the HCPA, LGBTQIA+ identifying individuals still face hate-fueled crimes.

When people who have experienced sexual-orientation or gender-identity hate crimes interact with police, they often report unhelpful communications and treatment. They report the police often have an attitude of indifference, or they are hostile in their questioning and handling of the case. LGBTQIA+ individuals have often experienced incidents of police misconduct, excessive force, entrapment, and arrest of the person reporting the crime. The attention to such cases in 2020 and the **Black Lives Matter** movement have raised awareness about the violence that people of color experience at the hands of police. However, women, especially trans women of color, are often left out of the media hype and the forefront of the movement. While the George Floyd and Breonna Taylor cases were brought to the forefront of the Black Lives Matter movement, the trans women who were killed by police in 2020 did not receive as much attention. For example, two Black transgender women, Dominique Fells and Riah Milton, and a Black transgender man, Tony McDade, were also killed by police in 2020. The lack of attention and discussion nationally about these deaths and about transgender people of color led grassroots activists to work toward initiatives such as **Black Trans Lives Matter.** Black Trans Lives Matters demonstrations started popping up nationally in the summer and fall of 2020, and groups started organizing to raise awareness about the specific issues and targeted victimizations that Black transgender individuals face. Activists also called for organizations dedicated to LGBTQIA+ issues that have traditionally been run by white cisgender individuals to transition leadership to people of color and from the LGBQTIA+ communities. The issue, as discussed in chapter 1, is one of cisgender privilege, as well as white privilege, because someone who is of a privileged class cannot know what it is like to live the life of someone who is not privileged.

INTIMATE PARTNER ABUSE

Prevalence

Research into the extent of intimate partner abuse (IPA) among LGBTQIA+ populations shows that the rates are similar to those in heterosexual relationships, and often higher. However, Messinger (2011) argues that LGBTQIA+ individuals are more likely to experience IPA than heterosexual individuals, but it may not be reported at the rate of heterosexual abuse. Researchers have found that 43.8 percent of lesbian women and 61 percent of bisexual women have experienced rape, physical violence and/or stalking by an intimate partner over the course of their lifetime. In comparison, the rates are 25 percent for heterosexual women, 26 percent for gay men, 37 percent for bisexual men, and 29 percent for heterosexual men (Walters, Chen and Breiding, 2013). However, other research conducted by Hellemans and colleagues (2015) found that those in same-sex and heterosexual relationships experienced IPA at the same rates, but that transgender women experience IPA at the highest rate. The prevalence of physical violence in same-sex relationships varies. Sand and Pepper (2015) found that it occurred in 20 percent of female-female relationships, while Bartholomew and colleagues (2008) found it occurred in 44 percent of the relationships of gay and bisexual men. These studies found that psychological or emotional abuse occurred in 95 percent of bisexual or gay male relationships and 67.5 percent of same-sex female relationships.

There is also another factor that is more common in IPA in non-heterosexual relationships: intersection between the person committing the crime and the person against whom it is committed, or dual victimization. In same-sex relationships in which IPA is present, it is more likely that individuals victimize each other than it is in heterosexual relationships in which IPA is present. Research has shown variations in the extent to which this occurs, with estimates from 22 percent of relationships (Edwards and Sylaska, 2013) to 31 percent (Balsam and Szymanski, 2005). However, Carvalho et al. (2011) found that almost all the research participants in same-sex relationships who were perpetrators of IPV also reported IPV victimization. More research is needed to better understand the rate of these occurrences as well as the context.

International research has shown that the IPA rates for LGBTQIA+ couples are similar to those for heterosexual couples or higher. The rates have been found to be higher for intimate partner abuse in Australia (Leonard et al., 2008), Hong Kong (Chong, Kwong, and Mak, 2019), South Africa (Eaton et al., 2008), Italy (Moscati, 2016; Arcilesbica, 2011), and Britain (Guasp, 2012). However, more research needs to be conducted both domestically and internationally to determine the exact amount of IPA occurring within LGBTQIA+ communities, as well as issues specific to this group.

Heterosexism and homophobia may play a part in the high number of individuals in same-sex relationships who both commit IPA and have IPA committed against them. The structural inequality that can weigh on a relationship as a result of both partners belonging to a sexual-orientation minority can influence the dynamic of power between the two, as well as the level of stress that people experience, which is often referred to as minority stress. **Minority stress** is psychosocial stress that comes from external and internal stressors related to being in a sexual minority or in a racial or ethnic minority. External stressors include homophobia and discrimination from society and people in one's life. Internal stressors can include internalized homophobia and the degree of one's outness or openness about their sexual or gender identity or sexual orientation (Messinger, 2011 Meyer, 1995). This extra stress can increase the likelihood of IPA and violence in relationships between LGBTQI+ individuals (Calton, Cattaneo, and Gebhard, 2016). Some individuals may respond by lashing out, often in a physical way at their partners.

Intimate partner abuse has also moved online with individuals being harassed, stalked, and experiencing sextortion and nonconsensual pornography online. LGBTQIA+ individuals have the added risk of being outed online and having images shared that would expose them to the world. This can cause anxiety, depression, and thoughts of suicide. Preliminary research has shown, as is the case with cyberbullying, that the rates for IPA online for those within LGBTQIA+ communities is the same or higher than for cisgender or heterosexual people (Navarro, Clevenger, and Marcum, 2016).

Effects on Those Who Experience IPA

IPA victimization research has shown that there are differing effects on individuals based on identity and stress. Individuals who belong to multiple minority groups, such as those who identify as LGBTQIA+ and who are also people of color and female, may have higher risks for stress, depression, health problems, and substance abuse. They may use substances as a form of self-medication and may internalize the abuse perpetrated against them, which can result in depression. IPA can be very isolating for anyone, but for those in LGBTQIA+ relationships, it can be especially isolating if they are estranged from family or friends or are not out to the people in their lives from whom they could seek assistance.

Research has revealed that a factor in same-sex IPA is **internalized homophobia.** This is the degree to which a LGBTQIA+ individual has internalized negative beliefs about their sexuality and sexual orientation. It is often a result of upbringing, family life, and religious background, but it can also be a result of messages from society. Internalized homophobia can also be related to violence committed against those who also identify as sexual minorities (Renzetti, 1992), such as an intimate partner. Individuals who experience internalized homophobia may take out their negative emotions on their intimate partner. Research has revealed a connection between internalized homophobia and IPA for lesbian and bisexual women (Balsam and Szymanski, 2005), for gay and bisexual men (Bartholomew et al., 2008), and for LGBTQ youth (Edwards and Sylaska, 2013). People who are raised to believe there is something wrong or bad about loving someone of the same sex or identifying as a different gender than what was assigned to them at birth may feel negatively about themselves and their relationship and express that in a violent way. Individuals who feel bad about their relationship may blame their partner for their feelings. That anger can manifest itself through physical abuse or through emotional or psychological abuse by saying damaging things to the partner to hurt them.

Same-sex IPA can also be affected by the degree to which an individual in the relationship is out (openly LGBTQIA+) or closeted (hiding LGBTQIA+ status). If important people in their lives do not know about their identification as LGBT-QIA+, that can be a stressor in romantic relationships. Individuals who are not open about their identification, who are in the closet, can experience more stress and conflict in an intimate partner relationship than individuals who are out. High levels of strain on both parties result from keeping the relationship a secret, which isolates the individuals from support networks of family or friends, and in turn increases the risk for IPA. However, research has shown a relationship between the degree of outness and IPA in same-sex relationships, with greater outness posing greater risk (Bartholomew et al., 2008; Carvalho et al., 2011; Edwards and Sylaska, 2013). Being more out can lead to an overall increased risk for lifetime IPA victimization among lesbian women and gay men (Carvalho et al., 2011), as well as increased psychological IPA for gay and bisexual men (Bartholomew et al., 2008; Carvalho et al., 2011). Two other studies found that lower levels of disclosure of one's sexual orientation were related to an increased risk for physical IPA perpetration in current relationships among LGBTQ youth (Edwards and Sylaska, 2013) and among gay and bisexual men (Kelley et al., 2014).

No wanting to identify as or be outed as LGBTQIA+ may be the result of stigma consciousness. Individuals may not want to be labeled or stereotyped based on their identity. This is especially salient for LGBTQIA+ people of color who have experienced stigmatization based on race. If a person has experienced racism or discrimination based on their race, they may be less willing to let the world know this part of their identity because of those past experiences (Pinel, 1999). Individuals may fear the reactions of their loved ones, coworkers and friends but they also may fear additional violence in what they perceive to be homophobic and/or racist criminal-legal system (Carvalho, 2006). An individual's level of stigma consciousness is positively correlated with the commission of IPA against lesbian women and gay men, meaning that the more aware the individual is of the level of stigma or maltreatment they could face as a result of identifying as LGBTQIA+, the more likely they are to commit acts of abuse on their partner (Carvalho et al., 2011).

The consensus in the general public is that IPA within LGBTQIA+ communities is rare, particularly between two women. This often is a result of stereotypes associated with women, that women cannot be violent and that two women in a relationship would be in a peaceful and idealistic relationship that would be free of behaviors that are seen in a relationship that includes a male (Glass and Hassouneh, 2008; Barnes, 2010). This sort of stereotypical thinking may create an obstacle for women in lesbian relationships to identify behavior that is occurring that is abusive as they may falsely believe that women cannot be abusers (Seelau and Seelau, 2005).

LGBTQIA+ individuals who experience IPA may not seek assistance, or may be reluctant to, due to the barriers associated with their sexual identity or

---

MEDIA BYTE 8.2   Serving All Those Who Experience Domestic
Violence/IPA

Please watch the following video clip about a shelter that serves LGBTQIA+
individuals experiencing IPA: https://www.mcall.com/news/local/mc-lgbt-
domestic-violence-outreach-20160910-story.html. Afterward, answer the
following questions:

1. What do you think about this organization's approach?
2. What are some things that it is doing to make this shelter and its services
   more LGBTQIA+ friendly?
3. Do you think that more shelters and organizations will follow the example of
   this organization? Why or why not?

---

sexual orientation (Messinger, 2011). They may be hesitant to report out of fear
of being outed to family, friends, and coworkers. They also may fear risking
rejection from the agency or center they reach out to or that it will not have
resources that apply to LGBTQIA+ individuals. In making a report to law
enforcement, there is trepidation regarding how they will be treated, and there
may be a problem with charging the abuser if the legal definition of domestic
violence or IPA excludes same-sex couples (Brown and Herman, 2015).

For individuals who seek assistance, counselors have been found to be the
most beneficial. Shelters for women and men who are in a sexual minority or
are transgender individuals have not proven helpful. In some cases those who
go to shelters experience a great deal of homophobia; in others shelters are not
available or are not open to them. (See Media Byte 8.2.) In seeking healthcare
for IPA, those in the transgender community reported that healthcare providers were unfamiliar with the medical concerns and needs of transgender individuals. Law enforcement was also not found to be helpful, and many LGBT-
QIA+ individuals have reported that they experienced bias or discrimination
when interacting with law enforcement (Brown and Herman, 2015).

SEXUAL ASSAULT

Prevalence

People within the LGBTQIA+ communities experience sexual assault at the
same level or higher than individuals who identify as heterosexual. There is not
a current consensus on the true extent of sexual assault against the LGBTQIA+
individuals, as more in-depth research needs to be conducted. However, existing early research show lifetime estimates between 3.1 percent (Messinger,

2011) and 13 percent (Turell, 1999). Certain populations are more vulnerable to sexual assault than others. LGBTQIA+ individuals who are homeless are more likely to be assaulted, as are those who are undocumented. Native American, Black, and Hispanic LGBTQIA+ identifying individuals have the highest victimization for sexual assault while incarcerated in jail or prison (Grant et al., 2011).

Effects on Those Who Experience Sexual Assault

As with domestic violence, LGBTQIA+ individuals who have been sexually assaulted may have increased problems with depression, physical health, and substance abuse. In terms of seeking assistance, LGBTQIA+ individuals may not feel comfortable interacting with police or criminal-legal officials for many of the reasons mentioned in the discussion of IPA. LGBTQIA+ people often are blamed, harassed, or not taken seriously when reporting a sexual assault. Many worry that they will not be believed if it is a same-sex assault. This is particularly salient for men due to the common myth that men cannot be raped. There is further complication if the person who experienced the assault is not out and may be fearful to report because the case could become public and could out their sexual identity or sexual orientation (RAINN, 2021a).

LGBTQIA+ individuals may also receive unequal treatment when reporting sexual assault to authorities. Evidence of sexual assault may not be collected consistently and in the same manner from LGBTQIA+ individuals as from those that experience a heterosexual assault. For example, in a heterosexual sexual assault case, a rape kit is taken. However, this is not routinely done for LGBTQIA+ individuals who are sexually assaulted. There is often lack of knowledge of victimization within this population, and many medical professionals do not understand how to take a rape kit for someone who is transgender or in the process of transition. This can lead to cases and charges being dismissed and to those who experienced sexual assault not receiving their fair chance to have their case heard in court.

In order to better assist individuals who identify as LGBTQIA+ who have experienced sexual assault, it is important for medical facilities, police, and rape crisis centers to understand and acknowledge the special needs of this population and behave accordingly and treat them with dignity and respect. Intake forms and other documents should allow individuals to write in a response to questions about sex or gender or have an option for transgender or intersex, and not the term "other," which can be very offensive and is not helpful in understanding individual needs. There should also be sensitivity when either verbally asking or having individuals answer questions on medical forms about sexual history and sexual partners. Asking what a person's preferred pronouns are and then using them is also a positive step that can help a person reporting sexual assault feel more at ease. It is also important for those working with LGBTQIA+ people who have experienced sexual assault to understand that their loved ones may not know about their gender identity or sexual orientation and to treat that matter with confidentiality and privacy (SafeTA, 2021).

Many LGBTQIA+ individuals have had negative experiences at rape crisis centers when seeking assistance because the services are predominantly aimed at cisgender women who have experienced heterosexual assault. Most of the signs, pamphlets, and books, as well as the support services, at these centers are aimed at cisgender, heterosexual women who have experienced assault. It can be very hard for individuals within LGBTQIA+ communities to find assistance tailored to their needs (Grant et al., 2011). They may find themselves excluded from very valuable services that rape crisis centers provide if the centers are not serving LGBTQIA+ people or are not making them feel welcome.

LGBTQIA+ people who do not or cannot access the services of rape crisis centers are missing out on many benefits that help those who have experienced sexual assault through the coping process. From the start of a sexual assault case, rape crisis center advocates can accompany those who have experience sexual assault to the initial medical exam and follow-up appointments and also provide them with clothing if their clothes are taken as evidence. Consequently, rape crisis centers should have gender-neutral clothing available, and center advocates should understand the needs of this population while they are with them at the hospital. Advocates from rape crisis centers can also be with people through the whole criminal-legal process, which can not only provide much emotional support but also help with logistics during this sometimes daunting process. Many rape crisis and sexual assault centers have free or low-cost individual and group counseling and advocacy services, and advocates also can assist people in obtaining crime victim compensation and securing social service benefits if needed. There has been some progress among rape crisis centers, like domestic violence shelters across the United States, in being more inclusive of those who identify as LGBTQIA+, but there is still room for improvement because most centers are still predominantly focused on cisgender females who experience a heterosexual sexual assault.

GLOBAL VICTIMIZATIONS

One of the major issues of concern regarding LGBTQIA+ identifying individuals is the way that they are viewed and often persecuted across the globe. Transgender individuals have historically been classified as having a mental illness, which often resulted in their being treated differently and often seen by society as less important than cisgender heterosexual individuals. The World Health Organization has reclassified "gender incongruence" from a mental disorder to a condition related to sexual health. However, for decades, transgender individuals were often treated as "mentally ill" and were subject to a great deal of stigma and persecution from the medical and psychiatric community and, as result, their friends and family. Globally, transgender individuals still receive unfair treatment, unequal access to services, discrimination, and violent victimizations.

Transgender individuals suffer from HIV at the highest rates, with transgender women being forty-nine times more likely to be living with HIV than any other group worldwide. In some countries, transgender women are eighty times more likely to be living with HIV. Being HIV positive and transgender increases the chances for victimization for transgender women, because there is a great deal of stigma surrounding HIV as well. Globally, HIV-positive transgender women have extremely high rates for victimization (World Health Organization, 2019).

Individuals who identify as gay, lesbian, or bisexual are often persecuted and harassed, as well as facing being charged, imprisoned, or put to death in some countries, as discussed in chapter 5. Internationally, LGBTQIA+ individuals face discrimination, harassment, and violent attacks at a higher rate than those who are not part of these groups (Amnesty International, 2019). Although government-implemented and legally sanctioned in many countries, the arrest, torture, imprisonment, and death of LGBTQIA+ individuals can be viewed as victimizations because they are a result of biased and heteronormative laws designed to persecute part of the population. LGBTQIA+ individuals do not receive the same legal protections as heterosexuals, which can pose problems and incite bias that leads to victimization.

ACTIVE LEARNING ASSIGNMENT 8.2

Explore the World's LGBTQ Policies

Use the World Policy Center page on constitutions, at https://www.worldpolicycenter.org/topics/constitutions/policies, to complete the following activity:

1. Pick a country (*not* the United States).
2. For each of the following issues, describe your country's stance:

   Equality and non-discrimination (sexual orientation)
   Education rights (gender)
   Workplace rights (sexual orientation)
   Health rights (right to health)
   Marriage rights
   Civil and political rights

3. What is your reaction to your findings? Please explain.
4. How do these positions differ from the laws in the United States?
5. How could these policies relate to the potential victimization and prevention of victimization of those that identify as LGBTQIA+?

Only five countries in the world (Bolivia, Ecuador, Fiji, Malta, and the United Kingdom) guarantee equality for citizens of any sexual orientation or sexual identity (Amnesty International, 2019). Most nations do not specifically give citizens rights based on sexual orientation or gender identity. Additionally, the right to same-sex marriage was also not part of any nation's main governing document but was enacted later as part of case law or legislation. Without specific legal protections, LGBTQIA+ individuals worldwide are vulnerable to victimization and discrimination because they are not viewed as equal under the law and granted the same protections as others.

The UN Human Rights Council has ruled that nations and states are under international obligation to treat people equally and protect individuals from differing treatment based on sexual orientation or gender. However, in the ever-changing political climate, even countries that signed can change their position. (See Active Learning Assignment 8.2.)

SUMMARY

In this chapter we explored the ways in which LGBTQIA+ individuals can be victimized. The victimizations that individuals within these communities face are often a result of their identity and the bias that people have against LGBTQIA+ individuals. There are policies and laws in place in the United States, as well as in other countries, that allow for systematic discrimination and victimization of LGBTQIA+ individuals. This has left LGBTQIA+ people with limited recourse for justice. However, grassroots organizations and allies are working to raise awareness and assist those that experience victimization as result of their identity.

As evidenced by the extent and nature of victimizations perpetrated against LGBTQIA+ individuals, collectively we need to reduce the bias and stigma against people in these communities. If there were equality for all people from a systematic standpoint, a lot of these victimizations would not occur and the challenges that LGBTQIA+ individuals who experience crimes against them face would not exist. As time moves on and social movements influence the public consciousness, it is our hope that the victimizations that are experienced by LGBTQIA+ individuals will decrease and the laws that contribute to harming people within these communities will be repealed.

Policing Crime   9

How Gender Influences Arrest Decisions and Court Cases

KEY TERMS
- chivalry theory
- discretion
- dual arrest
- evil woman hypothesis
- intimate partner terrorism
- mandatory arrest
- sexism
- victim blaming

LEARNING OBJECTIVES
- Understand the impact of gender on arrest decisions within the system.
- Recognize the role gender plays in court cases.
- Be able to determine the issues associated with gender that can led to victimization.

As we have discussed throughout this text, gender underpins why individuals engage in crime as well as shapes victimization experiences. In this chapter and the next, we will examine the role of gender in shaping case outcomes from arrest and prosecution to punishment and sentencing. This chapter discusses the role of gender in influencing arrest decisions and prosecution, with attention to individuals involved in the judicial phase, such as defense attorneys, prosecution, judges, and jurors. In the next chapter, we look at types of punishment imposed (diversion programs, probation, incarceration, parole) and how gender informs (or not) each of these punishments.

The power associated with gender in guiding behavior stems from the wider social constructions of femininity and masculinity in the United States, which relate the femininity with nurturance and passivity and masculinity with aggressiveness and strength (Connell, 1987). In addition to shaping the criminal event itself, gender affects arrest and court case processing decisions both indirectly (e.g., by unconsciously shaping thoughts about "perfect" and "imperfect" people in the "survivor" role) and directly (e.g., by relying on gender norms to inform decisions that have long-term consequences). We will begin by noting important perspectives pertinent to this discussion and then segue into explaining the role of gender in influencing decisions made by the major players involved case processing: police, lawyers, judges, and jurors. Finally, we will apply this material by examining specific crimes against persons.

The criminal-legal system is a massive entity of social control, which employs over500,000 law enforcement officers and interacts with millions of individuals every day (FBI, 2017a). These employees are vital as the criminal-legal system handles administering justice via arrests, prosecutions, and incarcerations as well as working toward prevention. Thus, the system is complex, with multiple missions (such as intervention and prevention) and multiple moving parts (such as law enforcement, judiciary, and corrections). To support the general functioning of the system, state agents use **discretion** in their decisions to arrest, prosecute, and if prosecuting, court case processing. It is our belief that gender influences all of these decisions. But before undertaking that discussion, we will introduce two concepts that are central to this chapter: chivalry theory and the evil woman hypothesis.

MADONNA VERSUS MEDUSA: PERSPECTIVES ABOUT THE ROLE OF GENDER IN CRIME

The chivalry theory and the evil woman hypothesis are dueling explanations to frame offending by women. Even though they are separate concepts, these ideas are both related to hegemonic masculinity and emphasized femininity. To reiterate, Connell (1987) proposed that the general social structure prescribes ideal behaviors that align with femininity and masculinity. The term *hegemonic masculinity* refers to an ideal form of masculinity: attractiveness, aggressiveness, financial and personal independence, sexual prowess, and emotional and physical strength. All other forms of masculinity, as well as all women, are inherently subordinate to the hegemonic man.

Emphasized femininity is the natural complement to hegemonic masculinity. According to Connell, *emphasized femininity* describes ideal traits associated with women within the wider culture: attractiveness, passivity, nurturance, sexual availability, and weakness. As with hegemonic masculinity, those not adhering to these ideals are inherently subordinated to those who closely align. For example, cyberbullying studies have found that women have higher odds of experiencing "weight-based" tormenting than men do (Puhl, Peterson, and Luedicke, 2013). Though not explicitly connected to gender ideals, one cannot deny the potential relationship given that femininity is associated with beauty and sexual attractiveness to men.

Although the chivalry theory is a separate concept from hegemonic masculinity and emphasized femininity, the three are intimately related. First raised in the early 1980s and 1990s, the **chivalry theory** is about the leniency of the criminal-legal system toward system-involved women but not system-involved

ACTIVE LEARNING ASSIGNMENT 9.1

Active Learning Assignment 9.1: Gender and Punishment

Research news stories about the sexual abuse of pupils by their teachers in the United States. Find at least five stories of male teachers and female students and five stories of female teachers and male students. Try to find cases that are as close as possible in incident details (e.g., ages of those involved, school levels). Then, try to find the charge and sentence for each system-involved person. After gathering these data, investigate whether there are any differences by gender. If so, as a gender scholar, explain what those differences are and why they exist. If not, explain why there are no differences from a gender perspective. It might be helpful to use the following matrix:

	System-involved person details	Student(s) details	Charges	Sentencing outcome
Male teacher/female student				
Case 1				
Case 2				
Case 3				
Case 4				
Case 5				
Female teacher/male student				
Case 1				
Case 2				
(continue. . .)				

men. Scholars argue that this leniency stems from social conceptions that associate women with compliance and weakness (emphasized femininity), which means they need protection from the patriarchy (Connell, 1987; Herzog and Oreg, 2008; Nagel and Hagan, 1983). Thus, although the system punishes violent men, as their use of violence aligns with dominant gender ideals, the reaction to violent women varies by situational characteristics. (See Active Learning Assignment 9.1.)

While studies suggest that the criminal-legal system affords women adhering to dominant gender norms some leniency for certain offenses, the pendulum also swings the other way (Herzog and Oreg, 2008). In other words, the system more severely punishes "evil women" (the **evil woman hypothesis**), or those who engage in actions that are in stark contrast to notions of emphasized femininity, than it punishes men who engage in the same actions (Erez, 1992; Nagel and Hagan, 1983). This difference holds true for both adolescent and adult women (Chesney-Lind and Shelden, 2014), in the case of the latter, it can set them on a pathway toward further deviance or victimization (Pasko and Chesney-Lind, 2016). These patterns explain how dominant gender ideals like hegemonic masculinity and emphasized femininity not only shape everyday social interaction but also the administration of justice.

Similar to the premises of chivalry theory and evil woman hypothesis, Glick and Fiske (1997) argue that **sexism**, or the belief that one sex is inferior to another, shapes everyday experiences and perceptions, rather than simply gender norms. From their perspective, sexism is not necessarily hostile (although it often manifests as such) but it can motivate believers to think that the "inferior" sex is in need of protection from those who are "stronger." Hence, believing that one gender is inferior to the other can result in contradictory beliefs, or "ambivalent sexism," which contributes to the persistence of the overall patriarchal structure.

In an analysis of the interrelationships of chivalry theory and ambivalent sexism, Herzog and Oreg (2008) found that these concepts influenced beliefs about individuals involved in the criminal-legal system. In a study with residents in Israel, they found that ambivalent sexist beliefs were less likely among young, highly educated, and high-income earners. Moreover, women, including married women with children, scored significantly lower than men on the hostile sexism scale (assessing overt negative perceptions of women). When they committed similar crimes, men were judged more harshly than women. As scores on the benevolent sexism scale increased (assessing beliefs that are not overtly hostile but still in alignment with sex inferiority), there was a corresponding increase in the leniency afforded to system-involved women, especially to those who adhered to traditional gender norms, compared to similarly situated men. On the other hand, high scores on the hostile sexism scale were associated with beliefs that crimes perpetrated by men were less serious relative to similarly situated women, especially women who did not adhere to traditional gender norms.

The Role of Mass Media in Reinforcing the "Good versus Evil" Dichotomy

Ambivalent sexism, chivalry theory, and the evil woman hypothesis not only shape the administration of justice but also influence crime reporting (see Case Study 9.1). Crime and media scholars have found that news organizations often frame women who engage in offenses that are incongruent with traditional

---

CASE STUDY 9.1

Andrea Yates

The story of Andrea Yates is tragic, but it also serves as an excellent example of how gender underscores beliefs about criminal engagement as well as punishment. We introduce her case in this chapter and discuss her punishment in the next chapter.

In 2001, Yates drowned her five children in the bathtub. During the progression of her criminal case, news agencies reported on the event through two different lenses: one was sympa-

thetic to Yates's history of mental illness, and one framed her as a monster. The article written by Wallwork (2016) and the images included in it show this polarization.

1. Find at least ten news articles about the event.
2. After reading each article, classify whether it casts Yates as an "evil woman" or as an individual in need of protection from a benevolent patriarchy (akin to chivalry theory).

---

gender norms (such as child abuse and murder) as "evil" and "monsters" (Wilczynski, 1991). The stories written about these individuals include descriptive wording and pictures that underscore those characterizations. On the other hand, the criminal-legal system, and ostensibly the mass media, react more sympathetically to women who engage in offenses that conform to traditional gender roles (such as excessive self-defense of a child) (Herzog and Oreg, 2008). While mass media is only one socialization agent, in the age where technology permeates every aspect of our social lives, one cannot understate the role of news in shaping our beliefs.

Aside from projecting an aura of evil or good onto individuals who engage in crime, mass media also reinforces widely held gender norms vis-à-vis victim blaming. To reiterate, **victim blaming** is direct and indirect spoken or written statements that assign fault to those who experience offense against them. For example, when questioning a person who experienced sexual assault, a law enforcement officer asks, "But why did you go back to his house?" Regardless of the intention, that question places emphasis on the person's own behavior as potentially contributing to the assault. This has led some to advocate avoiding specific words and phrases, such as "at least" (as in "at least you survived"), in conversations with traumatized individuals to avoid treading into judgement and instead to build empathy (Thieda, 2014). Moreover, public awareness has increased about the importance of being aware of one's body language and messages that it communicates to those who have experienced offenses against them. For example, imagine a person answering questions about their experience and the interviewer appearing disinterested or rolling their eyes. While this not a direct form of victim blaming, the indirect message is that the interviewer is not seriously reflecting on the information being shared. (See

---

ACTIVE LEARNING ASSIGNMENT 9.2

Gender and Victim Blaming in Popular TV

Please watch the *Law & Order: Special Victims Unit* episode entitled "Funny Valentine," (season 14, episode 16). Identify all instances of victim blaming and whether men or women perpetrate them. Also, make note of whether law enforcement engages in victim blaming. Finally, note any communication (body language, spoken, written) that points to the role of gender in shaping behavior and response to crime.

Active Learning Assignment 9.2.) Research shows that these kinds of interactions can revictimize the person who experienced the offense (Maier, 2008), hinder their willingness to report a crime (Rich and Seffrin, 2012), and negatively contribute to the physical and psychological consequences of the crime itself.

Gender and gender norms like emphasized femininity and hegemonic masculinity shape victim-blaming beliefs. Put another way, women who deviate from notions of emphasized femininity, such as exercising sexual agency, may experience victim blaming from those who consider their behavior "unlady-like." Likewise, men who deviate from notions of hegemonic masculinity, by showing emotional vulnerability, for instance, may experience victim blaming from those who consider their behavior as a significant departure from being "a man." In the court of public opinion, such responses result in the figurative trial of the individual who was victimized rather than the person who harmed them. This is especially clear in sexual assault cases with women who were victimized (Suarez and Gadalla, 2010). In the next sections of this chapter, we will discuss how these concepts influence people directly involved in the criminal-legal system.

The Role of Gender in Police Officers' Behaviors and Arrest Decisions

We have discussed important gender perspectives and the reinforcement of these frameworks in mass media. Now we move to discussing how these frameworks and mass media shape individual everyday interactions between law enforcement officers (LEOs) and citizens. For example, Rabe-Hemp (2008a) studied how women and men LEOs interacted with citizens across three types of control: extreme control (through direct methods like arrest or interrogation), lower-level control (mainly through verbal commands), and supportive control (mainly through advising individuals about potential next steps). She found that men LEOs were more likely than women LEOs to engage in extreme and supportive types of control. While women LEOs were less likely than men LEOs to use extreme control, when they used that tactic, it was related to interactions with their supervisor. In the absence of supervisors, women LEOs were less likely to use extreme control than when supervisors were involved. Rabe-Hemp concludes that although gender is an important consideration in assessing LEO behaviors, it would be a mistake to believe all women conform to dominant gender norms while "wearing the badge" because, if that were the case, they would be more (not less) likely than their men colleagues to use supportive control, which is a gender-congruent behavior. Finally, and relatedly, Rabe-Hemp found that the gender of the person who engaged in the offense was also important in assessing LEO control technique. Unsurprisingly, given the content of this book, men were more likely than women to experience extreme control.

In an analysis that built on Rabe-Hemp's study, Novak, Brown, and Frank (2011) evaluated factors influencing arrest decisions by men and women LEOs. They found that several factors differed across the two groups: offense seriousness, citizen race, citizen-LEO interaction, presence of a crime, and supervisor presence. In terms of agreement between the two, only two factors were consistent. Across men and women LEOs, women citizens were less likely to be arrested, but the odds of arrest were more likely if the individual was intoxicated. Factors that increased the likelihood of arrest by women LEOs were how serious the offense was (odds increased with seriousness), how much evidence was present (odds increased with increasing amount), whether or not the citizen was a person of color, whether or not the citizen was deferential, and whether a supervisor was present. The only factor that decreased the odds of arrest by women officers was the presence of other officers. For men LEOs, the latter was also important, but it led to *higher* odds of arrest, or the opposite of women LEOs. Arrest by men LEOs was also more likely if the citizen was a juvenile or if the officer saw the crime.

Finally, a related study reviewing arrest decisions between white and people of color LEOs found that several of the prior relationships were still important. For instance, increasing offense seriousness, suspect disrespect, intoxication, or juvenile status all corresponded to an increase in likelihood of arrest across both groups of officers (Brown and Frank, 2006). On the other hand, the only factor that led to a decrease in odds of arrest across both groups was the presence of a woman suspected of an offense. These three studies all suggest that women experience leniency by LEOs, which underscores the applicability of the frameworks of ambivalent sexism, chivalry theory, and the evil woman hypothesis. We will now turn to whether there is evidence of these patterns as cases progress through the courts prior to punishment (chapter 10 will discuss gender and punishment).

The Role of Gender in Court Case Processing

Like law enforcement, the judiciary has been and continues to be a man-dominated profession. According to data published by the National Association of

Women Judges (2019), fewer than 40 percent of judges are women: state final appellate jurisdiction courts (36%), state intermediate appellate jurisdiction courts (39%), state general jurisdiction courts (33%), and state limited and special jurisdiction courts (36%). Likewise, US Census data shows a persistent under-representation of women lawyers (38% vs. 62%) and a significant gender pay gap in the profession (Day, 2018). Finally, data from the Bureau of Labor Statistics for 2019 shows a substantial pay gap between men and women involved in the professional security field, which includes corrections. Given these data, it is not surprising that women involved in the legal profession have reported various instances of overt and unconscious bias (Lee, 2015).

In a thoughtful discussion of gender bias within the judicial system, Lee (2015) notes that women attorneys reported experiencing various examples of bias, such as others assuming they were in a supportive role, being chastised for deviating from gender-congruent communication styles, being subjected to infantilizing or paternalistic comments, and encountering hostility or indifference. These negative reactions to women in the legal profession extend to the courtroom, where engaging in gender-incongruent behavior (such as being "overly assertive") can backfire on jurors and ultimately the client. Thus, women in the legal profession must walk a fine line every day and, if they notice bias, they risk potential personal or professional consequences for calling the behavior out. (See Case Study 9.2.) Studies discussed by Lee note these challenges are aggravated for women of color in the legal profession as they must battle both racism and sexism.

As well as affecting individuals employed within the legal system, gender shapes case processing as well. For instance, data show that various demographic factors influence whether cases involving juveniles are handled in juvenile court or in adult court. In examining the likelihood of transfers to adult

---

CASE STUDY 9.2

Ruth Bader Ginsburg

"The Notorious RBG," as she was affectionally known across social media, knew the sting of sexism first hand. As a young female lawyer with prestigious credentials, she met great difficulty in securing employment.

1. Research the life of the late Supreme Court justice Ruth Bader Ginsburg.

2. Create a one-page write-up that discusses the various challenges she encountered due to merely being a woman.

3. Compare her life story to information presented in this chapter and propose three potential programs to address the under-representation of women in the legal profession—particularly women who are underrepresented because of ableism, class, ethnicity, race, or other characteristics.

court, Brown and Sorensen (2013) found that individuals who were people of color, Hispanic, and men were most likely to have their cases transferred. Additionally, transfer to adult court was more likely if the offense involved a crime against a person or a first-degree or capital felony or if the defendant had a prior record. The only factor that decreased a juvenile's odds of transfer to adult court was being 14 or 15 years old. Brown and Sorensen point out that the lower risk of adult transfer for women likely stems from social conceptions that young men are more dangerous. Not only does gender influence where cases are heard, but also whether cases are tried at all.

Follingstad and colleagues (2015) investigated what factors influenced prosecutorial decisions in intimate partner abuse (IPA) homicide cases by presenting law students with hypothetical vignettes. The students were most likely to prosecute in instances where the woman behaved as an "imperfect victim" (see Active Learning Assignment 9.2. to revisit victim blaming). In other words, if the homicide followed a potential cooling-off period, the students were more likely to prosecute. Moreover, they were more likely to prosecute if the woman had been drinking during the incident, was overweight, was not well liked in the community, was rumored to be having an affair, was quiet following the event (compared to hysterical), and was unable to clearly articulate fear. Though not directly associated with gender frameworks discussed earlier, these behaviors all align with the notion that women who engage in "masculine" crimes (like extreme violence) and who do not align with traditional notions of femininity—such as being compliant and well-mannered (articulate, loyal, not drinking excessively), fragile (not overweight, but small, which warrants protection), nurturing (emotionally devastated at the loss of loved one), and pleasant in interacting with others (reputation)—will be treated as "evil women" by a patriarchal criminal-legal system (Nagel and Hagan, 1983).

Aside from factors related to the woman herself, the law students were also more likely to prosecute if incident characteristics did not align with dominant (and gendered) notions of how women "should" react following IPA or what IPA "should" look like. For example, many forms of abuse (e.g., financial, psychological) are not always visible. However, the law students were more likely to prosecute in cases where women did not have a history of medical injuries (Follingstad et al., 2015). Similarly, prosecution was more likely if women had no prior history of calls to police despite it being well-known that individuals who are victimized sometimes resist calling police because it can put them in even more danger. Additionally, the law students were more likely to prosecute if a woman fired multiple shots rather than only one in a homicide despite ample evidence that sometimes individuals who are victimized react violently (even using preemptive violence) to ongoing abuse (Johnson, 1995). These findings are simply a sampling of the factors noted in the study by Follingstad and colleagues, but they present a telling picture that dominant gender norms shape our perceptions of men and women and how they should "act" and "react" in situations like IPA. For example, instead of hiding abuse, "perfect victims" should call LEOs for help—even though this might increase the risk of murder by the abusive partner.

If gender norms influence prosecutorial decisions, what about the decisions of jurors? In a study investigating what factors influenced mock jurors' decisions about guilt in IPA homicide cases, Hodell and colleagues (2014) found more support for the argument that gender underscores every facet of involvement in the criminal-legal system. More specifically, the scholars found that mock jurors were more lenient toward women in heterosexual relationships than to men both when they were the ones who experienced an offense against them and when they were the ones who perpetrated the abuse. Mock jurors were also more likely to decide the defendant was guilty if a child was absent during the event. To drill down on the thinking behind these decisions, the scholars collected notes about mock jurors' reasoning. Their findings to show that gender shapes our beliefs about events and appropriate actions within those events. For example, mock jurors reported more leniency to defendants if a child was present, because of the widely held belief that children are inherently vulnerable and must be protected at all costs. On the other hand, if evidence of self-defense (either as an individual or in defense of a child) was not compelling, mock jurors were more likely to convict.

Indeed, the role of gender in informing mock jurors' decisions was especially pronounced when voting to convict defendants of murder: "If she needed to be protected, she could [have] gone to the police" (502). That statement underscores several concepts addressed in this chapter and again shows that women are afforded leniency in the criminal-legal system only when their behavior conforms to notions of emphasized femininity. If women deviate from those prescribed social behaviors (by using extreme violence in lieu of patriarchal protection through law enforcement), they risk harsh punishment by the criminal-legal system. Because we have discussed important gender concepts and frameworks as well as how they affect individuals involved in the processing of cases through the criminal-legal system, we will now turn to looking at these factors across specific gender-based offenses.

THE ROLE OF GENDER AND GENDER FRAMEWORKS IN CRIMES AGAINST PERSONS

Although more offenses exist than child abuse, intimate partner abuse, and sexual violence, we selected these crimes to discuss for several reasons: (1) they are often co-occurring within homes and, thus, are intimately related (Herrenkohl et al., 2008), (2) they are recognized forms of gender-based violence (Heise, Ellsberg, and Gottmoeller, 2002), (3) the role of gender in shaping the aftermath of these events is particularly pronounced, and (4) we have already discussed the role of gender as an undercurrent in other crimes.

Child Abuse

As discussed in prior chapters, most system-involved individuals and most people who experience violent crime are men (FBI, 2017b) except within the home when confronted by intimate partners (BJS, 2012–2017). Indeed, within the home, children and women are at more risk of suffering violence (BJS, 2012–2017). This does not mean that women are never system-involved individuals, though. Research shows that both parents are more likely than strangers to harm their children (Fox, Levin, and Quinet, 2018). This statement includes mothers. According to data from the most recent child maltreatment report by the US Department of Health and Human Services (2019), most individuals who perpetrated child maltreatment were mothers.

Although child abuse is horrific regardless of the background of the person engaging in the abuse, gender influences the processing of these cases from start to finish. Scholars have found that men's use of violence, especially toward vulnerable populations, is judged more severely than similar actions by women (Franklin and Fearn, 2008). This pattern is thought to stem from the societal association of anger and violence with masculinity (Messerschmidt, 1993), and thus, the public is quick to severely punish those who commit crimes. On the other hand, because women are socialized to nurture and be passive, their perpetration of violence is less easy to accept by the public. Consequently, the public may seek more insight into violence perpetrated by women, because it is such an affront to how society conceptualizes femininity (Whiteley, 2012).

Evidence shows a variety of characteristics could function as guilt mitigators in cases involving women who offend, but less so among men: prior abuse, mental illness, and substance use (Deering and Mellor, 2009). While mitigators can lessen sentence severity, they also connect to wider gender norms and potential difficulty in accepting violence perpetrated by women without a "rational" reason (Wilczynski, 1991). This is not to suggest that these factors are not legitimate considerations, only that they more often appear as considerations in cases involving women than men, which points to a need to rationalize gender incongruent behavior. For example, in an analysis of infanticide, Wilczynski (1991) named two dominant groups of system-involved women: "the mad" and "the bad" (71).

Gender underscores understandings of not only child maltreatment, which can entail any form of abuse (educational, medical, physical, psychological), but also specific subtypes like child sexual abuse (Deering and Mellor, 2009). Because masculinity is associated with protecting one's family (Connell, 1987), child sexual abuse is an obvious deviation. Likewise, femininity is associated with caring and nurturing one's family, from which child sexual abuse is, again, an obvious deviation. However, as studies have found, the chivalry theory and evil woman hypothesis are applicable in these cases of child abuse as well. More specifically, research shows that women received less severe sentences for child sexual abuse than men (Deering and Mellor, 2009). Moreover, as previously mentioned, mitigating factors like prior abuse, mental illness, and substance use were greater considerations among system-involved women compared to men.

Intimate Partner Abuse

IPA is not simply the use of violence out of anger or frustration. Although research shows that couples are sometimes generally violent with each other, these events, broadly referred to as situational couple violence, are not caused by an insidious desire to exert power and control over one's partner, as seen in **intimate partner terrorism** (Johnson, 1995). In the latter, gender underscores the offense as well as shapes how agents of formal social control react to calls for service. Unfortunately, for men and women who are victimized and seek help, gender and adherence to traditional gender norms can have consequences. Research shows the dynamics are even worse for those in same-sex relationships or identifying outside of the gender binary.

Revisiting IPA as a Gender-Based Crime: An Overview of Societal Recognition

Before the 1970s, the public widely considered IPA a "private trouble" (Pastoor, 1984) and it was minimally policed. The dominant gender ideals that continue to shape society today were strongly adhered to within the home. In other words, the public characterized men as the "breadwinners," the de facto "heads of households," and the protectors of their family (Allan and Coltrane, 1996). On the other hand, the public characterized women as the "caretakers" and "supporters" of the family leadership (that is, the husband). The use of abuse and violence to keep children and women within their assigned roles, as ultimately supportive of husbands/fathers, was common during this time and still is a social problem today according to national statistics (Catalano, 2013). (See Active Learning Assignment 9.3.)

Despite social advances since the 1970s, IPA is still a serious form of gender-based violence where the chivalry theory and evil woman hypothesis both have applicability in decision-making about arrest and prosecution. Broadly speaking, during the battered women's movement of the 1970s, considerable effort was placed into raising awareness about the various forms of violence and creating resources for individuals seeking an escape. Activists focused their efforts on the public as well as on law enforcement. Realizing that the criminal-legal system needed a sea change, the Domestic Abuse Intervention Project

---

ACTIVE LEARNING ASSIGNMENT 9.3

The Burning Bed

The Burning Bed is based on the real-life story of Francine Hughes. During the movie, make notes about the portrayal of femininity and masculinity. Additionally, take note of how law enforcement and the public respond to Mickey's abuse of Francine. After watching the film, answer the following questions by referring to information from this chapter as well as prior chapters:

1. Compare and contrast Francine's behavior with emphasized femininity.
2. Compare and contrast Mickey's behavior with hegemonic (or toxic) masculinity.
3. Explain how the adherence to traditional gender roles affected the relationship between Francine and Mickey.
4. Explain how the adherence to traditional gender roles affected Francine's options to escape Mickey's violence.
5. Explain how formal entities of social control (such as law enforcement, the judiciary) responded to the intimate partner abuse and whether their responses have changed over the last decades.

(DAIP) in Duluth, Minnesota, offered a different path forward in policing violence (Pence, 1983).

The DAIP program began as an experiment with coordinated community action response to intimate partner abuse (Shepard and Pence, 1999). Initially, the experiment involved partially instituting guidelines that standardized the response of the local criminal-legal system to IPA, covering the entirety of each case from arrest to case resolution. For example, one requirement of the program was the **mandatory arrest** of the individual engaging in the abuse, which removed variations across cases due to officer discretion. Following an evaluation that showed the effectiveness of mandatory arrest as well as other initiatives, the DAIP program became a model intervention to combat IPA. Research supporting this shift in policing appeared shortly afterward, based on the Minneapolis Domestic Violence Experiment, which also showed that arrest reduced the likelihood of re-offense (Maxwell, Garner, and Fagan, 2002). Although research supporting the role of mandatory arrest in reducing later violence is inconsistent, or even contradictory to assumptions (Sherman and Harris, 2015), the practice is still in use today.

The paternalistic nature of the criminal-legal system toward women is also visible through the potential defenses invoked during court proceedings (such as "battered woman syndrome") that were not applicable to similarly situated men until the late 1990s, when "battered woman syndrome" became "battered person syndrome" (*Chester v. State*, 1996). This defense stems from Lenore Walker's seminal study (1989), which named the cycle of domestic violence and explained the entrapment of women within abusive relationships. One controversial aspect of her work was the idea of learned helplessness as a plausible reason why individuals who are abused stop trying to leave violent relationships and potentially became violent themselves (hence, "battered woman syndrome"). Essentially, Walker argued that individuals who are abused who experienced multiple failures in their attempts to leave are at risk of giving up their efforts altogether. Because these individuals are trapped and suffer abuse for prolonged periods of time, their mental and physical health rapidly deteriorate to the point where they may react violently if they perceive no other way out of the relationship.

As mentioned earlier, the gender pendulum also swings in the other direction and points to a system that harshly punishes women who deviate from dominant gender ideals associated with emphasized femininity: the evil woman hypothesis (Nagel and Hagan, 1983). Similarly, strong adherence to traditional gender norms also presents barriers to men who are victimized reaching out to help from law enforcement. For example, given that statistics continue to show that a greater percentage of IPA is men-to-women perpetrated (Smith et al., 2018), men who are victimized who decide to reach out for help face the real risk of arrest by law enforcement if incorrectly perceived as the primary aggressor (Shuler, 2010). Women who deviate from dominant conceptions of emphasized femininity also face the real risks not only of labeling and victim blaming by those strongly adhering to those traditional views (Lloyd and Ramon, 2017; Notestine et al., 2017) but also of being harshly sentenced by the criminal-legal system (Gavin, 2014). (See Active Learning Assignment 9.4.)

ACTIVE LEARNING ASSIGNMENT 9.4

Violence in Media

Find two music videos: one that depicts male-on-female intimate partner abuse and one that depicts female-on-male intimate partner abuse. After finding the videos, analyze the portrayal of femininity and masculinity in the actions and lyrics. Please pay attention to the level of seriousness assigned to male-perpetrated abuse versus female-perpetrated abuse. Use your notes to answer the following questions:

1. Discuss the portrayal of masculinity in each music video and whether or not it aligns with hegemonic masculinity.
2. Discuss the portrayal of femininity in each music video and whether or not it aligns with emphasized femininity.
3. Discuss whether there are depictions of chivalry theory or the evil woman hypothesis in the music videos.
4. Discuss whether the music videos treat intimate partner abuse with the level of seriousness it deserves or minimize it.

IPA among Individuals Identifying as LGBTQIA+

Until this point, we have focused on heterosexual couples. However, a review of the research on intimate partner abuse within same-sex relationships shows that IPA occurs at a greater rate within same-sex relationships (Brown and Herman, 2015). Moreover, these individuals experience unique challenges in accessing the legal system to pursue justice. Individuals who are abusive may leverage their knowledge of the stigma associated with IPA and individuals identifying as LGBTQIA+ to trap their partners (Ard and Makadon, 2011). For instance, an individual who abuses their partner can threaten to disclose their partner's status without their consent (forced outing) or threaten to disclose their partner's HIV status without their consent (forced HIV outing). If a gay man who experienced IPA takes steps to call law enforcement, the partner who abused him may try to convince law enforcement that the first man was the primary aggressor as retribution (Douglas and Hines, 2011). This fear is a reality as the push for mandatory arrest has led to the **dual arrest** of individuals who were abusive and who were victimized in situations where the primary aggressor cannot be determined (Hamel and Russell, 2013). The entwinement of gender and sexuality with dominant conceptions of femininity and hegemonic masculinity affects IPA case processing for those identifying as LGBTQIA+ (Blumenstein and Guadalupe-Diaz, 2016).

Findings show that individuals who are abused within sexual minority relationships hesitate in contacting law enforcement for aid out of fear of experiencing homophobic and sexist reactions (Blumenstein and Guadalupe-Diaz, 2016). These reactions often relate to deviations from dominant gender ideals associated with hegemonic masculinity and emphasized femininity. Blumenstein and Guadalupe-Diaz note that these "cultural construct[s] [have] consequences in police reaction [in which] they may approach lesbian battering as a 'cat fight' or gay battering as a fight between roommates" (30). Aside from the obvious impacts, these potential reactions can minimize the abuse, which can escalate into extreme violence as in any other relationship.

Individuals involved in sexual minority relationships face difficulties not only in reaching out to law enforcement but also in finding social services that can help them escape a relationship (Ard and Makadon, 2011). Most social service resources for people who experience IPA are geared for cisgender women. As a result, those in sexual minority communities may perceive these resources as unavailable to them (Blumenstein and Guadalupe-Diaz, 2016). Even if they reach out for help, shelters may be unable to house men (cisgender or not) who have experienced IPA, given the proximity to women who may fear men as a result of the trauma of experiencing IPA (Ard and Makadon, 2011). In terms of aiding lesbian women, it is not unheard of that the person who abused them tries to gain access to a shelter in which the people who experienced the abuse is living (Patzel, 2006).

CASE STUDY 9.3

Brandon Teena

Study the case of Brandon Teena by watching the film entitled *Boys Don't Cry*. Brandon Teena was a transgender male who was brutally raped and murdered by acquaintances. Before his life was stolen from him, Teena had established a relationship with another woman, which infuriated the perpetrators. To "punish" Teena and "show him" what "real men" are, the two perpetrators raped him. After Teena reported the rape, the perpetrators killed him.

1. During the film, please pay attention to the unique challenges Brandon experiences as he tries to seek help from law enforcement and medical personnel.

2. Using sources such as the following, research the challenges *still* confronting transgender people who experience sexual assault:

Office for Victims of Crimes, US Department of Justice, "Sexual Assault in the Transgender Community": https://ovc.ojp.gov/sites/g/files/xyckuh226/files/pubs/forge/sexual_assault.html

National Center for Transgender Equality, "U.S. Transgender Survey":

https://transequality.org/issues/us-trans-survey.

Individuals who identify as LGBTQIA+ face unique barriers not only in accessing help from law enforcement and social services to escape from intimate partner abuse, but they often experience more challenges during the administration of justice. For example, writings on the topic have noted that some court personnel—judges included—use language that denies the identities of those who were victimized, are visibly and vocally uncomfortable in handling cases involving non-cisgender individuals who were victimized, and require individuals who were victimized to engage in actions that are blatantly insensitive (Goodmark, 2013). In addition, individuals who were victimized may meet difficulty in securing legal counsel and, if incarcerated, are at greater risk of victimization while in state custody. Considering all these realities, it should not be surprising that IPA, broadly, still is underreported, especially among sexual minority couples. (See Case Study 9.3.)

Although the challenges are different for cisgender individuals, their path through the court system is not any easier. For example, given dominant conceptions of femininity that emphasize passivity and compliance not only to hegemonic men but to the patriarchal state, it is not unheard of for court personnel to blame and shame women in the middle of court proceedings for their perceived failings (Rivera, Sullivan, and Zeoli, 2012). In one notorious example that spurred a national outcry, a Florida judge sentenced an individual who experienced intimate partner abuse to three days in jail for not taking part in her abuser's trial (Chan, 2015). Before her sentencing, the individual who experienced the abuse tried to explain why she did not show and was visibly distraught during the discussion, which did not sway the judge (Chan, 2015). This is merely one example of the barriers that individuals who experience intimate partner abuse face when confronted with individuals in positions of authority who lack understanding and sympathy about the consequences of abuse.

Sexual Abuse

This chapter has shown that decisions about arrest and prosecution are framed by dominant gender ideals like emphasized femininity and hegemonic masculinity and that these ideals are in turn related to the chivalry theory and evil woman hypothesis. Although these gender concepts are relevant across offense types, they have a profound impact on arrest and prosecution decisions in sexual violence cases. Because we focused on sexual violence toward children in the child abuse section of this chapter, this area will discuss abuse involving adults.

Sexual abuse, like domestic abuse, is known to be extensively underreported. Even though recent years have seen significant breakthroughs like the #MeToo movement, individuals who were victimized continue to experience significant barriers in the help-seeking process. These barriers litter their path in pursuing justice through the criminal-legal system and in the "figurative" trying of the case in the court of public opinion. As we have emphasized throughout this chapter, gender underscores all these difficulties.

The first barrier is interacting with first responders, whom individuals suffering victimization fear may engage in victim blaming or be outwardly skeptical of their assault. (See Media Byte 9.1.) Scholars have documented these reactions among individuals who were victimized who believe their case does not align with dominant ideals of the "perfect victim" (Weiss, 2010). As previously discussed, the "perfect victim" is a myth that no individual aligns with, nor should they have to. The public tends to associate the "perfect victim" of sexual abuse with cisgender women who do not "contribute" to their assault through actions, body language, clothing, gestures, words, past history with the abuser, or in any other conceivable manner (Larcombe, 2002). Although not explicitly related to gender, perfect victimhood overlaps emphasized femininity in several key areas: compliance [to one man], passivity, and weakness. In other words, women who exercise agency in how and with whom they sexually engage are "imperfect victims." Moreover, women who experience tonic immobility during an assault, in which the body and mind freeze in anticipation of experiencing severe trauma, are also "imperfect victims" due to the absence of physical resistance.

Barriers to pursuing the arrest of individuals who engage in sexual abuse exist not only for cisgender women but also for men and non-cisgender individuals, who are both inherently imperfect victims (Patterson, 2016). Myths that it is biologically and physically impossible to rape men continue to abound. Because hegemonic masculinity is intertwined with sexual prowess, rape

---

MEDIA BYTE 9.1   **Sexual Abuse at the University of Tennessee**

In 2016, the alumni and student community of the University of Tennessee received devastating news: several football players had sexually assaulted several women in 2013. As if that news was not bad enough, administrators and staff had evidently been aware of the assaults and had minimally addressed the women's reports. Although the women were successful in raising awareness and pursuing justice outside the university, doing so was not without cost. Online forums quickly ignited with victim-blaming posts that argued that the women themselves were solely responsible for the assaults. To see what victim blaming looks like online and how it discourages those who experience sexual assault from reaching out to law enforcement, please go to https://www.vocativ.com/283331/tennessee-fans-blame-rape-victims-for-messing-up-football/index.html.

ACTIVE LEARNING ASSIGNMENT 9.5

#MeToo Men

The #MeToo movement was profound step forward in the national conversation about sexual assault. While this movement brought attention to the many women who have experienced sexual assault, it also created a space for men who have experienced sexual assault to come forward. One of these, Alex Winter, is best known for his portrayal of Bill in the film *Bill and Ted's Excellent Adventure*.

Conduct research on Winter's disclosure and his opinion that "the problems [sexual abuse] aren't going to get sorted out overnight, because frankly, these issues are part of the fabric of human nature" (Burwick, 2018). Create a brochure that could be distributed in the movie industry and other settings of power imbalances where abuses of authority may occur. The brochure should have the following objectives: (1) to raise awareness about the different types of sexual abuse, (2) to challenge myths that apply to females, males, and individuals outside the gender binary, (3) to note appropriate responses to people who have experienced sexual abuse that are not victim blaming, and (4) to identify resources for reporting.

---

myths reinforce the idea that "real men" are always accepting of sexual activity (Struckman-Johnson and Struckman-Johnson, 1992). Thus, before any other incident characteristics are even considered, dominant gender ideals and norms discourage men from pursuing justice through formal entities of social control. (See Active Learning Assignment 9.5.)

Because all individuals grow up and are socialized into the same dominant culture, responding law enforcement officers are not immune to the effects of dominant gender ideals (emphasized femininity and hegemonic masculinity) and gender frameworks (chivalry theory, the evil woman hypothesis, the perfect victim). Research shows that officers consider several factors while investigating cases: (1) the relationship between the individuals involved, (2) how the individual who was victimized reacted during the assault, and (3) how the individual who was victimized reacted after the assault with law enforcement (Alderden and Ullman, 2012). While the connection is not explicit, each of these factors is related to dominant gender ideals.

For example, Alderden and Ullman found that officers were less likely to pursue cases involving strangers than known persons, because of the difficultly in identification and apprehension. However, this pattern does not mean law enforcement prefers these cases; on the contrary, stranger-perpetrated assaults more closely align with notions about "perfect victims." For women who were victimized, engaging in sexual activity outside of socially acceptable situations (e.g., marriage), is an affront to dominant gender ideals and can result in difficulties during the pursuit of justice. Similarly, because emphasized femininity views a woman's sexuality as the ultimate prize to a hegemonic male, veracity assessments may incorrectly rely on whether women who report sexual assault physically fought their attacker. Finally, because compliance and weakness are associated with femininity and lead to assumptions that women should readily accept protection from the state, veracity assessments may consider refusals to cooperate as indicators of deception. Although these statements refer to the sexual assault of women, they are just as applicable to men and non-binary people who were experience sexual assault.

Considering the prevalence of myths about rape of men and the challenges in pursuing these cases despite those beliefs, law enforcement officers are likely to consider the above factors in determining arrest decisions involving men who were victimized too. For example, given that hegemonic masculinity and rape myths point to men being always available for sexual activity, it could be more difficult for men who were experience sexual assault to pursue action against a known individual versus a stranger. As in the case of women, the stranger-rape aligns more with a "perfect victim" situation and the corresponding belief that the individual assaulted had limited control over events. Also, as in the case of women who were victimized, the absence of physical resistance by men who were victimized can cause others to be skeptical of their veracity. Although the reasons for the skepticism are like those for women, they are also specific to the dominant conceptualization of masculinity in society. Given the intertwinement of physical strength with masculinity, the absence of physical resistance during a sexual assault can lead to skepticism during the pursuit of justice. Finally, just as in cases involving women who were victimized, law enforcement may perceive refusals to cooperate as indicative of deception regardless of how logical and valid a man's reasons for noncooperation are.

In addition to incident characteristics, research shows that officer gender also affects arrest decision making (Alderden and Ullman, 2012). Although one might assume that women officers are more likely to pursue arrest in rape cases, since women are statistically more likely to experience rape, contradictory results appeared in this research. Put another way, women law enforcement officers were less likely to pursue arrest compared to their men counterparts. Alderden and Ullman note that this finding shows that arrest decisions are complex and go beyond the officer's gender. This finding may also relate to similar research that has found a relationship between hindsight bias, or the belief that an outcome was a given in a particular situation, and victim blaming of those who experience rape (Carli, 1999).

Just as gender shapes experiences of the person who experienced sexual assault during arrest and prosecution and decision making by agents of the state, it also affects the system-involved person. As in the other areas discussed in this chapter, there is a marked difference in the sentencing of system-involved women who commit sex offenses and system-involved men who commit sex offenses, which stems from dominant gender ideals as well as gender frameworks like the chivalry theory and the evil woman hypothesis. When people hear the term "sexual offender," most report visualizing a man. Moreover, they typically parse that conception even further to include men who appear abnormal or unstable. Rarely do people assume that a "sexual offender" could be an attractive and successful woman, despite statistics showing that women do engage in these offenses as well.

SUMMARY

In this chapter, we discussed critical frameworks for understanding the role of gender in arrest and prosecutorial decisions as well as in how cases move through the courts. These frameworks include ambivalent sexism, the chivalry theory, and the evil woman hypothesis. While they are three different perspectives, they all share the same basic premise: that alignment or deviation from widely held gender norms has ramifications for how responding LEOs perceive and make arrest decisions, which cases prosecutors decide to pursue, the challenges of attorneys (and by extension system-involved individuals) in processing those cases, and how judges and juries respond to all of the above. For women who align with the notions of emphasized femininity, studies indicate they are treated leniently by a paternalistic criminal-legal system; however, if they behave in a manner that is gender-incongruent, they risk being perceived as "evil women" who deserve severe punishment. Men who align with notions of hegemonic masculinity may be treated more harshly than their counterparts since violence is a gender-congruent behavior. These gender norms may also work against men who survive violence because "strength" is an ideal trait and, thus, many may find it improbable that "a manly man" would be victimized. Individuals outside the gender binary inherently violate dominant gender norms and experience a myriad of unique challenges during the help-seeking process as well as outright discrimination. Taken together, the information in this chapter paints a clear picture that gender concepts and frameworks reinforce a patriarchal system that subordinates all others but the hegemonic man. These gender concepts and frameworks continue to follow individuals as their cases are completed and punishment is administered, which we review in the next chapter.

The Gendered Nature of Punishment

LEARNING OBJECTIVES

▶ Understand how gender shapes punishment.
▶ Be able to identify key concepts related to gendered punishment.
▶ Apply these topics in various activities.

In chapter 9 we discussed the role of gender in shaping arrest and prosecution decisions. Broadly speaking, because society conceptualizes men as dominant and more willing to use violence as a source of social capital (Connell, 1987; Messerschmidt, 1993), the administration of justice is swift in cases of violence perpetrated by men. However, when women perpetrate violence, it is less easy to rationalize given dominant gender conceptions.

One method that laypersons and state agents use to "rationalize" crime by women entails considering the role of earlier traumatic experiences or substance use in motivating the offense (Deering and Mellor, 2009). Yet, the same consideration is typically absent for men. These treatment differences affect sentencing outcomes of system-involved women and men. The system may treat a woman with more leniency (the chivalry theory; Nagel and Hagan, 1983) than it treats a man. However, if state agents perceive that the system-involved woman grossly deviated from implicit gender norms, they may treat her even more severely than a man who committed the same act (e.g., the evil woman hypothesis; Nagel and Hagan, 1983). Gender shapes the nature of punishment at all stages of interaction, starting with diversion programs.

DIVERSION PROGRAMS

Diversion programs allow individuals involved with the criminal-legal system to avoid formal incarceration as well as the negative labels associated with it. These programs differ from probation in the sense that participants may not ever be convicted of the offense, provided that all requirements of the diversion program are satisfied. However, it would be a mistake to believe diversion programs are "free passes" to avoid incarceration; many require individuals to complete a series of tasks to avoid formal sanctions. These programs are often for first-time or nonviolent individuals; however, specialty programs also exist where the role of gender in pronounced in their design.

Because gender underscores every aspect of social life, including decisions about offending and related risks of victimization, states have created innovative diversion programs that recognize individual behavior is the result of many factors (in addition to gender). These programs, broadly referred to as "problem solving courts," encompass a wide range of issues and populations (Leon and Shdaimah, 2012). Two diversion programs affecting men involved in the criminal-legal system are designed to address intimate partner abuse and soliciting sexual services. Because men are most often arrested for those offenses, with women representing a majority of those who have these offenses committed against them, these diversion programs are inherently gendered and focus on challenging harmful societal attitudes.

In Florida, for example, there are diversion programs for domestic violence misdemeanors, driving with a suspended license, felony pretrial intervention (for third-degree or lower felonies), misdemeanors, and truancy (for parents with youth who have excessive absences from school) (Satz, n.d.). In the domestic violence misdemeanor diversion program, participants must complete a **batterer intervention program** (BIP) and other recommended treatments to avoid formal sanctions. Given the nature of intimate partner abuse and the fact that most abusers are men, BIP programs are inherently men-centric (Miller, Gregory, and Iovanni, 2005). This design presents challenges when women are arrested for intimate partner abuse, because the context is often different (Johnson, 2008).

Although there is an ongoing debate whether intimate partner abuse is gendered or gender neutral, BIP program design is based on addressing men's violence against women. In pursuit of that goal, programs usually adhere to the Duluth model, which situates intimate partner abuse within wider patriarchal society that contributes to violence within the home via harmful gender norms. Despite that goal, Miller and colleagues (2005) found that BIP programs did not effectively combat intimate partner abuse at the macro level because they failed to address systemic causes of violence, or at the micro level because they failed to hold program participants accountable for their abuse. The prior finding is especially interesting because there were clearer efforts in the compara-ble program delivered to system-involved women to link relationship conflict to the larger sociocultural framework.

Another diversion program that is men-centric in design, with strong undercurrents of gender and the challenging of harmful gender norms, is the "john school." This diversion program is targeted at the men who ask for serv-ices from sex workers (Kennedy et al., 2004). John schools are designed to edu-cate those who buy sex about the realities of this work; they also challenge harmful gender norms that can underscore johns' behaviors. For example, john schools challenge derogatory beliefs about sex workers and center them as people. These beliefs are important to challenge, because they are used to dis-miss women engaging in sex work as "evil women" or "imperfect women" who are not deserving of empathy or protection and are an affront to "ideal femininity."

In an evaluation study of 446 men who attended john schools, scholars found that the diversion program significantly altered attitudes about sex work (Kennedy et al., 2004). For example, there was stronger disagreement with the statements that there was "nothing wrong with sex work" and that "women are sex workers because they want to be." Moreover, there was stronger agreement with statements like "sex workers are victimized by others" and "most sex workers live in poverty." It is important to note though that this initiative addresses sex work that results from economic desperation or force (such as human trafficking) instead of sex work where individuals are exercising full agency in their actions. There are some movements to decriminalize the latter, but they are controversial.

There are also programs specifically targeting women involved in the crimi-nal-legal system. Like the prior examples, program content is grounded in prevailing gender norms and roles. For example, one jail diversion program, Tamar's Children, helps pregnant women battling substance abuse and the residual impacts of trauma with parenting (Cassidy et al., 2010). Within this program, participants receive various counseling, educational, and parenting services and training meant to both empower them as individuals and prevent the risk of their infants experiencing disorganized and insecure attachments. Although men involved in the criminal-legal system can also be parents, pro-grams like Tamar's Children are grounded in the gender norm that assigns the primary caretaker role to women.

To avoid the negative repercussions of unhealthy parenting during early life, Tamar's Children offers a different pathway for expectant mothers involved in the criminal-legal system. Indeed, at the conclusion of their study, the authors found that there was no difference in infant attachment between Tamar's Chil-dren participants and the study comparison group, who were not involved in the criminal-legal system. Moreover, there was no difference in mothering

---

ACTIVE LEARNING ASSIGNMENT 10.1

Liberation Thesis or Economic Marginalization Hypothesis

In chapter 7, we discussed two perspectives that emphasize the role of gender in structuring choices about offending, which also affects victimization risks: the liberation thesis and the economic marginalization hypothesis. In this chapter, the quote beginning with "My honest first thought" addresses possible reasons for engaging in prostitution. Apply both perspectives to theorize why women may engage in sex work. In the write up, ensure there is adequate explanation of the premise of each perspective. Following those explanations, discuss how a theorist adhering to a liberation perspective and an economic marginalization perspective would explain women's engagement in sex work.

---

styles between Tamar's Children participants and the study comparison group. Put another way, Tamar's Children may have entirely minimized the known negative consequences associated with involvement in the criminal-legal system on mothers and their children, but replication studies are necessary before firm conclusions can be drawn.

Another diversion program that recognizes the role of gender in shaping experiences, including decisions about offending and risks of victimization, focuses on individuals charged with supplying sexual services. These specialized courts arose out of the recognition that many individuals, particularly women, engage in sex work as a means for survival if they have limited access to conventional employment. (See Active Learning Assignment 10.1.) The following quote from an interviewee in Leon and Shdaimah's study (2012) poignantly expresses that realization: "My honest first thought—I really believed that all the prostitutes were going to need substance abuse treatment. And it was enlightening to find out that everyone that prostitute doesn't have a substance abuse issue. And maybe not even a mental health issue. Like a lot of times it's a financial issue that make these people go out and prostitute—sell themselves" (257).

Even though there are several negative aspects related to diversion programs, such as coerced guilty pleas (sometimes required to access a program), increased surveillance, and the "stacking" of charges, research has also found that program employees are empathetic to individuals involved with the criminal-legal system (Leon and Shdaimah, 2012). Programs that are heavily grounded in gender norms and roles can be counterproductive for certain offense types (such as violent resistance in intimate partner abuse). To reiterate, research has also found differing experiences between men and women in terms of challenging systemic inequalities (Miller et al., 2005). Nevertheless, diversion programs are still practical pathways to avoid the negative labels associated with involvement in the criminal-legal system.

PROBATION

Although laypersons use the terms **parole** and **probation** interchangeably, they have quite different meanings within the criminal-legal system. Parole, as in "life without parole," for example, refers to the possibility of release after serving a part of a sentence (Steiner, n.d.). Parole, which will be discussed further later in the chapter, entails serving time in a correctional institution. Probation, on the other hand, is an alternative to formal incarceration that places individuals under state control within the wider community during a period of either "unsupervised" or "supervised" observation. To force compliance, incarceration is a possibility if the terms of probation are not adhered to (Nolo, n.d.).

Although gender influences on the probation process may not be immediately obvious, there are clear gendered patterns that are worth exploring. First, because women are conceptualized in terms of emphasized femininity (as nurturing, passive, and weak), they are likely to be viewed as posing minimal risk to their surrounding community (Rodriguez, Curry, and Lee, 2006) if their offense did not deviate from expected gender norms so much that they would be considered "evil women" (Nagel and Hagan, 1983). Second, given that women interact with the criminal-legal system less often than men, they are unlikely to have extensive criminal histories, which is a significant consideration when determining a sentence (Streib, 1989). Finally, because women are often the primary caretakers of their children, the judicial system may hesitate to incarcerate them, given the serious negative repercussions to their dependents (Spohn and Beichner, 2000). For all these reasons, men are more likely to be incarcerated than women. Successful completion versus recidivism on probation also follows gender patterns.

Assessing the relationship between gender and probation outcomes is not easy given methodological challenges and inconsistent findings in prior research. Yet, in one large-scale study, Olson, Alderden, and Lurigio (2003) endeavored to examine the role of gender and probationer recidivism. They found that several demographic characteristics, aside from gender, were important. In terms of overall sample (men and women) and important demographic characteristics, young, unmarried men on probation without a high school diploma/GED and earning marginal income were most likely to recidivate. In addition to these demographic characteristics, probationers who were involved in gangs, had prior convictions (especially at the felony level), or had a history of substance abuse were also more likely to recidivate. While these results are interesting, there were differences across genders that are important to note.

Looking across genders, low educational attainment remained important and increased the likelihood of recidivism for men and women, but no other demographic variable reached statistical significance. Put another way, there was no difference among women in terms of age, martial status, or income and recidivism; however, most of these factors were important for men except for income. Likewise, the other variables previously noted remained important across genders apart from gang membership and substance abuse history. Those two variables increased the risk of recidivism for men on probation, but not for women on probation.

To further investigate these differences, this study also considered how men and women responded to probation conditions. Results suggest that men and women also differ in this area of the probation process. For instance, threatening a fine was not an effective method to encourage probation-condition compliance among women, but it was useful among men. Thus, not only do men and women differ in terms of risk factors of probation recidivism but also in how they respond to system interventions to encourage system compliance.

Finally, in Olson, Alderden, and Lurigio's assessment of the prior noted risk factors and likelihood of technical violations of a probation condition like curfew, many of the same relationships reappeared, with a few added characteristics worth noting. For example, individuals most at risk for technical violations were young, people of color, marginally educated individuals with low income. Additionally, those with prior convictions, especially misdemeanors, and substance abuse issues were most likely to receive technical violations. The only risk factors that reached statistical significance among women were educational attainment (low educational attainment correlated to higher risk of technical violation) and current substance use (current substance use correlated to higher risk of technical violation). In contrast, for men on probation, age (young most at risk), race (non-white most at risk), educational attainment (incomplete high school/GED most at risk), income (low income most at risk), gang membership (members most at risk), prior convictions (those with prior convictions, especially misdemeanors, most at risk), and substance abuse (past and current uses most at risk) were all significant factors influencing the likelihood of receiving a technical violation.

An examination into what sociodemographic characteristics influence parole and probation officers' responses to technical violations also points to gender. Results show that although there was no relationship between parole and probation officers' (PPOs) gender and support for formal responses to several types of violations (such as those concerning employment, meetings, curfew), women PPOs were more likely to pursue formal responses to community service violations than were men PPOs (Kerbs, Jones, and Jolley, 2009). These results again suggest that the whole probation process—from assignment to individual response, to program outcomes—differs by gender for all involved. Given these findings, it should be no surprise that gender also affects individual experiences during incarceration.

INCARCERATION

Gender shapes incarceration length and incarceration facility. As mentioned, scholars have repeatedly found that men receive harsher sentences than women for the same crime (the chivalry theory) (Doerner and Demuth, 2014) unless the woman's actions grossly deviated from gender norms (evil woman hypothesis) with no mitigating reason (Nagel and Hagan, 1983). The research we have presented shows that this leniency occurs through an informal process (that is, unconscious bias) and through the application of sentencing factors influenced by gender beliefs (Doerner and Demuth, 2014; Streib, 1989). This gendered application of punishment then affects the numbers of women and under formal state control, which in turn affect incarceration facility options (Kaeble and Cowhig, 2018).

Given the sheer number of men who are incarcerated compared to women, incarceration facilities differ widely in whom they house. Because fewer women are incarcerated, states often house all women in one or two facilities regardless of the security threat they pose. For example, as of this writing, South Carolina has two facilities that house women (Graham Correctional Institution and Leath Correctional Institution). Both facilities are level-2 facilities, or **medium security,** but house individuals who engaged in extreme violence (South Carolina Department of Corrections, n.d.). As an example, Susan Smith is at Leath Correctional Institution for the murder of her two sons (South Carolina Department of Corrections, Incarcerated Inmate Search, https://public.doc.state.sc.us/scdc-public/).

Due to more diversity in facilities, decisions about where to incarcerate men are related to the security threat they pose because of their crimes. For example, at the federal level, there are minimum-, low-, medium-, and high-security incarceration facilities (Federal Bureau of Prisons, n.d.). At **minimum-** and **low-security facilities,** there is a lower staff-to-prisoner ratio than at higher-security facilities and a stronger emphasis on future reintegration through work and other programming. As the level of security increases, so does the staff-to-prisoner ratio and the emphasis on social control. For instance, given the likelihood of escape and risk to the public, the criminal-legal system houses individuals who engaged in capital crimes at **maximum-security facilities** with death chambers. While laypersons may assume that higher levels of social control and staff provide a safer environment for all involved, there is inconsistent support for this belief across the literature (Briggs, Sundt, and Castellano, 2006).

The design and structure of correctional facilities also do not account for differences in gender of population, but rather emphasizes the social control of men. Housing women in facilities designed only for males can be problematic. For example, pregnant women need specialized prenatal care to ensure the health and safety of the growing fetus and mother, but a facility may not be able to afford such care (Tapia and Vaughn, 2010). Relatedly, pregnant women are more at risk of abuse from others given their inherent vulnerability. Finally, there may be a delay in correctional staff responding to medical crises that arise during pregnancy or problems that occur during labor.

During labor, women who are incarcerated need serious medical supervision to ensure the health of the infant and mother during delivery, which may require transportation to the closest medical facility (Tapia and Vaughn, 2010). At the medical facility, the pregnant incarcerated woman may be shackled to the hospital beds during labor. Aside from dehumanizing the woman, this practice prevents her from using various positions to aid in childbirth. Moreover, because the woman is under federal or state control, correctional personnel often limit the time she can spend with her infant before returning to the facility. Not only does this separation cause emotional stress for the infant and mother, but it also has health consequences for the infant in terms of access to breast milk and bonding. Finally, correctional facilities are limited in their ability to supply services following delivery, such as counseling if postpartum depression emerges. In a few pages, we discuss gender-responsive programming, which is meant to mitigate the consequences of these problems.

In addition to pregnancy, the simple biological functioning of female bodies presents special challenges to how women experience incarceration. Specifically, the monthly menstrual cycle is particularly dehumanizing and distressing for women who are incarcerated (Smith, 2009) because access to feminine products varies across correctional facilities (Polka, 2018). Moreover, women who are incarcerated have little agency in terms of coping with the body discomfort, fatigue, and headaches that can sometimes accompany the monthly cycle (Smith, 2009). The recent campaign entitled #letitflow addressed this dilemma. Through this innovative social media campaign, activists successfully pressured state lawmakers to ensure that women who are incarcerated have easy access to feminine hygiene products (Polka, 2018). There have been similar efforts at the federal level to address the needs of women who are incarcerated. For example, the Dignity of Incarcerated Women Act of 2017 would ensure women who are incarcerated had access to feminine products as well as take concrete steps to address their other unique needs, such as mothering (James, 2017). Despite being introduced, the bill had not yet moved out of committee in 2020.

Incarceration has long-term consequences even after release, chief among them poverty, and they vary across gender (Massoglia et al., 2014). For example, research shows a relationship between incarceration and early mortality among women but not men. One reason may be that the stigma of incarceration, particularly as framed through a gendered lens, has devastating consequences for the long-term health of women. In addition, because substance abuse is a persistent problem within correctional facilities, women may struggle with substance abuse post-incarceration, which may lead to early death. The relationship between women's incarceration and early mortality stems from a culmination of various risk factors, like health and stigma, that do not have the same impact on life outcomes for men. (See Active Learning Assignment 10.2.)

ACTIVE LEARNING ASSIGNMENT 10.2

Compassionate Social Control

As we have discussed in this text, the pathway to crime is indirect and varied across individuals. Often, the missed opportunities to intervene and help individuals off their destructive path become visible only in hindsight. Yet, even in cases of extreme violence, incarcerated individuals are still humans despite their flaws and are deserving of basic decency. Decent treatment is especially important because a significant percentage of the incarcerated population eventually reenters society.

Select at least six correctional facilities (three for men and three for women) and investigate the services they provide in terms of education, family, health, job training, mental and physical health, and so on. Then, discuss any differences between men's and women's facilities.

To summarize the chapter so far: gender influences men's and women's facility assignment, length of stay, and their experiences during their incarceration. Now we will focus on how men and women perform gender within the total institution that is government and state correctional control (Goffman, 1961). Men leave a social order that values hegemonic masculine ideals for an environment in which hyper and toxic masculinity reigns (Karp, 2010). As women are resocialized into correctional institutions, they also meet constraints on their behavior that are rooted in dominant gender ideals (Bosworth and Carrabine, 2001).

"Doing Gender" in Prison

Unlike conventional social life, where men perform masculinity through demonstrations of intelligence, strength, and wealth (Messerschmidt, 1993), incarceration strips them of these options and forces them to adopt a "prison code" of gender-congruent behaviors necessary for survival (Sabo, Kupers, and London, 2001, 10). These behaviors are akin to toxic masculinity, or the extreme adherence to hegemonic masculinity, and are necessary for survival in prison. The setting calls for men to be constantly emotionally, physically, and sexually dominant over other men. Part of this performance also entails self-reliance and supporting a culture of secrecy about the events occurring in prison.

In qualitative research on this topic, individuals who were formerly incarcerated reported acute awareness of the potential consequences if other system-involved individuals perceived that they are vulnerable (Ricciardelli, Maier, and Hannah-Moffat, 2015). One of the most significant threats, unsurprisingly, is the constant threat of physical harm. This led men to create handmade tools for survival (such as shanks) as well as to be always hyperaware of their surroundings. The research also showed that men who are incarcerated balanced their emotional vulnerability and seeking support from others to avoid appearing weak. Overall, within correctional facilities, men's violence was a tool that is defensive as well as offensive.

Men also engage in other methods to assert their masculinity and ward off conflict. For example, some join a prison gang for the symbolic capital as well as protection in numbers (Skarbek, 2011). Others may display their dominance through the sexual humiliation of others (Castle, Hensley, and Tewksbury, 2002; Man and Cronan, 2001). Indeed, even though engaging sexual activity with other men is typically stigmatizing for hegemonic men, it is different in prison, where effeminate men replace women as instruments for sexual gratification (Hefner, 2018; Just Detention International, 1994). Therefore, prison's hypermasculine environment is particularly dangerous for men who identify as sexual minorities (Hefner, 2018; Jenness and Fenstermaker, 2014). In one notorious example, cellmates repeatedly gang raped a fellow detainee in 1973 and he contracted HIV as a result (Just Detention International, 1994). That individual, who became the founding president of Stop Prisoner Rape, now called Just Detention International, died of AIDS. (See Active Learning Assignment 10.3.)

Women experience unique challenges during incarceration as well. While the threats to physical safety are not as plentiful as in correctional facilities housing men, women are not immune from violence. For example, although women who are incarcerated are less likely than men who are incarcerated to experience sexual violence, research shows they are more likely to experience non-consensual touching (Wolff and Shi, 2011). Moreover, while the difference was not statistically significant between genders, between 0.5 percent and 1.5 percent of women who are incarcerated reported experiencing rape by another individual who was also incarcerated—sometimes to secure protection (Wolff and Shi, 2011). Thus, both inside and outside of prison, sexual

---

ACTIVE LEARNING ASSIGNMENT 10.3

Prison Rape Elimination Act (PREA)

Please conduct research on the 2003 Prison Rape Elimination Act (PREA).
Next, navigate to the National PREA Resource Center's website (https://www
.prearesourcecenter.org) and select "Library." In the search panel, please select the term "LGBTI" and the type "Webinar." Select the webinar entitled "Understanding Lesbian, Gay, Bisexual, Transgender and Intersex Inmates, Residents, and Detainees." After you watch the video, create a one-page informational handout, designed for correctional employees, on what PREA is, important terminology, and the role of gender in shaping risks, experiences, and consequences of sexual violence.

violence remains a constant threat for women. This, as discussed throughout this text, stems from broader gender ideals, like emphasized femininity, that conceptualize women as instruments for pleasure who are constantly sexually available.

Gender ideals like hegemonic masculinity and emphasized femininity also shape interactions and the broader social structure within women's facilities. For example, unlike facilities housing men, where violence underscores the social order, relationships are important to keeping the social order at facilities housing women (Castle, Hensley, and Tewksbury, 2009). These relationships take the form of dyads and pseudo-families (Kolb and Palys, 2018). As in all social spheres, unwritten rules govern these relationships and there are sanctions for violations.

Studies have found that women who were incarcerated, including heterosexual women, form dyads, or romantic relationships with each other, in which each person assumes a heteronormative role (such as "femme," or feminine individual akin to girlfriend, and "butch," or masculine individual akin to boyfriend) for emotional and sexual comfort, for economic and physical protection, and to perform expected gender roles while doing time (Castle, Hensley, and Tewksbury, 2002; Kolb and Palys, 2018). These relationships mirror those outside prison, and "masculine" partners (also called "studs") are dominant in their interactions and relations both with their femme partner, who is submissive, and with other individuals broadly (Kolb and Palys, 2018). These roles are especially pronounced when another individual who is incarcerated, attached or not, appears to be making advances on an "attached" person. According to interview data collected by Kolb and Palys, such advances violate an unwritten rule, and the "violator" is likely to experience a physical confrontation in a scenario similar to a hypermasculine man asserting his dominance outside prison if he perceives another man making advances toward his partner.

Building solidarity and safety through setting up relationships, rather than using violence, is a gender-congruent method by which women navigate and protect themselves within their unfamiliar environment (Castle, Hensley, and Tewksbury, 2002). Aside from romantic partnerships, women who are incarcerated also form kinship networks or pseudo-families to secure emotional comfort, protection, and status and respect among their fellow incarcerated individuals (Kolb and Palys, 2018). These families mirror dominant sociocultural norms outside prison: individuals who are incarcerated performing masculinity via behaviors and in physical appearance are called "play dads," individuals who are incarcerated performing femininity are called "play moms," and younger individuals who are incarcerated are called "play children" or "play brother/sister." Unwritten rules govern pseudo-families, such as showing loyalty to "family members" even if it results in severe consequences, such as administrative punishment. In sum, gender on has a strong effect on prison experiences and identity performances. Thus, gender-responsive programs are immensely important for both the incarcerated individual and the wider society that will receive the individual upon release.

Gender-Responsive Programming

In recognition that the pathway to prison as well as the prison experience itself is complicated and varies across backgrounds, there was a push in the 1990s to create a "gender-responsive" correctional system that accounted for risk factor differences, with an emphasis on women, instead of the "one-size fits all" approach (Wright et al., 2012). Risk factors uniquely affecting women involved in the criminal-legal system include past criminal and victimization history, mental health, substance use, and sociocultural factors like pressures associated with motherhood. Since the 1990s, some prisons have become gender-responsive, but the approach is not universal. Nonetheless, gender responsiveness remains important given that most women become involved in the criminal-legal system because of nonviolent drug or property offenses, so planning for their success and eventual reentry into society should begin as quickly as possible. For example, because research has found women often engage in crime as a result of marginalization, especially economic marginalization, supplying occupational training is a way that correctional facilities could respond to women's needs.

Another gender-responsive program concerns women's multiple societal roles, such as mother and wife. For some mothers who are incarcerated, their children are positive motivators and encourage their success (Granja, 2016). On the other hand, separation from their children can be emotionally and psychologically harmful to mothers who are incarcerated and blame themselves for the distance. The importance of children is why diversion programs like Tamar's Children developed (discussed in "Diversion Programs" in this chapter). Aside from these direct impacts, mothers who are incarcerated experience the unique challenges of securing childcare and taking part, albeit from afar, in the raising of their children. Although many men who are incarcerated also have children, society places the onus on mothers as the primary caretakers. Thus, when the federal government or a state government incarcerates a mother, she must reconcile how to continue to be a "good mother" while also having deviated from the ideal notions of femininity by engaging in criminal activity. One route to mitigating that societal pressure is through gender-responsive programming. (See Active Learning Assignment 10.4.)

Other gender-responsive initiatives are programs that address the likelihood of recidivating by mitigating the challenges associated with mental health, confronting residual impacts of trauma, and addressing substance abuse issues (Wright et al., 2012). Another initiative is to encourage correctional staff to emphasize interpersonal communication rather than direct and punitive action, reflecting the interpersonal interaction differences between

---

ACTIVE LEARNING ASSIGNMENT 10.4

Helping Children of Incarcerated Parents

Please search Amazon or another resource for books designed for children of incarcerated parents. As you look through the previews of the books, take note of the gendered portrayal of fathers and mothers. Document any specific gender language and gendered themes (i.e., fathers as protectors, mothers as caretakers).

Then, please search for books designed for children of incarcerated parents identifying as LGBT-QIA+. After conducting the search, design a book for children of incarcerated parents with a focus on fathers or mothers, or both. However, avoid using any gender-specific roles or terminology in the presentation of fathers and mothers.

After completing the book, write a brief reaction statement about whether this assignment, and specifically the avoidance of gender-specific framing, was difficult and why.

---

men and women. By being gender-responsive, the criminal-legal system can make it more likely that women will successfully complete their sentence, reenter society, and avoid recidivating.

DEATH PENALTY

The United States is one of the few fully developed countries that uses the death penalty. Australia, Canada, and all of Europe (except for Belarus) have abolished it. The only comparable countries that still actively use it are Japan and Singapore (Smith, 2018). The abolition of the death penalty in so many countries stems from research that shows it is not an effective deterrent (Dölling et al., 2009) and that it has been unevenly applied across individuals of different genders and race (Dovidio et al., 1997; Mitchell, 2005). In other words, not only does research show there is no empirical or social benefit to administering the death penalty, but its application is influenced by social characteristics of defendants.

Research shows that the imposition of the death penalty varies across genders. The death penalty is less likely in cases involving women (Shatz and Shatz, 2012). This disparity likely stems from the broader patriarchal notion that women are weaker than men and in need of protection (Connell, 1987); therefore, women defendants are less likely to be sentenced to death than men defendants because they are widely perceived as posing little risk to others. However, the death penalty is more likely in cases where women defendants grossly deviate from their gender role and there is no mitigating explanation

Christa Pike

Research the case of Christa Pike and her role in the murder of Colleen Slemmer (Kern, 2001). Pike engaged in the offense while living in Knoxville, Tennessee, where she was participating in the University of Tennessee's Job Corps program. While in this program, Pike met her boyfriend, Tadaryl Shipp, who was a Satanist, and she was fiercely devoted to him. Pike was so devoted, in fact, that she hatched a plot to kill Slemmer, whom she believed was trying to lure Shipp away. Pike's murder of Slemmer, which involved torture and bashing in her skull, sent shockwaves across Tennessee. At the conclusion of the case, the judge sentenced Pike to death by electrocution, but case reporting openly acknowledged she would never experience it given her female gender and white race. To this day, Christa Pike remains incarcerated in Nashville. Moreover, she was not among the list of individuals executed in Tennessee between 2019 and 2020—all of whom were men (Wadhwani, 2018).

1. What is your opinion of this case?
2. How could this have been prevented? Please explain.

for their actions. For instance, Farr's (2000) research shows that receiving the death penalty is more likely among women viewed as "manly," who have committed "masculine" offenses, or who are perceived as lesbians (correctly or incorrectly). An "evil woman" is considered unworthy of leniency and protection. Yet, again, the death penalty is still more likely for a system-involved man than for a woman.

Gender concepts like emphasized femininity and gender frameworks like the chivalry theory and the evil woman hypothesis affect decisions about imposing the death penalty. Because of emphasized femininity in Western societies, which conceptualizes women as caring, nurturing, passive, sexually available, and submissive to hegemonic men, system-involved women who commit gender-incongruent crimes, such as murdering their children or their spouse, are severely punished by the patriarchal system as they are a threat to the prevailing social order (Shatz and Shatz, 2012). Put another way, they are "evil women" who deserve society's most extreme punishment. On the other hand, in some cases, women receive leniency (chivalry theory) where there is a gender-congruent rationale such as mental illness or where the defendant aligns with dominant gender ideals, such as overreaction in terms of self-defense (Nagel and Hagan, 1983).

Andrea Yates is an example of the evil woman hypothesis (see Case Study 9.1). In the summer of 2001, she drowned her five children at their Texas home. Her case garnered massive media attention, and news outlets labeled her "evil" and a "monster" (Hewitt, 2002). However, as the case progressed, reports surfaced that mental illness had plagued her for years (Lezon, 2006). Her psychiatrist had even advised Yates's husband against leaving her alone with the children.

At the conclusion of Yates's first trial, the jury convicted her of multiple counts of first-degree murder, and she was sentenced to life in prison with the possibility of parole. She was eligible for the death penalty, but a testimonial error by an expert witness might have swayed the jury away from that extreme punishment as he incorrectly implied that she had murdered her children after watching a *Law and Order* episode (*Yates v. Texas*, 2005). Although the prosecution argued that this error was minor and had no bearing on the case outcome, the Texas First District Court of Appeals decided it was important because it directly challenged whether Yates was insane at the time of the event. The court overturned the verdict and remanded the case back for retrial (Williams, 2005).

Yates's second trial had a similar, yet quite different, outcome. The jurors again found she had murdered her children, but they judged her not guilty because of insanity (Newman, 2006). In other words, even though she had engaged in a horrific event, she was not legally responsible because she could not distinguish between right and wrong at that moment, so it was excusable homicide. This outcome mirrored national sentiment about the case; a large percentage of the public believed Yates deserved mercy given her mental health history. Even though Texas could press more charges of capital murder that it did not pursue in the first two cases, prosecutors decided against it. Since that time, Yates has lived in various Texas mental health facilities, where she will remain until she shows that she is no longer a threat to society (Wilkinson and Spargo, 2016).

In contrast to the jury decisions about Andrea Yates, a jury in South Carolina sentenced Tim Jones Jr. to death for murdering his five children (Monk and Dulaney, 2019). Jones, like Andrea Yates, had five children and was struggling as a father. Though he had been employed in a prestigious job as a software engineer with a good salary, his defense attorneys shared details about his traumatic childhood history that (they alleged) informed his behavior. Like Yates's attorneys, Jones's attorneys argued that he suffered from crippling mental illness that included delusions. This information did not sway jurors: they convicted Jones and he was sentenced to death.

The cases of Tim Jones Jr., Christa Pike (Case Study 10.1), Karla Faye Tucker (Case Study 10.2), and Andrea Yates are real-life example of what gender and legal scholars continue to point out: that the imposing of the death penalty is a deeply gendered process. First, research continues to show that juries rarely impose the death penalty on women compared to similarly situated men, because they hesitate to do "the ultimate harm" to women (Streib, 2002). This pattern is so clear and pervasive that Supreme Court Justice Thurgood Marshall spoke to it in *Furman v. Georgia* (1972): "There is also overwhelming evidence that the death penalty is employed against men and not women. Only

32 women have been executed since 1930, while 3,827 men have met a similar fate. It is difficult to understand why women have received such favored treatment since the purposes served by capital punishment are applicable to both sexes."

Since *Furman v. Georgia* (1972), the gender gap in the imposition of the death penalty has not lessened. Women continue to engage in capital crimes, albeit much less often than men, but rarely are they executed for them. To support that claim, Reza (2005) reviewed the four cases of women on death row in North Carolina at that time with sentences imposed after *Furman*. In comparison, there were 187 men on death row in North Carolina. Although the sample was small, four characteristics were significant in imposing the ultimate punishment: (1) the crime was motivated (at least in part) by financial gain; (2) the crime was committed during the course of a felony, such as kidnapping or robbery; (3) the crime was especially heinous, atrocious, or cruel (for example, slow poisoning); and (4) the crime was not a "one-off" for the individual. Given these characteristics, these women greatly deviated from dominant gender norms associated with femininity and were easily seen as "evil women" and deserving of death.

Part of the reason for this continuing gender disparity is that the application of aggravating and mitigating factors in death penalty cases varies between women and men (Streib, 1989). In other words, as some legal scholars have pointed out, even though gender is not a recognized "aggravating" or

---

CASE STUDY 10.2

Karla Faye Tucker

The state of Texas executed Karla Faye Tucker for a particularly gruesome double murder in the 1980s. The murder occurred during a home invasion and robbery where Tucker took part in the execution of two individuals. The method of execution involved multiple blows to each individual by a pickax, with sexual undertones. Tucker reported that she had experienced multiple orgasms during the homicides (*Tucker v. State*, 1988). Given the nature of the homicides, it is not surprising that the jury sentenced Tucker to death.

However, what *is* surprising is how Tucker reinvented herself while on death row. By the time Texas was ready to impose the punishment, a large swath of the public was calling for a stay of execution. Governor George W. Bush even admitted to feeling uneasy about the execution of a woman but noted that he could not treat Tucker differently than any other defendant (Howarth, 2002).

1. Investigate how Tucker reinvented herself during her incarceration.
2. Frame this shift in public opinion through a gendered lens. In other words, discuss the role of concepts like emphasized femininity (Connell, 1987), the chivalry theory, and the evil woman hypothesis (Nagel & Hagan, 1983) in how laypersons viewed Tucker at sentencing versus shortly before her execution in 1998.

"mitigating" factor in state statutes, it underlies considerations about whether to impose the death penalty. For example, one often-noted aggravating factor is earlier criminal history, which is statistically less likely among women defendants than among men defendants. In addition, state statutes often include future criminality as an aggravating factor. Given dominant gender conceptions like emphasized femininity and hegemonic masculinity, jury members may perceive women as less dangerous than men. This punishment disparity also stems from mitigating factors, which can reduce sanctions imposed on system-involved women as compared to men. Even when the mitigating factors are very similar, Streib notes that men who break the law often receive harsher punishment than women who break the law.

Not only is there a clear gender disparity in the imposition of the death penalty, with gendered concepts like hegemonic masculinity and emphasized femininity affecting death penalty outcomes, but there are also disparities *within these groups*. In other words, the ramifications of whether a defendant adheres to dominant gender ideals are compounded by other societal methods of stratification such as ableism, classism, and racism. This intersectional perspective adds insight as to why certain groups of men, particularly men of color, are overrepresented among those who are paying the ultimate price (Cohen and Smith, 2010). Likewise, these interlocking systems of oppression help explain why certain groups of women, particularly those who challenge notions of emphasized femininity, are overrepresented among individuals paying the ultimate price (Farr, 2000). Thus, not only do beliefs about gender underscore the unequal imposition of the death penalty across men and women, but they also frame why (in part) there is difference within gender groups. This is unlikely to change because gender informs public attitudes about the death penalty as well.

In an analysis investigating support for the death penalty from 1972 to 2002, Cochran and Sanders (2009) found women have consistently and significantly been less supportive of the death penalty than men. To understand why this gap has persisted for years, these scholars evaluated several variables that accounted for gender norms and roles, structural gender inequality, and value dispositions. Contrary to some of the theoretical perspectives described in this chapter, none of the variables assessed in their study were successful in accounting for the gender gap in support for the death penalty. These findings suggest that the academic community needs better measures to understand the nature of the gender difference in support for the death penalty.

PAROLE

For most individuals involved in the criminal-legal system, there is a possibility of either completing their sentence or being released via parole. To reiterate, parole is awarded when an individual involved in the criminal-legal system has served part of their sentence and is granted release with conditions governing their behavior. If those conditions are violated, the rest of the sentence can be reimposed, and the individual can be reincarcerated. This happens to many individuals involved in the criminal-legal system according to data collected by the Bureau of Justice Statistics (Alper, Durose, and Markman, 2018).

In the decade following their release, 83 percent of individuals involved in the criminal-legal system are arrested again. This percentage includes all individuals released: those who have completed their sentence and those who are paroled. While the percentage of rearrests is highest during the first year (40%+), in the ninth year following release, the rearrest percentage is still 24 percent (Alper, Durose, and Markman, 2018). This study showed that rearrested individuals were less likely to be violent felons than those who had been arrested for property or drug crimes. If an individual had engaged in a violent felony prior to release though, they were most likely to be rearrested for engaging in similar offenses rather than a property or drug offense. There were gender differences in who was rearrested, but these were not critical differences.

As discussed in terms of sentencing guidelines, gender underscores parole decision factors as well as challenges with reentry. At the start of the parole process, gender is influential in later actions. For instance, one study found that when men were reviewed for possible parole, their risk score assessing future criminality was the principal factor influencing decisions (Erez, 1992). While other factors were considered, like emotional stability (2%), these did not have as much impact on final decisions. As Erez points out, this reflects dominant gender ideals that associate violence with masculinity, which in turn frames men who come to the attention of the criminal-legal system as inherently "dangerous men" (119). On the other hand, the risk score was not the most significant factor in decisions about women confronting possible parole. Instead, when considering a woman for parole, the important factors were her marital status and her skillset. These findings, coupled with qualitative statements like the following, show that gender ideals also shape decisions about parole: "These women do not have a husband to return to [and that's why marital status is important]" (121).

Although the emphasis on a husband's presence is not found elsewhere in the literature, studies do show that men and women face different challenges in their reentry to society that affect the likelihood of rearrest (Spjeldnes and Goodkind, 2009). For both genders, it is particularly important to reintroduce individuals who were formerly incarcerated into prosocial and positive social environments where the "criminal" label and associated stigma does not lead to relapse into problematic behavior. In studies noted by Spjeldnes and Goodkind, this was the most crucial need for women who were formerly incarcerated, but it was also important for men. Aside from supportive social environments, studies have found many women who relapsed into problematic behavior engaged in substance abuse offenses and prostitution; therefore, programs addressing economic sustainability and substance abuse counseling are also important for reintegration success. Finally, programs need to address the relationship between formerly parents who were formerly incarcerated and their children; because although society assigns women to the primary care-taker role, fathers' connections to their children are also important for success-ful post-release behavior.

One program that focuses on easing the transition from incarceration to successful reintegration is the Transition from Prison to Community Initiative (TPCI) (Holtfreter and Wattanaporn, 2014). This 2001 collaborative National Institute of Corrections program involved both academics and practitioners in its design and implementation and was launched to increase prosocial behavior post-release. To achieve that lofty goal, the program begins during incarcera-tion with an initial assessment and classification that informs a "success plan," which follows the participant throughout their incarceration and release. What is interesting about TPCI is that it is flexible enough to respond to the unique needs and background of each system-involved individual, unlike one-size-fits-all approaches. Holtfreter and Wattanaporn highlighted the program's ability to be gender-responsive as a notable strength. This finding again underscores the importance of accounting for gender in future social behavior.

SUMMARY

In this chapter, we discussed how gender underscores every aspect of the pun-ishment phase for individuals involved in the criminal-legal system. As we have discussed throughout this text, no social interaction or process is immune from the effect of gender, in addition to other forms of social stratification. We presented research that shows that the intertwining of concepts like empha-sized femininity and hegemonic masculinity with frameworks like the chivalry theory and the evil woman hypothesis often leads to harsh sentences imposed on men yet some leniency granted to women in certain situations. These pat-terns then affect the experiences men and women have within the correctional system, whether via formal incarceration or through alternatives to incarcera-tion like probation. While all individuals suffer consequences under federal or state control, the challenges and risks experienced by women and men do dif-fer. Even upon release, women and men suffer different long-term conse-quences from incarceration, which may lead to early mortality among women. Thus, as in all areas discussed in this text, awareness of how gender shapes our beliefs is critically important when imposing punishment on individuals.

"Boys' Clubs"

Gender and Employment in the Criminal-Legal System

KEY TERMS

► culture of corrections
► daddy bonus
► double-life strategy
► gendered organization
► glass ceiling
► glass wall
► harassment
► iron maiden
► leaking pipeline
► little sister
► mother
► motherhood penalty
► pay gap
► race matching
► seductress
► sexual harassment
► shrinking door
► tokenism

LEARNING OBJECTIVES

► Understand how gender can impact one's experience working in the criminal-legal system.
► Appreciate the history and current issues for women working in the criminal-legal system.
► Recognize the reasons why working in the criminal-legal system is different for women, people of color, and those who identify as LGBTQIA+.

The criminal-legal system, which typically includes policing, courts, and corrections, has been a male-dominated system since its inception. Traditionally most women who worked within this field were invisible and given clerical tasks or work guarding women or attending to juveniles— "women's work" (Barberet, 2014). The criminal-legal system has been, and in some places still is, a "boys' club" run by men and permeated with masculinity (Rabe-Hemp, 2008b; Rabe-Hemp, 2018). The physicality of police and corrections officers' work has contributed to viewing it a masculine field. Although working as a lawyer or within the legal profession is not physical, the ability to be cold, rational, and calculating is viewed as a more masculine trait (Barberet, 2014). The masculine culture and work environment in the criminal-legal system can pose challenges for women, people of color, and LGBT people. (Note that at times in this chapter we use the term LGBT and not LGBTQIA+, when referring to research that has specifically only examined lesbian, gay, bisexual, and transgender workers. Also, even though the discussions of women in this chapter may include transgender women, historically the research has focused on cisgender women or may have misgendered individuals. The section in this chapter on LGBTQIA+ individuals includes transgender women's experiences.)

THE CHALLENGES OF NOT BEING A "GOOD OLD BOY"

More women, people of color, and LGBTQIA+ individuals work in the criminal-legal system than ever before, but they face challenges that their male (especially white male) colleagues do not, such as tokenism, harassment, pay and benefits disparities, and discrimination. These challenges can make work difficult and cause emotional strain and distress, such as depression and anxiety, which lead to employee turnover. This chapter will explore what it is like for people who historically have not been working in the criminal-legal system to be working in a traditionally masculine and white environment.

Tokenism and Discrimination

While increasing numbers of women, individuals of color, and LGBTQIA+ individuals are working in the criminal-legal system, women, especially women of color, often face the challenge of tokenism. The term **tokenism** was coined by Kanter (1993) to describe the experiences of women employed in business, which had historically been very male-dominated. The one or two women working in an organization were often perceived as tokens of gender equality, hired for the sake of appearances. The term *token* usually has a negative connation, as the token individual is allegedly filling a slot because of a personal characteristic and not merit. The idea of being a token has been expanded and is now used to refer to anyone of an underrepresented group, thus representing a group, whether based on gender, race, ethnicity, or sexual orientation.

Kanter considered people to have a token status if they were members of a group that made up a small part of an organization's population, often 15 percent or less. These individuals face challenges that employees that are part of the majority group (whether it be gender, sexual orientation, or race) do not experience. This can make their work life much different and often harder than the work life of those who are part of the majority. An individual deemed a token by colleagues may experience discrimination, sexual harassment, verbal or physical harassment, exclusion, and/or segregation (Kanter, 1993).

According to Bureau of Labor Statistics (2019) estimates, white workers make up 78 percent of the US workforce, and men make up 53 percent of all those working today. Men make more money than women across all age groups. Men with children make more money than men who do not have children. However, women with children earn 10–15 percent less than women who do not have children. In a comparison of gender and race, white women earn 15.9 percent less than white men, Black women earn 3.7 percent less than Black men, Asian women earn 25.8 percent less than Asian men, and Hispanic women earn 10.8 percent less than Hispanic men (Bureau of Labor Statistics, 2019). The same trends hold true for those working in the criminal-legal system. Men, predominately white men, dominate policing and corrections.

Research on tokenism suggests that individuals of color working in the criminal-legal system still experience negative consequences at work because of their status. Surveys of female police officers reveals that they typically make up 15 percent or less of their departments and reported less job satisfaction, more occupation-related depression, and more issues with self-esteem related to their work environment. Stroshine and Brandl (2011) found that all police officers who were minorities in the department (that is, who belonged to a group that made up less than 15% of the department) experienced the effects of tokenism, but that Black men and women experienced it at the highest level, with harassment, bullying, and workplace stress.

The ill effects of tokenism are most often seen in discrimination within the workplace. Women of color face discrimination at higher rates than other groups (Crenshaw, 1989; Collins and Moyer, 2008). Research by the US Equal Employment Opportunity Commission found that Black women filed more claims of employment discrimination than any other group. Women of color are also more likely to lose discrimination cases than white women and men of all races (Best et al., 2011). (See Active Learning Assignment 11.1.)

Non-heterosexual employees often face discrimination and stigma when they do not follow the heteronormative rules and norms that exist in most workplaces (Warner, 1991). Although many organizations have enacted anti-discrimination policies, such policies focus on formal discrimination around promotion and recruitment (Jones et al., 2016) whereas the discrimination that

---

ACTIVE LEARNING ASSIGNMENT 11.1

Gender-Based Work Discrimination

Listen to the story (or read the transcript) "LaDonna" from *This American Life* (https://www.thisameri-canlife.org/647/ladonna) about race- and gender-based discrimination on the job.

 After listening to LaDonna's story, please write a one-page reflection on her experiences. Things to think about in your reflection:

   1. What is your reaction to what happened to LaDonna?
   2. Do you think that she experienced sexual harassment and/or discrimination? Why or why not?
   3. What is your opinion regarding how LaDonna handled what happened to her?
   4. Do you think that you would have reacted the same way? Why or why not?

LGBTQIA+ identifying individuals face is often more subtle and happens after they have been hired. For example, many LGBTQIA+ employees experience offhand comments, informal isolation, or segregation, such as exclusion from social gatherings and events (Hebl et al., 2002).

Harassment and Sexual Harassment

The Equal Employment Opportunity Commission (EEOC) is charged by the US government with enforcing federal laws prohibiting discrimination in the workplace and is empowered to investigate allegations of discrimination submitted by individual employees. The EEOC (2018) has defined **harassment,** which is considered a form of discrimination, as "unwelcome conduct that is based on race, color, religion, sex (including pregnancy), national origin, age, disability or genetic information." **Sexual harassment** includes unwelcome or unwanted sexual advances, sexual verbal or physical harassment, petitioning a person to perform sex favors, and making derogatory comments about a person's sex (which do not have to be sexual in nature). The person experiencing the harassment and person perpetrating the harassment can be of the same sex, and the person committing the harassment can be a woman. In work situations, the harasser can be a supervisor, coworker, client, or customer. (See Case Study 11.1, Active Learning Assignment 11.2, and Media Byte 11.1.)

 According to the EEOC (2020), 6,587 people filed complaints for sexual harassment in 2020. Of that number, 16.8 percent of complainants were male. Most incidents of sexual harassment are not reported, and many of those who experience them stay silent. Individuals who experience sexual harassment may not view what happened to them as sexual harassment. Even when an individual does perceive their experience as sexual harassment, they may worry about repercussions to their career or personal safety at work or home

#MeToo and Time's Up

The Me Too movement was founded by Tarana Burke in 2006, with the goal of assisting people who had experienced sexual violence in finding assistance and healing. Burke was particularly interested in focusing on young women of color from lower socioeconomic backgrounds. The use of the phrase "me too" was intended to empower women through empathy so that they would know that they were not alone. She wanted people to feel that others understood their pain and what they were going through. Burke wanted to create a community for those who have survived sexual violence and raise awareness, end the stigma that surrounds sexual violence, and work toward prevention of such violence.

In the fall of 2017, the movement gained national attention in the wake of allegations of abuse against Hollywood producer Harvey Weinstein, when it took the form of the hashtag #MeToo. As the hashtag spread, people all over the world used it to share their experiences on social media. Burke has said that this movement is the start of a larger conversation relating to the number of women who suffer sexual victimization and harassment and how society can work to change this.

In 2018, inspired by #MeToo and a string of allegations against men in Hollywood, nearly four hundred women in the entertainment industry, including Shonda Rimes, Reese Witherspoon, and Natalie Portman, announced the foundation of Time's Up, a legal defense fund and movement dedicated to ending sexual assault, harassment, and inequality in the workplace. This inequality is seen as the root of the criminal behavior that #MeToo has focused on. The organization is working to get policies and legislation passed, with a focus on equal pay and equal work environments, especially for low-wage jobs and women of color.

1. What are your thoughts about the #MeToo and Time's Up movement?
2. Do you think that these movements will prevent workplace harassment and violence for women? Why or why not?

Explore and Reflect on the #MeToo and Time's Up Movements

Please explore the official websites of the #MeToo (https://metoomvmt.org/) and Time's Up (www.timesupnow.com).

Write one to two pages describing your reaction to the content of the websites. Some things to consider in your response:

1. What is the mission of each group?
2. How are they working to meet their missions?
3. What did you learn exploring the websites that you did not know before?
4. What impact do you think that these movements will have on society? Please explain.
5. Do you think that these movements will help with arresting, prosecuting and sentencing abusers? Why or why not?

MEDIA BYTE 11.1   **#WhyWeWearBlack at the Emmy Awards**

Watch this clip, which discusses why many female celebrities opted to wear black at the 2018 Golden Globe Awards: https://variety.com/2018/film/news/whywewearblack-golden-globes-times-up-1202657554/. Then answer the following questions:

1. Do you think that this was an effective strategy to draw attention their cause? Why or why not?
2. What impact do you think that this has had? Please explain.
3. Why do you think that this happened only once?
4. Do you think that it drew attention to sexual assault? Please explain.

MEDIA BYTE 11.2   **I Am Student X**

While the #MeToo and Time's Up campaigns drew attention because of their connections to Hollywood, sexual harassment and assault occur in other fields, including in higher education. Please read this article about sexual harassment and victimization in higher education: https://www.vox.com/identities/2018/1/17/16880814/me-too-sexual-harassment-graduate-students-academia. Then answer the following questions:

1. What is your reaction to this article?
2. Do you think that sexual harassment and assault are an issue in higher education? Why or why not?
3. What types of initiatives do you think would be successful to prevent this from happening? Please explain.

---

and not file a report (Cochran, Frazier, and Olson, 1997). (See Media Byte 11.2 and Active Learning Assignment 11.3.)

The Pay Gap

The criminal-legal system, like other organizations and companies, traditionally has paid women less for their work, as women's work is often devalued (Padavic and Reskin, 2002). The **pay gap** is the difference between what working women earn and what working men earn. There are also differences in pay in terms of race. The US Bureau of Labor statistics (2019) quarterly reports regularly confirm that women make less than men, regardless of age group, race, or ethnicity, with white women receiving higher wages than women of color. (See Active Learning Assignment 11.4.)

ACTIVE LEARNING ASSIGNMENT 11.3

Your Institution's Sexual Harassment Policy and Procedures

Search your institution's website for "sexual harassment," "sexual harassment reporting procedure," and/or "sexual harassment policy" to find out how a person would go about reporting sexual assault, what the current policy is, and what resources are available for those who experience sexual assault.

In a one- to two-page double-spaced paper, reflect upon the process, the policy, and the services. Some things to consider may include:

1. How easy was it to find the information regarding sexual assault on your institution's website?
2. Was the language used to describe the policy and procedure clear and understandable? Please explain.
3. What do you think of the amount and types of services that are available to those who experience sexual assault?
4. Do you believe that there is enough information on your institution's website? What additional information might have been helpful to include?

ACTIVE LEARNING ASSIGNMENT 11.4

Investigate the Wage Gap

Check out the Bureau of Labor Statistics site that details earnings (https://www.bls.gov/cps/earnings.htm). Under the "Earnings by Demographics" section you will see "News Release: Usual Weekly Earnings of Wage and Salary Workers (Quarterly)." Please click on the PDF to view the most recent report on wages by demographic information.

Answer the following questions:

1. What were the median weekly earnings?
2. What was the women's-to-men's earnings ratio?
3. What were the differences in wages among the major race and ethnicity groups?
4. Did occupational group and educational attainment make a difference in wages. Please describe.
5. What is your reaction to seeing the wages based on demographics? Did anything surprise you? Please explain.

The global pandemic of COVID-19 also is likely to impact the pay gap between men and women. Women have been the ones who are trying to juggle full-time child care with working from home, and a greater number of women are taking the lead on household responsibilities. Women's unemployment rates have surpassed men's in the pandemic so far. Women of color in particular have been hit very hard and face higher unemployment and layoff rates than their white counterparts, which will increase the pay gap even more as women try to recover from the effects of the pandemic. Moreover, a disproportionate number of "essential workers" (such as those in the criminal-legal system) are women who have children. They need to have childcare if they are to work, and many women have had to decide whether to put their child in daycare (if it is available) or to stop working to protect their family but lose their job and earnings.

Parenthood affects earnings. Mothers earn less and fathers earn more than they did before becoming parents. This **daddy bonus** is higher for white men and Latinos, as well as men that are more highly educated. The reason that some men receive this daddy bonus, Hodges and Budig (2010) argue, is that men with more education and who are white and middle- or upper-class earn more, and men with those characteristics are often more likely to become fathers. This research indicates that *all* men experience a wage bonus, but the amount differs based race and ethnic group, education, professional level, and occupation. (See Media Byte 11.3.)

The US Census Bureau conducted research on the difference in pay of spouses and found that two years before having a child, men made only slightly more than their wives (Chung et al., 2017). But by the first birthday of their child, the gap in pay was more than $25,000 between husbands and wives. Some of this change may be attributed to women taking maternity leave and working less or not at all as result of having a baby, but the researchers believe that these reasons do not explain all of the difference, and that gender is a factor in regard to pay. For women under the age of thirty-five, the pay gap between women who are mothers and those who are not is more substantial than the gap between men and women.

Becker (1985) argued that mothers may be less productive in the workplace than nonmothers because of all the energy that they use on child-rearing. Mothers perform more domestic responsibilities than men do, often putting in

---

| MEDIA BYTE 11.3 | Equal Pay Day |

Equal Pay Day is a national day dedicated to raising awareness about pay inequity in the United States and globally. Read the following article and watch the accompanying video regarding equal pay and Equal Pay Day: http://fortune.com/2018/02/27/equal-pay-for-women-degree-education/. Then answer the following questions:

1. Do you think that Equal Pay Day will raise awareness and help to get a federal Equal Pay amendment passed? Why or why not?
2. Why do you think that the gender pay gap is different between races and gets wider as women age? Please explain.

a "second shift" after working all day, taking full responsibility for the care of the children and the house. Women typically have a full-time second profession as a parent, whereas men typically do not (Hochschild, 1990). Budig and England (2001) argue that the wage gap between mothers and nonmothers occurs not only because mothers may be less productive at work because of exhaustion and childcare demands, but also because there is discrimination against mothers. Anderson, Binder, and Kraus (2003) revisited this theory and examined the pay gap by education level. They found that the largest difference in pay between mothers and nonmothers was between those with only a high school education. However, as Correll, Benard and Paik (2007) point out, the ways that a company measures productivity may be very subjective. Unless scholars can easily quantify productivity in a neutral, unbiased way, such as the number of billable hours an attorney generates in a year, then the assessment of productivity may be flawed and assessment of productivity could be the result of bias.

Pregnancy and Family Responsibilities

Some of the biggest challenges that women face in the workplace are related to pregnancy and motherhood. In 1978, Congress passed the Pregnancy Discrimination Act. This law made it illegal to treat women differently than other employees who were "similar in their ability or inability to work." However, according to the EEOC, the number of pregnancy discrimination suits filed with it annually has been on the rise for two decades and is approaching an all-time high (EEOC, 2020). Women report unfair treatment with regard to pregnancy, as well as breastfeeding accommodations.

Being a good father and being a good worker are not seen as incompatible in our culture (Townsend, 2002). However, that is often not the case with motherhood. Correll, Benard, and Paik (2007) have found in their research that there is a **motherhood penalty**, which means that simply by being a mother, a woman is penalized both when applying for jobs and once she has job. The researchers tested this theory by having managers who were responsible for hiring examine two résumés from two equally qualified women. It was made known on half the résumés that the woman had a child. Managers were twice as likely to call the woman who did *not* appear to have a child. Other research has found similar results. Fuegen and colleagues (2004) discovered that when hypothetical individuals applied for a position as an attorney, women who had children were held to a higher standard than women who did not have children. In the same study, fathers were held to a significantly lower standard than women and men who did not have children. Cuddy, Fiske, and Glick (2004) found that adding "has a two-year-old child" to a description of an employee of any gender led to that person being rated as less competent than a comparable employee who did not have a child.

Gendered Identities and Categories at Work

Kanter (1993) argues that women are placed into different categories, or identities, within the workplace in a way that men are not. This is especially salient for male-dominated fields, such as those in the criminal-legal system. These four identities are very much associated with the classic societal gender conditioning of women. Coworkers and supervisors (both male and female) often place women into one of these categories, not necessarily consciously, but the interactions they have with female coworkers is often structured by their opinions of them. While these categories may appear to be dated, women are still viewed stereotypically by coworkers and supervisors and these categories are still of relevance today.

The first category is the **little sister**. This woman is viewed as incompetent, helpless, or needy. She needs someone to assist or take care of her and look after her. This is often how younger, newer female employees are viewed. In the criminal-legal system, this often how young women are viewed and treated when starting to work at agencies. The second category is the **seductress**, who is seen as overly sexual yet incompetent. Her friendliness may be misinterpreted as sexual interest in or flirtation with men at work. Often, if a woman is too friendly or uses physical touch at work, people may misconstrue her behavior as sexually motivated. The third category is the **iron maiden**. This woman is considered cold and harsh. She takes on masculine characteristics and has disregarded much of femininity. This woman tends to be older and may be in a more senior or supervisory position. Women working in criminal-legal system agencies may feel compelled to embrace the masculine nature of the organization in order to be successful. Finally, the **mother** takes care of others' needs, which can sometimes be seen as nagging or irritating, but also nurturing. These women are often the ones who will take on the work of others and go out of their way to please and help people. These categories are caricatures and do not fairly represent what women can do within the workplace or who they are (Lewis and Simpson, 2011). However, it is important to know that women may be viewed as one of these types by others based on their behavior or personality within the workplace. (See Media Byte 11.4.)

The Criminal-Legal System as a Gendered (Male) Organization

We begin the discussion of gender within the criminal-legal system by introducing the theory of **gendered organizations**. Acker (1990; 1992) argues that that organizations are inherently gendered and not gender-neutral. An organization has a structure, values, and individuals that work within it offering cultural ideas of gender that are prized and reinforced. This gendering of an organization is a contextual process seen throughout the day-to-day

> **MEDIA BYTE 11.4**   Changing Your Identity at Work
>
> Read "Being Black—but Not Too Black—in the Workplace," about individuals' experiences at work in relation to their identity: https://www.theatlantic.com /business/archive/2015/10/being-black-work/409990/. Afterward answer the following questions:
>
> 1. Do you think that feeling that you have to adhere to a certain ideal limits your potential for advancement? Why or why not?
> 2. What are some strategies that an organization could use if it wanted employees to be better able to be themselves? Please explain.

operations. It is not a characteristic that an individual possesses but rather how an organization functions and the structure it takes. It can also be seen in the types of behaviors, as well as the communication style and preferences, that are rewarded or ridiculed. A company that has family-friendly policies, work- and time-sharing between employees, benefits for same-sex partners, flexible schedules, relaxed dress codes, and an open-door policy for management may be seen as more feminine in nature because it appears to value individuality and a work-life balance, not just the bottom line or success at any cost.

Traditionally, the criminal-legal system legitimizes masculinity. This is not simply because criminal-legal system organizations consist mostly of men, although that is part of the reason. It is because of the structure and nature of the criminal-legal system as a paramilitary organization. It is a system that inherently values expediency, impartiality, and disregard for feelings and emotions—all qualities traditionally associated with masculinity. This may be in part due to the fact that men have molded its culture through policies, practices, and the way things are structured and handled on a daily basis (Acker, 2006).

When women or individuals from different backgrounds with different perspectives are employed in traditionally male-dominated institutions, this often changes the institutional culture (Wajcman, 1998). Men in organizations that have been male dominated may experience some trepidation, fearing change to their own work identities and their lifestyle and experience at work (Van Wijk and Finchilescu, 2008). For example, the first women working in the criminal-legal system were often met with discrimination and harassment (Brown and Heidensohn, 2000; Hunt, 1990).

To detect whether an organization has gender equality, we can look for official and unofficial markers. Official markers include the number of female employees and managers (Bowling et al., 2006). These numbers are facts that

---

ACTIVE LEARNING ASSIGNMENT 11.5

Reflecting on Gendered Organizations

Please describe an organization that you have worked in or been a part of that you felt was either masculine or feminine and describe why. Then share your experiences with a partner and encourage them to ask you questions.

---

cannot be disputed and are easily observable. Unofficial markers are more subjective and are often related to expectations and perceptions. For example, an organization may have 50 percent female supervisors, an official marker of equality, but those women may not have the same authority as their male peers in making decisions, which would be an unofficial marker. Both kinds of markers can provide insight into an organization's gender inclusivity. (See Active Learning Assignment 11.5.)

POLICING IN THE BOYS' CLUB

Research has shown that police have been homophobic (Bernstein and Kostelac, 2002; Burke, 1993; Burke, 1994; Colvin, 2008; Colvin, 2012; Colvin, 2015; Leinen, 1993; Miller, Forest, and Jurik, 2003; Panther, 2021), transphobic (Grant et al., 2011; Miles-Johnson, 2013), and sexist (Brown and Heidensohn, 2000; Rabe-Hemp, 2009; Rabe-Hemp, 2018; Westmarland, 2001). In addition, research has shown that there has been discrimination, prejudice, and violent acts committed against transgender individuals by law enforcement (Clements-Nolle, Marx, and Katz, 2006; Gagné, Tewksbury, and McGaughey, 1997; Grant et al., 2011; Grossman and D'Augelli, 2006; Hill, 2002; Leppel, 2016; Tee and Hegarty, 2006; Whittle et al., 2007; Witten and Eyler, 1999). This history may make people from those populations not overly enthusiastic to work as law enforcement. It can also make it difficult when people of color and/or women try to work within the policing organization. The difficulties are further complicated in the post–George Floyd and Breonna Taylor world, where the Black Lives Matter movement is drawing attention to the issues of bias and racism that arise in policing.

Female Police Officers

Although women have been involved in police organizations in the United States since before the 1970s (especially in clerical roles), that decade saw a major increase in the number of women working as sworn police officers

(Hunt, 1990; Rabe-Hemp, 2018). This increase can be attributed to the Equal Employment Opportunity Act (EEOA), passed in 1972, which allowed women to work as patrol officers alongside men (Rabe-Hemp, 2009). However, while women could now work as patrol officers, they were often excluded from much of the actual patrolling, or "action," which was left to the male officers (Bartlett and Rosenblum, 1977; Sichel et al., 1978). Research assessing women's performance as officers showed that they were equal to males in their duties and actually excelled at communication and defusing violence or hostile situations (Balkin, 1988; Rabe-Hemp, 2018; Schulz, 1995). In 1972, women were 2 percent of sworn police officers (Hickman and Reeves, 2006). Currently, there are an estimated 58,000 female police officers in the United Sates, which is about 12 percent of all sworn officers (Rabe-Hemp, 2018). The number of women in police organizations does not represent the communities that they serve in terms of gender and race as women make up a little over half the population in the United States, and the proportion of officers of color often does not reflect the demographics of most communities (Morabito and Shelley, 2015).

Research has shown that only a small percentage of female officers obtain promotions (Lonsway et al., 2002). An examination of female policing in England and Wales found that there was a lack of women in police leadership roles and a reduction in the number of women joining the ranks. Research in Australia has discovered that the proportion of female police officers typically peaks at around one third of all officers and then there will often be a period of decrease as women resign and leave the force, often as a result of not being promoted and lack of advancement opportunities (Prenzler and Sinclair, 2013). Cordner and Cordner (2011) found that the number of women who have been appointed to leadership positions in police forces in the United States has plateaued.

Challenges for Female Police

Collinson (2012) used Prozac as a metaphor when talking about the status and role of female police. Collison argues that Prozac, a drug that is used to treat depression, can induce what he refers to as "artificial happiness." If an organization does not allow any criticism or suggestions for improvement regarding issues of gender and instead reports that all is well with women in policing, then it is promoting what Collinson argues is akin to the effect of Prozac, an artificial happiness. This artificial façade is often employed by police agencies. If no problem is reported or identified, then there is no problem. While there are more women in policing than before, and many women report that they are thriving in law enforcement (Rabe-Hemp, 2008b; Rabe-Hemp, 2018), there are still problems pertaining to recruitment, promotion, and job satisfaction of female police officers, and they need to be addressed. The "Prozac" approach is not a sustainable one.

Promotion and Advancement

In examining why so few women take on supervisory or administrative positions within police organizations, research has shown that it is related to gender and the very gendered nature of the policing organization and promotion process. For a police officer to be promoted, the officer must first work hard as a patrol officer and gain the attention of senior officers. The officer must network within the police organization, making themselves known, often unofficially, to senior officers or administrators. Male officers benefit from this process as they are thought to be valuable patrol cops and good colleagues and partners, and they have an easier time finding and interacting with male mentors who are more senior officers and can assist them in promotion and advancement (Balkin, 1988; Franklin, 2007). The networking that leads to promotion for officers can be an informal process as well, which often benefits males more than females. Males are more likely to hang out together at bars or play sports off-duty, whereas women may not be invited or included. In these informal settings men can gain information, access to superiors, and advice for advancement. Female officers often struggle to take this same route to promotion as they are not invited to these informal networking opportunities and do not have the same sort of informal friendships (Shelley, Morabito, and Tobin-Gurley, 2011).

However, even when women would be under consideration for promotion, they may not elect to go forward. Whetstone's (2001) research revealed that women who were qualified for promotion often removed themselves from the process and/or did not take the needed exams. One of the main reasons cited was a concern that promotion would require a shift change that might conflict with child care and domestic responsibilities. Women often are the primary caregivers of their children and elderly family members and take on more household responsibilities than men, even in two-parent households where both adults work. As a result, women felt that they could not take on the additional work responsibilities, change their shifts, and also care for their family and household efficiently (Agocs, Langan, and Sanders, 2015).

Women also may not want a promotion because they do not want to provoke negative attention or take on a token status as a female leader in an organization filled with male leaders and employees. Archbold and Schulz (2008) found that female officers were encouraged to apply for positions not because of their qualifications but because of department initiatives to have more females in administrative roles. This led women to not apply out of fear of resentment or retaliation from colleagues. Women historically have encountered pushback from men when seeking advancement in their policing careers (Martin, 1978, 1979, 1989). Women have faced harassment, name calling, and further isolation or insubordination when they get promotions.

Research has shown that male officers have not been supportive of women joining police organizations and have not valued the work women do as officers, which can translate into administration (Balkin, 1988; Franklin, 2007; Herbert, 2001; Prokos and Padavic, 2002). As a result, women's applications are sometimes seen as less strong than men's for officer and administrative roles. Male officers may also balk at the idea of a woman in command as there is fear that she will not be respected or obeyed or that she will be "too emotional" to make the tough calls and be a strong leader.

As women have moved on from what was considered "women's work" in police departments, there has been pushback from within. In the past, women on patrol were forced to wear skirts or carry their gun in a purse so that they could still appear "ladylike," further separating them from their male counterparts (Franklin, 2007; Heidensohn, 1992), often to demean them. Today there may not be quite this level of reaction toward women, but the sentiment may linger in some departments that women are not equal to male officers and therefore not fit to lead.

Women in police departments often find both a glass ceiling and a glass wall. A **glass ceiling** is an invisible barrier preventing women and people of color from moving up the career ladder to the top levels of leadership in a company or organization. However, what is more common is a **glass wall**. This prevents women and people of color from moving laterally to a position with more possibility of climbing the career ladder. The ability to be promoted is also a matter of the opportunities available to women and people of color within the organization. Many policing organizations keep women out of certain sections of a department and in positions relating to women and children. Many women advance to sexual assault investigators or are promoted to task forces relating to children and human trafficking or domestic violence. Only rarely do they get positions in departments that lead to higher positions, such as homicide, gangs, or special weapons and tactics (SWAT) (Sneed, 2007).

Exclusion and maltreatment within the policing organization are other reasons that there are few female leaders. Female officers may resign before they can advance in their careers, which is referred to as a **leaking pipeline** (Bailyn, 2003). Due to the nature and challenges of police work, women may have a harder time coping and adapting than men. Policing is a job that is very demanding of time and energy. When starting out, officers often have rotating shifts, overtime, and little control over their schedules or assignments. This is often a challenge for women with childcare or family responsibilities who need stable schedules. Women who are promoted often have support from family and spouses along the way in order to deal with the challenges of police work. (See Media Byte 11.5.)

Job Satisfaction

Women, still a minority when it comes to policing, often have concerns to deal with that their male colleagues do not, which can lead to job dissatisfaction.

> **MEDIA BYTE 11.5**   Female Police Chiefs
>
> Please watch the following video clip and read the corresponding article about female police chiefs:
>
> http://www.sun-sentinel.com/news/florida/fl-sb-south-florida-female-police-chiefs-20171212-story.html
>
> 1. What is your reaction to this story?
> 2. Do you think that it is easier for women to become police chiefs today than in the past? Please explain.
> 3. Did the locations within the United States factor into these women becoming chiefs? Why or why not?
> 4. Do you think that the experiences of these women are similar to those of other women? Please explain.

Female officers often endure higher stress levels, more incidents of harassment, and greater discrimination than their male counterparts (Deschamps et al., 2003; Thompson, Kirk, and Brown, 2006; Chaiyavej and Morash, 2008). Women officers also have a more consistent lack of support and underestimation of their abilities by administration and peers (Morash, Kwak, and Haarr; 2006). Police departments are traditionally masculine and have not adapted to include women, which is a key driver in the high stress and burnout rates among female officers. But women are finding ways to cope and fit in. Rabe-Hemp (2009; 2018) found that female officers were able to find success in male-dominated organizations by accepting and thriving in roles that are stereotypically "women's work," such as acting as caretakers for those who experienced offenses against them and assisting them. Female officers take pride in being able to do a good job in these roles.

Lesbian, Gay, and Bisexual Individuals Working as Police Officers

Research on the experiences of lesbian, gay, and bisexual (LGB) officers has revealed that working in an environment where heterosexuality is overtly dominant can present challenges. Burke (1993; 1994), one of the pioneers in this research, interviewed LGB officers in England and Wales and found that whether they openly disclosed or were merely suspected of not being heterosexual, they experienced prejudice, discrimination, and harassment within their organizations. Officers reported that they endured professional humiliation, derogatory comments, and the refusal of colleagues to work with them, as well as physical violence and victimization. In addition, the officers said they experienced unfair distribution of work assignments and promotion and recruitment practices.

As a result of the challenges that these officers experienced in their work, many employed what Burke (1994) referred to as a **double-life strategy**, disguising their sexual orientation throughout their careers. They felt that in their work life, they were forced to hide who they were so that they could fit in and not be punished, harassed, threatened, or harmed. In their personal life, they tried to be more authentic but still felt oppression spill over from the pressure to conform in their work life. The findings of recent research by Collins and Rocco (2015) were similar to Burke's: gay male officers reported that law enforcement was still very much a heterosexual man's job, and they could not talk about their personal lives at work for fear of harassment or retaliation.

Research has shown that gay men often face more issues working in policing than lesbians or bisexual individuals do (Williams and Robinson 2004, 2007), and they experience discrimination at higher rates (Jones and Williams, 2015). Gay men are often stereotyped by their heterosexual colleagues, considered effeminate and not "tough" enough for the job. As a result, they may be rejected as candidates for policing (Praat and Tuffin, 1996) or, if employed as officers, they may be discriminated against in training, work assignments, and promotion opportunities (Jones and Williams, 2015). Many gay men limit their disclosures to other officers in order to avoid homophobic or bigoted comments or microaggressions (Charles and Arndt, 2013; Collins and Rocco, 2015). Praat and Tuffin argue that gay officers have such trouble with other (mostly male) officers because of the cultural ideal of the institution of policing as a "manly" profession. Furthermore, sodomy and homosexuality were once considered crimes. Gay officers tell their fellow officers they are gay first and every other characteristic or identity second.

Lesbians feel freer to talk with heterosexual male officers about their romantic life. They report that most male heterosexual officers just assume women in policing are all lesbians. More lesbians than gay men are "out" at work as they feel they are seen as strong and capable by their coworkers in a way that heterosexual women (seen as weak) and gay male officers (seen as less manly) are not (Mennicke et al., 2016).

Research in the San Diego Police Department found that while LGB police officers have experienced improvements in their overall working environment, they still face challenges. Participants reported issues obtaining promotion, difficulties in communication, derogatory and demeaning comments, and a feeling that their heterosexual colleagues resented them (Belkin and McNichol, 2002). In research conducted in the southwestern United States, Colvin (2008) found discrimination, unfair allocation of resources and work assignments, and fewer chances for promotion for LGB officers than for heterosexual officers. (See Media Byte 11.6.)

Colvin (2012) found these same issues to be pertinent in his comparative study between LGB officers in the United Kingdom and the United States. The research in the United Kingdom, with 836 LGB police officers from forty-three

---

MEDIA BYTE 11.6   Police Officer Proposes during Pride Parade

Read the following story and watch the accompanying video of a police officer proposing to his boyfriend at a PRIDE parade: https://www.theguardian.com /commentisfree/2017/jun/30/police-officer-proposal-gay-pride-london-social-media. Then answer the following questions:

1. What is your reaction to this story?
2. Were you surprised at the response of the public on social media to this proposal? Please explain.
3. Do you think that other gay or lesbian police officers will be empowered or disheartened by what happened? Please explain your answer.

---

police services (departments), revealed discrimination against LGB officers in training and placement, with those in smaller and larger forces more likely to experience discrimination than those in mid-size departments. This research also revealed that the rank of the officer was found to affect their perception of discrimination, with those of a senior rank perceiving more discrimination (Panther, 2021).

Transgender Police Officers

While the focus of research has been on women and LGB police officers, the empirical study of transgender individuals in law enforcement is an emerging area. Transgender police officers in the United States, England, and Wales reported a general lack of awareness within policing regarding transgender individuals. Transgender officers experienced varying levels of bias in their jobs, which seemed to correlate with the extent to which they conformed to the gender ideals of the organization they worked for. Officers who were transitioning on the job often faced a lack of understanding by colleagues about to what they were doing and why (Jones and Williams, 2015). (See Media Byte 11.7.)

However, some agencies are actively recruiting transgender officers, including in England and Wales. The Transgender Community of Police and Sheriffs (TCOPS) in the United States and the National Trans Police Association (NTPA) in the United Kingdom were both created to assist transgender officers and offer support networks of peers. (See Active Learning Assignment 11.6.) An examination by Panther (2021) of the membership of these two organizations indicates that fewer than 1 percent of officers in the United States and the United Kingdom openly identify as transgender. As with gay police officers, hiding who they are is often their strategy to work on the force without ridicule, discrimination, or victimization. Both TCOPS and NTPA reported an

---

MEDIA BYTE 11.7   **Working as a Transgender Police Officer**

Watch these two clips about transgender police officers and then respond to the questions below.
  https://www.nbcnews.com/video/transgender-police-officer-finds-acceptance-on-force-in-florida-983876163955
  https://youtu.be/Zl_RjjctHVw

1. What is your reaction to the stories of these two officers?
2. What was similar and different in what they shared?
3. Do you think that the experiences of these officers are similar to those of transgender officers of different racial or ethnic backgrounds? Why or why not?

ACTIVE LEARNING ASSIGNMENT 11.6

Check Out TCOPS

Please visit the Transgender Community of Police and Sheriffs (TCOPS) website (https://tcops-international.org/) and answer the following questions:

1. Describe the resources available on this site. How do you think these would be helpful to a transgender officer?
2. What are some allied transgender support communities? Why would it be important to list them?
3. In examining this site, what surprised you the most. Please explain.
4. If you were a transgender officer, do you think that you would utilize this website and the resources provided? Why or why not?

---

increase in membership from 2012 to 2015 (the most recent data available). This could mean that individuals are more willing to disclose that they are transgender or that more transgender individuals are beginning to work in policing. Many police departments have also been actively and publicly seeking transgender officers. Cities such as Houston, Austin, Aurora, and Cincinnati have encouraged transgender individuals to apply. There are also cities that have openly transgender officers who have received support from their departments and communities they serve (Astor, 2017). (See Media Byte 11.8.)

Policing for many is still a "boys' club," However, there is hope for female, lesbian, gay, bisexual, and transgender officers in the future. As communities and society become more tolerant of people who are different from themselves entering the force and moving into leadership roles, there will be a more accepting work environment. Officers have said that hearing "war stories" about the past treatment of LGB and officers of color has assisted them in see-

---

MEDIA BYTE 11.8   **First Transgender Police Officer Promoted to Captain in Portland**

Read this article about the first transgender police chief: https://patch.com /oregon/portland/ppb-promotes-first-transgender-captain. Then answer the following questions:

1. Do you think that the subordinates in this chief's department will be accepting and respectful? Why or why not?
2. What issues do you think that this person will face as a transgender chief, if any? Please explain your answer.
3. Do you think that your town or city would promote a transgender person to chief? Why or why not?

---

ing the positive changes that have occurred and makes them hopeful for more positive changes in the future (Collins and Rocco, 2015). However, more work needs to be done to ensure that all people have a place in policing and are treated with respect and equality.

CORRECTIONS

The main responsibility of corrections employees is to oversee and secure an unwilling, sometimes violent population. Research about corrections and gender has reached varying conclusions, with some detecting differences in attitudes and experiences between men and women, and others finding little differences. Researchers have acknowledged that there may be differences relating to gender that affect the perceptions of employees regarding their jobs (Camp, 1994; Lambert et al., 2005).

Female Corrections Officers

Historically, women in corrections (as in policing) worked in clerical roles and as security officers and counselors in juvenile and women-only gender-segregated facilities (Feinman, 1980). As in policing, the surge of women entering the field came in the 1970s with the women's rights movement and the passage of civil rights legislation. By 1978, thirty-three states had women working as correctional officers in men's prisons (Jurik, 1985). By the close of the 1980s, women were working in almost every correctional system in the nation (Carlson, Thomas, and Anson, 2004; Fry and Glaser, 1987). As the number of women employed in corrections has continued to grow, there has also been an increase in the number of Black and Hispanic women working in corrections (Belknap, 1991; Walters, 1992). The most recent statistics published by the Federal Bureau of Prisons (2018) indicate that 27.2 percent of federal corrections staff are female and 72.8 percent are male, with 62.8 percent white, 21.6 percent Black, 12.1 percent Hispanic, and 1.3 percent Native American.

The increase in the number of women and women of color in corrections can also be attributed to the fact that more women are receiving college educations and wanting to enter corrections, though for different reasons than men. Women often have more intrinsic reasons for wanting to work in corrections, such as a desire to help people, often through rehabilitation programming that is available in institutions (Farkas, 1999, Jurik and Halemba, 1984; Walters, 1992). Work opportunities for women within correctional institutions have been growing with mass incarceration and a growing population of incarcerated individuals. However, with the multifaceted nature of corrections in which officers wear many different hats on their job, there is a higher turnover rate for this occupation than for other jobs in the criminal-legal system (Camp and Camp, 2002).

Challenges for Female Officers: Will Someone Have Your Back?

Female correctional officers often struggle with working in a male-dominated environment, leading to less satisfaction with their jobs and careers and often higher stress levels. Overtime is often required in corrections, which means long shift work and time away from home and family. Women working in corrections work the same hours as men regardless of domestic and childcare responsibilities. In some correctional settings, corrections officers can work sixty to seventy (or more) hours per week, which can be difficult with the often-heavy domestic workload of women. This can cause women to have higher work-related stress and job dissatisfaction (McMahon, 1999; Watts, 2009).

One of the biggest daily challenges and job stressors for women corrections officers is acceptance by their male coworkers (*Beneath the Veneer*, 1990; Zimmer, 1987). This is often cited as a reason many women leave corrections. Some male correctional officers believe that women are not able to perform the job as well as men and they can be very vocal in expressing their opinion to their female coworkers (Camp and Langan, 2005; Camp, Steifer, and Batchelder, 1995). Male officers often feel the need to protect female officers from harm and "take care of them" within the institution. This often sends the message to women that they are not able to take care of themselves, are not as competent as males (Crewe, 2006), and are "soft" and need a man to help them (Camp and Langan, 2005). Many female correctional officers have reported paternalistic treatment by male coworkers, creating job stress or dissatisfaction at work (Farnworth, 1992; Hunt, 1990; Jurik, 1985; Pogrebin and Poole, 1998).

Research in the past twenty years has revealed that correctional institutions are still patriarchal in nature. Female correctional officers face high levels of hostility and sexual harassment from incarcerated people and fellow officers or superiors (Carlson, Thomas, and Anson, 2004; Savicki, Cooley, and Gjesvold, 2003), but many women do not report such treatment or say anything to their male colleagues out of fear of retaliation and losing out on promotion opportunities, reducing their ability to advance their career within the system (Matthews, Monk-Turner, and Sumter, 2010). Female officers also face issues with discrimination, sexism, and isolation as there are usually few female officers in an institution (Braid, 2012; Butler and Ferrier, 2000; Gleeson, 1996; Paap, 2006). As a result of these conditions, women also experience a lack of institutional socialization and do not make connections with coworkers in the same way that male officers do, which affects their satisfaction with the job (Belknap, 1991).

Female corrections officers struggle with comments and questions about their very presence in the institution (Britton, 1997; Jurik, 1985; Savicki, Cooley, and Gjesvold, 2003). Coworkers may challenge their abilities and their right to be working with them, often seeing them a token woman hired only to check a box for diversity's sake (McMahon, 1999). However, female officers have strengths that are different than male officers, which can be of use in the institution and give women a sense of value and accomplishment and build their self-esteem. Women are often seen as caregivers or nurturers, which can be an asset in some situations and in helping incarcerated individuals and the institution through challenging times (Camp and Langan, 2005; Crewe, 2006). (See Media Byte 11.9.)

MEDIA BYTE 11.9   ### Working as Female Corrections Officer

Read the following article about women working in male prisons: https://www
.washingtonpost.com/local/social-issues/women-working-in-male-prisons-face-
harassment-from-inmates-and-co-workers/2018/01/27/21552cee-01f1-11e8-
9d31-d72cf78dbeee_story.html?noredirect=on&utm_term=.adc2843e4ce3.
Afterward, answer the following questions:

1. What is your reaction to this story?
2. Do you think the conditions for female correctional officers reported in this story are normal? Why or why not?
3. What do you think that it would be like to work in the conditions described in the article? Please explain.

Promotion and Advancement

Research has shown that advancement in correctional careers has been difficult for women, just as it has been for women in policing. This may be a result of the fact that female correctional officers must navigate a hypermasculine culture of men in power, with colleagues questioning their capability at every turn. There is a **culture of corrections** (McMahon, 1999) in which male officers are seen as superior based on the traits of toughness and a capacity for violence and aggression if needed. Women are seen lacking these necessary traits for correctional institutional work, which often puts them at a disadvantage. This keeps women as officers often feeling powerless as they are unable to advance up the line for promotion (Burdett, Gouliquer and Poulin, 2018). Women often have difficulty relocating to correctional jobs in other areas that could offer opportunities for advancement as easily as men. Because of greater family and financial responsibilities, women correction officers often stay in the same institution long-term (Camp, 1994; Griffin, 2007; Lambert et al., 2005).

Lesbian, Gay, Bisexual, and Transgender Individuals Working as Corrections Officers

Research has shown that the discrimination that LGBT officers face is extensive (Colvin 2015, Panther, 2021), though more scholarship is needed, particularly about transgender officers. In 2015, the Williams Institute reported that 40 percent of discrimination reports from all public employers were from LGBT individuals and came from law enforcement and correctional facilities (Mallory, Hasenbush, and Sears, 2015). Mennicke and colleagues (2016) interviewed LGBT corrections officers in focus groups and found that gay and lesbian officers were stereotyped and discriminated against differently. Lesbian officers reported that they were expected by coworkers and superiors to be more masculine or tough than heterosexual women. Gay male officers said that they were expected to be more feminine and sensitive than heterosexual men. However, both lesbians and gay men said that their colleagues thought them to be hypersexual. This stereotype has real implications for the jobs of corrections officers. Two of the lesbians in this study reported that they had been falsely accused of sexual misconduct because they were taking too long to do their checks and evaluations of the incarcerated individuals in their section.

In this research, LGBT corrections officers also stated that they faced discrimination, such as same-sex coworkers refusing to work with them out of fear that they would sexually assault them). Participants also expressed concern about their job security, indicating that they felt that because of their sexual orientation or identity, their performance was more scrutinized than that of heterosexual cisgender employees. They felt that they always had to be on guard. This led to an overall feeling of a lack of support at work. LGBT corrections officers also reported that they worried that if they needed help, a coworker would either not come when called or would not step in to assist. The corrections officers who participated in this study discussed their experiences at an LGBT law enforcement conference. Although their superiors permitted them to attend the conference, they were instructed not to wear their uniforms while there. The officers took this to mean that their superiors did not want their institution publicly associated with them or with the conference, which was hurtful to many and sent a message to them they were not supported by leadership.

The shortage of scholarly research pertaining to the experiences of corrections officers who identify as LGBT speaks volumes to the importance that it has been given within academia and the criminal-legal system. As of this writing, there was no scholarly article that examined solely transgender officers, and only one that examined lesbian and gay officers. In order to understand the experiences of transgender corrections officers, more research needs to be done.

LEGAL PROFESSION

Within the past fifty years, the legal profession has transitioned from being almost exclusively white men to include women and people of color. However, there is debate as to whether these populations have been fully accepted into the profession. Women and people of color have the largest rate of attrition in the field (Hull and Nelson, 2000; Sander, 2006) and struggle with promotion and advancement (Kay and Gorman, 2008).

Challenges for Women in the Legal Profession: Still Largely a Boys' Club

Women were banned from working in the legal profession in the United States until 1869. The passage of the Civil Rights Act in 1964 led to the most notable increase of women in the legal profession. Women currently serve in leadership positions at almost half (46%) of the top fifty law schools as ranked by *U.S. News & World Report*, and the American Bar Association (2017) reports that 35 percent of its members are female. Despite these strides, however, women still face challenges associated with gender and race.

Exclusion

The first major challenge that women experience in the legal profession is exclusion. Much of the work in the legal profession is done outside the courtroom, which requires attorneys, judges, and other legal personnel to work together. The same people tend to work together repeatedly over time, building relationships and rapport and creating a **courtroom work group** (Galanter, 1974). This established relationship and trust can be a major advantage for negotiation (Johnson and Waldfogel, 2002; Gilson and Mnookin, 1994); past successful negotiations reinforce trust and allow attorneys and judges to reach mutually beneficial outcomes (Molm, Takahaski, and Peterson, 2000).

However, this reliance on relationships and established trust can be a challenge for women and people of color because of gender and racial biases. Individuals often are more trusting of members who are part of their own group, including their race and gender. Although there has been progress, white men are still the dominant group in the legal profession, and groups in power often exhibit bias toward those who are not part of the dominant group. White men also typically occupy different employment and social networks than women or people of color (Dinovitzer, 2011), which can pose challenges for making the connections and building the relationships that are necessary for successful negotiations on behalf of clients. Women and people of color have reported that there are exclusionary practices within their own firms and within the legal system at large, as they are often segregated and kept from opportunities that could lead to networking and opportunities for advancement (Kay and Gorman, 2014). As is the case with policing and corrections networking, women and people of color report that many connections happen over cocktails, on the golf course, and at social gatherings that they are not included in or invited to due to their race or gender.

Credibility and Stereotypes

Women and people of color working in the legal profession also face issues that their white male counterparts do not. Research has shown that female attorneys face credibility problems based solely on their gender (Nelson, 1994), and women lawyers and lawyers of color are viewed as less competent and capable than white male attorneys and are less respected by clients (Bogoch, 1997). Blacks and Latinos in the legal field are viewed as less intelligent and less hardworking than their white colleagues. Even if an individual has graduated from a prestigious school, he or she is still viewed as a product of affirmative action or tokenism (Rhode, 2011). As in other areas in the criminal-legal system, masculine characteristics are seen as desirable. Women who behave in too feminine a way are often viewed negatively because they are not performing the stereotypical tough-attorney role.

Attorneys of color experience incidents of racism, such as racist jokes, slurs, or comments from other attorneys or judges. Black attorneys report that they are often mistaken for criminal defendants (Rhode, 2011). Chicana attorneys report that they are mistaken for courtroom staff such as court reporters or interpreters (Garcia-López, 2008). Being a woman of color makes integration into the culture of legal professionals and law firms difficult, and many struggle in a way that white men do not. Attorneys of color report that they experience **race matching**, or being assigned to a case or a task because of their identity and not their particular expertise. For example, if a case involves a defendant of color, the only attorney of color may get assigned this case. In addition, attorneys of color may be assigned presentations in court or to clients, recruiting or marketing for the firm, to show diversity within the organization. This often makes employees feel like a show horses or mascots (Epner, 2006).

Advancement in the Legal Field

Research indicates that women still fall behind men in every indicator of success in the legal field (Wallace, 2019). At many law firms, the attorneys on track to make partner are disproportionately white men, putting others, such as women and people of color, into "workhorse" positions where they are tasked with work that needs to be done, but not the high-profile or large-budget cases that can earn a person a partnership (Epner, 2006). In the two hundred largest law firms in the United States, only 18 percent of managing partners are women (American Bar Association, 2017).

The term **shrinking door** describes a phenomenon experienced by women in the legal profession. From just starting in the legal profession to mid-career to judgeships, the number of women seems to dwindle. Women make up 35 percent of legal practitioners, 22 percent of state court judges, and 1 percent of state and federal judges (McKeig, 2021). Ninety percent of cases are heard at the state level, yet the demographics of judges do not reflect the demographics of the state or the nation. Currently at the state level, 8 percent of judges are women of color, 22 percent are white women, 12 percent are men of color, and 58 percent are white men. President Obama appointed 138 female federal judges, more than any other president to date, but the federal judiciary remains heavily male (National Association of Women Judges, 2018).

LGBT Individuals in Legal Careers

LGBT attorneys may face additional discrimination regarding sexual orientation or gender identity once hired, which makes working in the legal profession challenging. Partners often select more junior lawyers to work on cases with them and may choose a heterosexual cisgender attorney rather than an LGBT attorney because they worry how the client will respond. This can cause LGBT lawyers to hide their true identities or to alter their behavior or dress to conform to heterosexual standards (Rhode, 2011). See Active Learning Assignment 11.7.)

ACTIVE LEARNING ASSIGNMENT 11.7

Explore the LGBT Bar Association

Explore the website for the LGBT Bar Association (https://lgbtbar.org/) and answer the following questions:

1. What is the mission of this organization?
2. When was this organization founded?
3. What are three things this organization does?
4. How do you think this organization would help a LGBT legal professional?
5. What do you believe is the most beneficial service or program that the LGBT Bar Association provides? Please explain your answer.

SUMMARY: FURTHER EXPAND THE BOYS' CLUB

Although a great deal of progress has been made by women, people of color, and those within the LGBTQIA+ communities in the criminal-legal system, there is still work to be done in order for all individuals to feel that they are accepted, have equal opportunities, and will not suffer from bias, discrimination, and harassment. One of the ways that this can happen is through a renegotiation of the psychological contract between the employee and the employer. Instead of the work environment being strictly transactional in nature (in which an employee clocks in and gets paid for their time), there needs to be a mutually beneficial emotional and psychological investment between the employees and employer. This can be done through working with employees and allowing them input into the organization. Having input can allow them to feel a part of the process, as well as change or expand the gendered nature of the organization. If an employee feels that they can actively participate in the culture, environment, and decisions of their workplace, they feel more invested and satisfied. However, diversity must be a core value of this reform (Brown and Woolfenden, 2011).

As this chapter has shown, there needs to be greater inclusion of women, people of color, and LGBTQIA+ identifying individuals within all areas of the criminal-legal system. This will allow for all voices, not just those who have had power, to be heard and to have influence. It could also potentially help to remedy the challenges that all those who are minorities in criminal-legal system organizations experience. This is especially important given the historically masculine culture of the criminal-legal system. Adding new voices can help to change the system.

Gender, Crime, and the Media

LEARNING OBJECTIVES

▶ Understand how the media can impact societal views of gender, sexual orientation, race, and identity.
▶ Recognize ways in the which the media can reinforce stereotypes or myths related to gender, sexual orientation, race, and identity.
▶ Be able to identify different ways that the media has portrayed individuals based on sex, sexual orientation, gender, or race.

The media is a powerful force in our society. Because most citizens in the United States have access to smartphones or internet-capable devices, they access some form of social media daily, as well as other forms of media. The ease of access to the media allows people to experience and consume it in a way that has never been seen in human history. The increased amount of time that individuals spend consuming media can affect their world views, including their thoughts about gender and crime. This chapter will discuss the influence of the media on how we think about crime, particularly how media portrayals matter in regard to gender, sexual orientation, race, and identity.

THEORETICAL PERSPECTIVES ON THE INFLUENCE OF MEDIA

Mass Society Theory

When considering the impact that media has on gender, it is important to consider some theoretical connections about how we consume media and its effect on our perceptions. One of the first theories to relate media and behavior was **mass society theory**, which emerged in the later part of the nineteenth century after the term *mass society* gained recognition as a sociological concept. Initially, this was a negative term because *mass society* was characterized as large groups of people lacking individuality and prone to apathy. This theory is often seen as a predecessor to Durkheim's anomie theory. Durkheim (1897) argued that the group was becoming less valued as the individual became the main priority, and there was a breakdown in community culture as social controls weakened, leading to increased suicides. The Chicago School also studied mass society as large groups that can be controlled or manipulated by the media and ideas (Blumer, 1951). This theory has been used by more conservative scholars and thinkers to relate media to the decline of traditional family values (Swingewood, 1977). There can also be danger with the use of the media by certain individuals in power. Nazis in Germany and Communists in the USSR used the media to spread their messages. While not all within those societies adhered to the values and beliefs of those parties, their portrayal in media at the time and their control over the message did assist in altering the masses' viewpoints (Mills, 1956).

While this theory may appear dated, mass society theory is arguably very relevant today regarding the internet and its ability to distribute information instantaneously around the world (Lee, 2010). In relation to gender, a great deal of information online is misogynistic, perpetuating stereotypes of women and oversexualizing them. New terms have been coined to describe this misinformation, including *hate speech online, gendered cyberhate, online abuse, digital violence, technology-facilitated violence, online misogyny,* and *networked harassment.* Online misogyny also intersects with racism, homophobia, classism, ableism, and residency status (Ging and Siapera, 2018).

Misinformation in the media, particularly social media, can create biases against individuals or groups. Research has shown that about two-thirds of Americans get at least some of their news from social media (Shearer and Gottfreid, 2017). However, information on social media does not have to be vetted, or investigated and confirmed, the way that information on other news media does. Consequently, wrong or biased information can spread through an **online misinformation ecosystem**, comprising decentralized websites and "news" sources that can spread unwarranted conclusions, fabricate stories, and not vet sources or information. This misinformation can often be biased toward one viewpoint or political agenda. If individuals share what they read on social media, this can help to spread the misinformation and create media-generated mass misinformation (Starbird et al., 2018). Mass misinformation can cause people to believe that they are receiving correct and legitimate information about events and issues, which can influence their views on crime, who experiences crime, and who commits crime as well as the policies and political candidates they support. For example, people who see lots of social media news reports about "rampant violence and murder at the border" may be more likely to support policies related to harsher penalties for undocumented people or people trying to immigrate into the United States through Mexico.

Cultural Criminology

What a society considers criminal is expressed through its laws and practices, as well as through media information. **Cultural criminology** examines the connection between crime and the culture of a society. It seeks to dissect how crime and justice (and related concepts such as offenders, victims, and punishment) are conceived and portrayed within a culture, including the media. Media and culture often work together to perpetuate a society's beliefs about crime and its related components (Ferrell, Hayward, and Young, 2015). The media coverage of crimes, trials, and punishments indicates what crimes are considered heinous or more serious and which system-involved people are the worst. The portrayal of fictional crime and characters is part of a society's narrative as well. Certain system-involved individuals are often portrayed differently in comic books, film, and television. Cultural criminology, like other theoretical constructs, suggests that the ways in which the media portrays the criminal-legal system, crime, those who have crimes committed against them, and those who commit crimes affect people's perceptions and attitudes (Phillips and Strobl, 2006; Reyns and Henson, 2010).

Seen through a cultural criminology lens, the media can be a way for society to communicate what is acceptable based on gender, who or what to fear or loathe—or sometimes both—by means of the "other." **Others** are individuals who are excluded from society and denied the right to belong. Others are categorized through binary categories in which people either do or do not fit—for example, "Black or white," "us or them," "men or women," and "insiders or outsiders." Others are those who are different from us and whom we do not know or easily understand. Individuals who do not easily fit into any category are also often viewed as "other." The media is a powerful tool for conveying that to the public (Greer and Jewkes, 2005).

Cultivation Theory

Cultivation theory argues that as we watch or are exposed to media, our beliefs or ideas about the people or things being portrayed are affected (Gerbner et al., 2002). The representation of someone from a group that a viewer has little to no contact with, whether individuals who identify as LGBTQIA+, people of color, immigrants, system-involved individuals, or people against whom crimes are committed, can influence our perceptions. Media portrayal can also perpetuate traditional gender norms and roles regarding men and women and sexuality. According to cultivation theory, the perceptions that people have because of viewing media can have a positive or negative effect. If a white person is viewing media that shows individuals of color behaving, talking, or speaking in a stereotypical way, the viewer is more likely to support and endorse racial stereotypes (Busselle and Crandall, 2002; Morgan, Shanahan, and Signorielli, 2009). If the only exposure that a person has to people who could be considered "others," or who are of a different race, sexual orientation, gender identification, immigrant status, or gender, is a very stereotypical and incorrect version in the media, their view of those "others" may be skewed. This media-limited exposure can lead to biased opinions and beliefs, which can culminate in behaviors reflective of stereotype acceptance. However, portrayals of "others" that are positive or empowering may increase the media consumer's acceptance or tolerance of those that are different.

Representation in the media is important. It is vital that different races, ethnicities, genders, sexual orientation or identities, and residency statuses are represented in a positive way in the media and do not create or reinforce negative biases. In addition to introducing people to groups that they may not be familiar with and influencing perceptions, the media can influence whom young people see as role models. Traditionally, the popular media has focused on white males as the heroes or protagonists. However, there have been recent initiatives to ensure that more voices are represented. This is seen most notably in the superhero industry, whether in print comics or films. In the *Iron Man* comics, there is now a young, Black female Iron Man. In the *Incredible Hulk* comics, the Hulk is currently a brilliant young Asian man named Amadeus Cho. By redefining these two popular characters as people of color, Marvel has opened the door for many people to see these heroes in new people. In addition, superhero films are starting to focus on different heroes. There has tremendous success with *Black Panther* and *Wonder Woman*. Both the Black community and women everywhere rejoiced in seeing heroes who looked like them on the big screen. There have also been the reimaginings of female Ghostbusters and most recently, a female Doctor Who in the popular BBC show. (See Active Learning Assignment 12.1.) Media representation matters as it not only allows children to dream that they could grow up and be the champions they see on the screen or in the pages of a comic, but it allows adults to identify with them as well, and to feel connected to these characters in new ways. Incorporating more diverse characters also allows people to see new and different individuals in roles of power, which has the potential to shift biases in the male- and white-dominated entertainment industry.

However, it is important to note that the changes in the comics and films were met with resistance. There was much racist and misogynist backlash on the internet, as well as protests from the mostly male fans of the original superheroes. Almost daily, men, but women too, have been writing and streaming videos about the "corruption" of these characters, and even threatening harm and violence. Actors who portray these characters have faced online and in-person harassment and threats, as well as cyberstalking. For example, Leslie

---

ACTIVE LEARNING ASSIGNMENT 12.1

Female Dr. Who Backlash

After fifty-four years, the popular British science-fiction series *Dr. Who* cast a woman in the lead role. Here is an article about the backlash: https://www.huffingtonpost.com/entry/doctor-who-backlash-exposed-the-irony-of-men-who-dont-want-women-in-fandom_us_596f642ce4b0000eb1978720.

After reading it, answer the following questions:

1. Were you surprised that the naked photos of the actress playing Dr. Who were published but the naked pictures of the actors who had played the role were not published? Please explain.
2. A quote in the article says that many men see gains by women and/or LGBTQ people as a loss for men. What is your reaction to this?
3. Do you think that as more changes are made to characters to be inclusive of other populations, it will be more accepted? Why or why not?
4. How does the reaction of some fans to the new female Dr. Who relate to the general treatment of women in society? Please explain.

Jones, a Black actress who portrayed one of the female Ghostbusters in the 2016 reboot of the film, received racist comments and rape and death threats and even had her personal website hacked. This caused her much personal anguish and fear for her safety.

THE PORTRAYAL OF WOMEN IN THE MEDIA

"Girl Power!" The Rise of Female Power?

Feminism and "girl power" have been popularized in mainstream media through music, film, television, and literature. However, recently the media has also been responsible for contradictory and simplified examples or notions of feminism, often referred to as "postfeminist" (Genz and Brabon, 2009; Gill, 2016; Keller and Ringrose, 2015). Postfeminism developed as a response to previous versions of feminism and asserts that gender equality has been attained and that other versions of feminism prevent women from maintaining feminine standards of beauty (Lazar, 2009). Postfeminism also promoted "girl power" in various ways through the media of the 1980s and 1990s (Genz and Brabon, 2009; Lazar, 2009). In girl power and postfeminism as presented in the media, women can display femininity without apology or without the constraints of being viewed as not feminist or pro-women (Nguyen, 2013). However, postfeminist portrayals in the media are often seen as reinforcing problematic issues of privilege and beauty perpetuated by patriarchal systems (Lazar, 2009).

Postfeminism and girl power in the popular media in the 1980s, 1990s, 2000s, and arguably still today, show females who do whatever they want, but still look physically good doing it. However, girl power and postfeminism in the media typically do not challenge the white heteronormative patriarchal systems of society but rather perpetuate cultural norms in relation to race and gender (Lazar, 2009). Feminist analyses of media show that postfeminist ideals can duplicate repressive gendered ideals (Brunner, 2010; Feasey, 2012; Keller and Ringrose, 2015; Lazar, 2009; Petersen, 2012). For example, the media typically portray women who can "have it all"—a career, motherhood, physical beauty, and a great sex life and relationship—as cisgender, thin, white, educated or from a middle-or upper-class background, conventionally attractive, with a substantial amount of privilege. This woman also does not have it all as a result of her own hard work, but through the consumption of pills, makeup, lotions, exercise, cosmetic surgery, style, accessories, and convenience foods (Gamble, 2006). The women portrayed in the media in the postfeminist ideal way "have it all" but they use their money and privilege to attain it.

The media portrayal of the powerful, successful woman, this woman who "has it all," is often a very masculine and privileged example and reflects Sandberg's (2013) advice for women to "lean in." The mantra of "lean in" means that women who hope to succeed in the professional world must behave like men in order to fit into the heteronormative patriarchal institutions where they are employed (Gill, 2016; Keller and Ringrose, 2015). These media representations of women behaving like men in order to be successful, that is, leaning in, uphold the gender binary system and promote the masculine way of achieving success. Feminist activists who use other methods for success or refuse to lean in are not promoted in the media as readily or as positively (Gill, 2016) but often are portrayed as unattractive, ugly, or villainous (Genz and Brabon, 2009). The advice to "lean in" has been hotly debated within the corporate world and among feminists. However, the most favorable media portrayals of successful women have been those that have leaned in or taken on a masculine persona in their professional life (Gill 2007, 2016). (See Active Learning Assignment 12.2.)

In pop culture, two portrayals of women are often in direct opposition with each other. On one hand, there are the strong, smart, independent, and powerful women both as fictional characters and in real life (such as Ruth Bader Ginsberg) who provide hope and inspiration to young girls and women. On the other hand, the media oversexualizes women, objectifies them, and scrutinizes their appearance or looks. Sometimes, these things occur all at the same time. In today's media, women's bodies are often seen as their mode of success or failure and are constantly scrutinized by men and women. One example is the degree to which women can bounce back to their original form, or an improved

---

ACTIVE LEARNING ASSIGNMENT 12.2

Lean In?

Please explore the Lean In organization's website (https://leanin.org/) and then read this article about Michelle Obama's feelings about the Lean In philosophy (https://www.vox.com/culture/2018/12/3/18123796/michelle-obama-criticizes-lean-in-becoming-tour).

Answer the following questions:

1. In examining the Lean In website, how are women portrayed? Please provide details.
2. Do you think that the Lean In ethos works for women in all professions? Please provide some examples of where it could and could not work.
3. Do you think the Michelle Obama's statements about leaning in are on point? Please explain your answer.

---

version, after having a baby. There is often coverage in the media about celebrities and their post-baby bodies and how "successful" they are at being new mothers and still looking thin and fit (Gill, 2007). Regular everyday women also face this issue with pressure from magazines, mothering sites, and even medical professionals about looking thin after a baby. The "mommy makeover," a combination of liposuction and a tummy tuck, is marketed to new mothers nationwide. If a woman has a desirable body, that is often viewed as a form of power by men and women, and this is perpetuated by media representations of women in both fiction and real life.

The most popular film genres in the United States currently are fantasy, superhero, and action adventure, which have recently embraced the girl power movement. In films such as *Star Wars: The Last Jedi* and *Rise of Skywalker,* Rey, a young woman, is the Jedi hero leading the resistance. She is strong and makes her own rules for how to be a Jedi. In *Captain Marvel,* it is Carol Danvers, a young woman, who will be the hero saving the day and the world from destruction. In the *Harry Potter* series (and books), Hermione Granger is the "cleverest witch of her age" and saves her male friends time and time again with her knowledge, making her arguably the hero of the franchise. There is also Katniss Everdeen in *The Hunger Games.* She is a young woman able to lead a fight that brings down an oppressive government. However, all these young women are white, thin, fit, and beautiful. Their looks and bodies are commodities that attract men and women alike, although for different reasons. Women often want to be these characters because they are strong and possess a physically desirable form, and most heterosexual males would be attracted to them.

The looks of everyday women, especially those in the public eye, are subject to much criticism. When Hillary Clinton was running for president of the

United States in 2008 and 2016, her wardrobe, hair, and makeup were the subject of national news. Throughout her career and public life, her appearance has been the topic of many discussions. She received harsh criticism about her use of scrunchies, blue eye shadow, and pantsuits (Clinton, 2014). Women in politics often face much more scrutiny than their male counterparts about their clothes or hair. There are also reality television shows and segments on national news programs such as the *Today Show* and *Good Morning America* that are completely dedicated to "improving" women through a makeover. *What Not to Wear* was a long-running program that made over everyday women, often insulting their body and overall physical appearance in the process. There have also been more drastic shows such as *Extreme Makeover* in which the participants not only got a hair and makeup makeover but also received plastic surgery. The intended result of these endeavors was to make women feel better about themselves and arguably to inspire those watching at home to act similarly for self-improvement. However, this type of programming reinforces the idea that a woman's body is her source of power and respect (Gill, 2007).

While there is the media focus on women's bodies, there are also positive portrayals in the media. In spite of the scrutiny about the physical appearance of Hillary Clinton in the presidential race against Donald Trump in 2016, there were news media outlets that heralded the rise in the power and abilities of women. Her run was history in the making. After her loss, there was extensive media coverage of the Women's March in Washington, DC, and in cities nationwide in 2017. This coverage showed women mobilizing to fight misogyny and wrongful acts against women. In February 2017, Senator Elizabeth Warren, during her speech regarding President Trump's nomination of Jeff Sessions as US Attorney General, was interrupted by Senate Majority Leader Mitch McConnell but refused to be silenced. McConnell said that Warren had violated Senate Rule 19, which forbids a senator from accusing another senator of motive or conduct unworthy of a senator. The party then voted to stop her from speaking. "Senator Warren was giving a lengthy speech," McConnell said, defending the move. "She had appeared to violate the rule. She was warned. She was given an explanation. Nevertheless, she persisted" (Reilly, 2018). While Mitch McConnell meant this comment in a negative way and to essentially put Warren in her place, "Nevertheless, she persisted" was used in the media positively as an example to show that women do not have to be silenced when they have something important to say. It arguably has become part of inspiring the movement of women who will "persist" against patriarchal systems of oppression.

The Pornification of Women in the Media

Although there has been a movement for girl power and female empowerment, women are still portrayed in popular culture as objects, usually in reference to their physical appearance, sexuality, and age, which are closely tied to their worth and viability. Women in American culture are often overly sexualized (; Attwood, 2002; Olfman, 2009) or even **"pornified"** (Paul, 2005; Dines, 2010; Paasonen, Nikunen, Saarenmaa, 2007), meaning that women are portrayed within media and popular culture as if they exist only as objects for sex and to be consumed by men. There have been other names given to this phenomenon such as **"striptease culture"** (MacNair, 2002), as we are shown women scantily clad and/or appearing as teases for sex for heterosexual males. The photographs and videos that women appear in are often sexually objectifying or sexual in nature (Gill, 2007). This can be seen in advertisements, books, print media, comic books, television, films, and video games.

The pornification of women can be seen not only in pop culture but in the statistics related to pornography consumption. Pornhub's (2020) most recent annual statistics indicate that in 2019 there were 42 billion visits to the site, with an average of 115 million visits per day. While not all these visits or searches are necessarily related to the pornification or oversexualization of women, many were. Pornography uploaded to this site can be amateur and can include people who may not consent to having these images made public. There is promotion of rape and sexual assault on this site with videos of individuals forcing women and girls to have vaginal or anal sex. For example, there is dramatized pornography of a man raping his stepdaughter while she is sleeping. There is also pornography of men having sex with young-looking girls, with aspects of child sexual assault and abuse. While the individuals appear to be adults in these videos, this sort of media is promoting the rape and the oversexualization of young girls. (See Active Learning Assignment 12.3.)

The portrayal of women as sex objects and the pornification of women sends the message that this is a socially acceptable way for women and girls to "do gender" and be female, or "do femininity" (West and Fenstermaker, 1995; West and Zimmerman, 1987). This can be detrimental as young girls and women as they may begin to believe that this is how they should act if they want to be viewed as feminine, worthy, valued, and accepted. This oversexualization of the female body can affect how females view their body and produce increasing unhappiness, promoting eating disorders and unrealistic body expectations (Aubrey, 2006a; Aubrey, 2006b; Aubrey et al., 2009; Hargreaves, 1994; Hargreaves and Tiggemann, 2004).

This depiction of women in the media can also have real world implications in the treatment of women. Research has shown that sexualizing women and girls in the media can contribute to the legitimization or exacerbation of violence against women. A link has been found between pornography consumption and abuse inflicted on partners; attitudes supporting violence against women are strongly correlated with pornography consumption (DeKeseredy and Corsianos, 2016; DeKeseredy and Hall-Sanchez, 2016; DeKeseredy, Muzzatti and Donnermeyer, 2014). When women are viewed only as sexual objects

---

ACTIVE LEARNING ASSIGNMENT 12.3

Explore the Trends in Pornography

Please explore the statistics related to the most searched and downloaded pornography for 2019 (https://www.pornhub.com/insights/2019-year-in-review) and answer the following questions:

1. What was the most-searched-for genre for 2019?
2. What was the most-searched-for term of 2019?
3. What country has the most traffic on Pornhub?
4. What were the most-viewed categories for the United States?
5. What is the most-viewed category by gender?
6. After examining these statistics, do you think that women are being pornified or oversexualized?
7. What is your opinion about the statistics you found? Were you surprised by anything?
8. Do you think that the portrayal of women and sex on Pornhub is positive or negative? Please explain your answer.

---

and that image is presented again and again in the media, that can encourage the violent treatment of women because they are seen only as objects and not as people.

While there has been oversexualization and pornification of women within the media, there has also been an intentional national media movement to inspire young girls through female empowerment initiatives not related to appearance or body, such as focusing on recruitment of girls into STEM (science, technology, engineering and math) or STEAM (science, technology, engineering, art, and math) fields, which have been traditionally male dominated. The "She Can STEM" national media campaign has been created by the Advertising Council in partnership with Microsoft, Google, IBM, Verizon and General Electric. There is also Black Girls Code and Girls Who Code, which promote the depiction of girls and women in these fields in the media, as well as raise awareness that not only men can be in these fields. Seeing young girls and women in these roles using their minds can help other girls and women to see themselves in those roles. Such portrayals also allow girls and women to see that they have other commodities than their body and that their mind can be valuable too. Changing the media representation of a group can change the views people have of that group and the views they have of themselves.

There are also media campaigns to change the conversation about girls and women's bodies. Instead of focusing on female bodies as objects of desire and sex, the media occasionally depicts what women can do with their bodies through activity or sport. There has been increased media attention through various groups and initiatives promoting the idea that women do not need to

---

MEDIA BYTE 12.1   Redefining Exercise for Women

Watch the video clip and read the accompanying article about a British campaign to reduce the gender gap in sports participation: https://www.marketingweek .com/2017/02/24/sport-england-this-girl-can-tv/. Then answer the following questions:

1. What is your opinion of this campaign? Please explain.
2. How is this campaign different than other ones you have seen?
3. Do you think that incorporating women of different body images will encourage women and girls to feel differently about their bodies and/or participation in exercise? Why or why not?
4. Do you think that this campaign will decrease the sexualization or pornification of women?

---

be a certain size, body type, or age to enjoy physical activity. An example is ad campaigns by companies such as Nike. The victory of the United States Women's National Team in the World Cup in 2019 is a great example of media attention being paid to what women of different shapes, races, and backgrounds can do with their bodies. Also, media attention to females in the Olympics can also help to inspire women. (See Media Byte 12.1.)

The portrayal of girls and young women as smart and successful because of using their brains and not their bodies and sexual attractiveness can change the way that girls view themselves. But feminism still often carries a negative denotation as the "F word," with some women not wanting to be associated with that label out of the fear they will be viewed or perceived as anti-male or man hating. Many women fear that they may be seen as too tough or too masculine. However, as result of the Women's March and the positive promotion of feminism in the media and the "cool" association with feminism courtesy of Beyoncé, who had FEMINIST in bright lights behind her at the Video Music Awards, feminism has become "in" in a way that it may not have been before. Progress is being made in expanding the national conversation to include all people and to open feminism to women of color and transgender women. (See Active Learning Assignment 12.4.)

Media Portrayal of System-Involved Women and Women against Whom Crimes Are Committed

The issues in the representation of women in the media also apply to the portrayal of both women who are system-involved and women against whom crimes have been committed. System-involved women and women against

ACTIVE LEARNING ASSIGNMENT 12.4

"F" is for Feminism!

Explore these sites relating to feminism. Then answer the following questions.
   https://www.facebook.com/fisforfeminism/
   https://www.thefword.org.uk/
   https://twitter.com/fisforfeminism?lang=en

1. What did you see on these sites that was the most interesting? Please provide details.
2. Do you think that these sites (and those like them) will promote the acceptance of feminism and/or the willingness of people to identify as feminist? Why or why not?
3. What was missing from the sites that you think could promote feminism better or reach more individuals? Please explain.

whom crimes are committed are often portrayed as inherently different, as "other." A system-involved woman often gains attention from the media in both positive and negative ways. Women who commit violent offenses are an aberration and therefore interesting, which leads the news and popular entertainment media to focus on what makes them different and caused them to commit such crimes. The media often places women into categories such as **mad, sad, or bad** to frame their offenses (Noh, Lee and Feltey, 2010). These categories help society understand how and why a woman offended, because crime, especially violent crime, is in direct opposition to society's ideals and norms associated with women. If a woman is "mad," then a mental illness or disorder must have led to her offending or can be cited as the reason why. If she is "sad," something happened to her to cause her pain and sadness that led her to commit crime. Finally, if a woman is deemed "bad," then she committed the crime because she is just bad, or evil. For many people, being able to separate system-involved women into categories that make them seem different than themselves is important. Women are thought of as caretakers, as nurturers, and as gentle, kind, and obedient. The idea of females as made of "sugar and spice and everything nice" is often still very common. When a woman steps out of that role, it is often very unsettling to many in society and their need to know why is urgent. Even though the categories are too simplistic, they may help people process the reason behind the crime. (See Case Study 12.1.)

These three categories of mad, sad, and bad can also be applied to women who have offenses committed against them. Women who are victimized are judged in way that men are often not (Noh, Lee and Feltey, 2010). The public not only is curious about why a woman would commit a crime, but also is interested in why and how a woman is the target of a crime. This often results in the media

Monster

The 2002 film *Monster* was about serial killer Aileen Wuornos (Case Study 7.1). Charlize Theron portrayed Wuornos. This film illustrates how society views women who kill as different, and the societal reaction to this movie was unlike that to films about male serial killers based on true events. Actors who have played real-life serial killers in films have not garnered the attention that Theron received. She received accolades for gaining weight and making a physical transformation to become the heavier-set, masculine Wuornos. She even received the Academy Award for Best Actress.

The very name of the film, *Monster,* conveys how people view Wuornos. She was seen as a monster by society at the time of her crimes, trial, and execution. She was an unattractive, uneducated, masculine, lesbian woman who worked as a prostitute at truck stops. In the eyes of the public, she was an "other," or someone so far from themselves that they could not identify with her. However, what is often overlooked when considering what influenced Wuornos's crimes is the childhood physical and sexual abuse she suffered, as well as the hard life she endured as an adult. Many women who become "monsters" have often been victimized in horrible ways, leading them to offend.

1. Watch this interview with Charlize Theron and director Patty Jenkins about *Monster:* https://youtu.be/ObgXaoZg4wM.
2. What are your thoughts about this interview?
3. Do you think that the term *Monster* was appropriate for the story of Aileen Wuornos? Why or why not?

scrutinizing her life and behavior to understand what led to her victimization. She was either mad, sad, or bad, and that is what led to her victimization.

Examples are the women murdered by Jack the Ripper and the Yorkshire Ripper. These women worked as prostitutes. The gory details of the crimes were often the focus of newspaper stories at the time and they continue to be portrayed in popular culture. Particulars about the women as mothers, daughters, partners, or human beings are often not included. Instead, the media has depicted these women as faceless victims who were selling their bodies to men in the streets and therefore put themselves in danger of being brutally murdered. The portrayal of them at the time of their death as "whores," "strumpets," and "degenerates" othered them, meaning the way the media wrote about them reassured the public that they were not likely to be murdered because only this segment was being murdered, and they might be to blame due to their position in society.

While it is important to portray women as more than objects and show that women are smart, strong, and capable, it is also important to acknowledge that women can be sexual and enjoy sex without it being wrong or criminal. Women who are deemed promiscuous, lesbians, or sex workers are deemed as "others" and ridiculed in the media negatively portrayed in popular culture, which reflects society's heterosexual and patriarchal ideals. Women who are sexually unrestrained and enjoy sex are seen as "sluts" or "whores." Women who are virgins or waiting until marriage to engage in intercourse are "prudes." There seems to be no sexual middle ground for women and their portrayal in the media and popular culture (Jewkes, 2015). Even when women are victimized, it is often their sexuality that comes in to play when the crime is being covered by the media.

The blaming of females for their own victimization, particularly sexual victimization, and the intense scrutiny of their lives and behavior by media and society can be attributed to rape culture. **Rape culture** is an environment in which rape is common and the violence committed against women is normalized and excused by the media and the public. Rape culture can be perpetuated by the media through the oversexualization and objectification of women and making violence against women seem normal, glamorous, or even part of regular sex. The promulgation of women as objects for consumption by the media makes the sexual assault of a woman partly her fault. This may be why people ask, "What was she wearing?" or "Was she drinking?" Such questions imply that she in some way "asked" for her victimization or that there was a "misunderstanding" and there was no victimization at all.

Lesbians are often deemed as outsiders, or others, by the media, which often links being a lesbian with being more aggressive or more masculine. *Lesbian* is a label given to women who are deviant or criminal, whether or not that is actually the case. There may be no evidence that a woman is a lesbian, but if she committed a particularly aggressive or violent (inherently male) crime, she may be deemed a lesbian, in part to explain why she committed that crime. Women who are lesbians, or who are thought to be lesbians, are punished more severely and receive harsher and more destructive coverage in the media (Chesney-Lind and Eliason, 2006). The label is a way for the public to understand why a woman committed crime.

THE PORTRAYAL OF MALES IN THE MEDIA

Men as Heroes, Sexual Brutes, and Romantic Ideals

In the United States, the ruling type of masculinity has been heterosexual and white. This is what has been portrayed in the media, whether the news or popular culture mediums such as films, television, books, or comic books. Historically, most leading characters or "heroes" have been white men. Even today, with the purposeful inclusion of non-white, non-male characters to create equity, and some changes in reporting in the news media, white men continue to be the leading characters. This can be attributed to the privilege and power that have been historically afforded to them within society and within the media industry, as white males typically have been the ones creating media of all forms. There is also a lack of men of color in leading roles in popular media. The roles for most people of color in film and television historically have been as a secondary or supporting character, or as the villain or criminal. Research into four decades of media has shown that there is often stereotypical or unappealing representation of people of color (Mastro, 2009). Tyler Perry's films have often been viewed as breakthroughs for Black culture, even though there are criticisms from the community about some tropes and depictions. However, because Perry's films feature Black protagonists and Black casts and tell stories that can be identified with, they allow mainstream America to see the Black community portrayed in a new way.

Popular media, whether movies, television, video games, or print, often portray masculinity in terms of **hegemonic male fantasies** or ideals, in which males are the dominant and powerful group in society and women are subjugated. Most of these hegemonic fantasies are often brutish and sexual in nature (MacKinnon, 2003). This is often through enjoying male-focused action toys (Pope et al., 1999), consuming depictions of the female form and pornography (Leit, Pope, and Gray, 2001), and participating in or watching organized sports. (See Case Study 12.2 and Active Learning Assignment 12.5.)

While hegemonic male fantasies are common, the metrosexual male, or a male who is often more embracing of his feminine side, arguably has become more accepted within the mainstream public thanks to the television program *Queer Eye for the Straight Guy* (Aldrich, 2004). The term *metrosexual male* is now imbedded in our vocabulary, and many might think that this is a new concept associated with white middle- or upper-class males if their only exposure to it was *Queer Eye*. However, some may view a metrosexual male or a male who does not perpetuate the hegemonic male stereotype as gay or bisexual (Coad, 2008).

The idea of a fashion- or image-conscious male, or a male who appears to be in touch with his feminine identity, has roots in the Black culture. The nineteenth-century American **dandy** was a stylish Black man who reclaimed his post-slavery body by dressing and appearing well-groomed and elegant on his own terms (Kaye, 2009; White and White, 1998) and as part of the barbershop culture, which has had some representation in the media (Barber, 2008). Some Black men today are once again adopting this idea of the dandy in their dress and attitude and putting time and care into their appearance. (See Media Byte 12.2.) In the media today, there is often a stereotype regarding Black men as having a gangster-like appearance in terms of dress and overall look, and a violent or rough demeanor. Historically, in the media Black men have been depicted as unprofessionally and often provocatively dressed, with the suggestion that they are unemployed, blue collar, or involved in crime (Mastro and Greenberg, 2000). That is not an accurate depiction of Black men, as there are many variations of masculinity.

Bang Bus

Bang Bus is a reality show created and produced by a company called Bang Bros that streams online. Members pay a $34.95 subscription to view videos. However, they often will save the videos and then share them. The premise of *Bang Bus* is that a bus (really an unmarked white van) travels around a city (Miami), picks up real women (not actresses), and convinces them to perform a sexual act on camera for money while the bus is moving. After they have performed the act, one of the men creates a reason for the bus to stop, and the woman gets out of the bus. At this point, the woman is left as the bus drives away, never receiving her money. On occasion, a "guest" is a professional adult actress/actor or performer. The producers also solicit couples to work together and have sex for money. The key theme in all the videos is that the women are solicited for money, humiliated, degraded, and treated like sexual objects.

The *Bang Bus* was investigated after women reporting having been cheated and/or extorted. For example, a twenty-year-old college student, "Lori," desperate for money for rent and an abortion, was told she could get $1,200 and that her video would only be up for two weeks. She and her boyfriend at the time signed the paperwork, not reading it closely but believing what they were told in their meeting with the business representative. The video was up much longer and she did not receive her money as the company had paid all of the money to her boyfriend and he took off with the entire amount. People she knew and worked with recognized her on the video and began sharing it and distributing it. When Lori called the company after two weeks and the video could still be viewed, Bang Bros informed her that she would have to pay the amount of money that they had made thus far on the video in order to get it removed from the site, which in this case was $50,000. The video remains up (Conesa, 2004). The police in Miami were contacted to determine if this was illegal as the videos portray men soliciting women with money on the street. The police indicated that this is not illegal because that part is staged and the women have agreed to participate and have signed release contracts, and the "bus" has tinted windows so there is no risk for indecent exposure ("Police Look at Local 10 Porn Bus Investigation," 2004).

Those who view the videos and/or subscribe to *Bang Bus* may have their perceptions altered regarding women and men and the nature of gender roles and sex, which is harmful to both. In these videos, women are reduced to objects of sexual pleasure for men to first humiliate and degrade and then consume. This sends the message that this is how a man should behave and that a woman can and should expect this from her male partners and it is acceptable.

1. What is your reaction to *Bang Bus*?
2. Do you think that this portrays women *and* men in a negative way? Please explain your answer.
3. Do you think that the *Bang Bus* and similar programs should be legal?

ACTIVE LEARNING ASSIGNMENT 12.5

Male Fantasies/Pleasure in Media

Select a type of media (film, video game, advertisement, magazine, comic book, music video, etc.). Select a specific example of that media that focuses on male fantasies or pleasures (e.g., the film *The Hangover*).

1. Describe, using examples, how this form of media reinforces or speaks to the male fantasies or pleasures of men (heterosexual or homosexual) over others.
2. Why do you think that this is the case with this particular example? What was the influence for its creation?
3. How do you think that the example you chose could have been reconceptualized or reimagined to be more inclusive of others? Please explain.

MEDIA BYTE 12.2   The Resurgence of Black Dandyism

Read this article pertaining to the return of Black dandyism: https://howwegettonext.com/black-dandyism-is-back-and-its-both-oppositional-fashion-and-therapy-at-once-11735833b37. Then answer the following questions:

1. Do you think that dress and/or appearance will affect stereotypes of Black men?
2. Do you think that if Black men were portrayed more like dandies in the media that it would shape people's perceptions differently? Please explain.

Media Portrayal of System-Involved Men and Men against Whom Crimes Are Committed

In popular media, men are more often shown as system-involved than as people against whom crimes are committed, and men are more likely than women to be shown as law enforcement, government officials, or superheroes saving the day. Depending on the type of media and the narrative, even the system-involved males in popular culture may be the ones the audience roots for. Men are often portrayed as the "tough guy" in any role, whether the person committing the crime, the person experiencing the crime, or the one saving the day. In *Godfather II* and *Scarface,* Al Pacino depicts a ruthless, cruel criminal who is an alpha male. In films such as *The Bourne Identity* and the James Bond and Mission Impossible series, the men are technically committing crimes, making them system-involved individuals, even if their crimes are sanctioned by a government agency. Batman is a vigilante who works outside the law to catch the "bad guy," but he himself is a criminal. All these characters are portrayed as men who are taking the law into their own hands in one way or another, but the audiences still root for them and love them even when they are not acting like the "good" guy.

The media also may capitalize on current issues within a community or country regarding race, which may intersect with gender, sexual orientation, class, and residency status. The particular angle taken by a news outlet or depiction in popular media may vary. One of the best-known examples of media coverage relating to race, but also gender, sexual orientation, and class, was the O.J. Simpson case. This trial received enormous amounts of media attention, and more recently has intrigued people with an award-winning mini-series. The reason that this case captured the media and the nation's attention is that O.J. Simpson ("The Juice") was at the time a hero to the Black community and beloved in the nation. It also involved issues with the police and past problems with police treatment of Black men and women in the area, Simpson's record of domestic violence, and the high-powered "dream team" of attorneys Simpson hired. It was also one of the first times in history that a rich Black man accused of a crime was garnering so much attention nationally.

When examining the portrayal of race in the media, there is a long history of misrepresentation and poor portrayals of people of color, emphasizing criminality and offending, particularly by males (Greenberg, Mastro, and Brand, 2002). Black and Hispanic men are often vilified in news media and in television and film. Even before modern media, Black men in particular, in the slavery and Jim Crow eras, were depicted as violent sexual predators and ultimately as villains. The portrayal of a group in the media can impact how that group is viewed by society.

Research has uncovered stigma and a lack of empathy for Black Americans, as well as support for their differential treatment in the criminal-legal system or in general within society. Individuals often have exaggerated and inaccurate beliefs about the violence committed both overall and within Black communities (Ramasubramanian, 2011; Entman, 1994) and as a result support harsher laws to imprison Black people (Hetey and Eberhardt, 2014). The portrayal of Black Americans in the media as "other" affects public opinion. Phelps et al. (2000) discovered in their research that even though the white people in their sample reported neutral attitudes about race, when they saw unfamiliar Black people, the areas of the brain that indicate fear were activated. The white individuals in the sample were frightened just by seeing someone of that race.

Believing that Black Americans, principally men, are criminal and out to harm society has dangerous implications. Black men receive harsher sentences by judges and unfair treatment in the criminal-legal system at every stage (Marable, Middlemass, and Steinberg, 2007). They also have an increased likelihood of being harassed and fatally shot by the police (Greenwald, Oakes, and Hoffman, 2003). Black individuals receive less attention from doctors, and there is often a false belief that they are "tougher," so they are administered less pain medication (Rachlinski et al., 2009). Black Americans have a decreased likelihood of being hired or admitted to a school (Entman, 2006) and are less likely to receive loans (Greenwald, Oakes, and Hoffman, 2003). The negative portrayal of Black men in the media and society also hurts their self-esteem and self-expectations and can lead to implicit bias against their own race Schmader, Johns, and Forbes, 2008).

The media rarely acknowledges that men of any race have crimes committed against them, particularly the crimes of intimate partner violence or sexual assault. However, about 14 percent of rapes reported to law enforcement involve boys or men, one in six sexual assaults are against boys, and most perpetrators against men and boys are white heterosexual men (RAINN, 2021b). The reason so few of these crimes are reported is the myth that men cannot be experience sexual assault or intimate partner violence because they are "strong" and should be able to defend themselves. What is universally missing in the media's portrayal of men who experience offenses against them is the suffering of men. When men experience any type of crime, there is often the "strong and silent" response. The race of a man also matters in terms of news coverage or portrayal within fictional media. White people who experience crime are more likely to be named on the news and to have specific details provided about them, often in a positive light, whereas people of color who experience crime are not typically named or any details given (Entman and Rojecki, 2001). For example, a news headline for a murdered Black person might read "Black Man Shot," but for a murdered white person, "Local Businessman Killed." These send very different messages.

THE PORTRAYAL OF LGBTQIA+ IN THE MEDIA

The Impact of *Will and Grace* and *Ellen*

The positive portrayal of LGBTQIA+ characters in the media and popular culture can assist the general public in understanding issues and experiences of this community as well help to create empathy for someone who is different than themselves. In the past, LGBTQIA+ individuals were often ridiculed, mocked, parodied, or chastised in mainstream media. While there is still room for improvement regarding the representation of the LGBTQIA+ community, there have been some strides made that have led to more LGBTQIA+ characters being incorporated and shown in a positive light, as well as improved coverage of LGBTQIA+ issues in the news media.

In the early 2000s *Will and Grace* was one of the highest rated television shows. It appeared on a major national network during prime time. Also during that time, Ellen DeGeneres, who came out publicly as a lesbian in the 1990s, started a television day-time talk show, *Ellen*, in 2003, which was watched by millions until it was halted over allegations of a hostile work environment. Her show has also earned twenty-seven Emmy awards and made her one of the highest-paid television stars. Kris Franklin (2001) originated the term "the **Ellen Effect**," referring to mainstream society viewing lesbians and gay men as culturally significant and not intimidating or scary, as a result of watching her show. Ellen was "safe." She allowed America to see that individuals who do not adhere to heteronormative gender norms in terms of dress and appearance are not threatening or scary.

In 2005, LOGO was launched, a television station aimed specifically at the LGBTQIA+ communities. It maintained substantial number of viewers and created original programming for audiences that include cisgender heterosexual viewers rather than exclusively focusing on the LGBTQIA+ community (Ciriaco, 2012). Also, during the 2000s, the widespread use of social media and smartphones gave a platform for those in the LGBTQIA+ community, as well as allies, to connect and to inform the world about issues that matter. For example, the tweet made by President Obama in 2013 regarding his support of marriage equality reached 150 million people via Twitter. Today, social media has created a new way for people to connect or share their thoughts. However, while there have been gains for LGBTQIA+ individuals in the media and in characters on television, there have also been negative portrayals. GLAAD (2017b) conducted an analysis of the number of LGBTQIA+ characters and their portrayal on television during the 2016–17 season. They found that some of the portrayals were stereotypical and unflattering. There is also the issue of individuals and groups on social media spewing hate against the LGBTQIA+ communities, promoting policies and actions against them.

Many young LGBTQIA+ individuals do not have role models within their daily lives or community that they can turn to, and some youth may have no one to look to for guidance or to model behavior (Raley and Lucas, 2006). As a result, they may turn to figures in the media or pop culture in order try to find their identity within the LGBTQIA+ communities. What these young people see portrayed may be their first introduction to this community, and what they view can influence their journey and even whether to "come out" or identify as their true selves (Padva, 2007). Positive portrayals help them on their journey as they can see that you can be yourself and still be accepted and in the world. Negative or stereotypical portrayals may cause them to believe that they must behave in a certain, often parodied way that may not be authentic. Derogatory comments or negative reactions in the media may influence them to keep their identity a secret.

The It Gets Better project was created to help LGBTQIA+ youth everywhere. In 2010, Dan Savage and his partner Terry Miller said, "It gets better" to help youth who were struggling. It began as a social media campaign with people from the LGBTQIA+ communities sharing their stories to inspire and encourage LGBTQIA+ youth. The goal was to give hope to youth who might be experiencing bullying or not being accepted by family and friends. Today, It

Gets Better has evolved into an international organization with a multimedia platform to utilize the media for inspiration for youth, but the organization also has community-based service providers to help LGBTQIA+ youth. It Gets Better has worked with schools to create materials and facilitate learning in states that have passed the FAIR Education Act, which mandates that all K–12 history and social studies curriculums within participating states (California, Colorado, Illinois, Maryland, and New Jersey) include contributions and news from the LGBTQIA+ community.

Media Portrayal of LGBTQIA+ System-Involved Individuals and LGBTQIA+ Individuals against Whom Crimes Are Committed

When examining media for the depiction of LGBTQIA+ individuals who experience crime, one of the most prominent ways that the community is featured is in cases of bullying, as well as teenage or young adult suicides. While this arguably has always been an issue for individuals who identify as LGBTQIA+, it did not hit mainstream news as an issue until the 2000s. There have been fictional accounts in media dating back to the 1980s in which youth were bullied not necessarily for being gay but for not living up to expected gender norms, such as being too effeminate (Padva, 2007).

As bullying and suicide among LGBTQIA+ youth gained attention from the media, the general public began a discussion about the experiences of young people who do not identify as cisgender or heterosexual. This discussion recently gained momentum as a result of issues relating to transgender children and the bullying, harassment, and ridicule that they can face in school. When examining the coverage in the news, young white men who are thought to be gay seem to be the most at risk for bullying and for suicide. Females who are lesbian, bisexual, or transgender do not experience the same degree of bullying, or their victimization is not covered in news reports. (See Active Learning Assignment 12.6.) The increased risk for young white men thought to be gay may be attributed to toxic masculinity in the sense that males who do not meet these ideals are seen as "others" and therefore ridiculed.

ACTIVE LEARNING ASSIGNMENT 12.6

LGBTQIA+ Individuals in the Media

Find a case in the news media or popular culture media (TV, movie, book, video game) that focuses on an LGBTQIA+ individual.

1. Describe how this individual is portrayed.
2. Write a reaction to this portrayal. Consider how and/or why the individual is portrayed this way and how this portrayal could affect the way that people view them and their actions.

SUMMARY

This chapter examined the portrayal of gender, sexual orientation, race, and identity in the media and the potential impact on public perceptions. Negative portrayals, or those that reinforce harmful stereotypes, can be detrimental. People who do not have regular interactions with anyone with a different gender, sexual orientation, race or sexual identity will only have the depiction in the media to use as reference. The media representation can, in part, affect individuals' thoughts and beliefs about those groups. Media portrayals can also impact individuals who are members of those groups. For example, if young people who are struggling with gender or sexual identity see a person like them in the media being represented in a positive and accurate way, that can help them to see themselves in that light and may assist them to share who they are with the world or to live as their authentic self.

References

Acker, J. (1990). "Hierarchies, Jobs, Bodies: A Theory of Gendered Organizations." *Gender & Society* 4(2): 139–58.

———. (1992). "Gendering Organizational Theory." In *Gendering Organizational Theory*, edited by A. J. Mills and P. Tancred. Thousand Oaks, CA: Sage.

———. (2006). *Class Questions: Feminist Answers*. Lanham, MD: Rowman and Littlefield.

Adam, A. (2005). "Hacking into Hacking: Gender and the Hacker Phenomenon." In *Gender, Ethics and Information Technology*. London: Palgrave Macmillan. https://doi.org/10.1057/9780230000520_7.

Adler, F. (1975). *Sisters in Crime: The Rise of the New Female Criminal*. New York: McGraw-Hill.

Adler, P. A. (1993). *Wheeling and Dealing an Ethnography of an Upper-Level Drug Dealing and Smuggling Community*. New York: Columbia University Press.

Agnew, R. (1992). "Foundation for a General Strain Theory of Crime and Delinquency." *Criminology* 30:1: 47–88. https://doi.org/10.1111/j.1745-9125.1992.tb01093.x.Agnew, R. (2016). "Strain, Economic Status, and Crime." In *The Handbook of Criminological Theory*, edited by A. R. Piquero, 210–29. Malden, MA: Wiley.

Agocs, T., D. Langan, and C. B. Sanders. (2015). "Police Mothers at Home: Police Work and Danger-Protection Parenting Practices." *Gender & Society* 29(2): 265–89.

Akbulut, Y., and B. Eristi. (2011). "Cyberbullying and Victimisation among Turkish University Students." *Australasian Journal of Educational Technology* 27(7): 1155–70.

Akers, R. L. (1990). "Rational Choice, Deterrence, and Social Learning Theory in Criminology: The Path Not Taken." *Journal of Criminal Law and Criminology* 81(3): 653–76.

———. (1991). "Self-Control as a General Theory of Crime." *Journal of Quantitative Criminology* 7(2): 201–11.

Akers, R. L., and W. G. Jennings. (2016). "Social Learning Theory." In *The Handbook of Criminological Theory*, edited by A. R. Piquero, 231–40. Malden, MA: Wiley.

Alarid, L. F., V. S. Burton Jr., and F. T. Cullen. (2000). "Gender and Crime among Felony Offenders: Assessing the Generality of Social Control and Differential Association Theories." *Journal of Research in Crime and Delinquency* 37(2): 171–99.

Alderden, M. A., and S. E. Ullman. (2012). "Gender Difference or Indifference? Detective Decision Making in Sexual Assault Cases." *Journal of Interpersonal Violence* 27(1): 3–22.

Aldrich, R. (2004). "Homosexuality and the City: An Historical Overview." *Urban Studies* 41(9): 1719–37.

Allan, K., and S. Coltrane. (1996). "Gender Displaying Television Commercials: A Comparative Study of Television Commercials in the 1950s and 1980s." *Sex Roles* 35(3–4): 185–203.

Allen, K. P. (2012). "Off the Radar and Ubiquitous: Text Messaging and Its Relationship to 'Drama' and Cyberbullying in an Affluent, Academically Rigorous U.S. High School." *Journal of Youth Studies* 15(1): 99–117.

Alper, M., M. R. Durose, and J. Markman. (2018). *2018 Update on Prisoner Recidivism: A 9-Year Follow-up Period (2005–2014)*. US Department of Justice, Office of Justice Programs, Bureau of Justice Statistics. https://www.bjs.gov/content/pub/pdf/18upr9yfup0514.pdf.

American Bar Association. (2017.) *A Current Glance at Women in the Law*. https://www.americanbar.org/content/dam/aba/marketing/women/current_glance_statistics_january2017.authcheckdam.pdf.

American Civil Liberties Union. (2019). "LGBT Rights." https://www.aclu.org/issues/lgbt-rights.

American Immigration Council. (2019). "Immigrant Women and Girls in the United States: A Portrait of Demographic Diversity." Fact sheet. https://www.americanimmigrationcouncil.org/research/immigrant-women-united-states.

American Psychological Association, Task Force on Gender Identity, Gender Variance, and Intersex Conditions. (2006). *Answers to Your Questions about Individuals with Intersex Conditions*. https://www.apa.org/topics/lgbt/intersex.pdf.

Amnesty International. (2019). "LGBTI Rights." Accessed 2021, https://www.amnesty.org/en/what-we-do/discrimination/lgbt-rights/.

Anderson, D. J., M. Binder, and K. Kraus. (2003). "The Motherhood Wage Penalty Revisited: Experience, Heterogeneity, Work Effort and Work-Schedule Flexibility." *Industrial and Labor Relations Review* 56(2): 273–94.

Anderson, E. (1999). *Code of the Street*. New York: W. W. Norton.

Anderson, T. L. (2005). "Dimensions of Women's Power in the Illicit Drug Economy." *Theoretical Criminology* 9(4): 371–400.

Andrews, J. (2016). "Tennessee Fans Blame Rape Victims for Messing Up Football." *Vocative*, February 11, 2016. https://www.vocativ.com/283331/tennessee-fans-blame-rape-victims-for-messing-up-football/index.html.

Aosved, A. C., P. J. Long, and E. K. Voller. (2011). "Sexual Revictimization and Adjustment in College Men." *Psychology of Men and Masculinity* 12(3): 285–96.

Appleby L. (1996). "Suicidal Behaviour in Childbearing Women." *International Review of Psychiatry* 8(1): 107–15.

Archbold, C. A., and D. M. Schulz. (2008). "Making Rank: The Lingering Effects of Tokenism on Female Police Officers' Promotion Aspirations." *Police Quarterly* 11(1): 50–73.

Arcilesbica. (2011). *Eva contro Eva: I convegno sulla violenza di genere*. Rome: Arcilesbica Roma.

Ard, K. L., and H. J. Makadon. (2011). "Addressing Intimate Partner Violence in Lesbian, Gay, Bisexual, and Transgender Patients." *Journal of General Internal Medicine* 26(8): 930–33.

Aricak, T., S. Siyahhan, A. Uzunhasanoglu, S. Saribeyoglu, S. Ciplak, N. Yilmaz, and C. Memmedov. (2008). "Cyberbullying among Turkish Adolescents." *Cyberpsychology & Behavior* 11(3): 253–61.

Astor, M. (2017). "Transgender Recruits Welcome at Police Departments, Even if Trump Doesn't Want Them." *New York Times,* May 3, 2017. https://www.nytimes.com/2017/08/03/us/transgender-military-police-trump.html.

Attwood, F. (2002). "Reading Porn: The Paradigm Shift in Pornography Research." *Sexualities* 5(1): 91–105.

Aubrey, J. S. (2006a). "Effects of Sexually Objectifying Media on Self-Objectification and Body Surveillance in Undergraduates: Results of a Two-Year Panel Study." *Journal of Communication* 56(2): 366–86.

———. (2006b). "Exposure to Sexually Objectifying Media on Negative Body Emotions and Sexual Self-Perceptions: Investigating the Mediating Role of Body Self-Consciousness." *Mass Communication and Society* 10(1): 1–23.

Aubrey, J. S., J. Henson, K. M. Hopper, and S. E. Smith. (2009). "A Picture Is Worth Twenty Words (About the Self):Testing the Priming Influence of Visual Sexual Objectification on Women's Self-Objectification." *Communication Research Reports* 26(4): 271–84. doi:10.1080/08824090903293551.

Axelrod, J. (2018). "Anchorage Becomes First U.S. City to Vote Down Transgender 'Bathroom Bill' Proposition." *American City and County,* April 16, 2018. https://www.americancityandcounty.com/2018/04/16/anchorage-becomes-first-us-city-to-vote-down-transgender-bathroom-bill-proposition/.

Bailyn, L. (2003). "Academic Careers and Gender Equity: Lessons Learned from MIT." *Gender, Work & Organization* 10(2): 137–53.

Baker, S. J. (2010). "Exploring the Dimensions of Gay Taunting." Paper presented at the National Communication Association annual conference, San Francisco, CA.

Baker, S. J., and K. Lucas. (2017). "Is It Safe to Bring Myself to Work? Understanding LGBTQ Experiences of Workplace Dignity." *Canadian Journal of Administrative Sciences Revue* 34(2): 133–48. doi: 10.1002/CJAS.1439.

Balkin, J. (1988). "Why Policemen Don't Like Policewomen." *Journal of Police Science and Administration* 16: 29–38.

Ball, M. (2016a). *Criminology and Queer Theory: Dangerous Bedfellows?* Basingstoke: Palgrave Macmillan.

———. (2016b). "Queer Criminology as Activism." *Critical Criminology* 24(4): 473–87. doi 10.1007/s10612–016–9329–4.

Balsam, K. F., and D. M. Szymanski. (2005). "Relationship Quality and Domestic Violence in Women's Same-Sex Relationships: The Role of Minority Stress." *Psychology of Women Quarterly* 29(3): 258–69. doi: 10.1111/j.1471–6402.2005.00220.x.

Banister, J. (2004). "Shortage of Girls in China Today." *Journal of Population Research* 21(1): 19–45.

Barber, K. (2008). "The Well-Coiffed Man: Class, Race, and Heterosexual Masculinity in the Hair Salon." *Gender & Society* 22(4): 455–76.

Barberet, R. (2014). *Women, Crime and Criminal Justice: A Global Enquiry.* New York: Routledge.

Barlett, C., and S. M. Coyne. (2014). "A Meta-Analysis of Sex Differences in Cyber-Bullying Behavior: The Moderating Role of Age." *Aggressive Behavior* 40(5): 474–88.

Barnes, J. C., and M. TenEyck. (2017). "Prenatal and Perinatal Risk Factors for Delinquency." *The Encyclopedia of Juvenile Delinquency and Justice,* edited by C. J. Schreck. Malden, MA: Wiley.

Barnes, R. (2010). "'Suffering in a Silent Vacuum': Woman-to-Woman Partner Abuse as a Challenge to the Lesbian Feminist Vision." *Feminism & Psychology* 21(2): 233–39. 10.1177/0959353510370183.

Bartholomew, K., K. V. Regan, D. Oram, and M. A. White. (2008). "Correlates of Partner Abuse in Male Same-Sex Relationships." *Violence and Victims* 23(3): 344–60. doi: 10.1891/0886-6708.23.3.344.

Bartlett, H. W., and A. Rosenblum. (1977). *Policewomen Effectiveness.* Denver: Denver Civil Service Commission.

Bartusch, D. J., and R. L. Matsueda. (1996). "Gender, Reflected Appraisals, and Labeling: A Cross-Group Test of an Interactionist Theory of Delinquency." *Social Forces* 75(1): 147–77.

Bates, E. (2019) "'No One Would Ever Believe Me': An Exploration of the Impact of Intimate Partner Violence Victimization on Men." *Psychology of Men and Masculinity* 21(4): 497–507.

Bauman, S., R. B. Toomey, and J. L. Walker. (2013). "Associations among Bullying, Cyberbullying, and Suicide in High School Students." *Journal of Adolescence* 36(2): 341–50.

BBC News. (2018). "Elliot Rodger: How Misogynist Killer Became 'Incel Hero.'" *BBC News,* April 26, 2018. https://www.bbc.com/news/world-us-canada-43892189.

Beaver, K. M., J. C. Barnes, and B. B. Boutwell, eds. (2015). *The Nurture versus Biosocial Debate in Criminology: On the Origins of Criminal Behavior and Criminality.* Thousand Oaks, CA: SAGE Publications.

Becker, G. S. (1985). "Human Capital, Effort and the Sexual Division of Labor." *Journal of Labor Economics* 3(1–2): 33–58.

Becker, H. S. (1963). *Outsiders.* New York: Free Press.

Bedgett, M. V. L., H. Lau, B. Sears, and D. Ho. (2007). *Bias in the Workplace: Consistent Evidence of Sexual Orientation and Gender Identity Discrimination.* Los Angeles: Williams Institute.

Beesley, F., and J. McGuire. (2009). "Gender-Role Identity and Hypermasculinity in Violent Offending." *Psychology, Crime and Law* 15(2–3): 251–68.

Belkin, A.. and J. McNichol. (2002). "Pink and Blue: Outcomes Associated with the Integration of Open Gay and Lesbian Personnel in the San Diego Police Department." *Police Quarterly* 5(1): 63–95.

Belknap, J. (1991). "Women in Conflict: An Analysis of Women Correctional Officers." *Women & Criminal Justice* 2(2): 89–115.

———. (2015). "Activist Criminology: Criminologists' Responsibility to Advocate for Social and Legal Justice." *Criminology* 53(1): 1–22.

———. (2016). "Feminist Theories." In *The Handbook of Criminological Theory,* edited by A. R. Piquero, 290–300. Malden, MA: Wiley.

Belknap, J., A. T. Chu, and A. P. DePrince. (2012). "The Roles of Phones and Computers in Threatening and Abusing Women Victims of Male Intimate Partner Abuse." *Duke Journal of Gender Law and Policy* 19: 373–406.

Bell, C., and T. Puckett. 2020. "I Want To Learn but They Won't Let Me: Exploring the Impact of School Discipline on Academic Achievement." *Urban Education.* November 2020. doi:10.1177/0042085920968629.

Beneath the Veneer: The Report of the Task Force on Barriers to Women in the Public Service. (1990). DSS cat. no. BT22–19/1–1990E. Ottawa: Canadian Publishing Centre, Supply and Services Canada.

Beran, T., and Q. Li. (2007). "The Relationship between Cyberbullying and School Bullying." *Journal of Student Wellbeing* 1(2): 16–33.

Beran, T. N., C. Rinaldi, D. S. Bickham, and M. Rich. (2012). "Evidence for the Need to Support Adolescents Dealing with Harassment and Cyber-harassment: Prevalence, Progression, and Impact." *School Psychology International* 33(5): 562–76.

Berg, M., M. Mimiaga, and S. A. Safren. (2008). "Mental Health Concerns of Gay and Bisexual Men Seeking Mental Health Services." *Journal of Homosexuality* 54(3): 293–306.

Bernburg, J. G. (2009). "Labeling Theory." In *Handbook on Crime and Deviance*, edited by M. D. Krohn, A. J. Lizotte, and G. P. Hall, 187–207. New York: Springer.

Bernburg, J. G., M. D. Krohn, and C. J. Rivera. (2006). "Official Labeling, Criminal Embeddedness, and Subsequent Delinquency: A Longitudinal Test of Labeling Theory." *Journal of Research in Crime and Delinquency* 43(1): 67–88.

Berne, S., A. Frisén, and J. Kling. (2014). "Appearance-Related Cyberbullying: A Qualitative Investigation of Characteristics, Content, Reasons, and Effects." *Body Image* 11(4): 527–33.

Bernstein, M., and C. Kostelac. (2002). "Lavender and Blue Attitudes about Homosexuality and Behavior toward Lesbians and Gay Men among Police Officers." *Journal of Contemporary Criminal Justice* 18(3): 302–28.

Best, R. K., L. D. Edelman, L. H. Krieger, and S. R Eliason. (2011). "Multiple Disadvantages: An Empirical Test of Intersectionality Theory in EEO Litigation." *Law & Society Review* 45(4): 991–1025.

Bettcher, T. M. (2007). "Evil Deceivers and Make-Believers: On Transphobic Violence and the Politics of Illusion." *Hypatia* 22(3): 43–65.

Birkett, M., D. L. Espelage, and B. Koenig. (2009). "LGB and Questioning Students in Schools: The Moderating Effects of Homophobic Bullying and School Climate on Negative Outcomes." *Journal of Youth and Adolescence* 38(7): 989–1000. https://doi.org/10.1007/s10964-008-9389-1.

Blakemore, E. (2019). "Chinese Americans Were Once Forbidden to Testify in Court. A Murder Changed That." *History.com*, May 7, 2019. https://www.history.com/news/chinese-exclusion-act-yee-shun-legal-rights.

Blanco, C., J. Grant, N. M. Petry, H. B. Simpson, A. Alegria, S.-M. Liu, and D. Hasin. (2008). "Prevalence and Correlates of Shoplifting in the United States: Results from the National Epidemiologic Survey on Alcohol and Related Conditions (NESARC)." *American Journal of Psychiatry* 165(7): 905–13.

Blumenstein, L., and X. Guadalupe-Diaz. (2016). "Intimate Partner Abuse." In *The Intersection between Intimate Partner Abuse, Technology, and Cybercrime: Examining the Virtual Enemy*, edited by J. N. Navarro, S. Clevenger, and C. D. Marcum. Durham, NC: Carolina Academic Press.

Blumer, H. (1951). "The Field of Collective Behavior." In *Principles of Sociology*, edited by A. M. Lee. New York: Barnes & Noble.

Bogoch, B. (1997). "Gendered Lawyering: Difference and Dominance in Lawyer–Client Interaction." *Law & Society Review* 31(4): 677–712. https://doi.org/10.2307/3053984.

Bosworth, M., and E. Carrabine. (2001). "Reassessing Resistance: Race, Gender and Sexuality in Prison." *Punishment and Society* 3(4): 501–15.

Botchkovar, E., I. H. Marshall, M. Rocque, and C. Posick. (2015). "The Importance of Parenting in the Development of Self-Control in Boys and Girls: Results from a Multinational Study of Youth." *Journal of Criminal Justice* 43(2): 133–41.

Bowie, B. H. (2007). "Relational Aggression, Gender, and the Developmental Process." *Journal of Child and Adolescent Psychiatric Nursing* 20(2): 107–15.

Bowling., C. J., C. A. Kelleher., J. Jones, and D. S. Wright. (2006). "Cracked Ceilings, Firmer Floors, and Weakening Walls: Trends and Patterns in Gender Representation among Executives Leading American State Agencies." *Public Administration Review* 66(6): 823–36.

Braid, K. (2012). *Journeywoman: Swinging a Hammer in a Man's World*. Halfmoon Bay, BC: Caitlin Press.

Branch, K., C. M. Hilinski-Rosick, E. Johnson, and G. Solano. (2017). "Revenge Porn Victimization of College Students in the United States: An Exploratory Analysis." *International Journal of Cyber Criminology* 11(1): 128–42.

Brantingham, P., and P. Brantingham. (2013). "Crime Pattern Theory." In *Environmental Criminology and Crime Analysis*, edited by R. Wortley and L. Mazerolle, 100–16. Oxfordshire: Willan.

Briggs, C. S., J. L. Sundt, and T. C. Castellano. (2006). "The Effect of Supermaximum Security Prisons on Aggregate Levels of Institutional Violence." *Criminology* 41(4): 1341–76.

Britton, D.M. (1997). "Perceptions of the Work Environment among Correctional Officers: Do Race and Sex Matter?" *Criminology* 35(1): 85–105.

Broadus, K. W. (2009). "The Criminal-Legal System and Trans People." *Temple Political and Civil Rights Law Review* 18(2): 561–72.

Broidy, L., and R. Agnew. (1997). "Gender and Crime: A General Strain Theory Perspective." *Journal of Research in Crime and Delinquency* 34(3): 275–306.

Brookman, F., C. Mullins, T. Bennett, and R. Wright. (2007). "Gender, Motivation, and the Accomplishment of Street Robbery in the United Kingdom." *British Journal of Criminology* 47(6): 861–84.

Broverman, N. (2018). "Don't Let History Forget About Compton's Cafeteria Riot." *Advocate*, August 2, 2018. https://www.advocate.com/transgender/2018/8/02/dont-let-history-forget-about-comptons-cafeteria-riot.

Brown, J., and F. Heidensohn. (2000). *Gender and Policing: Comparative Perspectives*. Basingstoke: MacMillan.

Brown, J., and S. Woolfenden. (2011). "Implications of the Changing Gender Ratio amongst Warranted Police Officers." *Policing* 5(4): 356–64. doi: 10.1093/police/par043.

Brown, J. M., and J. R. Sorensen. (2013). "Race, Ethnicity, Gender, and Waiver to Adult Court." *Journal of Ethnicity in Criminal Justice* 11(3): 181–95.

Brown, N. T., and J. L. Herman. (2015). *Intimate Partner Violence and Sexual Abuse among LGBT People*. Los Angeles: Williams Institute. https://williamsinstitute.law.ucla.edu/wp-content/uploads/Intimate-Partner-Violence-and-Sexual-Abuse-among-LGBT-People.pdf.

Brown, R. A., and J. Frank. (2006). "Race and Officer Decision Making: Examining Differences in Arrest Outcomes between Black and White Officers." *Justice Quarterly* 23(1): 96–126.

Brunner, L. A. K. (2010). "How Big Is Big Enough? Steve, Big, and Phallic Masculinity in Sex and the City." *Feminist Media Studies* 10(1): 87–98.

Budig, M., and P. England. (2001). "The Wage Penalty for Motherhood." *American Sociological Review* 66: 204–25.

Buist, C., and E. Lenning. (2016). *Queer Criminology: New Directions in Critical Criminology*. New York: Routledge.

Buist, C.L., and C. Stone. (2014). "Transgender Victims and Offenders: Failures of the United States Criminal Justice

System and the Necessity of Queer Criminology." *Critical Criminology* 22(1): 35–47. https://doi.org/10.1007/s10612-013-9224-1.

Bureau of Justice Statistics (BJS). (2012–2016a). "Number of Violent Victimizations by Victim-Offender Relationship and Sex, 2012–2016." Generated with NCVS Victimization Analysis Tool at www.bjs.gov.

———. (2012–2016b). "Number of Serious Violent Victimizations, Rape/Sexual Assaults, Robberies, and Aggravated Assaults by Sex and Victim-Offender Relationship,1993–2016." Generated with NCVS Victimization Analysis Tool at www.bjs.gov.

———. (2012–2017). "Number of Violent Victimizations, Serious Violent Victimizations, Rape/Sexual Assaults, Aggravated Assaults, and Simple Assaults by Sex and Victim-Offender Relationship, 2012–2017." Generated with the NCVS Victimization Analysis Tool at www.bjs.gov.

Burke, M. (1993). *Coming Out of the Blue*. London: Continuum.

———. (1994). "Homosexuality as Deviance: The Case of the Gay Police Officer." *British Journal of Criminology* 34(2): 192–203.

Burton, P. R., D. E. McNiel, and R. L. Binder. (2012). "Firesetting, Arson, Pyromania, and the Forensic Mental Health Expert." *Journal of the American Academy of Psychiatry and the Law Online* 40(3): 355–365.

Burton, V. S., Jr., F. T. Cullen, T. D. Evans, L. F. Alarid, and R.G. Dunaway. (1998). "Gender, Self-Control, and Crime." *Journal of Research in Crime and Delinquency* 35(2): 123–47.

Burwick, K. (2018). "Bill and Ted Star Alex Winter Recounts Hellish Sexual Abuse as Child Actor." *MovieWeb*, February 2, 2018. https://movieweb.com/alex-winter-sexual-abuse-young-actor-hollywood-pedophiles/.

Bush-Baskette, S. (2004). "The War on Drugs as a War Against Black Women." In *Girls, Women, and Crime*, edited by M. Chesney-Lind and L. Pasko. London: Sage.

Busselle, R., and H. Crandall. (2002). "Television Viewing and Perceptions about Race Differences in Socioeconomic Success." *Journal of Broadcasting and Electronic Media* 46(2): 265–82. DOI: 10.1207/s15506878jobem4602_6.

Butler, E., and F. Ferrier. (2000). *Don't Be Too Polite, Girls! Women, Work and Vocational Education and Training: A Critical Review of the Literature*. Leabrook, Australia: National Centre for Vocational Education Research.

Butler, J. (1990). *Gender Trouble*. London: Routledge.

Button, D. M. (2015). "A General Strain Approach Comparing the Effects of Victimization, Social Support, and Perceived Self-Efficacy on LGBQ and Heterosexual Youth Suicidality." *Criminal Justice Studies* 28(4): 484–502.

Button, D. M., and M. G. F. Worthen. (2014). "General Strain Theory for LGBQ and SSB Youth: The Importance of Intersectionality in the Future of Feminist Criminology." *Feminist Criminology* 9(4): 270–97.

Calton, J., L. Cattaneo, and K. Gebhard. (2016). "Barriers to Help Seeking for Lesbian, Gay, Bisexual, Transgender, and Queer Survivors of Intimate Partner Violence." *Trauma, Violence & Abuse* 17(5): 585–600.

Calvete, E., I. Orue, A. Estévez, L. Villardón, and P. Padilla. (2010). "Cyberbullying in Adolescents: Modalities and Aggressors' Profile." *Computers in Human Behavior* 26(5): 1128–35.

Camp, C., and G. Camp. (2002). *The Corrections Yearbook 2001: Adult Systems*. Middletown, CT: Criminal Justice Institute.

Camp, S. D. (1994). "Assessing the Effects of Organizational Commitment and Job Satisfaction on Turnover: An Event History Approach." *Prison Journal* 74(3): 279–305.

Camp, S. D., and N. P. Langan. (2005). "Perceptions about Minority and Female Opportunities for Job Advancements: Are Beliefs about Equal Opportunities Fixed?" *Prison Journal* 85(4): 399–419.

Camp, S. D., T. L. Steifer, and J. A. Batchelder. (1995). *Perceptions of Job Advancement Opportunities: A Multilevel Investigation of Race and Gender Effects*. Federal Bureau of Prisons and Indiana State University.

Campbell, A. (1981). *Girl Delinquents*. Oxford: Blackwell.

———. (1990). "Female Participation in Gangs." In *Gangs in America*, edited by C.R. Huff. Newbury Park, CA: Sage.

Campbell, H. (2005). "Drug Trafficking Stories: Everyday Forms of Narco-Folklore on the U.S.-Mexico Border." *International Journal of Drug Policy* 16(5): 326–33.

———. (2008). "Female Drug Smugglers on the U.S.-Mexico Border: Gender, Crime, and Empowerment." *Anthropological Quarterly* 81(1): 233–67.

Carli, L. L. (1999). "Cognitive Reconstruction, Hindsight, and Reactions to Victims and Perpetrators." *Personality and Social Psychology Bulletin* 25(8): 966–79.

Carlson, J. R., G. Thomas, and R. H. Anson. (2004). "Cross-Gender Perceptions of Corrections Officers in Gender-Segregated Prisons." *Journal of Offender Rehabilitation* 39(1): 83–103.

Carroll, A., and L. R. Mendos. (2017). *State Sponsored Homophobia 2017; A World Survey of Sexual Orientation Laws: Criminalisation, Protection and Recognition*. Geneva: International Lesbian, Gay, Bisexual and Intersex Association. https://ilga.org/downloads/2017/ILGA_State_Sponsored_Homophobia_2017_WEB.pdf.

Carvalho, A. F. (2006). "Gay Men's and Lesbians' Perceptions of Intimate Partner Abuse in Same-Sex and Opposite-Sex Relationships." PhD diss., Virginia Consortium Program in Clinical Psychology, Virginia Beach.

Carvalho, A.M., R.J. Lewis, V.J. Derlega, B. A. Winstead, and C. Viggiano. (2011). "Internalized Sexual Minority Stressors and Same-Sex Intimate Partner Violence." *Journal of Family Violence* 26(7): 501–9. doi: 10.1007/s10896–011–9384–2.

Cassidy, J., Y. Ziv, B. Stupica, L. J. Sherman, H. Butler, A. Karfgin, G. Cooper, K. T. Hoffman, and B. Powell. (2010). "Enhancing Attachment Security in the Infants of Women in a Jail-Diversion Program." *Attachment and Human Development* 12(4): 333–53.

Castle, T., C. Hensley, and R. Tewksbury. (2002). "Argot Roles and Prison Sexual Hierarchy." *Prison Sex: Practice and Policy*, edited by Christopher Hensley, 13–26. Boulder, CO: Lynne Reinner.

Catalano, S. (2012). *Stalking Victims in the United States—Revised*. Washington, DC: US Department of Justice, Office of Justice Programs, Bureau of Justice Statistics. https://bjs.gov/content/pub/pdf/svus_rev.pdf.

Catalano, S. M. (2013). *Intimate Partner Violence: Attributes of Victimization, 1993–2001*. Bureau of Justice Statistics. https://www.bjs.gov/index.cfm?ty=pbdetail&iid=4801.

Cauffman, E., A. R. Piquero, E. Kimonis, L. Steinberg, L. Chassin, and J. Fagan. (2007). "Legal, Individual, and Contextual Predictors of Court Disposition in a Sample of Serious Adolescent Offenders." *Law and Human Behavior* 31(6): 519–35.

Caulkins, J. P., H. Burnett, and E. Leslie. (2009.) "How Illegal Drugs Enter an Island Country: Insights from Interviews with Interviews with Incarcerated Traffickers." *Global Crime* 10(102): 66–96.

CBS News. (2014). "Thwarted in His Plan, California Gunman Improvised." *CBS News*, May 25, 2014. https://www

.cbsnews.com/news/thwarted-in-his-plan-california-gunman-improvised/.

Centers for Disease Control and Prevention. (2015). Youth Risk Behavior Study. https://www.cdc.gov/healthyyouth/data/yrbs/index.htm.

———. (2018). "LGBT Health." https://www.cdc.gov/lgbthealth/.

———. (2019). *HIV in the United States: At a Glance.* http://www.cdc.gov/hiv/statistics/overview/ataglance.html.

———. (2021). *Teen Dating Violence.* https://www.cdc.gov/violenceprevention/pdf/ipv/TDV-factsheet_508.pdf.

Chaiyavej, S., and M. Morash. (2008). "Dynamics of Sexual Harassment for Policewomen Working alongside Men." *Policing: An International Journal of Police Strategies and Management* 31(3): 485–98.

Chambliss, W. J., and R. B. Seidman. (1971). *Law, Order, and Power.* Reading, MA: Addison-Wesley.

Chan, M. (2015). "See It: Florida Judge Berates Domestic Abuse Victim, Sentences Sobbing Woman to Jail: 'You Haven't Even Seen Anxiety.'" *Daily News,* October 9, 2015. https://www.nydailynews.com/news/national/judge-berates-domestic-abuse-victim-sentences-jail-article-1.2389943?cid=bitly.

Chaplin, T. M., P. M. Cole, and C. Zahn-Waxler. (2005). "Parental Socialization of Emotion Expression: Gender Differences and Relations to Child Adjustment." *Emotion* 5(1): 80–88.

Chapple, C. L., J. Vaske, and T. L. Hope. (2010). "Sex Differences in the Causes of Self-Control: An Examination of Mediation, Moderation, and Gendered Etiologies." *Journal of Criminal Justice* 38(6): 1122–31.

Charles, M. W., and L. M. R. Arndt. (2013). "Gay- and Lesbian-Identified Law Enforcement Officers: Intersection of Career and Sexual Identity." *Counseling Psychologist* 41(8): 1153–85.

Chesney-Lind, M., and M. Eliason. (2006). "From Invisible to Incorrigible: The Demonization of Marginalized Women and Girls." *Crime, Media, Culture* 2(1): 29–47.

Chesney-Lind, M., and L. Pasko. (2013). *The Female Offender: Girls, Women, and Crime.* Thousand Oaks, CA: Sage.

Chesney-Lind, M., and R. G. Shelden. (2014). *Girls, Delinquency, and Juvenile Justice.* Hoboken, NJ: Wiley.

Chester v. State, 471 S.E.2nd 836. (1996). https://law.justia.com/cases/georgia/supreme-court/1996/s96a0236-1.html.

Chong E. S., M. M. Kwong, and W. W. Mak. (2010). "Prevalence of Same-Sex Intimate Partner Violence in Hong Kong." *Public Health* 124(3): 149–52. doi: 10.1016/j.puhe.2010.02.002.

Chung, Y., B. Downs, D. H. Sandler, and B. Sienkiewicz. (2017). *The Parental Gender Earnings Gap in the United States.* Washington, DC: Center for Economic Studies, U.S. Census Bureau.

Ciriaco, M. (2012). "Exclusive: Logo's New Programming Slate Reveals Shift Away from Gay-Centric Shows." *Queerty,* February 21, 2012, https://www.queerty.com/exclusive-logos-new-programming-slate-reveals-shift-away-from-gay-centric-shows-20120221.

Clarke, R. V. G., ed. (1997). *Situational Crime Prevention.* Monsey, NY: Criminal Justice Press.

Clements-Nolle, K., R. Marx, and M. Katz. (2006). "Attempted Suicide among Transgender Persons: The Influence of Gender-Based Discrimination and Victimization." *Journal of Homosexuality* 51(3): 53–69.

Clinton, H. (2014). *Hard Choices.* New York: Simon & Schuster.

Coad, D. (2008). *The Metrosexual: Gender, Sexuality, and Sport.* Albany: SUNY Press.

Cochran, C., P. Frazier, and A. Olson. (1997). "Predictors of Responses to Unwanted Sexual Attention." *Psychology of Women Quarterly* 21(1): 201–26.

Cochran, J. K., and B. A. Sanders. (2009). "The Gender Gap in Death Penalty Support: An Exploratory Study." *Journal of Criminal Justice* 37(6): 525–33.

Cohen, G. B., and R. J. Smith. (2010). "The Racial Geography of the Federal Death Penalty." *Washington Law Review* 85: 425.

Cohen, L. E., and M. E. Felson. (1979). "Social Change and Crime Rate Trends: A Routine Activity Approach." *American Sociological Review* 44: 588–608.

Collins, J. C., and T. S. Rocco. (2015). "Rules of Engagement as Survival Consciousness: Gay Male Law Enforcement Officers' Experiential Learning in a Masculinized Industry." *Adult Education Quarterly* 65(4): 295–312.

Collins, T. A., and L. Moyer. (2008). "Gender, Race, and Intersectionality on the Federal Appellate Bench." *Political Research Quarterly* 61(2): 219–27.

Collinson, D. (2012). "Prozac Leadership and the Limits of Positive Thinking." *Leadership* 8(2): 87–107. https://doi.org/10.1177%2F1742715011434738.

Colvin, R. (2008). "Shared Perceptions among Lesbian and Gay Police Officers: Barriers and Opportunities in the Law Enforcement Work Environment." *Police Quarterly* 12(1): 86–101.

———. (2012). *Gay and Lesbian Cops: Diversity and Effective Policing.* Boulder, CO: Lynne Rienner.

———. (2015). "Shared Workplace Experiences of Lesbian and Gay Police Officers in the United Kingdom." *Policing: An International Journal of Police Strategies and Management* 38(2): 333–49.

Conesa, K. (2004). "The Ride to Perdition." *Miami New Times,* October 14, 2004. https://www.miaminewtimes.com/news/the-ride-to-perdition-6367591

Connell, R. W. (1987). *Gender and Power: Society, the Person and Sexual Politics.* Stanford, CA: Stanford University Press.

Connell, R. W., and J. W. Messerschmidt. (2005). "Hegemonic Masculinity: Rethinking the Concept." *Gender & Society* 19(6): 829–59.

Cooper, R. M., and W. J. Blumenfeld. (2012). "Responses to Cyberbullying: A Descriptive Analysis of the Frequency of and Impact on LGBT and Allied Youth." *Journal of LGBT Youth* 9(2): 153–77. doi: 10.1080/19361653.2011.649616.

Copes, H., and A. Hochstetler. (2003). "Situational Construction of Masculinity among Male Street Thieves." *Journal of Contemporary Ethnography* 32(3): 279–304.

Cordner, G., and A. Cordner. (2011). "Stuck on a Plateau? Obstacles to Recruitment, Selection, and Retention of Women Police." *Police Quarterly* 14(3): 207–26. doi: 10.1177/1098611111413990.

Cornish, D. B., and R. V. Clarke, eds. (1986). *The Reasoning Criminal: Rational Choice Perspectives on Offending.* Secaucus, NJ: Springer-Verlag.

Correll, S. J., S. Benard, and I. Paik. (2007). "Getting a Job: Is There a Motherhood Penalty?" *American Journal of Sociology* 112(5): 1297–338.

Costello, M. (2018). "We Don't Like Your Type Around Here: Regional and Residential Differences in Exposure to Online Material Targeting Sexuality." *Deviant Behavior* 40(3). Published online January 19, 2018. https://doi.org/10.1080/01639625.2018.1426266.

Cowan, K. (2007). *Living Together: British Attitudes towards Lesbian, Gay, and Bisexual People in 2012.* London: Stonewall.

Crane, D. (2001). *Fashion and Its Social Agendas: Class, Gender and Identity in Clothing*. Chicago: University of Chicago Press.

Creighton, G., and J. L. Oliffe. (2010). "Theorising Masculinities and Men's Health: A Brief History with a View to Practice." *Health Sociology Review* 19(4): 409–18.

Crenshaw, K. (1989). "Demarginalizing the Intersection of Race and Sex: A Black Feminist Critique of Antidiscrimination Doctrine, Feminist Theory, and Antiracist Doctrine, Feminist Theory, and Antiracist Politics." *University of Chicago Legal Forum* 140: 139–67.

Crewe, B. (2006). "Male Prisoners' Orientations towards Women Officers in an England Prison." *Punishment & Society* 8(4): 395–421.

Cuddy, A. J. C., S. T. Fiske, and P. Glick. (2004). "When Professionals Become Mothers, Warmth Doesn't Cut the Ice." *Journal of Social Issues* 60: 701–18.

Curry, D., R. A. Ball, and R. J. Fox. (1994). *Gang Crime and Law Enforcement Recordkeeping, Research in Brief*. Washington, DC: US Department of Justice, Office of Justice Programs, National Institute of Justice.

Curtis, M. A., S. Garlington, and L. Schottenfeld. (2013). "Alcohol, Drug and Criminal History Restrictions to Public Housing." *Cityscape: A Journal of Policy Development and Research* 15(3): 37–52. https://www.huduser.gov/portal/periodicals/cityscpe/vol15num3/ch2.pdf.

Dabney, D. A., R. C. Hollinger, and L. Dugan. (2004). "Who Actually Steals? A Study of Covertly Observed Shoplifters." *Justice Quarterly* 21(4): 693–728.

Dalhuisen, L., F. Koenraadt, and M. Liem. (2015). "Psychotic versus Non-psychotic Firesetters: Similarities and Differences in Characteristics." *Journal of Forensic Psychiatry and Psychology* 26(4): 439–60.

Dalton, D. (2016). "Reflections on the Emergence, Efficacy, and Value of Queer Criminology." In *Queering Criminology*, edited by A. Dwyer, M. Ball, and T. Crofts, 15–35. Basingstoke: Palgrave Macmillan.

Daly, K. (1989). "Gender and Varieties of White-Collar Crime." *Criminology* 27(4): 769–94.

———. (1994). *Gender, Crime, and Punishment*. New Haven, CT: Yale University Press.

Daly, M., and M. Wilson. (1988). "Evolutionary Social Psychology and Family Homicide." *Science* 242(4878): 519–52.

Dank, M., J. Yahner, K. Madden, I. Banuelos, L. Yu, A. Ritchie, M. Mora, and B. Conner. (2012). *Surviving the Streets of New York: Experiences of LGBTQ Youth, YMSM, YWSW Engaged in Survival Sex*. New York: Urban Institute.

Das, A. (2009). "Sexual Harassment at Work in the United States." *Archives of Sexual Behavior* 38(6): 909–21. https://doi.org/10.1007/s10508-008-9354-9.

Davies, P. A. (2003). "Is Economic Crime a Man's Game?" *Feminist Theory* 4(3): 283–303.

Davis, A. Y. (2003). *Are Prisons Obsolete?* New York: Seven Stories Press.

Day, J. C. (2018). "More Than 1 in 3 Lawyers Are Women." U.S. Census Bureau, May 8, 2018. https://www.census.gov/library/stories/2018/05/women-lawyers.html.

Day, S. (2007). *On the Game: Women and Sex Work*. London: Pluto Press.

Deering, R., and D. Mellor. (2009). "Sentencing of Male and Female Child Sex Offenders: Australian Study." *Psychiatry, Psychology and Law* 16(3): 394–412.

DeKeseredy, W., and M. Corsianos. (2016). *Violence against Women in Pornography*. New York: Routledge.

DeKeseredy, W. S., and A. Hall-Sanchez. (2016). "Adult Pornography and Violence against Women in the Heartland: Results from a Rural Southeast Ohio Study." *Violence against Women* 23(7): 830–49. doi: 10.177/1077801216648795.

DeKeseredy, W. S., S. L. Muzzatti, and J. F. Donnermeyer. (2014). "Mad Men in Bib Overalls: Media's Horrification and Pornification of Rural Culture." *Critical Criminology* 22(2): 179–97.

Depraetere, J., C. Vandeviver, T. V. Beken, and I. Keygnaert. (2018). "Big Boys Don't Cry: A Critical Interpretive Synthesis of Male Sexual Victimization." *Trauma, Violence, and Abuse* 21(5): 991–1010.

Deschamps, F., I. Paganon-Badinier, A. C. Marchand, and C. Merle. (2003). "Sources and Assessment of Occupational Stress in the Police." *Journal of Occupational Health* 45(6): 358.

Dettlaff. A. J., M. Washburn, L. C. Carr, and A. Vogel. (2018). "Lesbian, Gay, and Bisexual (LGB) Youth within in Welfare: Prevalence, Risk and Outcomes." *Child Abuse and Neglect* 80: 183–93. https://doi.org/10.1016/j.chiabu.2018.03.009.

Detrow, S. (2021). "Biden Repeals Trump-Era Ban on Transgender Troops." *NPR*, January 25, 2021. https://www.npr.org/sections/president-biden-takes-office/2021/01/25/960338217/biden-repeals-trump-era-ban-on-transgender-soldiers.

de Vogue, A., and Z. Cohen. (2019). "Supreme Court Allows Transgender Military Ban to Go into Effect." *CNN*, January 22, 2019. https://www.cnn.com/2019/01/22/politics/scotus-transgender-ban/index.html.

Dick, R. N., H. L. McCauley, K. A. Jones, D. J. Tancredi, S. Goldstein, S. Blackburn, E. Monasterio, L. James, J. G. Silverman, and E. Miller. (2014). "Cyber Dating Abuse among Teens Using School-Based Health Centers." *Pediatrics* 134(6): e1560–67. doi: 10.1542/peds.2014–0537.

Didden, R., R. H. Scholte, H. Korzilius, J. M. de Moor, A. Vermeulen, M. O'Reilly, R. Lang, and G. E. Lancioni. (2009). "Cyberbullying among Students with Intellectual and Developmental Disability in Special Education Settings." *Developmental Neurorehabilitation* 12(3): 146–51.

Dilmac, B. (2009). "Psychological Needs as a Predictor of Cyber Bullying: A Preliminary Report on College Students." *Educational Sciences: Theory and Practice* 9(3): 1307–25.

Dines, G. (2010). *Pornland: How Porn Has Hijacked Our Sexuality*. Boston: Beacon Press.

Dinovitzer, R. (2011). "The Financial Rewards of Elite Status in the Legal Profession." *Law & Social Inquiry* 36(4): 971–98.

Dixon, A., P. Howie, and J. Starling. (2004). "Psychopathology in Female Juvenile Offenders." *Journal of Child Psychology and Psychiatry* 45(5): 1150–58.

Dixon, D., and Dixon, J. (1998). "She-Male Prostitutes: Who Are They, What Do They Do and Why Do They Do It?" In *Prostitution: On Whores, Hustlers and Johns*, edited by J. Elias, V. Bullough, V. Elias, and G. Brewer. New York: Prometheus Books.

Dobash, R. E., and R. P. Dobash. (1998). "Violent Men and Violent Contexts." In *Rethinking Violence against Women*, edited by R. E. Dobash and R. P. Dobash, 141–68. Sage Series on Violence against Women, 9. Thousand Oaks, CA: Sage Publications.

Dodge, M. (2000). "Our Juvenile Court Has Become More Like a Criminal Court: A Century of Reform at the Cook County (Chicago) Juvenile Court." *Michigan Historical Review* 26 (Fall): 51–89.

———. (2009). *Women and White-Collar Crime*. Upper Saddle River, NJ: Prentice Hall.

Doerner, J. K., and S. Demuth. (2014). "Gender and Sentencing in the Federal Courts: Are Women Treated More Leniently?" *Criminal Justice Policy* 25(2): 242–69.

Dölling, D., H. Entorf, D. Hermann, and T. Rupp. (2009). "Is Deterrence Effective? Results of a Meta-analysis of Punishment." *European Journal on Criminal Policy and Research* 15(1–2): 201–24.

Douglas, E. M., and D. A. Hines. (2011). "The Helpseeking Experiences of Men who Sustain Intimate Partner Violence: An Overlooked Population and Implications for Practice." *Journal of Family Violence* 26(6): 473–85.

Dovidio, J. F., J. K. Smith, A. G. Donnella, and S. L. Gaertner. (1997). "Racial Attitudes and the Death Penalty." *Journal of Applied Social Psychology* 27(16): 1468–87.

Draucker, C. B., and D. S. Martsolf. (2010). "The Role of Electronic Communication Technology in Adolescent Dating Violence." *Journal of Child and Adolescent Psychiatric Nursing* 23(3): 133–42.

Dreßing, H., J. Bailer, A. Anders, H. Wagner, and C. Gallas. (2014). "Cyberstalking in a Large Sample of Social Network Users: Prevalence, Characteristics, and Impact upon Victims." *Cyberpsychology, Behavior, and Social Networking* 17(2): 61–67.

Drijber, B. C., U. J. Reijnders, and M. Ceelen. (2013). "Male Victims of Domestic Violence." *Journal of Family Violence* 28(2): 173–78.

Duberman, M. B. (1986). *About Time: Exploring the Gay Past.* New York City: Gay Presses of America.

Durkheim, E. (1897). *Suicide.* New York: Free Press.

Eaklor, V. L. (2008). *Queer America: A GLBT History of the Twentieth Century.* New York: New Press.

Eaton, A., H., Jacobs, and Y. Ruvalcaba. (2017). "Nationwide Online Study of Nonconsensual Porn Victimization and Perpetration." *Cyber Civil Rights Initiative.* https://www .cybercivilrights.org/wp-content/uploads/2017/06/CCRI-2017-Research-Report.pdf.

Eaton, L., M. Kaufman, A. Fuhrel, D. Cain, C. Cherry, H. Pope, and S. Kalichman. (2008). "Examining Factors Co-existing with Interpersonal Violence in Lesbian Relationships." *Journal of Family Violence* 23(8): 697–705. doi:10.1007/s10896–008–9194–3.

Edwards, K. M., and D. M. Sylaska. (2013). "The Perpetration of Intimate Partner Violence among LGBTQ College Youth: The Role of Minority Stress." *Journal of Youth and Adolescence* 42(11): 1721–31. doi: 10.1007/s10964–012–9880–6.

Effrig, J. C., K. J. Bieschke, and B. D. Locke. (2011). "Examining Victimization and Psychological Distress in Transgender College Students." *Journal of College Counseling* 14(2): 143–57. https://doi.org/10.1002/j.2161–1882.2011.tb00269.x.

Ehrmann, S., N. Hyland, and C. Puzzanchera. (2019). "Girls in the Juvenile Justice System." *Juvenile Justice Statistics,* April. Office of Juvenile Justice and Delinquency Prevention. https:// ojjdp.ojp.gov/sites/g/files/xyckuh176/files/pubs/251486.pdf.

Eitle, D., F. Niedrist, and T. M. Eitle. (2014). "Gender, Race, and Delinquent Behavior: An Extension of Power-Control Theory to American Indian Adolescents." *Deviant Behavior* 35(12): 1023–42.

Elder, G. H., Jr., M. K. Johnson, and R. Crosnoe. (2003). "The Emergence and Development of Life Course Theory." In *Handbook of the Life Course,* edited by J. T. Mortimer and M. J. Shanahan, 3–19. New York: Springer.

Embrick, D. G., C. S. Walther, and C. M. Wickens. (2007). "Working Class Masculinity: Keeping Gay Men and Lesbians Out of the Workplace." *Sex Roles* 56(11): 757–66. https://doi.org /10.1007/ s11199–007–9234–0.

Entman, R. M. (1994). "Representation and Reality in the Portrayal of Blacks on Network Television News." *Journalism Quarterly* 71(3): 509–20.

———. (2006). *Young Men of Color in the Media: Images and Impacts.* Washington, DC: Joint Center for Political and Economic Studies, Health Policy Institute.

Entman, R. M., and A. Rojecki. (2001). *The Black Image in the White Mind: Media and Race in America.* Chicago: University of Chicago Press.

Epner, J. E. G. (2006). *Visible Invisibility: Women of Color in Law Firms.* Chicago: American Bar Association.

Epstein, R., J. Blake, and T. Gonzalez. (2017). "Girlhood Interrupted: The Erasure of Black Girls' Childhood." *SSRN Electronic Journal,* June 27, 2021. doi:10.2139/ssrn.3000695.

Equaldex. (2021). "LGBTQ+ Rights by Country." https://www .equaldex.com/.Erez, E. (1992). "Dangerous Men, Evil Women: Gender and Parole-Decision Making." *Justice Quarterly* 9(1): 105–26.

Equal Opportunity Employment Commission (EEOC). (2020). "Enforcement and Litigation Statistics." https://www.eeoc .gov/statistics/enforcement-and-litigation-statistics.

Eskridge, W. M. (2008). *Dishonorable Passions: Sodomy Laws in America, 1861–2003.* New York City: Viking Press.

Espelage, D., and G. Merrin. (2016). "Violence Victimization among Sexual Minority High School Students: Impact of School Disorganization on Mental Health Outcomes." *Journal of the American Academy of Child and Adolescent Psychiatry* 55(10): S279–87. https://doi.org/10.1016/j.jaac.2016.07.228.

Espelage, D. L., S. R. Aragon, M. Birkett, and B. W. Koening. (2008). "Homophobic Teasing, Psychological Outcomes, and Sexual Orientation among High School Students: What Influence do Parents and Schools Have?" *School Psychology Review* 37(2): 202–16.

Fabelo, T., M. D. Thompson, M. Plotkin, D. Carmichael, M. P. Marchbanks, and E. A. Booth. (2011). *Breaking Schools' Rules: A Statewide Study of How School Discipline Relates to Students' Success and Juvenile Justice Involvement.* New York: Council of State Governments Justice Center. http:// justicecenter.csg.org/resource.

Farkas, M. (1999). "Inmate Supervisory Style: Does Gender Make a Difference?" *Women & Criminal Justice* 10(4): 25–45.

Farnworth, L. (1992). "Women Doing a Man's Job: Female Prison Officers Working in a Male Prison." *Australian and New Zealand Journal of Criminology* 25(3): 278–29.

Farr, K. A. (2000). "Defeminizing and Dehumanizing Female Murderers: Depictions of Lesbians on Death Row." *Women and Criminal Justice* 11(1): 49–66.

Feasey, R. (2012). "Absent, Ineffectual and Intoxicated Mothers: Representing the Maternal in Teen Television." *Feminist Media Studies* 12(1): 155–59. doi: 10.1080/14680777.2011.640011.

Featherly, K. (2016). s.v. "ARPANET." *Encyclopedia Britannica.* https://www.britannica.com/topic/ARPANET.

Federal Bureau of Investigation (FBI). (2010). *Offense Definitions.* Uniform Crime Reporting Program. https://ucr.fbi.gov /crime-in-the-u.s/2010/crime-in-the-u.s.-2010/offense-definitions.

———. (1995–2019). "Crime in the United States." https://ucr.fbi .gov/crime-in-the-u.s.

———. (2015). *Crime in the United States: 2015.* https://ucr.fbi.gov /crime-in-the-u.s/2015/crime-in-the-u.s.-2015.

———. (2016a). *Crime in the United States: 2016.* https://ucr.fbi .gov/crime-in-the-u.s/2016/crime-in-the-u.s.-2016.

———. (2016b). "Tables with All Offenses." National Incident-Based Reporting System. https://ucr.fbi.gov/nibrs/2016/tables /data-tables.

———. (2017a). "Full-Time Law Enforcement Employees." Uniform Crime Reporting Program. https://ucr.fbi.gov/crime-in-the-u.s/2017/crime-in-the-u.s.-2017/tables/table-70.

———. (2017b). National Incident-Based Reporting System Data Tables. https://ucr.fbi.gov/nibrs/2017/tables/data-tables.

———. (2017c). "Preliminary Report of Crime in the United States." https://ucr.fbi.gov/crime-in-the-u.s/2017/preliminary-report.

———. (2017d). UCR Data Tables. https://ucr.fbi.gov/crime-in-the-u.s/2017/crime-in-the-u.s.-2017/home.

———. (2017e). "UCR Offense Definitions." https://www .ucrdatatool.gov/offenses.cfm.

———. (2019a). "Hate Crimes." What We Investigate. https://www .fbi.gov/investigate/civil-rights/hate-crimes.

———. (2019b). "National Incident-Base Reporting System." https:// ucr.fbi.gov/nibrs/2019/tables/data-tables.

Federal Bureau of Prisons. (n.d.). "About Our Facilities." https:// www.bop.gov/about/facilities/federal_prisons.jsp.

———. (2018.) "Staff Ethnicity/Race." https://www.bop.gov/about /statistics/statistics_staff_ethnicity_race.jsp.

Feinman, C. (1980). *Women in the Criminal-Legal System.* New York: Praeger,

Felson, M. (2006). *Crime and Nature.* Thousand Oaks, CA: Sage.

Fergusson, D. M., L. J. Horwood, and D. S. Nagin. (2000). "Offending Trajectories in a New Zealand Birth Cohort." *Criminology* 38(2): 525–52.

Fernando Rodriguez, S., T. R. Curry, and G. Lee. (2006). "Gender Differences in Criminal Sentencing: Do Effects Vary across Violent, Property, and Drug Offenses?" *Social Science Quarterly* 87(2): 318–39.

Ferrell, J., K. Hayward, and J. Young. (2015). *Cultural Criminology: An Invitation.* London: Sage Publications.

Ferrell, J., and C. R. Sanders. (1995). "Cultural Criminology." Boston: Northeastern University Press.

Finkelhor, D. (2008). *Childhood Victimization: Violence, Crime, and Abuse in the Lives of Young People.* New York: Oxford University Press.

Finkelhor, D., and Ormrod, R. (2001). "Homicides of Children and Youth." *Juvenile Justice Bulletin.* Washington, DC: US Government Printing Office.

Finley, N., and H. Grasmick. (1985). "Gender Roles and Social Control." *Sociological Spectrum* 5(4): 317–30.

Finn, J. (2004). A Survey of Online Harassment at a University Campus. *Journal of Interpersonal Violence* 19(4): 468–83.

Fisher, B., F. T. Cullen, and M. G. Turner. (1999). *The Extent and Nature of the Sexual Victimization of College Women: A National Level Analysis.* Washington, DC: National Institute of Justice.

Fleetwood, J. (2010). "Drug Mules in the International Cocaine Trade: Diversity and Relative Deprivation." *Service Prison Journal* 192(1): 3–8.

———. (2015). *Drug Mules: Women in the International Cocaine Trade.* Basingstoke: Palgrave MacMillan.

Flowers, R. B. (2001). "The Sex Trade Industry's Worldwide Exploitation of Children." *Annals of the American Academy of Political and Social Science* 575(1): 147–57. doi:10.1177/000271620157500109.

Follingstad, D. R., M. J. Rogers, S. N. Welling, and F. J. Priesmeyer. (2015). "Decisions to Prosecute Battered Women's Homicide Cases: An Exploratory Study." *Journal of Family Violence* 30(7): 859–74.

Follman, M., G. Aronsen, and D. Pan. (2019). "US Mass Shootings, 1982–2019: Data from *Mother Jones* Investigation." *Mother Jones*, December 11, 2019. https://www.motherjones.com /politics/2012/12/mass-shootings-mother-jones-full-data/.

Fontenot, K., J. Semega, and M. Kollar. (2018). *Income and Poverty in the United States: 2017.* US Census Bureau. https://www .census.gov/library/publications/2018/demo/p60–263.html.

Forsyth, C., and T. Marckese. (1995). "Female Participation in Three Minor Crimes: A Note on the Relationship between Opportunity and Crime." *International Journal of Sociology of the Family* 25(1): 127–32.

Fowler, H. (2020). "'Act of Genocide': Eugenics Program Tried to 'Breed Out' Black People in NC, Report Says." [North Carolina] *News & Observer*, July 22, 2020. https://www .newsobserver.com/news/state/north-carolina/ article244411987.html.

Fox, J., and K. M. Warber. (2015). "Queer Identity Management and Political Self-Expression on Social Networking Sites: A Co-cultural Approach to the Spiral of Silence." *Journal of Communication* 65(1): 79–100. http://dx.doi.org/10.1111 /jcom.12137.

Fox, J. A., J. Levin, and K. Quinet. (2018). *The Will to Kill: Making Sense of Senseless Murder.* Thousand Oaks, CA: Sage Publications.

Franklin, C. A. (2007). "Male Peer Support and the Police Culture: Understanding the Resistance and Opposition of Women in Policing." *Women & Criminal Justice* 16(3): 1–25.

Franklin, C. A., and N. Fearn. (2008). "Gender, Race, and Formal Court Decision-Making Outcomes: Chivalry/Paternalism, Conflict Theory or Gender Conflict?" *Journal of Criminal Justice* 36(3): 279–90.

Franklin, K. (2001). "The Rhetorics of Legal Authority Constructing Authoritativeness, the 'Ellen Effect,' and the Example of Sodomy Law." *Rutgers Law Journal* 33: 49–104.

Fridel, E. E. (2017). "A Multivariate Comparison of Family, Felony, and Public Mass Murders in the United States." *Journal of Interpersonal Violence* 36(3–4): 1092–118.

Fry, L., and D. Glaser. (1987). "Gender Differences in Work Adjustment of Prison Employees." *Journal of Offender Counseling, Services, and Rehabilitation* 12(1): 39–52.

Fuegen, K., M. Biernat, E. Haines, and K. Deaux. (2004). "Mothers and Fathers in the Workplace: How Gender and Parental Status Influence Judgments of Job-Related Competence." *Journal of Social Issues* 60(4): 737–54.

Furman, W., and D. Buhrmester. (1992). "Age and Sex Differences in Perceptions of Networks of Personal Relationships." *Child Development* 63(1): 103–15. https://doi.org/10.2307 /1130905.

Furman v. Georgia. 408 U.S. 238, 92 S. Ct. 2726, 33 L. Ed. 2d 346 (1972).

Gabbidon, S. L., H. Taylor Greene, and K. Wilder. (2004). "Still Excluded? An Update on the Status of African American Scholars in the Discipline of Criminology and Criminal Justice." *Journal of Research in Crime and Delinquency* 41(4): 384–406.

Gagné, P., R. Tewksbury, and D. McGaughey. (1997). "Coming Out and Crossing Over: Identity Formation and Proclamation in a Transgender Community." *Gender and Society* 11(4): 478–508.

Galanter, M. (1974). "Why the 'Haves' Come Out Ahead: Speculations on the Limits of Legal Change." *Law & Society Review* 9: 95–160.

Gallagher, P. (2015). "Ashley Madison Hack: Leaking Personal Email Addresses Puts Gay Lives at Risk Around the World."

Independent, August 20, 2015. http://www.independent.co.uk/news/world/ashley-madison-hack-leaking-personal-email-addresses-puts-gay-lives-at-risk-around-theworld-10464546.html.

Gamble, S. (2006). "Postfeminism." In *The Routledge Companion to Feminism and Postfeminism,* edited by S. Gamble, 36–46. London: Routledge.

Garcia, E., C. M. Rodriguez, M. Martín-Fernández, and M. Lila (2017). "Acceptability of Family Violence: Underlying Ties between Intimate Partner Violence and Child Abuse." *Journal of Interpersonal Violence* 35(17–18): 3217–36.

García-López, G. (2008). "'Nunca te toman en cuenta' [They Never Take You into Account]: The Challenges of Inclusion and Strategies for Success of Chicana Attorneys." *Gender & Society* 22(5): 590–612.

Gavin, H. (2014). "Jealous Men but Evil Women: The Double Standard in Cases of Domestic Homicide." Paper presented at 6th Global Conference: Evil, Woman and the Feminine, May 2–4, 2014, Lisbon, Portugal.

Geiger, B. (2006). "Crime, Prostitution, Drugs, and Malingered Insanity: Female Offenders' Resistant Strategies to Abuse and Domination." *International Journal of Offender Therapy and Comparative Criminology* 50(5): 582–94.

Genz, S., and B. B. Brabon. (2009). *Postfeminism: Cultural Texts and Theories.* Edinburgh: Edinburgh University Press.

Gerbner, G., L. Gross, M. Morgan, N. Signorielli, and J. Shanahan. (2002). "Growing Up with Television: Cultivation Processes." In *Media Effects,* edited by J. Bryant and M. B. Oliver, 53–78. New York: Routledge.

Giacomello, C. (2013). "Women, Drug Offenses and Penitentiary Systems in Latin America." *IDPC Briefing Paper,* October 2013. International Drug Policy Consortium. https://idpc.net/publications/2013/11/idpc-briefing-paper-women-drug-offenses-and-penitentiary-systems-in-latin-america.

Gill, R. (2007). *Gender and the Media.* Cambridge: Polity.

———. (2016). "Post-Postfeminism? New Feminist Visibilities in Postfeminist Times." *Feminist Media Studies* 16(4): 610–30. DOI: 10.1080/14680777.2016.1193293.

Gilman, S. L. (1985). *Difference and Pathology: Stereotypes of Sexuality, Race, and Madness.* Ithaca, NY: Cornell University Press.

Gilson, R. J., and R. H. Mnookin. (1994). "Disputing through Agents: Cooperation and Conflict Between Lawyers in Litigation." *Columbia Law Review* 94(2): 509–66.

Ging, D. (2019). "Alphas, Betas, and Incels: Theorizing the Masculinities of the Manosphere." *Men and Masculinities* 22(4): 638–57.

Ging, D., and E. Siapera. (2018). "Special Issue on Online Misogyny." *Feminist Media Studies* 18(4): 515–24. DOI: 10.1080/14680777.2018.1447345.

Giordano, P. C., and S. A. Cernkovich. (1979). "On Complicating the Relationship between Liberation and Delinquency." *Social Problems* 26(4): 467–75.

GLAAD. (2017a). "Debunking the 'Bathroom Bill' Myth." https://www.glaad.org/sites/default/files/Debunking_the_Bathroom_Bill_Myth_2017.pdf.

———. (2017b). "Where We Are on TV." https://www.glaad.org/whereweareontv17.

———. (2021). "Glossary of Terms: Lesbian/Gay/Bisexual/Queer." https://www.glaad.org/reference/lgbtq.

Glass, N., and D. Hassouneh. (2008). "The Influence of Gender Role Stereotyping on Women's Experiences of Female Same-Sex Intimate Partner Violence." *Violence against Women* 14(3): 310–25. doi: 10.1177/1077801207313734.

Gleeson, P. (1996). "Women in 'Men's' Work: An Issue of Identity." *Journal of Vocational Education and Training* 48(3): 261–76.

Glick, P., and S. T. Fiske. (1997). "Hostile and Benevolent Sexism: Measuring Ambivalent Sexist Attitudes toward Women." *Psychology of Women Quarterly* 21(1): 119–35.

Godoy, M., and D. Wood. (2020). "What Do Coronavirus Racial Disparities Look Like State By State?" *NPR Health Shots,* May 6, 2020. https://www.npr.org/sections/health-shots/2020/05/30/865413079/what-do-coronavirus-racial-disparities-look-like-state-by-state.

Goffman, E. (1961). *Asylums.* New York: Doubleday Archer.

González, T. (2012). "Keeping Kids in Schools: Restorative Justice, Punitive Discipline, and the School to Prison Pipeline." *Journal of Law and Education* 41(2): 281–35.

Goodmark, L. (2013). "Transgender People, Intimate Partner Abuse, and the Legal System." *Harvard Civil Rights–Civil Liberties Law Review* 48: 51–104.

Görzig, A., and K. Ólafsson. (2013). "What Makes a Bully a Cyberbully? Unravelling the Characteristics of Cyberbullies across Twenty-Five European Countries." *Journal of Children and Media* 7(1): 9–27.

Gottfredson, M. R. (2017). "The Empirical Status of Control Theory in Criminology." In *Taking Stock: The Status of Criminological Theory,* edited by F. T. Cullen, J. P. Wright, and K. R. Blevins, 77–100. New York: Routledge.

Gottfredson, M. R., and T. Hirschi. (1990). *A General Theory of Crime.* Stanford, CA: Stanford University Press.

Granja, R. (2016). "Beyond Prison Walls: The Experiences of Prisoners' Relatives and Meanings Associated with Imprisonment." *Probation Journal* 63(3): 273–92.

Grant, J., L. Mottet, J. Tanis, J. Harrison, J. Herman, and M. Keisling. (2011). *Injustice at Every Turn: A Report of the National Transgender Discrimination Survey.* Washington, DC: National Center for Transgender Equality and National Gay and Lesbian Task Force. http://www.thetaskforce.org/downloads/reports/reports/ntds_full.pdf.

Green, K. E., and B. A. Feinstein. (2012). "Substance Use in Lesbian, Gay, and Bisexual Populations: An Update on Empirical Research and Implications for Treatment." *Psychology of Addictive Behaviors* 26(2): 265–78.

Green, P., C. Mills, and T. Read. (1994). "The Characteristics and Sentencing of Illegal Drug Importers." *British Journal of Criminology* 34(4): 479–86.

Greenberg, B., D. Mastro, and J. Brand. (2002). "Minorities and the Mass Media: Television into the 21st Century." In *Media Effects: Advances in Theory and Research,* edited by J. Bryant and D. Zillmann, 333–51. Mahwah, NJ: Lawrence Erlbaum Associates.

Greenwald, A. G., M. A. Oakes, and H. G. Hoffman (2003). "Targets of Discrimination: Effects of Race on Responses to Weapons Holders." *Journal of Experimental Social Psychology* 39(4): 399–405. doi:10.1016/s0022–1031(03)00020–9.

Greer, J., and Y. Jewkes. (2005). "Extremes of Otherness: Media Images of Social Exclusion." *Social Justice* 32(1): 20–31.

Grossman, A., and A. D'Augelli. (2006). "Transgender Youth: Invisible and Vulnerable." *Journal of Homosexuality* 51(1): 111–28.

Groth, A. N., and H. J. Birnbaum. (1979). *Men Who Rape: The Psychology of the Offender.* New York: Plenum.

Groth, A. N., A. Burgess, and L. Holmstrom. (1977). "Rape, Power, Anger and Sexuality." *American Journal of Psychiatry* 134(11): 1239–43.

Guasp, A. (2012). *Gay and Bisexual Men's Health Survey.* London: Stonewall.

Gudelunas, D. (2012). "There's an App for That: The Uses and Gratifications of Online Social Networks for Gay Men." *Sexuality & Culture* 16(4): 347–65.

Gun Violence Archive. (2020). "Mass Shootings." https://www.gunviolencearchive.org/mass-shooting.

Gupta, M. D. (1987). "Selective Discrimination against Female Children in Rural Punjab, India." *Population and Development Review* 13: 77–100.

Hagan, J. (1989). "Why is There So Little Criminal Justice Theory? Neglected Macro- and Micro-Level Links between Organization and Power." *Journal of Research in Crime and Delinquency* 26(2): 116–35. doi:10.1177/0022427889026002002.

Hagan, J., A. R. Gillis, and J. Simpson. (1985). "The Class Structure of Gender and Delinquency: Toward a Power-Control Theory of Common Delinquent Behavior." *American Journal of Sociology* 90(6): 1151–78. https://doi.org/10.1086/228206.

———. (1990). "Clarifying and Extending Power-Control Theory." *American Journal of Sociology* 95(4): 1027–37.

———. (1987). "Class in the Household: A Power-Control Theory of Gender and Delinquency." *American Journal of Sociology* 92(4): 788–816.

Haider, S. (2016). "The Shooting in Orlando: Terrorism or Toxic Masculinity (or Both?)." *Men and Masculinities* 19(5): 555–65.

Haines, R. J., J. L. Johnson, C. I. Carter, and K. Arora. (2009). "'I Couldn't Say, I'm Not a Girl': Adolescents Talk about Gender and Marijuana Use." *Social Science and Medicine* 68(11): 2029–36.

Hamel, J., and B. L. Russell. (2013). "The Partner Abuse State of Knowledge Project: Implications for Law Enforcement Responses to Domestic Violence." In *Perceptions of Female Offenders*, edited by B. L. Russell, 151–79. New York: Springer.

Hamill, J. (2015). "HIV Dating App HZone 'Leaks 5,000 People's Private Details' during Devastating Alleged Data Breach." *Mirror*, December 16, 2015. http://www.mirror.co.uk/news/technology-science/technology/hiv-dating-app-hzone-leaks-7021486.

Hargreaves, D. A., and M. Tiggemann. (2004). "Idealized Media Images and Adolescent Body Image: 'Comparing' Boys and Girls." *Body Image* 1(4): 351–61. https://doi.org/10.1016/j.bodyim.2004.10.002.

Hargreaves, J. (1994). *Sporting Women*. London: Routledge.

Harper, R., G. C. Harper, and J. E. Stockdale. (2000). "The Role and Sentencing of Women in Drug Trafficking Crime." *Legal and Criminological Psychology* 7(1): 101–14.

Harrell, E. (2011). *Special Report: Workplace Violence, 1993–2009*. U.S. Department of Justice, Office of Justice Programs, Bureau of Justice Statistics. https://www.bjs.gov/content/pub/pdf/wv09.pdf.

Hasenbush, A., A. Miyashita, and B. D. M. Wilson. (2015). *HIV Criminalization in California: Penal Implications for People Living with HIV/AIDS*. Williams Institute. https://williamsinstitute.law.ucla.edu/publications/hiv-criminalization-ca-penal/.

Hassan, C. (2016). "Teen Who Was Relentlessly Bullied Kills Herself in Front of Her Family." CNN, December 1, 2016. https://www.cnn.com/2016/12/01/health/teen-suicide-cyberbullying-trnd/index.html.

Hatters-Friedman, S., D. R. Hrouda, C. E. Holden, S. G. Noffsinger, and P. J. Resnick. (2005). "Filicide-Suicide: Common Factors in Parents Who Kill Their Children and Themselves."

Journal of American Academic Psychiatry Law 33(4): 496–504.

Hawker, D. S. J., and M. J. Boulton. (2000). "Twenty Years' Research on Peer Victimization and Psychosocial Maladjustment: A Meta-analytic Review of Cross-sectional Studies." *Journal of Child Psychology and Psychiatry* 41(4): 441–55. https://doi.org/10.1111/1469-7610.00629.

Hawton, K., C. C. Comabella, C. Haw, and K. Saunders. (2013). "Risk Factors for Suicide in Individuals with Depression: A Systematic Review." *Journal of Affective Disorders* 147(1–3): 17–28. https://doi.org/10.1016/j.jad.2013.01.004.

Hebl, M. R., J. Bigazzi, L. M. Mannix, and J. F. Dovidio. (2002). "Formal and Interpersonal Discrimination: A Field Study of Bias toward Homosexual Applicants." *Personality and Social Psychology Bulletin* 28(6): 815–25.

Health Resources and Services Administration. (2020). "About the Ryan White HIV/AIDS Program." https://hab.hrsa.gov/about-ryan-white-hivaids-program/about-ryan-white-hivaids-program.

Hefner, M. K. (2018). "Queering Prison Masculinity: Exploring the Organization of Gender and Sexuality within Men's Prisons." Men and Masculinities 21(2): 230–53.

Heidensohn, F. (1992). *Women in Control? The Role of Women in Law Enforcement*. Oxford: Clarendon Press.

Heise, L., M. Ellsberg, and M. Gottmoeller. (2002). "A Global Overview of Gender-Based Violence." *International Journal of Gynecology and Obstetrics* 78(S1): S5-S14

Hellemans, S., T. Loeys, A. Buysse, A. Dewaele, and O. De Smet. (2015). "Intimate Partner Violence Victimization among Non-Heterosexuals: Prevalence and Associations with Mental and Sexual Well-Being. *Journal of Family Violence* 30(2): 171–88.

Herbert, S. (2001). "'Hard Charger' or 'Station Queen'? Policing and the Masculinist State." *Gender, Place and Culture: A Journal of Feminist Geography* 8(1): 55–71.

Herrenkohl, T. I., Sousa, C., Tajima, E. A., Herrenkohl, R. C., and Moylan, C. A. (2008). "Intersection of Child Abuse and Children's Exposure to Domestic Violence." *Trauma, Violence, and Abuse* 9(2): 84–99.

Herrero, J., F. J. Rodríguez, and A. Torres. (2017). "Acceptability of Partner Violence in 51 Societies: The Role of Sexism and Attitudes toward Violence in Social Relationships." *Violence against Women* 23(3): 351–67.

Herrero, J., A. Torres, F. J. Rodríguez, and J. Juarros-Basterretxea (2017). "Intimate Partner Violence against Women in the European Union: The Influence of Male Partners' Traditional Gender Roles and General Violence." *Psychology of Violence* 7(3): 385–94.

Herzog, S., and S. Oreg. (2008). "Chivalry and the Moderating Effect of Ambivalent Sexism: Individual Differences in Crime Seriousness Judgments." *Law & Society Review* 42(1): 45–74.

Hetey, R. C., and J. L. Eberhardt. (2014). "Racial Disparities in Incarceration Increase Acceptance of Punitive Policies." *Psychological Science* 25(10): 1949–54.. DOI: 10.1177/0956797614540307.

Hewitt, B. (2002). "Villain or Victim?" *People*, March 4, 2002.

Hickman, M. J., and B. A. Reeves. (2006). *Law Enforcement Management and Administrative Statistics: Local Police Departments, 2003*. Washington, DC: U.S. Department of Justice, Office of Justice Programs. https://www.bjs.gov/content/pub/pdf/lpd03.pdf.

Higgins, G. E. (2006). "Gender Differences in Software Piracy: The Mediating Roles of Self-Control Theory and Social Learning Theory." *Journal of Economic Crime Management* 4(1): 1–30.

Higgins, G. E., B. D. Fell, and A. L. Wilson. (2007). "Digital Piracy: Assessing the Contributions of an Integrated Self-Control Theory and Social Learning Theory Using Structural Equation Modeling." *Criminal Justice Studies* 19(1): 3–22.

Hightow-Weidman, L. B., G. Phillips, K. C. Jones, A. Y. Outlaw, S. D. Fields, and J. C. Smith. (2011). "Racial and Sexual Identity Related Maltreatment among Minority YMSM: Prevalence, Perceptions, and the Association with Emotional Distress." *AIDS Patient Care and STDs* 25(S1): 39–45. https://doi.org/10.1089/apc.2011.9877.

Hill, D. (2002). "Genderism, Transphobia and Gender Bashing: A Framework for Interpreting Anti-Transgender Violence." In *Understanding and Dealing with Violence: A Multicultural Approach*, edited by B. Wallace, and R. Carter, 113–36. Thousand Oaks, CA: Sage.

Hindelang, M. J., M. R. Gottfredson, and J. Garofalo. (1978). *Victims of Personal Crime*. Cambridge, MA: Ballinger.

Hinduja, S., and J. W. Patchin. (2008). "Cyberbullying: An Exploratory Analysis of Factors Related to Offending and Victimization." *Deviant Behavior* 29(2): 129–56.

Hirschi, T. (2004). "Self-Control and Crime." In *Handbook of Self-Regulation: Research, Theory, and Applications*, edited by R. F. Baumeister and K. D. Vohs, 537–52. New York: Guilford Press.

Hochschild, A. R. (1990). *The Second Shift: Working Parents and the Revolution in the Home*. New York: Penguin Putnam.

Hodell, E. C., N. E. Wasarhaley, K. R. Lynch, and J. M. Golding. (2014). "Mock Juror Gender Biases and Perceptions of Self-Defense Claims in Intimate Partner Homicide." *Journal of Family Violence* 29(5): 495–506.

Hodges, M., and M. Budig. (2010). "Who Gets the Daddy Bonus? Markers of Hegemonic Masculinity and the Impact of First-time Fatherhood on Men's Earnings." *Gender & Society* 24(6): 717–45.

Hollis, M. E., M. Felson, and B. C. Welsh. (2013). "The Capable Guardian in Routine Activities Theory: A Theoretical and Conceptual Reappraisal." *Crime Prevention and Community Safety* 15(1): 65–79.

Holt, T. J., J. N. Navarro, and S. L. Clevenger. (2019). "Exploring the Moderating Role of Gender in Juvenile Hacking Behaviors." *Crime & Delinquency* 66(11): 1533–55.

Holt, T. J., and B. H. Schell. (2013). *Hackers and Hacking: A Reference Handbook*. Santa Barbara, CA: ABC-CLIO.

Holtfreter, K. (2005). "Is Occupational Fraud 'Typical' White-Collar Crime? A Comparison of Individual and Organizational Characteristics." *Journal of Criminal Justice* 33(4): 153–56.

Holtfreter, K., and K. A. Wattanaporn. (2014). "The Transition from Prison to Community Initiative: An Examination of Gender Responsiveness for Female Offender Reentry." *Criminal Justice and Behavior* 41(1): 41–57.

Howarth, J. W. (2002). "Executing White Masculinities: Learning from Karla Faye Tucker." *Oregon Law Review* 81(1): 183–203.

Howell, J. (2007). "Menacing or Mimicking? The Realities of Youth Gangs." *Juvenile and Family Court Journal* 58(2): 39–50.

Howell, J. C., and E. Griffiths. (2018). *Gangs in America's Communities*. Los Angeles: Sage.

Hoynck, T., U. Zahringer, and M. Behnsen. (2012). *Neonaticide. A Study in the Project: Anonymous Birth Giving and Baby Hatches in Germany Number of Cases and Contexts*. Munich: Deutsches Jugendinstitut.

Hoyt, S., and D. G. Scherer. (1998). "Female Juvenile Delinquency: Misunderstood by the Juvenile Justice System, Neglected by Social Science." *Law and Human Behavior* 22(1): 81–107.

Huling, T. (1995). "Women Drug Couriers: Sentencing Reform Needed for Prisoners of War." *Criminal Justice* 9: 15–19.

———. (1996). "Prisoners of War: Drug Couriers in the United States." In *Drug Couriers: A New Perspective*, edited by P. Green. London: Quartet.

Hull, K. E., and R. L. Nelson. (2000). "Assimilation, Choice, or Constraint? Testing Theories of Gender Differences in the Careers of Lawyers." *Social Forces, 7*, 79(1): 229–64. https://doi.org/10.1093/sf/79.1.229.

Human Rights Campaign. (2013). *Growing Up LGBT in America*. https://assets2.hrc.org/files/assets/resources/Growing-Up-LGBT-in-America_Report.pdf.

———. (2018). *LGBTQ Youth Report*. Williams Institute. UCLA Law School. https://www.hrc.org/resources/2018-lgbtq-youth-report.

Hunnicutt, G., and L. M. Broidy. (2004). "Liberation and Economic Marginalization: A Reformulation and Test of (Formerly?) Competing Models." *Journal of Research in Crime and Delinquency* 41(2): 130–55.

Hunt, J. (1990). "The Logic Underlying Police Sexism." *Women & Criminal Justice* 1(2): 3–30.

Hunt, R., and S. Dick. (2008). *Serves You Right*. London: Stonewall.

Iakobishvili, E. (2012). *Cause for Alarm: The Incarceration of Women for Drug Offences in Europe, Central Asia and the Need for Legislative and Sentencing Reform*. London: International Harm Reduction Association. https://www.hri.global/files/2014/08/06/IHRA_WomenInPrisonReport_Aug2013_A5_Web.pdf.

Intersex Society of North America. (2008). "What Is Intersex?" Accessed in 2017. http://www.isna.org/faq/what_is_intersex.

Irvine, A. (2010). "We've Had Three of Them: Addressing the Invisibility of Lesbian, Gay, Bisexual, and Gender Nonconforming Youths in the Juvenile Justice System." *Columbia Journal of Gender and Law* 19(3). https://doi.org/10.7916/cjgl.v19i3.2603.

———. (2015). "Time to Expand the Lens on Girls in the Juvenile Justice System." *Evident Change*, March 26, 2015. https://www.evidentchange.org/blog/time-expand-lens-girls-juvenile-justice-system.

Jagose, A. (1996). *Queer Theory*. Melbourne: Melbourne University Press.

James, K. (2017). "Upholding the Dignity of Incarcerated Women." *Center for American Progress*, December 22, 2017. https://www.americanprogress.org/issues/women/news/2017/12/22/444468/upholding-dignity-incarcerated-women/.

James, S. E., J. L. Herman, S. Rankin, M. Keisling, L. Mottet, and M. Anafi. (2016). *The Report of the 2015 U.S. Transgender Survey*. Washington, DC: National Center for Transgender Equality. https://transequality.org/sites/default/files/docs/usts/USTS-Full-Report-Dec17.pdf.

Jankowski, P. J., S. J. Sandage, M. W. Cornell, C. Bissonette, A. J. Johnson, S. A. Crabtree, and M. L. Jensen. (2018). "Religious Beliefs and Domestic Violence Myths." *Psychology of Religion and Spirituality* 10(4): 386–97.

Jenness, V., and S. Fenstermaker. (2014). "Agnes Goes to Prison: Gender Authenticity, Transgender Inmates in Prisons for Men, and Pursuit of 'the Real Deal.'" *Gender & Society* 28(1): 5–31.

Jewkes, Y. (2015). *Media and Crime*. London: Sage.

Joe, K. A., and Chesney-Lind, M. (1995). "'Just Every Mother's Angel': An Analysis of Gender and Ethnic Variations in Young Gang Membership." *Gender & Society* 9(4): 408–31. https://doi.org/10.1177/089124395009004002.

Johnson, M. P. (1995). "Patriarchal Terrorism and Common Couple Violence: Two Forms of Violence against Women." *Journal of Marriage and the Family* 57(2): 283–94.

———. (2008). *A Typology of Domestic Violence: Intimate Terrorism, Violent Resistance, and Situational Couple Violence*. Boston: Northeastern University Press.

Johnston, J. S., and J. Waldfogel. (2002). "Does Repeat Play Elicit Cooperation? Evidence from Federal Civil Litigation." *Journal of Legal Studies* 31(1): 1–30.

Jones, A. (1980). *Women Who Kill*. Boston: Beacon Press.

Jones, K. P., C. I. Peddie, V. L. Gilrane, E. B. King, and A. L. Gray. (2016). "Not So Subtle: A Meta-analytic Investigation of the Correlates of Subtle and Overt Discrimination." *Journal of Management* 42(6): 1588–613.

Jones, M., and M. L. Williams. (2015). "Twenty Years On: Lesbian, Gay and Bisexual Police Officers' Experiences of Workplace Discrimination in England and Wales." *Policing and Society* 25(2): 188–211.

Jurik, N. C. (1985). "An Officer and a Lady: Organizational Barriers to Women Working as Correctional Officers in Men's Prisons." *Social Problems* 32(4): 375–88.

Jurik, N. C., and G. J. Halemba. (1984). "Gender, Working Conditions and the Job Satisfaction of Women in a Non-traditional Occupation: Female Correctional Officers in Men's Prisons." *Sociological Quarterly* 25(4): 551–66.

Just Detention International. (1994). "SPR Files Brief in *Farmer v. Brennan*." January 11, 1994. https://justdetention.org/spr-files-brief-in-farmer-v-brennan/.

Juvonen, J., and E. F. Gross. (2008). "Extending the School Grounds? Bullying Experiences in Cyberspace." *Journal of School Health* 78(9): 496–505.

Kaeble, D., and M. Cowhig. (2018). "Correctional Populations in the United States, 2016." Bureau of Justice Statistics. https://www.bjs.gov/index.cfm?ty=pbdetail&iid=6226.

Kågesten, A., S. Gibbs, R. W. Blum, C. Moreau, V. Chandra-Mouli, A. Herbert, and A. Amin. (2016). "Understanding Factors That Shape Gender Attitudes in Early Adolescence Globally: A Mixed-Methods Systematic Review." *PloS One* 11(6): e0157805.

Kailas, M., H. M. S. Lu, E. F. Rothman, et al. (2017). "Prevalence and Types of Gender-Affirming Surgery among a Sample of Transgender Endocrinology Patients prior to State Expansion of Insurance Coverage." *Endocrine Practice* 23(7): 780–86. doi: 10.4158/EP161727.

Kakar, S. (2005). "Gang Membership, Delinquent Friends and Criminal Family Members: Determining the Connections." *Journal of Gang Research* 13(1): 41–52.

Kanter, R. M. (1993). *Men and Women of the Corporation*. New York: Basic Books. First published in 1977.

Karp, D. R. (2010). "Unlocking Men, Unmasking Masculinities: Doing Men's Work in Prison." *Journal of Men's Studies* 18(1): 63–83.

Kauppi, A., K. Kumpulainen, K. Karkola, T. Vanamo, and J. Merikanto. (2010). "Maternal and Paternal Filicides: A Retrospective Review of Filicides in Finland." *Journal of the American Academy of Psychiatry and Law* 38(2): 229–38.

Kay, F., and E. Gorman. (2008). "Women in the Legal Profession." *Annual Review of Law and Social Science* 4: 299–322. 10.1146/annurev.lawsocsci.4.110707.172309.

Kaye, J. (2009). "Twenty-First-Century Victorian Dandy: What Metrosexuality and the Heterosexual Matrix Reveal about Victorian Men." *Journal of Popular Culture* 42(1): 103–25.

Keane, C., A. R. Gillis, and J. Hagan. (1989). "Deterrence and Amplification of Juvenile Delinquency by Police Contact: The Importance of Gender and Risk-Orientation." *British Journal of Criminology* 29(4): 336–52.

Keane, C., P. S. Maxim, and J. J. Teevan. (1993). "Drinking and Driving, Self-Control, and Gender: Testing a General Theory of Crime." *Journal of Research in Crime and Delinquency* 30(1): 30–46.

Keefe, P. R. (2013). "A Loaded Gun: A Mass Shooter's Tragic Past." *New Yorker*, February 11 and 18, 2013. https://www.newyorker.com/magazine/2013/02/11/a-loaded-gun.

Keller, J., and J. Ringrose. (2015). "But Then Feminism Goes Out the Window! Exploring Teenage Girls' Critical Response to Celebrity Feminism." *Celebrity Studies* 6(1): 132–35. doi:10.1080/19392397.2015.1005402.

Kelley, T. M., D. B. Kennedy, and R. J. Homant. (2003). "Evaluation of an Individualized Treatment Program for Adolescent Shoplifters." *Adolescence* 38(152): 725–33.

Kelly, D. M., S. Pomerantz, and D. Currie. (2005). "Skater Girlhood and Emphasized Femininity: 'You Can't Land an Ollie Properly in Heels.'" *Gender and Education* 17(3): 229–48.

Kempf, E. J. (1920). "The Psychopathology of the Acute Homosexual Panic. Acute Pernicious Dissociation Neuroses." In *Psychopathology*, edited by E. J. Kempf, 477–515. St. Louis: C. V. Mosby. https://doi.org/10.1037/10580–010.

Kennedy, M. A., C. Klein, B. B. Gorzalka, and J. C. Yuille. (2004). "Attitude Change following a Diversion Program for Men Who Solicit Sex." *Journal of Offender Rehabilitation* 40(1–2): 41–60.

Kerbs, J. J., M. Jones, and J. M. Jolley. (2009). "Discretionary Decision Making by Probation and Parole Officers." *Journal of Contemporary Criminal Justice* 25(4): 424–41.

Kern, W. (2001). "Angel's Face, Devil's Heart." *Straits Times*, April 22, 2001. http://www.willkern.com/pike.html.

Kimmel, M. (2017). *Angry White Men: American Masculinity at the End of an Era*. New York: Bold Type Books.

Kinkade, P. T., M. Bachmann, and B. Smith-Bachmann. (2013). "Hacker Woodstock: Observations on an Off-line Cyber Culture at the Chaos Communication Camp 2011." In *Crime On-Line: Correlates, Causes, Context*, edited by T. J. Holt, 27–60. Durham, NC: Carolina Academic Press.

Klenowski, P. M., H. Copes, and C. W. Mullins. (2011). "Gender, Identity, and Accounts: How White-Collar Offenders Do Gender When Making Sense of Their Crimes." *Justice Quarterly* 28(1): 46–69.

Kolb, A., and T. Palys. (2018). "Playing the Part: Pseudo-Families, Wives, and the Politics of Relationships in Women's Prisons in California." *Prison Journal* 98(6): 678–99.

Kopp, C., R. Layton, J. Sillitoe, and I. Gondal. (2015). "The Role of Love Stories in Romance Scams: A Qualitative Analysis of Fraudulent Profiles." *International Journal of Cyber Criminology* 9(2): 205–17.

Kopp, P. M. (2014). "Burglary." In *The Encyclopedia of Criminology and Criminal Justice*, edited by J. S. Albanese. Hoboken, NJ: Wiley.

Kosciw, J. G., E. A. Greytak, N. M. Giga, C. Villenas, and D. J. Danischewski. (2016). *The 2015 National School Climate Survey: The Experiences of Lesbian, Gay, Bisexual, Transgender, and Queer Youth in Our Nation's Schools*. New York: Gay, Lesbian and Straight Education Network (GLSEN).

Kowalski, R. M., C. A. Morgan, K. Drake-Lavelle, and B. Allison. (2016). "Cyberbullying among College Students with Disabilities." *Computers in Human Behavior* 57: 416–27.

Kulick, D. (1998). *Travesti: Sex, Gender and Culture among Brazilian Transgendered Prostitutes*. Chicago: University of Chicago Press.

Kupers, T. A. (2005). "Toxic Masculinity as a Barrier to Mental Health Treatment in Prison." *Journal of Clinical Psychology* 61(6): 713–24.

Kwan, G. C. E., and M. M. Skoric. (2013). "Facebook Bullying: An Extension of Battles in School." *Computers in Human Behavior* 29(1): 16–25.

Labree, W., H. Nijman, H. Van Marle, and E. Rassin (2010). "Backgrounds and Characteristics of Arsonists." *International Journal of Law and Psychiatry* 33(3): 149–53.

Laidler, K. J., and G. Hunt. (2001). "Accomplishing Femininity among the Girls in the Gang." *British Journal of Criminology* 41(4): 656–78.

Lambert, E., C. Edwards, S. Camp, and W. Saylor. (2005). "Here Today, Gone Tomorrow, Back Again the Next Day: Antecedents of Correctional Absenteeism." *Journal of Criminal Justice* 33(2): 165–75.

Lamontagne, Y., R. Boyer, C. Hetu, and C. Lacerte-Lamontagne. (2000). "Anxiety, Significant Losses, Depression, and Irrational Beliefs in First-Offence Shoplifters." *Canadian Journal of Psychiatry* 45(1): 63–66.

Lamphere, R. D., and K. T. Pikciunas. (2016). "Sexting, Sextortion, and Other Internet Sexual Offenses." In *The Intersection between Intimate Partner Abuse, Technology, and Cybercrime: Examining the Virtual Enemy*, edited by J. N. Navarro, S. Clevenger, and C. D. Marcum. Durham, NC: Carolina Academic Press.

Larcombe, W. (2002). "The Ideal Victim v Successful Rape Complainants: Not What You Might Expect." *Feminist Legal Studies* 10(2): 131–48.

Lauritsen, J., K. Heimer, and J. P. Lynch. (2009). "Trends in the Gender Gap in Violent Offending: New Evidence from the National Crime Victimization Survey." *Criminology* 47(2): 361–99.

Lazar, M. M. (2009). "Entitled to Consume: Postfeminist Femininity and a Culture of Post-Critic." *Discourse & Communication* 3(4): 371–400. doi:10.1177/1750481309343872.

Leach, D. L. (2007). "Managing Lesbian, Gay, Bisexual, Transgender, and Intersex Inmates: Is Your Jail Ready?" In *LJN Exchange*, edited by C. Clem, 25–30. Washington, DC: National Institute of Corrections.

Lee, C. (2015). "Gender Bias in the Courtroom: Combating Implicit Bias against Women Trial Attorneys and Litigators." *Cardozo Journal of Law and Gender* 22: 229–51.

Lee, C., and N. Shin. (2017). "Prevalence of Cyberbullying and Predictors of Cyberbullying Perpetration among Korean Adolescents." *Computers in Human Behavior* 68: 352–58.

Lee, R. L. M. (2002). "Globalization and Mass Society Theory." *International Review of Sociology* 12(1): 45–60. DOI: 10.1080/03906700220135318.

Leinen, S., 1993. *Gay Cops*. New Brunswick, NJ: Rutgers University Press.

Leiner, B. M., V. G. Cerf, D. D. Clark, R. E. Kahn, L. Kleinrock, D. C. Lynch, J. Postel, L. G. Roberts, and S. Wolff. (2009). "A Brief History of the Internet." *Computer Communication Review* 39(5): 22–31.

Leit, A., H. G. Pope, and J. J. Gray. (2001). "Cultural Expectations of Muscularity in Men: The Evolution of Playgirl Centerfolds." *International Journal of Eating Disorders* 29(1): 90–93.

Lenhart, A. (2015). "Teens, Social Media and Technology Overview 2015." Pew Research Center: Internet and Technology. http://www.pewinternet.org/2015/04/09/teens-social-media-technology-2015/.

Leon, C. S. and C. S. Shdaimah. (2012). "JUSTifying Scrutiny: State Power in Prostitution Diversion Programs." *Journal of Poverty* 16(3): 250–73.

Leonard, W., A. Mitchell, S. Patel, and M. Pitts. (2008). *Coming Forward: The Underreporting of Heterosexist Violence and Same-Sex Partner Abuse in Victoria*. Melbourne: La Trobe University.

Leppel, K. (2016). "The Labor Force Status of Transgender Men and Women." *International Journal of Transgenderism* 17(3–4): 155–64.

Leve, L. D., and P. Chamberlain. (2007). "A Randomized Evaluation of Multidimensional Treatment Foster Care: Effects on School Attendance and Homework Completion in Juvenile Justice Girls." *Research on Social Work Practice* 17: 657–63. doi: 10.1177/1049731506293971.

Levitzky, S., and R. Cooper. (2000). "Infant Colic Syndrome—Maternal Fantasies of Aggression and Infanticide." *Clinical Pediatrics* 39(7): 395–400.

Lewis, A. P. (2006). *Communicating Lesbian Identity: A Critical Analysis of Popular Culture Representations and Police Officer Narratives*. Tempe: Arizona State University Press.

———. (2009). "Destructive Organizational Communication and LGBT Workers' Experiences." In *Destructive Organizational Communication: Processes, Consequences, and Constructive Ways of Organizing*, edited by P. Lutgen-Sandvik and B. D. Sypher, 184–202. New York: Routledge.

Lewis, P., and R. Simpson. (2012). "Kanter Revisited: Gender, Power and (In)visibility." *International Journal of Management Reviews* 14(2): 141–58.

Lezon, D. (2006). "Yates Not 'Grossly Psychotic' before Drownings, Dietz Testifies." *Houston Chronicle*, July 13, 2006. https://www.chron.com/news/houston-texas/article/Yates-not-grossly-psychotic-before-drownings-1875541.php.

Liem, M., and F. Koenraadt. (2008). "Filicide: A Comparative Study of Maternal versus Paternal Child Homicide." *Criminal Behaviour and Mental Health* 18(3): 166–76.

Liem, M., J. Levin, C. Holland, and J. A. Fox, (2013). "The Nature and Prevalence of Familicide in the United States, 2000–2009." *Journal of Family Violence* 28(4): 351–58.

Lindberg, N., M. M. Holi, P. Tani, and M. Virkkunen. (2005). "Looking for Pyromania: Characteristics of a Consecutive Sample of Finnish Male Criminals with Histories of Recidivist Fire-Setting between 1973 and 1993." *BMC Psychiatry* 5(1): 47–52.

Little, J. (2017). "Understanding Domestic Violence in Rural Spaces: A Research Agenda." *Progress in Human Geography* 41(4): 472–88.

Lloyd, M., and S. Ramon. (2017). "Smoke and Mirrors: UK Newspaper Representations of Intimate Partner Domestic Violence." *Violence against Women* 23(1): 114–39.

Lo, L. (1994). "Exploring Teenage Shoplifting Behavior: A Choice and Constraint Approach." *Environment and Behavior* 26(5): 613–39.

Lombroso, C. (1911). *Crime, Its Causes and Remedies*. Vol. 3. Boston: Little, Brown.

Lonsway, K., S. Carrington, P. Aguirre, M. Wood, M. Moore, P. Harrington, E. Smeal, and K. Spillar. (2002). *Equality Denied: The Status of Women in Policing: 2001*. National Center for Women and Policing, a Division of the Feminist Majority Foundation. http://www.womenandpolicing.org/PDF/2002_Status_Report.pdf.

Lopes, G., M. D. Krohn, A. J. Lizotte, N. M. Schmidt, B. E. Vasquez, and J. G. Bernburg. (2012). "Labeling and Cumulative Disadvantage: The Impact of Formal Police Intervention on Life Chances and Crime during Emerging Adulthood." *Crime and Delinquency* 58(3): 456–88.

Loughran, T. A., R. Paternoster, and D. B. Weiss. (2016). "Deterrence." In *The Handbook of Criminological Theory*, edited by A. R. Piquero, 50–74. Malden, MA: Wiley.

MacKinnon, K. (2003). *Representing Men: Maleness and Masculinity in the Media*. New York: Oxford University Press.

Maglaty, J. (2011). "When Did Girls Start Wearing Pink? Every Generation Brings a New Definition of Masculinity and Femininity That Manifests Itself in Children's Dress." *Smithsonian*, April 7, 2011. https://www.smithsonianmag.com/arts-culture/when-did-girls-start-wearing-pink-1370097/.

Maher, L. (1997). *Sexed Work: Gender, Race, and Resistance in a Brooklyn Drug Market*. Oxford: Clarendon Press.

Maier, S. L. (2008). "'I Have Heard Horrible Stories . . .' Rape Victim Advocates' Perceptions of the Revictimization of Rape Victims by the Police and Medical System." *Violence against Women* 14(7): 786–808.

Mallory, C., A. Hasenbush, and B. Sears. (2015). "Discrimination and Harassment by Law Enforcement Officers in the LGBT Community." Williams Institute. https://williamsinstitute.law.ucla.edu/wp-content/uploads/LGBT-Discrimination-by-Law-Enforcement-Mar-2015.pdf.

Man, C. D., and J. P. Cronan. (2001). "Forecasting Sexual Abuse in Prison: The Prison Subculture of Masculinity as a Backdrop for Deliberate Indifference." *Journal of Criminal Law & Criminology* 92: 127.

Marable, M., K. Middlemass, and I. Steinberg, eds. (2007). *Racializing Justice, Disenfranchising Lives: The Racism, Criminal Justice, and Law Reader*. New York: Springer.

Marchini, K. and A. Pascual. (2019). "2019 Identity Fraud Study: Fraudsters Seek New Targets and Victims Bear the Brunt." *Javelin*. https://www.javelinstrategy.com/coverage-area/2019-identity-fraud-report-fraudsters-seek-new-targets-and-victims-bear-brunt.

Marcum, C. D. (2015). *Cyber Crime*. New York: Wolters Kluwer Law & Business.

Martin, S. (1978). "Sexual Politics in the Workplace: The Interactional World of Policewomen." *Symbolic Interaction* 1(2): 44–60.

———. (1979). "Policewomen and Policewomen: Occupational Role Dilemmas and the Choices of Female Officers." *Journal of Police Science and Administration* 7(3): 314–23.

———. (1989). "Women on the Move? A Report on the Status of Women in Policing." *Women & Criminal Justice* 1(1): 21–40.

Marzullo, M. A., and A. J. Libman. (2009). *Hate Crimes and Violence Against Lesbian, Gay, Bisexual and Transgender People*. Washington, DC: Human Rights Campaign Foundation.

Massoglia, M., P. P. Pare, J. Schnittker, and A. Gagnon. (2014). "The Relationship between Incarceration and Premature Adult Mortality: Gender Specific Evidence." *Social Science Research* 46: 142–54.

Mastro, D. (2009). "Effects of Racial and Ethnic Stereotyping." In *Media Effects: Advances in Theory and Research*, edited by J. Bryant and M. B. Oliver, 325–41. 3rd ed. Hillsdale, NJ: Lawrence Erlbaum.

Mastro, D., and B. Greenberg. (2000). "The Portrayal of Racial Minorities on Prime Time Television." *Journal of Broadcasting and Electronic Media* 44(4): 690–703.

Masucci, M., and L. Langton. (2017). *Hate Crime Victimization, 2004–2015*. Washington, DC: US Department of Justice, Bureau of Justice Statistics. https://www.bjs.gov/content/pub/pdf/hcv0415.pdf.

Matthews, C., E. Monk-Turner, M. Sumter. (2010). "Promotional Opportunities: How Women in Corrections Perceive their Chances for Advancement at Work." *Gender Issues* 27(1): 53–66. DOI 10.1007/s12147–010–9089–5.

Maxwell, C. D., J. H. Garner, and J. A. Fagan. (2002). "The Preventive Effects of Arrest on Intimate Partner Violence: Research, Policy and Theory." *Criminology & Public Policy* 2(1): 51–80.

May, C. A. (2014). "Arson." In *The Encyclopedia of Criminology and Criminal Justice*, edited by J. S. Albanese. Hoboken, NJ: Wiley.

McCartan, L. M., and E. Gunnison. (2010). "Individual and Relationship Factors That Differentiate Female Offenders With and Without a Sexual Abuse History." *Journal of Interpersonal Violence* 25(8): 1449–69. doi:10.1177/0886260509354585.

McCormick, M., and R. S. Barthelemy. (2020). "Excluded from 'Inclusive' Communities: LGBTQ Youths' Perception of 'Their' Community." *Journal of Gay and Lesbian Social Services* 33(1): 103–22.

McFarlane, L., and P. Bocij. (2003). "An Exploration of Predatory Behaviour in Cyberspace: Towards a Typology of Cyberstalkers." *First Monday* 8(9). https://doi.org/10.5210/fm.v8i9.1076.

McGee, T. R., and D. P. Farrington. (2016). "Developmental and Life-Course Theories of Crime." In *The Handbook of Criminological Theory*, edited by A. R. Piquero, 336–54. Malden, MA: Wiley.

McIntosh, P. (1988). "White Privilege: Unpacking the Invisible Knapsack." In *Race, Class, Gender in the United States*, edited by Paula Rothenberg. New York: Worth Publishers.

McKeganey, N. P., and M. Barnard. (1996). *Sex Work on the Streets: Prostitutes and Their Clients*. Buckingham: Open University Press.

McKeig, A. (2021). "'No One Succeeds Alone': The Critical Importance of Role Models in Empowering Women of Color to Succeed in the Legal Field." American Constitution Society, *Expert Forum*, March 12, 2021. https://www.acslaw.org/expertforum/no-one-succeeds-alone-the-critical-importance-of-role-models-in-empowering-women-of-color-to-succeed-in-the-legal-field/.

McLaughlin, E. C. (2018). "Florida Yoga Studio Shooter Was Arrested for Groping Women and Trespassing on FSU Campus." *CNN*, November 5, 2018. https://www.cnn.com/2018/11/05/us/florida-yoga-studio-shooting/index.html.

McMahon, M. (1999). *Women on Guard: Discrimination and Harassment in Corrections*. Toronto: University of Toronto Press.

McNair, B. (2002). *Striptease Culture: Sex, Media and the Democratization of Desire*. London: Routledge.

Melander, L. A. (2010). "College Students' Perceptions of Intimate Partner Cyber Harassment." *Cyberpsychology, Behavior, and Social Networking* 13(3): 263–68.

Ménard, K. S., and A. L. Pincus. (2012). "Predicting Overt and Cyber Stalking Perpetration by Male and Female College Students." *Journal of Interpersonal Violence* 27(11): 2183–2207.

Mendelsohn, B. (1976). "Victimology and Contemporary Society's Trends." *Victimology: An International Journal* 1(1): 8–28.

Mennicke, A., J. Gromer, K. Oehme, and L. MacConnie. (2016): "Workplace Experiences of Gay and Lesbian Criminal Justice Officers in the United States: A Qualitative Investigation of Officers Attending a LGBT Law Enforcement Conference." *Policing and Society* 28(6): 712–29. doi: 10.1080/10439463.2016.1238918.

Merton, R. K. (1938). "Social Structure and Anomie." *American Sociological Review* 3(5): 672–82.

Mesch, G. S. (2009). "Parental Mediation, Online Activities, and Cyberbullying." *CyberPsychology & Behavior* 12: 387–93.

Messerschmidt, J. (1993). *Masculinities and Crime: Critique and Reconceptualization of Theory.* Lanham, MD: Rowman and Littlefield.

———. (1997). *Crime as Structured Action: Gender, Race, Class, and Crime in the Making.* Thousand Oaks, CA: Sage.

Messerschmidt, J. W., and S. Tomsen. (2018). "Masculinities and Crime." In *The Routledge Handbook of Critical Criminology,* edited by W. DeKeseredy and M. Dragiewicz, 177–88. New York: Routledge.

Messinger, A. M. (2011). "Invisible Victims: Same-Sex IPV in the National Violence Against Women Survey." *Journal of Interpersonal Violence* 26(11): 2228–43.

Meyer, C. L., and M. Oberman. (2001). *Mothers Who Kill Their Children: Understanding the Acts of Moms from Susan Smith to the "Prom Mom."* New York: New York University Press.

Meyer, I. H. (1995). "Minority Stress and Mental Health in Gay Men." *Journal of Health and Social Behavior* 36(March): 38–56.

Miles-Johnson, T. (2013). "Confidence and Trust in Police: How Sexual Identity Difference Shapes Perceptions of Police." *Current Issues Criminal Justice* 25(2): 685–702.

Miller, B. D. (1997). *The Endangered Sex: Neglect of Female Children in Rural North India.* New York: Oxford University Press.

Miller, J. (1998). "Gender and Victimization Risk among Young Women in Gangs." *Journal of Research in Crime and Delinquency* 35(4): 429–53. https://doi.org/10.1177/0022427898035004004.

———. (2001). *One of the Guys: Girls, Gangs and Gender.* New York: Oxford University Press.

Miller, J., and S. H. Decker. (2001). "Young Women and Gang Violence: Gender, Street Offending, and Violent Victimization in Gangs." *Justice Quarterly* 18(1): 115–40.

Miller, J., and C. W. Mullins. (2017). "The Status of Feminist Theories." In *Taking Stock: The Status of Criminological Theory,* edited by F. T. Cullen, J. P. Wright, and K. R. Blevins, 217–50. New York: Routledge.

Miller, S. L., K. B. Forest, and N. C. Jurik. 2003. "Diversity in Blue: Lesbian and Gay Police Officers in a Masculine Occupation." *Men and Masculinities* 5(4): 355–85.

Miller, S. L., C. Gregory, and L. Iovanni. (2005). "One Size Fits All? A Gender-Neutral Approach to a Gender-Specific Problem: Contrasting Batterer Treatment Programs for Male and Female Offenders." *Criminal Justice Policy Review* 16(3): 336–59.

Miller, W. B. (1975). *Violence by Youth Gangs and Youth Gangs as Crime Problem in Major American Cities.* Washington, DC: US Department of Justice.

Mills, C. W. (1956). *The Power Elite.* New York: Oxford University Press.

Mitchell, O. (2005). "A Meta-analysis of Race and Sentencing Research: Explaining the Inconsistencies." *Journal of Quantitative Criminology* 21(4): 439–66.

Moffitt, T. E. (1993). "Adolescence-Limited and Life-Course-Persistent Antisocial Behavior: A Developmental Taxonomy." *Psychological Review* 100(4): 674–701.

Moffitt, T. E., and Caspi, A. (2001). "Childhood Predictors Differentiate Life-Course Persistent and Adolescence-Limited Antisocial Pathways among Males and Females." *Development and Psychopathology* 13(2): 355–75.

Mogul, J. L., A. J. Ritchie, and K. Whitlock. (2011). *Queer (In)justice: The Criminalization of LGBT People in the United States.* Boston: Beacon Press.

Molm, L. D., N. Takahashi, and G. Peterson. (2000). "Risk and Trust in Social Exchange: An Experimental Test of a Classical Proposition." *American Journal of Sociology* 105: 1396– 427.

Monk, J. and C. Dulaney. (2019). "God-Fearing, Computer Whiz on Death Row: The Twisted Journey of Child Killer Tim Jones." *The State,* June 23, 2019. https://www.thestate.com/news/local/crime/article231479443.html.

Moore, C. (2001). *Sunshine and Rainbows: The Development of Gay and Lesbian Culture in Queensland.* St. Lucia: University of Queensland Press.

Moore, J. W. (1991). *Going Down to the Barrio.* Philadelphia: Temple University Press.

Morabito, M., and T. Shelley. (2015). "Representative Bureaucracy: Understanding the Correlates of the Lagging Progress of Diversity in Policing." *Race and Justice: An International Journal* 5(4): 330–55. 10.1177/2153368715575376.

Moran, T. E., C. Y.-C. Chen, and G. S. Tryon. (2018). "Bully Victimization, Depression, and the Role of Protective Factors among College LGBTQ Students." *Journal of Community Psychology* 46(7): 871–84.

Morash, M., and R. N. Haarr. (2012). "Doing, Redoing, and Undoing Gender: Variation in Gender Identities of Women Working as Police Officers." *Feminist Criminology* 7(1): 3–23.

Morash, M., D. H. Kwak, and R. Haarr (2006). "Gender Differences in the Predictors of Police Stress." *Policing* 29(3): 541–63.

Morgan, M., J. Shanahan, and N. Signorielli. (2009). "Growing Up with Television: Cultivation Processes." In *Media Effects: Advances in Theory and Research,* edited by J. Bryant and M. B. Oliver, 34–49. 3rd ed. New York: Routledge.

Moscati, M. F. (2016). "Italia." In *La violenza domestica e di appuntamento verso donne LBT nell'Unione Europea,* edited by G. Viggiani, 87–105. London: Wildy, Simmonds and Hill.

Movement Advancement Project. (2020). "LGBTQ People." Accessed in 2020. https://www.lgbtmap.org/lgbtq-people.

Movement Advancement Program and Center for American Progress. (2016). *Unjust: How the Broken Criminal-Legal System Fails LGBT People.* https://www.lgbtmap.org/policy-and-issue-analysis/criminal-justice-youth.

Movement Advancement Project and GLSEN. (2018). *Separation and Stigma: Transgender Youth and School Facilities.* http://lgbtmap.org/transgender-youth-school.

Mullins, C. W. (2006). *Holding Your Square: Masculinities, Streetlife, and Violence.* New York: Routledge.

Mullins, C. W., and R. Wright. (2003). "Gender, Social Networks, and Residential Burglary." *Criminology* 41(3): 813–40.

Mullins, C. W., R. Wright, and B. A. Jacobs. (2004). "Gender, Streetlife and Criminal Retaliation." *Criminology* 42(4): 911–40.

Murnen, S. K., C. Wright, and G. Kaluzny. (2002) "If 'Boys Will Be Boys,' Then Girls Will Be Victims? A Meta-analytic Review of the Research That Relates Masculine Ideology to Sexual Aggression." *Sex Roles* 46(11/12): 359–75.

Mustaine, E. E., and R. Tewksbury. (2009). "Transforming Potential Offenders into Motivated Ones: Are Sex Offenders Tempted by Alcohol and Pornography?" *Deviant Behavior* 30(7): 561–88.

Nadal, K. L., V. Vargas, V. Meterko, S. Hamit, and K. Mclean. (2012). "Transgender Female Sex Workers: Personal Perspectives, Gender Identity Development, and Psychological Processes." In *Managing Diversity in Today's Workplace,* edited by M. A. Paludi, 123–53. Santa Barbara, CA: Praeger.

Nagel, I. H., and J. Hagan. (1983). "Gender and Crime: Offense Patterns and Criminal Court Sanctions." *Crime and Justice* 4: 91–144.

National Association of Women Judges. (2018). "2018 US State Court Women Judges." https://www.nawj.org/statistics/2018-us-state-court-women-judges.

———. (2019). "2019 Representation of United States State Court Women Judges." https://www.nawj.org/statistics/2019-us-state-court-women-judges.

National Center for Lesbian Rights. (2006). *Rights of Transgender Prisoners.* http://www.nclrights.org/site/DocServer/RightsofTransgenderPrisoners.pdf?docID=6381.

Navarro, J. N., and S. Clevenger. (2017). "Calling Attention to the Importance of Assisting Male Survivors of Sexual Victimization." *Journal of School Violence* 16(2): 222–35.

———. (2021). "Understanding Cyberinterpersonal Abuse." In *Crime Online: Correlates, Causes, and Context,* edited by T. Holt, 203–30. Durham, NC: Carolina Academic Press.

Navarro, J. N., S. Clevenger, M. E. Beasley, and L. K. Jackson. (2017). "One Step Forward, Two Steps Back: Cyberbullying within Social Networking Sites." *Security Journal* 30(3): 844–58.

Navarro, J., S. Clevenger, and C. Marcum. (2016). *The Intersection between Intimate Partner Abuse, Technology, and Cybercrime: Examining the Virtual Enemy.* Durham, NC: Carolina Academic Press.

Navarro, J. N., and J. L. Jasinski. (2012). "Going Cyber: Using Routine Activities Theory to Predict Cyberbullying Experiences." *Sociological Spectrum* 32(1): 81–94.

———. (2013). "Why Girls? Using Routine Activities Theory to Predict Cyberbullying Experiences between Girls And Boys." *Women & Criminal Justice* 23(4): 286–303.

———. (2014). "Identity Theft and Social Networks." In *Social Networking as a Criminal Enterprise,* edited by C. D. Marcum and G. E. Higgins, 86–107. Boca Raton, FL: CRC Press.

Navarro, J. N., J. L. Jasinski, and C. Wick. (2014). "Working for Change: Empowering Employees and Employers to 'Recognize, Respond, and Refer' for Intimate Partner Abuse." *Journal of Workplace Behavioral Health* 29(3): 224–39.

Navarro, J. N., C. D. Marcum, G. E. Higgins, and M. L. Ricketts. (2016). "Addicted to the Thrill of the Virtual Hunt: Examining the Effects of Internet Addiction on the Cyberstalking Behaviors of Juveniles." *Deviant Behavior* 37(8): 893–903.

Nelson, R. (1994). "The Futures of American Lawyers: A Demographic Profile of a Changing Profession in a Changing Society." *Case Western Reserve Law Review* 44: 345–506.

Newman, M. (2006). "Yates Found Not Guilty by Reason of Insanity." *New York Times,* July 26, 2006. https://www.nytimes.com/2006/07/26/us/26cnd-yates.html.

Nguyen, T. (2013). "From Slutwalks to Suicidegirls: Feminist Resistance in the Third Wave and Postfeminist Era." *Women's Studies Quarterly* 41(3/4): 157–72. doi:10.1353/wsq.2013.0102

Nock, M. K., and P. M. Marzuk. (1999). "Murder-Suicide: Phenomenology and Clinical Implications." In *Guide to Suicide Assessment and Intervention,* edited by D. G. Jacobs, 188–209. San Francisco: Jossey-Bass.

Noh, M. S., M. T. Lee, and K. M. Feltey. (2010). "Mad, Bad, or Reasonable? Newspaper Portrayals of the Battered Woman Who Kills." *Gender Issues* 27(3): 110–30.

Nolo. "Probation." (n.d.). https://www.nolo.com/legal-encyclopedia/probation.

Norton, A. T., and G. M. Herek. (2013). "Heterosexuals' Attitudes toward Transgender People: Findings from a National Probability Sample of U.S. Adults." *Sex Roles* 68(11–12): 738–53. http://dx.doi.org/10.1007/s11199–011–0110–6.

Notestine, L. E., C. E. Murray, L. D. Borders, and T. A. Ackerman. (2017). "Counselors' Attributions of Blame toward Female Survivors of Battering." *Journal of Mental Health Counseling* 39(1): 56–70.

Novak, K. J., R. A., Brown, and J. Frank. (2011). "Women on Patrol: An Analysis of Differences in Officer Arrest Behavior." *Policing: An International Journal of Police Strategies and Management* 34(4): 566–87.

Oberman M. (1996.) "Mothers Who Kill: Coming to Terms with Modern American Infanticide." *American Criminal Law Review* 34: 102–9.

O'Connell Davidson, J. (1998). *Prostitution, Power and Freedom.* Ann Arbor: University of Michigan Press.

O'Connor, C., and K. Kelly. (2006). "Auto Theft and Youth Culture: A Nexus of Masculinities, Femininities and Car Culture." *Journal of Youth Studies* 9(3): 247–67.

Office for Civil Rights. (2021). "Section 1557 of the Patient Protection and Affordable Care Act." HHS.gov. Updated May 10, 2021. https://www.hhs.gov/civil-rights/for-individuals/section-1557/index.html.

Office of Juvenile Justice and Delinquency Prevention (OJJDP). (2019). *Arrest Rates.* https://www.ojjdp.gov/ojstatbb/crime/JAR.asp.

Olfman, S. (2009). *The Sexualization of Childhood.* Westport, CT: Praeger.

Olmo, R. (1990). "The Economic Crisis and the Criminalization of Latin American Women." *Social Justice* 17(2): 40–53.

Olson, D. E., M. Alderden, and A. J. Lurigio. (2003). "Men Are from Mars, Women Are from Venus, but What Role Does Gender Play in Probation Recidivism?" *Justice Research & Policy* 5(2): 33–54.

O'Neill, M. (1997). "Prostitute Women Now." In *Rethinking Prostitution: Purchasing Sex in Britain in the 1990s,* edited by G. Scambler and A. Scambler. London: Routledge.

———. (2001). *Prostitution and Feminism.* Cambridge: Polity.

O'Neill, M., and R. Campbell (2006). "Street Sex Work and Local Communities: Creating Discursive Spaces for Genuine Consultation and Inclusion." In *Sex Work Now,* edited by R. Campbell and M. O'Neill, 33–61. Cullompton: Willan.

Paap, K. (2006). *Working Constructions: Why White Working Class Men Put Themselves—and the Labor Movement—in Harm's Way.* Ithaca, NY: Cornell University Press.

Paasonen, S., K. Nikunen, and L. Saarenmaa, eds. (2007). *Pornification: Sex and Sexuality in Media Culture.* New York: Berg.

Padavic, I., and B. F. Reskin. (2002). *Women and Men at Work.* Newbury Park, CA: Pine Forge Press.

Padva, G. (2007). "Media and Popular Culture Representations of LGBT Bullying." *Journal of Gay and Lesbian Social Services* 19(3–4): 105–18.

Palmer, N. A., and E. A. Greytak. (2017). "LGBTQ Student Victimization and Its Relationship to School Discipline and Justice System Involvement." *Criminal Justice Review* 42(2): 163–87.

Panther, H. (2021). *Transgender Cops: The Intersection of Gender and Sexuality Expectations in Police Cultures.* New York: Routlege.

Pasko, L. and M. Chesney-Lind. (2016). "Running the Gauntlet: Understanding Commercial Sexual Exploitation and the Pathways Perspective to Female Offending." *Journal of Developmental and Life-Course Criminology* 2(3): 275–95.

Pastoor, M. K. (1984). "Police Training and the Effectiveness of Minnesota Domestic Abuse Laws." *Law & Inequality* 2: 557–607.

Patchin, J. W., and S. Hinduja. (2006). "Bullies Move beyond the Schoolyard: A Preliminary Look at Cyberbullying." *Youth Violence and Juvenile Justice* 4(2): 148–69.

———, eds. (2012). *Cyberbullying Prevention and Response: Expert Perspectives.* New York: Routledge.

Paternoster, R., and L. Iovanni. (1989). "The Labeling Perspective and Delinquency: An Elaboration of the Theory and an Assessment of Evidence." *Justice Quarterly* 6(3): 359–94.

Patterson, G. R., B. DeBaryshe, and E. Ramsey. (1990). "A Developmental Perspective on Antisocial Behavior." *American Psychologist* 44(2): 329–35.

Patterson, J. (2016). *Queering Sexual Violence: Radical Voices from within the Anti-violence Movement.* Bronx, NY: Riverdale Avenue Books.

Patzel, B. (2006). "What Blocked Heterosexual Women and Lesbians in Leaving Their Abusive Relationships." *Journal of the American Psychiatric Nurses Association* 12(4): 208–15.

Paul, P. (2005). *Pornified: How Pornography Is Transforming Our Lives, Our Relationships, and Our Families.* New York: Times Books.

Pearce, J., M. Williams, and C. Galvin. (2002) *"It's Someone Taking a Part of You": A Study of Young Women and Sexual Exploitation.* London: National Children's Bureau for Joseph Rowntree Foundation.

Pearlstein, T., M. Howard, A. Salisbury, and C. Zlotnick. (2009). "Postpartum Depression." *American Journal of Obstetrics & Gynecology* 200(4): 357–64.

Pecora, N. (1992). "Superman/Superboys/Supermen: The Comic Book Hero as Socializing Agent." In *Men, Masculinity, and the Media,* edited by S. Craig, 61–77. Research on Men and Masculinities Series, 1. Thousand Oaks, CA: Sage Publications.

Pemberton, S. (2013). "Enforcing Gender: The Constitution of Sex and Gender in Prison Regimes." *Signs* 39(1): 151–75.

Pence, E. (1983). "The Duluth Domestic Abuse Intervention Project." *Hamline Law Review* 6: 247–75.

Petersen, A. (2012). "That Teenage Feeling: *Twilight,* Fantasy, and Feminist Readers." *Feminist Media Studies* 12(1): 51–67.

Peterson, R. D., and L. J. Krivo. (2010). *Divergent Social Worlds: Neighborhood Crime and the Racial-Spatial Divide.* New York: Russell Sage Foundation.

Phelps, E. A., K. J. O'Connor, W. A. Cunningham, E. S. Funayam, J. C. Gatenby, J. C. Gore, and M. R. Banaji. (2000). "Performance on Indirect Measures of Race Evaluation Predicts Amygdala Activation." *Journal of Cognitive Neuroscience* 12(5): 729–38.

Phillips, N. D., and S. Strobl. (2006). "Cultural Criminology and Kryptonite: Apocalyptic and Retributive Constructions of Crime and Justice in Comic Books." *Crime, Media, Culture* 2(3): 304–31.

Pinel, E. C. (1999). "Stigma Consciousness: The Psychological Legacy of Social Stereotypes." *Journal of Personality and Social Psychology* 76(1): 114–28. doi:10.1037/0022-3514.76.1.114.

Pinto, S. (2015). "Is the Death Penalty the Answer to Drug Crime?" *Amnesty International,* October 9, 2015. https://www.amnesty.org/en/latest/campaigns/2015/10/is-the-death-penalty-the-answer-to-drug-crime/.

Pitcher, J. (2006). "Support Services for Women Working in the Sex Industry." In *Sex Work Now,* edited by R. Campbell and M. O'Neill. Cullompton: Willan.

Plant, S. (1997). *Zeros + Ones: Digital Women + the New Technoculture.* London: Fourth Estate.

Pogarsky, G. (2002). "Identifying 'Deterrable' Offenders: Implications for Research on Deterrence." *Justice Quarterly* 19(3): 431–52. https://doi.org/10.1080/07418820200095301.

Pogrebin, M. R., and E. D. Poole. (1998). "Sex, Gender, and Work: The Case of Women Jail Officers." In *Sociology of Crime, Law, and Deviance,* vol. 1, edited by J. T. Ulmer, 105–24. Bingley, UK: JAI Press.

Polaris Project. (2019). "Sex Trafficking and LGBTQ Youth." https://polarisproject.org/wp-content/uploads/2019/09/LGBTQ-Sex-Trafficking.pdf.

"Police Look at Local 10 Porn Bus Investigation." (2004). *Local10.com,* November 18, 2004. Available at https://web.archive.org/web/20070606135045/http://www.local10.com/news/3930251/detail.html.

Polka, E. (2018). "The Monthly Shaming of Women in State Prisons." *Public Health Post,* September 4, 2018. https://www.publichealthpost.org/news/sanitary-products-women-state-prisons/.

Pope, H. G., R. Olivardia, A. Gruber, and J. Borowiecki. (1999). "Evolving Ideals of Male Body Image as Seen through Action Toys." *International Journal of Eating Disorders* 26: 65–72.

Popp, A. M., and A. A. Peguero. (2011). "Routine Activities Theory and Victimization at School: The Significance of Gender." *Journal of Interpersonal Violence* 26(12): 2413–36.

Pornhub. (2020). *Year in Review; 2019.* https://www.pornhub.com/insights/2019-year-in-review.

Porter, T., and H. Gavin. (2010). "Infanticide and Neonaticide: A Review of 40 Years of Research Literature on Incidence and Causes." *Trauma, Violence, & Abuse* 11(3): 99–112.

Portillos, E., and M. S. Zatz. (1995). "Positive and Negative Aspects of Chicano Youth Gangs." Presented at annual meeting of the American Society of Criminology, Boston.

Postmus, J. L., S. Plummer, S. McMahon, N. S. Murshid, and M. S. Kim. (2011). "Understanding Economic Abuse in the Lives of Survivors." *Journal of Interpersonal Violence* 27(3): 411–30.

Praat, F., and K. F. Tuffin. (1996). "Police Discourses of Homosexual Men in New Zealand." *Journal of Homosexuality* 31(4): 57–73.

Pratt, T. C., K. R. Blevins, L. E. Daigle, and T. D. Madensen. (2017). "The Empirical Status of Deterrence Theory: A Meta-Analysis." In *Taking Stock: The Status of Criminological Theory,* edited by F. T. Cullen, J. P. Wright, and K. R. Blevins, 367–96. New York: Routledge.

Price, G. N., and W. A. Darity Jr. (2010). "The Economics of Race and Eugenic Sterilization in North Carolina: 1958–1968." *Economics and Human Biology* 8(2): 261–72.

Prenzler, T., and G. Sinclair. (2013). "The Status of Women Police Officers: An International Review." *International Journal of Law, Crime and Justice* 41(2): 115–31.

Prokos, A., and I. Padavic. (2002). "'There Oughtta Be a Law against Bitches': Masculinity Lessons in Police Academy Training." *Gender, Work & Organization* 9(4): 439–59.

Puhl, R. M., J. L. Peterson, and J. Luedicke. (2013). "Weight-Based Victimization: Bullying Experiences of Weight Loss Treatment–Seeking Youth." *Pediatrics* 131(1): e1–e9. doi:10.1542/peds.2012–1106.

Quinney, R. (1970). *The Social Reality of Crime.* New Brunswick, NJ: Transaction.

Rabe-Hemp, C. (2008a). "Female Officers and the Ethic of Care: Does Officer Gender Impact Police Behaviors?" *Journal of Criminal Justice* 36(5): 426–34.

———. (2008b). "Survival in an 'All Boys Club': Policewomen and Their Fight for Acceptance." *Policing: An International Journal of Police Strategies and Management* 31(2): 251–70.

———. (2009). "POLICEwomen or policeWOMEN? Doing Gender and Police Work." *Feminist Criminology* 4(2): 114–29.

———. (2018). *Thriving in an All Boys Club: Female Police Officers and Their Fight for Equity.* Lanham, MD: Rowman and Littlefield.

Rachlinski, J., S. Johnson, A. Wistrich, and C. Guthrie. (2009). "Does Unconscious Racial Bias Affect Trial Judges?" *SSRN Electronic Journal* 84. 10.2139/ssrn.999490.

Raffaelli, M., and L. L. Ontai. (2004). "Gender Socialization in Latino/a Families: Results from Two Retrospective Studies." *Sex Roles* 50(5–6): 287–99.

Ragg, D. M., D. Patrick, and M. Ziefert. (2006). "Slamming the Closet Door: Working with Gay and Lesbian Youth in Care." *Child Welfare* 85(2): 243–65.

RAINN. (2021a). "LGBTQ Survivors of Sexual Violence." https:// www.rainn.org/articles/lgbtq-survivors-sexual-violence.

———. (2021b). "Child Sexual Abuse." https://www.rainn.org /articles/child-sexual-abuse. Raley, A. B., and J. L. Lucas. (2006). "Stereotype or Success? Prime-Time Television's Portrayals of Gay Male, Lesbian, and Bisexual Characters." Journal of Homosexuality 51(2): 19–38.

Ramasubramanian, S. (2011). "The Impact of Stereotypical Versus Counterstereotypical Media Exemplars on Racial Attitudes, Causal Attributions, and Support for Affirmative Action." *Communication Research* 38(4): 497–516.

Reed, L. A., R. M. Tolman, and L. M. Ward. (2016). "Snooping and Sexting: Digital Media as a Context for Dating Aggression and Abuse among College Students." *Violence against Women* 22(13): 1556–76.

Reilly, K. (2018). "Why 'Nevertheless, She Persisted' Is the Theme for This Year's Women's History Month." *Time*, March 1, 2018. http://time.com/5175901/elizabeth-warren-nevertheless-she-persisted-meaning/.

Rentoul, L., and N. Appleboom. (1997). "Understanding the Psychological Impact of Rape and Serious Sexual Assault of Men: A Literature Review." *Journal of Psychiatric and Mental Health Nursing* 4(4): 267–74.

Renzetti, C. M. (1992). *Violent Betrayal: Partner Abuse in Lesbian Relationships.* Thousand Oaks, CA: Sage. https://doi .org/10.4135/9781483325767.

Resnick, P. J. (1969). "Child Murder by Parents: A Psychiatric Review of Filicide." *American Journal of Psychiatry* 126(3): 325–34.

———. (1970). "Murder of the Newborn: A Psychiatric Review of Neonaticide." *American Journal of Psychiatry* 126(10): 1414–20. doi:10.1176/ajp.126.10.1414.

Reyns, B. W. (2013). "Online Routines and Identity Theft Victimization: Further Expanding Routine Activity Theory beyond Direct-Contact Offenses." *Journal of Research in Crime and Delinquency* 50(2): 216–38.

Reyns, B. W., and B. Henson. (2010). "Superhero Justice: The Depiction of Crime and Justice in Modern-Age Comic Books and Graphic Novels." In *Popular Culture, Crime and Social Control*, edited by M. Deflem, 45–66. Bingley, UK: Emerald Group Publishing.

———. (2016). "The Thief with a Thousand Faces and the Victim with None: Identifying Determinants for Online Identity Theft Victimization with Routine Activity Theory." *International Journal of Offender Therapy and Comparative Criminology* 60(10): 1119–39.

Reza, E. M. (2005). "Gender Bias in North Carolina's Death Penalty." *Duke Journal of Gender Law & Policy* 12(179): 179–214.

Rhode, D. L. (2011). "From Platitudes to Priorities: Diversity and Gender Equity in Law Firms." *Georgetown Journal of Legal Ethics* 24: 1041–53.

Ricciardelli, R., K. Maier, and K. Hannah-Moffat. (2015). "Strategic Masculinities: Vulnerabilities, Risk and the Production of Prison Masculinities." *Theoretical Criminology* 19(4): 491–513.

Rich, K., and P. Seffrin, (2012). "Police Interviews of Sexual Assault Reporters: Do Attitudes Matter?" *Violence and Victims* 27(2): 263–79.

Richards, S. C., and J. I. Ross. (2001). "Introducing the New School of Convict Criminology." *Social Justice* 28(1): 177–90.

Rivera, E. A., C. M. Sullivan, and A. M. Zeoli. (2012). "Secondary Victimization of Abused Mothers by Family Court Mediators." *Feminist Criminology* 7(3): 234–52.

Robinson, D. T., and L. Smith-Lovin. (2001). "Getting a Laugh: Gender, Status, and Humor in Task Discussions." *Social Forces* 80(1): 123–58.

Robinson, J. P., and D. L. Espelage. (2013). "Peer Victimization and Sexual Risk Differences between Lesbian, Gay, Bisexual, Transgender, or Questioning and Nontransgender Heterosexual Youths in Grades 7–12." *American Journal of Public Health* 103(10): 1810–19.

Rocque, M. (2012). "Exploring School Rampage Shootings: Research, Theory, and Policy." *Social Science Journal* 49(3): 304–13.

Roe-Sepowitz, D., and K. Hickle. (2011). "Comparing Boy and Girl Arsonists: Crisis, Family, and Crime Scene Characteristics." *Legal and Criminological Psychology* 16(2): 277–88.

Rosoff, S. M., H. N. Pontell, and R. Tillman. (2007). *Profit without Honor: White-Collar Crime and the Looting of America*, 4th ed. Upper Saddle River, NJ: Prentice-Hall.

Ross, J. I., S. Richards, G. Newbold, M. Lenza, and R. Grigsby. (2011). "Convict Criminology." In *The Routledge Handbook of Critical Criminology*, edited by W. DeKeseredy and M. Dragiewicz, 177–88. New York: Routledge.

Rumney, P. N. (2008). "Policing Male Rape and Sexual Assault." *Journal of Criminal Law* 72(1): 67–86.

Sabo, D. F., T. A. Kupers, and W. J. London, eds. (2001). *Prison Masculinities.* Philadelphia: Temple University Press.

SafeTA. (2021). "Victim Centered Care: Lesbian, Gay, Bisexual, or Transgender (LGBT) Victims." https://www.safeta.org /page/VictimCenteredLGBTQ.

Salcido, O., and C. Menjívar. (2012). "Gendered Paths to Legal Citizenship: The Case of Latin American Immigrants in Phoenix, Arizona." *Law & Society Review* 46(2): 335–68.

Sanchez, M., and S. Adams. (2018). "The Trans Trap: Women Who Identify as Men Are NOT Offered Routine NHS Breast Cancer Screening . . . But Men Who Identify as Women WILL Get Smear Tests." *Daily Mail*, January 13, 2018. http:// www.dailymail.co.uk/news/article-5266833/NHS-breast-cancer-screening-not-offered-trans-men.html.

Sand, S., and B. Pepper. (2015.) "Internalized Homophobia and Intimate Partner Violence in Young Adult Women's Same-Sex Relationships." *Journal of Aggression, Maltreatment, and Trauma* 24(6): 656–73. doi: 10.1080/10926771.2015 .1049764.

Sandberg, S. (2013). *Lean In: Women, Work, and the Will to Lead.* Toronto: Random House.

Sander, W. (2006). "Educational Attainment and Residential Location." *Education and Urban Society* 38(3): 307–26. doi:10.1177/0013124506286944.

Sanders, J. M. (2011). "Coming of Age: How Adolescent Boys Construct Masculinities via Substance Use, Juvenile

Delinquency, and Recreation." *Journal of Ethnicity in Substance Abuse* 10(1): 48–70.

Sanders, T., M. O'Neil, and J. Pitcher. (2009). *Prostitution: Sex Work, Policy and Politics.* London: Sage.

Satchell, E. (2014). "11-Year-Old Bullied Watching 'My Little Pony' Attempts Suicide." *CBS 6*, February 9, 2014. https://wtvr.com/2014/02/09/11-year-old-bullied-for-watching-my-little-pony-attempts-suicide.

Satz, M. J. (n.d.). "Diversion Programs." Office of the State Attorney, Florida. http://www.sao17.state.fl.us/diversion-programs.html.

Savicki, V., E. Cooley, and J. Gjesvold. (2003). "Harassment as a Predictor of Job Burnout in Correctional Officers." *Criminal Justice and Behavior* 30(5): 602–19.

Schemenauer, E. (2012). "Victims and Vamps, Madonnas and Whores: The Construction of Female Drug Couriers and the Practices of the US Security State." *International Feminist Journal of Politics* 14(1): 83–102.

Schilt, K. (2006). "Just One of the Guys?: How Transmen Make Gender Visible at Work." *Gender & Society* 20(4): 465–90. https://doi.org/10.1177/0891243206288077.

Schlesinger, L. B., and E. Revitch. (1999). "Sexual Burglaries and Sexual Homicide: Clinical, Forensic, and Investigative Considerations." *Journal of the American Academy of Psychiatry and the Law Online* 27(2): 227–38.

Schmader, T., M. Johns, and C. Forbes. (2008). "An Integrated Process Model of Stereotype Threat Effects on Performance." *Psychological Review* 115(2): 336–56.

Schneider, H. J. (2001). "Victimological Developments in the World during the Past Three Decades (I): A Study of Comparative Victimology." *International Journal of Offender Therapy and Comparative Criminology* 45(4): 449–68.

Schneider, S. K., L. O'Donnell, A. Stueve, and R. W. Coulter. (2012). "Cyberbullying, School Bullying, and Psychological Distress: A Regional Census of High School Students." *American Journal of Public Health* 102(1): 171–77.

Schreck, C. J. (1999). "Criminal Victimization and Low Self-Control: An Extension and Test of a General Theory of Crime." *Justice Quarterly* 16(3): 633–54.

Schulz, D. M. (1995). *From Social Worker to Crimefighter: Women in United States Municipal Policing.* Westport, CT: Praeger.

———. (2004). *Breaking the Brass Ceiling: Women Police Chiefs and Their Paths to the Top.* Westport, CT: Praeger.

Schulze, C. and V. Bryan. (2017). "The Gendered Monitoring of Juvenile Delinquents: A Test of Power-Control Theory Using a Retrospective Cohort Study." *Youth and Society* 49(1): 72–95.

Scott, M. C., and K. Dedel. (2006). "Street Prostitution," 2nd ed. ASU Center for Problem-Oriented Policing, guide 2. https://popcenter.asu.edu/content/street-prostitution-2nd-edition.

Sears, B., and C. Mallory. (2011). "Documented Evidence of Employment Discrimination and Its Effects on LGBT People. *The Williams Institute.* Retrieved from https://escholarship.org/uc/item/03m1g5sg.

Seddon, T. (2008). "Women, Harm Reduction and History: Gender Perspectives on the Emergence of the 'British System' of Drug Control." *International Journal of Drug Policy* 19(2): 99–105.

Seelau, E. P., and S. M. Seelau. (2005). "Gender-Role Stereotypes and Perceptions of Heterosexual, Gay and Lesbian Domestic Violence." *Journal of Family Violence* 20(6): 363–71. doi: 10.1007/s10896–005–7798–4.

Segan, S. (2000). "Female Hackers Battle Sexism to Get Ahead." *Mujeres en Red: El Periódico Feminista.* http://www.mujeresenred.net/spip.php?article1543.

Seiler, S. J., and J. N. Navarro. (2014). "Bullying on the Pixel Playground: Investigating Risk Factors of Cyberbullying at the Intersection of Children's Online-Offline Social Lives." *Cyberpsychology: Journal of Psychosocial Research on Cyberspace* 8(4): article 6.

Sellin, T. (1938). "Culture Conflict and Crime" *American Journal of Sociology* 44(1): 97–103.

Sentencing Project. (2020). "Incarcerated Women and Girls." Updated November 24, 2020. https://www.sentencingproject.org/publications/incarcerated-women-and-girls/.

Serrano, J. (2016.) *Whipping Girl: A Transsexual Woman on Sexism and the Scapegoating of Femininity.* Seattle: Seal Press.

Shadel, D., and D. Dudley, (n.d.). "'Are You Real?'—Inside an Online Dating Scam." AARP, Money: Scams and Frauds. https://www.aarp.org/money/scams-fraud/info-2015/online-dating-scam.html.

Shah, B. (2010). "Lost in the Gender Maze: Placement of Transgender Inmates in the Prison System." *Journal of Race, Gender, and Ethnicity* 5(1): 39–56.

Sharp, S. (2009). "Feminist Criminology." In *21st Century Criminology: A Reference Handbook*, edited by J. M. Miller, 184–200. Thousand Oaks, CA: Sage.

Shatz, S. F., and N. R. Shatz. (2012). "Chivalry Is Not Dead: Murder, Gender, and the Death Penalty." *Berkeley Journal of Gender Law and Justice* 27: 64.

Shearer, E., and J. Gottfried. (2017). *News Use Across Social Media Platforms 2017.* Pew Research Center. https://www.journalism.org/2017/09/07/news-use-across-social-media-platforms-2017/.

Shelley, T. O., M. S. Morabito, and J. Tobin-Gurley. (2011). "Gender Roles and Gendered Institutions: The Current State of Women in Policing." *Criminal Justice Studies: A Critical Journal of Crime, Law and Society* 24: 351–67.

Shelton, A. K., and P. Skalski. (2013). "Blinded by the Light: Illuminating the Dark Side of Social Network Use through Content Analysis." *Computers in Human Behavior* 33: 339–48. http://dx.doi.org/10.1016/j.chb.2013.08.017.

Shepard, M. F., and E. L. Pence, eds. (1999). *Coordinating Community Responses to Domestic Violence: Lessons from Duluth and Beyond.* Vol. 12. Thousand Oaks, CA: Sage Publications.

Sherman, L. W., and H. M. Harris, (2015). "Increased Death Rates of Domestic Violence Victims from Arresting vs. Warning Suspects in the Milwaukee Domestic Violence Experiment (MilDVE)." *Journal of Experimental Criminology* 11(1): 1–20.

Short, E., A. Guppy, J. A. Hart, and J. Barnes. (2015). "The Impact of Cyberstalking." *Studies in Media and Communication* 3(2): 23–37.

Shuler, C. A. (2010). "Male Victims of Intimate Partner Violence in the United States: An Examination of the Review of Literature through the Critical Theoretical Perspective." *International Journal of Criminal Justice Sciences* 5(1): 163–73.

Sichel, J. L., L. N. Friedman, J. C. Quint, and M. C. Smith. (1978). *Women on Patrol: A Pilot Study of Police Performance in New York.* New York: Vera Institute.

Sifakis, C. (2001). *Frauds, Deceptions and Swindles.* New York: Checkmark Books.

Silverman, R. A., and L. W. Kennedy. (1988). "Women Who Kill Their Children." *Violence and Victims* 3(2): 113–27.

Silverschanz, P., L. M. Cortina, J. Konik, and V. Magley. (2008). "Slurs, Snubs, and Queer Jokes: Incidence and Impact of Heterosexist Harassment in Academia." *Sex Roles* 58(3–4): 179–91. https://doi.org/10.1007/s/11199–007–9329–7.

Silverstein, M. J., and K. Sayre. (2009). "The Female Economy." *Harvard Business Review,* September. https://hbr.org /2009/09/the-female-economy.

Simmons-Brown, A. (2015). "Creative Embezzlement." Association of Certified Fraud Examiners. https://www.acfe.com/article .aspx?id=4294991086.

Simon, R., and H. Ahn-Redding. (2005). *Crimes Women Commit: The Punishments They Receive.* Lexington, MA: Lexington Books.

Simon, R. J. (1975). *Women and Crime.* Lexington, MA: Lexington Books.

Simpson, S. S., J. L. Yahner, and L. Dugan. (2008). "Understanding Women's Pathways to Jail: Analysing the Lives of Incarcerated Women." *Australian and New Zealand Journal of Criminology* 41(1): 84–108.

Sineath, R. C., C. Woodyatt, T. Sanchez, et al. (2016). "Determinants of and Barriers to Hormonal and Surgical Treatment Receipt among Transgender People." *Transgender Health* 1(1): 129–36. doi: 10.1089/trgh.2016.0013.

Skarbek, D. (2011). "Governance and Prison Gangs." *American Political Science Review* 105(4): 702–16.

Skiba, R., R. Horner, C.-G. Chung, M. Rausch, S. May, and T. Tobin. (2011). "Race Is Not Neutral: A National Investigation of African American and Latino Disproportionality in School Discipline." *School Psychology Review* 40(1): 85–107.

Skinner, B. F. (1953). *Science and Human Behavior.* New York: Simon and Schuster.

Skjelsbaek, I. (2001). "Sexual Violence and War: Mapping Out a Complex Relationship." *European Journal of International Relations* 7(2): 211–37.

Slonje, R., and P. K. Smith. (2008). "Cyberbullying: Another Main Type of Bullying?" *Scandinavian Journal of Psychology* 49(2): 147–54.

Smith, A. (2010a). "Indigeneity, Settler Colonialism, White Supremacy." *Global Dialogue* 12(2). http://www .worlddialogue.org/content.php?id=488.

———. (2010b). "Queer Theory and Native Studies: The Heteronormativity of Settler Colonialism." *Glq—A Journal of Lesbian and Gay Studies* 16(1–2): 41–68. 10.1215 /10642684–2009–012.

———. (2015). *Conquest: Sexual Violence and American Indian Genocide.* Chapel Hill, NC: Duke University Press.

Smith, C. (2009). "A Period in Custody: Menstruation and the Body." *Internet Journal of Criminology* 1–22.

Smith, D. A., and R. Paternoster. (1987). "The Gender Gap in Theories of Deviance: Issues and Evidence." *Journal of Research in Crime and Delinquency* 24(2): 140–72.

Smith, O. (2018). "Mapped: The 53 Places That Still Have the Death Penalty—including Japan." *Telegraph,* July 6, 2018. https:// www.telegraph.co.uk/travel/maps-and-graphics/countries- that-still-have-the-death-penalty/.

Smith, P. K., J. Mahdavi, M. Carvalho, S. Fisher, S. Russell, and N. Tippett. (2008). "Cyberbullying: Its Nature and Impact in Secondary School Pupils." *Journal of Child Psychology and Psychiatry* 49(4): 376–85.

Smith, S. G., J. Chen, K. C. Basile, L. K. Gilbert, M. T. Merrick, N. Patel, M. Walling, and A. Jain. (2017). *The National Intimate Partner and Sexual Violence Survey (NISVS): 2010–2012 State Report.* Atlanta, GA: National Center for Injury Prevention and Control, Centers for Disease Control

and Prevention. https://stacks.cdc.gov/view/cdc/46305 /cdc_46305_DS1.pdf.

Smith, S. G., X. Zhang, K. C. Basile, M. T. Merrick, J. Wang, M. Kresnow, and J. Chen. (2018). *The National Intimate Partner and Sexual Violence Survey (NISVS): 2015 Data Brief—Updated Release.* Atlanta: National Center for Injury Prevention and Control, Centers for Disease Control and Prevention. https://www.cdc.gov/violenceprevention /pdf/2015data-brief508.pdf.

Sneed, B. G. (2007). "Glass Walls in State Bureaucracies: Examining the Difference Departmental Function Can Make." *Public Administration Review* 67(5): 880–91.

Softley, I., dir. (1995). *Hackers.* Starring Jonny Lee Miller and Angelina Jolie. MGM/UA Distribution Company.

South Carolina Department of Corrections. (n.d.). "Institutions." http://www.doc.sc.gov/institutions/institutions.html.

Spade, D. (2011). *Normal Life: Administrative Violence, Critical Trans Politics, and the Limits of Law.* Brooklyn, NY: South End Press.

Spinelli, M. G. (2004). "Maternal Infanticide Associated with Mental Illness: Prevention and the Promise of Saved Lives." *American Journal of Psychiatry* 161(9): 1548–57.

Spjeldnes, S., and S. Goodkind. (2009). "Gender Differences and Offender Reentry: A Review of the Literature." *Journal of Offender Rehabilitation* 48(4): 314–35.

Spohn, C., and D. Beichner. (2000). "Is Preferential Treatment of Female Offenders a Thing of the Past? A Multisite Study of Gender, Race, and Imprisonment." *Criminal Justice Policy Review* 11(2): 149–84.

Springdale, M., ed. (2016). *LGBTQ America: A Theme Study of Lesbian, Gay, Bisexual, Transgender, and Queer History.* Washington, DC: National Park Foundation. https://www .nps.gov/subjects/lgbtqheritage/upload/lgbtqtheme-law.pdf.

Starbird, K., A. Arif, T. Wilson, K. Van Koevering, K. Yefimova, and D. P. Scarnecchia. (2018). "Ecosystem or Echo-System ? Exploring Content Sharing across Alternative Media Domains." In *12th International AAAI Conference on Web and Social Media,* 365–74. Association for the Advancement of Artificial Intelligence. Palo Alto, CA: AAAI Press. Available at http://faculty.washington.edu/kstarbi /Starbird-et-al-ICWSM-2018-Echosystem-final.pdf.

Stark, E. (2009). *Coercive Control: The Entrapment of Women in Personal Life.* New York: Oxford University Press.

Steiner, M. (n.d.). "What Is Parole? How Does Parole Work?" Nolo. https://www.nolo.com/legal-encyclopedia/how-does- parole-work.html.

Steinmetz, K. F., T. J. Holt, and K. M. Holt, (2019). "Decoding the Binary: Reconsidering the Hacker Subculture through a Gendered Lens." *Deviant Behavior* 41(8): 936–48.

Stemple, L., and I. H. Meyer. (2014). "The Sexual Victimization of Men in America: New Data Challenge Old Assumptions." *American Journal of Public Health* 104(6): e19–26.

Stewart-Winter, T. (2015). "Queer Law and Order: Sex, Criminality, and Policing in the Late Twentieth-Century United States." *Journal of American History* 102(1): 61–72. doi: 10.1093 /jahist/jav283.

Sticca, F., and S. Perren. (2012). "Is Cyberbullying Worse than Traditional Bullying? Examining the Differential Roles of Medium, Publicity, and Anonymity for the Perceived Severity of Bullying." *Journal of Youth and Adolescence* 42(5): 739–50. http://dx.doi.org/10.1007/s10964–012– 9867–3.

Stinson, P. (2020). *Criminology Explains: Police Violence.* Oakland: University of California Press.

Stoltenborgh, M., M. J. Bakermans-Kranenburg, L. R. Alink, and M. H. van Ijzendoorn. (2015). "The Prevalence of Child Maltreatment across the Globe: Review of a Series of Meta-analyses." *Child Abuse Review* 24(1): 37–50.

Stonard, K. E., E. Bowen, T. R. Lawrence, and S. A. Price. (2014). "The Relevance of Technology to the Nature, Prevalence and Impact of Adolescent Dating Violence and Abuse: A Research Synthesis." *Aggression and Violent Behavior* 19(4): 390–417.

Strauss, S. A. (2007). "Same-Sex Desire, Suicidality, and the School Climate: Extending Hirschi's Theory of Social Control." PhD diss., Columbia University.

Streib, V. L. (1989). "Death Penalty for Female Offenders." *University of Cincinnati Law Review* 58: 845–80..

———. (2002). "Gendering the Death Penalty: Countering Sex Bias in a Masculine Sanctuary." *Ohio State Law Journal* 63: 433–74.

Stroshine, M. S., and S. G. Brandl. (2011). "Race, Gender, and Tokenism in Policing: An Empirical Elaboration." *Police Quarterly* 4(4): 344–65.

Struckman-Johnson, C., and D. Struckman-Johnson. (1992). "Acceptance of Male Rape Myths among College Men and Women." *Sex Roles* 27(3): 85–100.

Stryker, Susan. (2008). "Transgender History, Homonormativity, and Disciplinarity." *Radical History Review* 100: 145–57. https://doi.org/10.1215/01636545-2007-026.

Suarez, E., and T. M. Gadalla. (2010). "Stop Blaming the Victim: A Meta-analysis on Rape Myths." *Journal of Interpersonal Violence* 25(11): 2010–35.

Sullivan, N. (2003). *A Critical Introduction to Queer Theory.* New York: New York University Press.

Sutherland, E. H. (1950). "The Sexual Psychopath Laws." *Journal of Criminal Law and Criminology* 40: 543–54.

Sutherland, E. H., D. R. Cressey, and D. Luckenbill. (1995). "The Theory of Differential Association." In *Deviance: A Symbolic Interactionist Approach*, edited by N. Herman, 64–68. New York: General Hall.

Swanson, A. H. (1960). "Sexual Psychopath Statutes: Summary and Analysis." *Journal of Criminal Law, Criminology, and Police Science* 51(2): 215–35.

Swingewood, A. (1977). *The Myth of Mass Culture.* Atlantic Highlands, NJ: Humanities Press.

SyndicatedNews. (2014). "Elliot Rodger's YouTube Video and 140 Page Manifesto on SyndicatedNews.NET." May 24, 2014. Video, 6:55.https://www.youtube.com/watch?v=-okAStQbGLo.

Tapia, N. D., and M. S. Vaughn. (2010). "Legal Issues regarding Medical Care for Pregnant Inmates." *Prison Journal* 90(4): 417–46.

Taylor, C. A., and S. B. Sorenson. (2005). "Community-Based Norms about Intimate Partner Violence: Putting Attributions of Fault and Responsibility into Context." *Sex Roles* 53(7–8): 573–89.

Tee, N., and P. Hegarty. (2006). "Predicting Opposition to the Civil Rights of Transpersons in the United Kingdom." *Journal of Community and Applied Social Psychology* 16(1): 70–80.

Thieda, K. (2014). "Brené Brown on Empathy vs. Sympathy." *Psychology Today*, August 12, 2014. https://www.psychologytoday.com/us/blog/partnering-in-mental-health/201408/bren-brown-empathy-vs-sympathy-0.

Thomas, P., M. Levine, J. Cloherty, and J. Date. (2014). "Columbine Shootings' Grim Legacy: More Than 50 School Attacks, Plots." *ABC News*, October 7, 2014. https://abcnews.go.com/US/columbine-shootings-grim-legacy-50-school-attacks-plots/story?id=26007119.

Thompson, B. M., A. Kirk, and D. Brown. (2006). "Sources of Stress in Policewomen: A Three Factor Model." *International Journal of Stress Management* 13(3): 309–328.

Thornberry, T. P., M. D. Krohn, A. J. Lizotte, and D. Chard-Wierschem. (1993). "The Role of Juvenile Gangs in Facilitating Delinquent Behavior." *Journal of Research in Crime and Delinquency* 30(1): 55–87.

Tibbetts, S. G., and D. C. Herz. (1996). "Gender Differences in Factors of Social Control and Rational Choice." *Deviant Behavior* 17(2): 183–208.

Tokunaga, R. S. (2010). "Following You Home from School: A Critical Review and Synthesis of Research on Cyberbullying Victimization." *Computers in Human Behavior* 26(3): 277–87.

Tontodonato, P., and B. K. Crew. (1992). "Dating Violence, Social Learning Theory, and Gender: A Multivariate Analysis." *Violence and Victims* 7(1): 3–14.

Townsend, N. W. (2002). *The Package Deal: Marriage, Work and Fatherhood in Men's Lives.* Philadelphia: Temple University Press.

Trexler, R. C. (1995). *Sex and Conquest: Gendered Violence, Political Order, and the European Conquest of the Americas.* Ithaca, NY: Cornell University Press.

Triplett, R., and L. Upton. (2016). "Labeling Theory." In *The Handbook of Criminological Theory*, edited by A. R. Piquero, 271–89. Malden, MA: Wiley.

Tucker v. State. 771 S.W.2d 523 (Tex. Crim. App. 1988).

Turell, S. C. (1999). "Seeking Help for Same-Sex Relationship Abuses." *Journal of Gay & Lesbian Social Services* 10(2): 35–49.

Turk, A. T. (1969). "Political Criminality." In *Criminology Theory: Selected Classic Readings*, edited by F. P. Williams III and M. D. McShane, 81–108. New York: Elsevier.

Turkewitz, J. (2018). "9-Year-Old Boy Killed Himself after Being Bullied, His Mom Says." *New York Times*. August 28, 2018. https://www.nytimes.com/2018/08/28/us/jamel-myles-suicide-denver.html.

Turner, S., H. Copes, K. R. Kerley, and G. Warner. (2013). "Understanding Online Work-at-Home Scams through an Analysis of Electronic Mail and Websites." In *Crime On-Line: Correlates, Causes, Context*, edited by T. J. Holt, 81–108. Durham, NC: Carolina Academic Press.

Tursz, A., and J. M. Cook. (2011). "A Population-Based Survey of Neonaticides Using Judicial Data." *Archives of Disease in Childhood: Fetal and Neonatal Edition* 96: F259–63. doi:10.1136/ adc.2010.192278.

Ulrich, M. (2010). "Deviance and a Social Construct: An In-Class Activity." *TRAILS: Teaching Resources and Innovations Library for Sociology.* Originally published in 2003 in *Deviance and Social Control*, edited by B. Hoffman and A. Demyan. Washington, DC: American Sociological Association.

United Nations. (2010). "Impunity for Domestic Violence, 'Honour Killings' Cannot cCntinue – UN Official." *UN News*, March 4, 2010. https://news.un.org/en/story/2010/03/331422.

———. (2017). "Intersex Awareness." UN Free and Equal. https://www.unfe.org/intersex-awareness/.

———. (2015b). "Executive Summary." *World Drug Report 2015.* https://www.unodc.org/documents/wdr2015/World_Drug_Report_2015.pdf.

United States v. Swartz, 2012 W.L. 4341933 (2012).

US Bureau of Labor Statistics. (2019). "Labor Force Statistics from the *Current Population Survey*, Household Data Annual Averages (table 39)." https://www.bls.gov/cps/cpsaat39.htm.

US Census Bureau (2019). *Quick Facts: United States*. Retrieved from https://www.census.gov/quickfacts/fact/table/US/AGE775219.

US Department of Defense. (2019). *Transgender Service Members*. https://dod.defense.gov/News/Special-Reports/0616_transgender-policy-archive/.

US Department of Health and Human Services, Administration for Children and Families, Children's Bureau. (2013). *Guidance to States and Services on Addressing Human Trafficking of Children and Youth in the United States*. https://www.acf.hhs.gov/cb/policy-guidance/guidance-states-and-services-addressing-human-trafficking-children-and-youth.

———. (2019). *Child Maltreatment 2017*. https://www.acf.hhs.gov/cb/research-data-technology/statistics-research/child-maltreatment.

US Department of Justice, Office of Justice Programs, Bureau of Justice Statistics. (2015). *National Inmate Survey, 2011–2012*. Ann Arbor, MI: Inter-university Consortium for Political and Social Research. https://doi.org/10.3886/ICPSR35009.v1.

US State Department. (2021). "2021 Trafficking in Persons Report." https://www.state.gov/reports/2021-trafficking-in-persons-report/

Van Ouytsel, J., E. Torres, H. J. Choi, K. Ponnet, M. Walrave, and J. R. Temple. (2017). "The Associations between Substance Use, Sexual Behaviors, Bullying, Deviant Behaviors, Health, and Cyber Dating Abuse Perpetration." *Journal of School Nursing* 33(2): 116–22.

Van Wijk, C., and G. Finchilescu. (2008). "Symbols of Organisational Culture: Describing and Prescribing Gender Integration of Navy Ships." *Journal of Gender Studies* 17(3): 237–49. 10.1080/09589230802204266.

Vaske, J. C. (2017). "Using Biosocial Criminology to Understand and Improve Treatment Outcomes." *Criminal Justice and Behavior* 44(8): 1050–72.

Vigil, D. (2002). "Community Dynamics and the Rise of Street Gangs." In *Latinos: Remaking America*, edited by Marcelo Suarez-Orozco and Mariela Paez, 97–109. Berkeley: University of California Press.

Violence Policy Center. (2018). *When Men Murder Women: An Analysis of 2016 Homicide Data*. http://vpc.org/studies/wmmw2018.pdf.

Vlachová, M., and L. Biason. (2005). *Women in an Insecure World: Violence against Women: Facts, Figures and Analysis*. Geneva: Geneva Centre for the Democratic Control of Armed Forces (DCAF).

Vold, G. B. (1958). *Theoretical Criminology*. New York: Oxford University Press.

Wadhwani, A. (2018). "Tennessee Supreme Court sets 6 Execution Dates in the Next Two Years." *Tennessean*, November 16, 2018. https://www.tennessean.com/story/news/2018/11/16/tennessee-death-row-inmates-six-executions-two-years/2026379002/.

Wajcman, J. (1998). *Managing Like a Man: Women and Men in Corporate Management*. University Park: Pennsylvania State University Press.

———. (2006). "Technocapitalism Meets Technofeminism: Women and Technology in a Wireless World." *Labour and Industry: A Journal of the Social and Economic Relations of Work* 16(3): 7–20.

Walker, L. E. (1989). "Psychology and Violence against Women." *American Psychologist* 44(4): 695–702.

Wall, D. S. (2001). *Crime and the Internet: Cybercrimes and Cyberfears*. New York: Routledge.

Wallace, W. C. (2019). "Sexual Discrimination in the Legal Profession." *The Encyclopedia of Women and Crime*, edited by Nicole Hahn Rafter, 1–4. New York: John Wiley and Sons.

Wallwork, E. (2016). "Changing the Way We View Mums with Postpartum Psychosis Who Kill Their Children." *Huffington Post*, November 3, 2016. https://www.huffingtonpost.co.uk/entry/mums-who-kill-their-children-postpartum-psychosis_uk_56e292e2e4b05c52666e7e7a?guccounter=1.

Walters, M. J., J. Chen, and M. J. Breiding. (2013). *National Intimate Partner and Sexual Violence Survey (NISVS): 2010 Findings on Victimization by Sexual Orientation*. https://www.ojp.gov/ncjrs/virtual-library/abstracts/national-intimate-partner-and-sexual-violence-survey-nisvs-2010.

Walters, S. (1992). "Attitudinal and Demographic Differences between Male and Female Correctional Officers: A Study in Three Midwestern Prisons." *Journal of Offender Rehabilitation* 18(1–2): 173–89.

Wang, K., Y. Chen, J. Zhang, and B. A. Oudekerk. (2020). "Indicators of School Crime and Safety: 2019." *National Center for Education Statistics*, 2020–063/NCJ 254485.

Warner, M. (1991). "Introduction: Fear of a Queer Planet." *Social Text* 29: 3–17.

Wattanaporn, K. A., and K. Holtfreter. (2014). "The Impact of Feminist Pathways Research on Gender-Responsive Policy and Practice." *Feminist Criminology* 9(3): 191–207.

Watts, J. H. (2009). "Leaders of Men: Women 'Managing' in Construction." *Work, Employment and Society* 23(3): 512–30. doi:10.1177/0950017009337074.

Websdale, N. (2010). *Familicidal Hearts: The Emotional Styles of 211 Killers*. New York: Oxford University Press.

Weiss, J. (2003). "GLvs.BT: The Archaeology of Biphobia and Transphobia within the U.S. Gay and Lesbian Community." *Journal of Bisexuality* 3(3/4): 25–55. https://doi.org/10.1300/J159v03n03_02.

Weiss, K. G. (2010). "Too Ashamed to Report: Deconstructing the Shame of Sexual Victimization." *Feminist Criminology* 5(3): 286–310.

Weitzer, R. (2005). "New Directions in Research on Prostitution." *Crime, Law and Social Change* 43(4): 211–35.

Wertz, J., D. Azrael, J. Berrigan, et al. (2020). "A Typology of Civilians Shot and Killed by US Police: A Latent Class Analysis of Firearm Legal Intervention Homicide in the 2014–2015 National Violent Death Reporting System." *Journal of Urban Health* 97(3): 317–28. https://doi.org/10.1007/s11524-020-00430-0.

West, C., and S. Fenstermaker. (1995). "Doing Difference." *Gender & Society* 9(1): 8–37.

West, C., and D. H. Zimmerman. (1987). "Doing Gender." *Gender & Society* 1(2): 125–51.

Westmarland, M. (2001). *Gender and Policing: Sex, Power and Police Culture*. New York: Willan.

Whetstone, T. S. (2001). "Copping Out: Why Police Officers Decline to Participate in the Sergeant's Promotion Process." *American Journal of Criminal Justice* 25(2): 147–59.

White, S., and G. White. (1998). *Stylin'*. Ithaca, NY: Cornell University Press.

Whiteley, K. (2012). "Monstrous, Demonic and Evil: Media Constructs of Women Who Kill." In *The Harms of Crime Media: Essays on the Perpetuation of Racism, Sexism and Class Stereotypes*, edited by D. L. Bissler and J. L. Conners, 91–110. Jefferson, NC: McFarland.

Whittle, S., L. Turner, M. Al-Alami, E. Rundall, and B. Thom. (2007). *Engendered Penalties: Transgender and Transsexual People's*

Experiences of Inequality and Discrimination. Wetherby, UK: Communities and Local Government.

Whitty, M.T. (2018). "Do You Love Me? Psychological Characteristics of Romance Scam Victims." *Cyberpsychology, Behavior, and Social Networking* 21(2): 105–9.

Wick, S. E., C. Nagoshi, R. Basham, C. Jordan, Y. K. Kim, A. P. Nguyen, and P. Lehmann. (2017). "Patterns of Cyber Harassment and Perpetration among College Students in the United States: A Test of Routine Activities Theory." *International Journal of Cyber Criminology* 11(1): 24–38.

Wilczynski, A. (1991). "Images of Women Who Kill Their Infants: The Mad and the Bad." *Women and Criminal Justice* 2(2): 71–88.

Wilkinson, J. and C. Spargo. (2016). "15 Years, Says 'She Grieves EVERY DAY for Her Five Kids She Drowned in the Bathtub.'" *Daily Mail,* September 1, 2016. https://www.dailymail.co.uk/news/article-3769609/Andrea-Yates-grieves-day-five-children-drowned-tub-15-years-ago-likely-never-leave-Texas-mental-hospital.html.

Williams, M., and A. L. Robinson. (2004). "Problems and Prospects with Policing the Lesbian, Gay and Bisexual Community in Wales." *Policing & Society* 14 (3): 213–32.

———. (2007). *Counted In! The All Wales Survey of Lesbian, Gay and Bisexual People.* London: Stonewall.

Williams, P. (2005). "Convictions Overturned for Mom Who Drowned 5 Kids." *NBC News.com,* January 6, 2005. http://www.nbcnews.com/id/6794098/ns/us_news-crime_and_courts/t/convictions-overturned-mom-who-drowned-kids/#.XHLhzlxKiUk.

Wilson, B. D. M., K. Cooper, A. Kastanis, and S. Nezhad. (2014). *Sexual and Gender Minority Youth in Foster Care: Assessing Disproportionality and Disparities in Los Angeles.* Los Angeles: Williams Institute. http://williamsinstitute.law.ucla.edu/wp-content/uploads/LAFYS_report_final-aug-2014.pdf.

Wilson, X. (2018). "David Matusiewicz, Amy Gonzalez Appeal Cyberstalking Convictions, Claim Trial Tainted." *Delaware Online,* February 7, 2018. https://www.delawareonline.com/story/news/crime/2018/02/07/david-matusiewicz-amy-gonzalez-appeal-cyberstalking-convictions-led-life-terms/316277002/.

Witten, T., and E. Eyler. (1999). "Hate Crimes and Violence against the Transgendered." *Peace Review* 11(3): 481–69.

Wittes, B., C. Poplin, Q. Jurecic, and C. Spera. (2016). *Sextortion: Cybersecurity, Teenagers, and Remote Sexual Assault.* Center for Technology at Brookings. https://www.brookings.edu/wp-content/uploads/2016/05/sextortion1-1.pdf.

Wolak, J., D. Finkelhor, and K. Mitchell. (2007). "1 in 7 Youth: The Statistics about Online Sexual Solicitations." Fact sheet. Crimes against Children Research Center. http://unh.edu/ccrc/internet-crimes/factsheet_1in7.html.

Wolff, N., and J. Shi. (2011). "Patterns of Victimization and Feelings of Safety inside Prison: The Experience of Male and Female Inmates." *Crime & Delinquency* 57(1): 29–55.

Wolford-Clevenger, C., H. Zapor, H. Brasfield, J. Elmquist, M. Brem, R. C. Shorey, and G. L. Stuart. (2016). "An Examination of the Partner Cyber Abuse Questionnaire in a College Student Sample." *Psychology of Violence* 6(1): 156–62.

Wong, R. Y., C. M. Cheung, and B. Xiao. (2018). "Does Gender Matter in Cyberbullying Perpetration? An Empirical Investigation." *Computers in Human Behavior* 79: 247–57.

Woodford, M. R., A. Kulick, B. R. Sinco, and J. S. Hong. (2014). "Contemporary Heterosexism on Campus and

Psychological Distress among LGBQ Students: The Mediating Role of Self-Acceptance." *American Journal of Orthopsychiatry* 84(5): 519–29. https://doi.org/10.1037/ort0000015.

Woodlock, D. (2017). "The Abuse of Technology in Domestic Violence and Stalking." *Violence Against Women* 23(5): 584–602.

Woods, J. B. (2014). "'Queering Criminology': Overview of the State of the Field." In *The Handbook of LGBT Communities, Crime, and Justice,* edited by D. Peterson and V. Panfil, 15–41. New York: Springer.

World Health Organization. (2017). "Violence against Women: Key Facts." http://www.who.int/news-room/fact-sheets/detail/violence-against-women.

———. (2018). *WHO: Addressing Violence against Women: Key Achievements and Priorities.* No. WHO/RHR/18.18. Geneva: WHO.

———. (2019). "Transgender People." Global HIV, Hepatitis and STIs Programmes. Accessed in 2019. https://www.who.int/hiv/topics/transgender/en/.

Wright, E. M., P. Van Voorhis, E. J. Salisbury, and A. Bauman. (2012). "Gender-Responsive Lessons Learned and Policy Implications for Women in Prison: A Review." *Criminal Justice and Behavior* 39(12): 1612–32.

Wright, J. P., and F. T. Cullen. (2012). "The Future of Biosocial Criminology: Beyond Scholars' Professional Ideology." *Journal of Contemporary Criminal Justice* 28(3): 237–53..

Yates v. State, 171 S.W.3d 215 (Tex. App. 2005).

Zeitz, D. (1981). *Women Who Embezzle or Defraud: A Study of Convicted Felons.* New York: Praeger.

Zetter, K. (2008). "Palin E-mail Hacker Says It Was Easy." *Wired.* https://www.wired.com/2008/09/palin-e-mail-ha/.

Zillman, C. (2017). "Congress's 'No Sleeveless' Dress Code Is Another Arbitrary Barrier for Women." *Fortune.* July 7, 2017. https://fortune.com/2017/07/07/congress-dress-code/.

Zimmer, L. (1987). "How Women Reshape the Prison Guard Role." *Gender & Society* 1(4): 415–31.

Zsila, Á., R. Urbán, M. D. Griffiths, and Z. Demetrovics. (2018). "Gender Differences in the Association between Cyberbullying Victimization and Perpetration: The Role of Anger Rumination and Traditional Bullying Experiences." *International Journal of Mental Health and Addiction* 17(5): 1252–67.

Zweig, J. M., M. Dank, J. Yahner, and P. Lachman. (2013). "The Rate of Cyber Dating Abuse among Teens and How It Relates to Other Forms of Teen Dating Violence." *Journal of Youth and Adolescence* 42(7): 1063–77.

RECOMMENDED WEBSITES

Biosocial Criminology Association. https://www.biosocialcrim.org/.

Centers for Disease Control and Prevention. "LGBTQ Health." https://www.cdc.gov/lgbthealth/index.htm.

Equaldex. http://www.equaldex.com/.

GLAAD. https://www.glaad.org/.

It Gets Better. https://itgetsbetter.org/about/.

National Coalition of Anti-Violence Programs. https://avp.org/ncavp/.

Rainbow Railroad. https://www.rainbowrailroad.com/.

RAINN. https://www.rainn.org/.

Transgender Law Center. https://transgenderlawcenter.org.

Index

Founded in 1893,
UNIVERSITY OF CALIFORNIA PRESS
publishes bold, progressive books and journals
on topics in the arts, humanities, social sciences,
and natural sciences—with a focus on social
justice issues—that inspire thought and action
among readers worldwide.

The UC PRESS FOUNDATION
raises funds to uphold the press's vital role
as an independent, nonprofit publisher, and
receives philanthropic support from a wide
range of individuals and institutions—and from
committed readers like you. To learn more, visit
ucpress.edu/supportus.